T0380022

Taiwan and the 'China Impact'

There can be no doubt that China's economic and political rise is having a stronger effect on Taiwan than on any other country, given the Chinese government's claim to sovereignty over Taiwan and Taiwan's quest to maintain its democratic achievements and political identity as a sovereign state. Against this background, this volume deals with the 'bigger picture' of evolving relations across the Taiwan Strait, taking as a starting point the observation that China's impact on Taiwan has become stronger over the last 20 years.

This book analyses the 'China impact' on Taiwan in terms of its social, political and security space from both an empirical and a conceptual point of view. It is the first comprehensive account of China's multifaceted impact on the politics and society of contemporary Taiwan, written by renowned scholars from Taiwan, Europe and the US. The book covers a wide range of topics including Taiwan's party alignment, elections, generational politics, cross-Strait political economy, immigration policy and security. The contributors – political scientists and sociologists – highlight both the dangers and the opportunities of the 'China impact' for Taiwan and draw a realistic picture of the island republic's current situation and future options in the shadow of its giant neighbour.

Based on qualitative and quantitative data, this volume is intended to fill a gap in the Taiwan studies field by studying the 'China impact' on Taiwan's politics and society systematically and from a comparative perspective. By doing so, it will be of great interest to students and scholars of Taiwan studies and of East Asian politics and society more generally.

Gunter Schubert is Professor of Greater China Studies at the Institute of Asian and Oriental Studies, University of Tübingen, Germany. He is also the founder and Director of the European Research Centre on Contemporary Taiwan at that university.

Routledge Research on Taiwan
Series Editor: Dafydd Fell
SOAS, UK

The *Routledge Research on Taiwan Series* seeks to publish quality research on all aspects of Taiwan studies. Taking an interdisciplinary approach, the books will cover topics such as politics, economic development, culture, society, anthropology and history.

This new book series will include the best possible scholarship from the social sciences and the humanities and welcomes submissions from established authors in the field as well as from younger authors. In addition to research monographs and edited volumes, general works or textbooks with a broader appeal will be considered.

The series is advised by an international editorial board and edited by *Dafydd Fell* of the Centre of Taiwan Studies at the School of Oriental and African Studies.

1 **Taiwan, Humanitarianism and Global Governance**
   Alain Guilloux

2 **Planning in Taiwan**
   Spatial planning in the twenty-first century
   Edited by Roger Bristow

3 **Popular Culture in Taiwan**
   Charismatic modernity
   Edited by Marc L. Moskowitz

4 **Politics of Difference in Taiwan**
   Edited by Tak-Wing Ngo and Hong-Zen Wang

5 **Taiwanese Identity in the 21st Century**
   Domestic, regional and global perspectives
   Edited by Gunter Schubert and Jens Damm

6 **Taiwan's Democracy**
   Economic and political challenges
   Edited by Robert Ash, John Garver and Penelope B. Prime

7 **Taiwan's Economic Transformation**
   Leadership, property rights and institutional change
   Tai-Chun Kuo and Ramon H. Myers

8 **Government and Politics in Taiwan**
   Dafydd Fell

9 **Documenting Taiwan on Film**
   Issues and methods in new documentaries
   Edited by Sylvia Li-Chun Lin and Tze-Lan D. Sang

10 **Technology Transfer Between the US, China and Taiwan**
   Moving knowledge
   Edited by Douglas B. Fuller and Murray A. Rubinstein

11 **Migration to and from Taiwan**
   Edited by Kuei-Fen Chiu, Dafydd Fell and Lin Ping

12 **Political Changes in Taiwan under Ma Ying-jeou**
   Continuity, change and future challenges
   Edited by Jean-Pierre Cabestan and Jacques deLisle

13 **Border Crossing in Greater China**
   Production, community and identity
   Edited by Jenn-Hwan Wang

14 **Language, Politics and Identity in Taiwan**
   Naming China
   Hui-Ching Chang and Richard Holt

15 **Place, Identity, and National Imagination in Post-war Taiwan**
   Bi-Yu Chang

16 **Environmental Governance in Taiwan**
   A new generation of activists and stakeholders
   Simona A. Grano

17 **Taiwan and the 'China Impact'**
   Challenges and opportunities
   Edited by Gunter Schubert

Taiwan and the 'China Impact'

Challenges and opportunities

Edited by Gunter Schubert

Routledge
Taylor & Francis Group

LONDON AND NEW YORK

First published 2016
by Routledge
2 Park Square, Milton Park, Abingdon, Oxon OX14 4RN

and by Routledge
711 Third Avenue, New York, NY 10017

Routledge is an imprint of the Taylor and Francis Group, an informa business

© 2016 Gunter Schubert

The right of the editor to be identified as the author of the editorial matter, and of the authors for their individual chapters, has been asserted in accordance with sections 77 and 78 of the Copyright, Designs and Patents Act 1988.

British Library Cataloguing in Publication Data
A catalogue record for this book is available from the British Library

Library of Congress Cataloging in Publication Data
Names: Schubert, Gunter, 1963– editor.
Title: Taiwan and the 'China impact' : challenges and opportunities / edited by Gunter Schubert.
Description: New York, NY : Routledge, 2016. | Series: Routledge research on Taiwan ; 17 | Includes bibliographical references and index.
Identifiers: LCCN 2015021686| ISBN 1138945927 (hardback) | ISBN 1315671115 (ebook)
Subjects: LCSH: Taiwan–Politics and government–2000– | Taiwan–Relations–China. | China–Relations–Taiwan.
Classification: LCC DS799.847 .T3473 2016 | DDC 951.24905–dc23
LC record available at http://lccn.loc.gov/2015021686

ISBN: 978-1-138-94592-0 (hbk)
ISBN: 978-1-315-67111-6 (ebk)

Typeset in Times New Roman
by Wearset Ltd, Boldon, Tyne and Wear

Contents

List of figures   x
List of tables   xi
Notes on contributors   xiii
Foreword   xvii
MICHAEL H.H. HSIAO

1 **Introduction**   1
GUNTER SCHUBERT

PART I
The China impact on Taiwan's domestic politics   13

2 **The PRC as a player in Taiwan's domestic politics:**
   a two-level game analysis   15
   JIH-WEN LIN

3 **Cross-Strait relations as an 'easy' issue: China's impact on**
   evidence provision in negative political campaigning in
   Taiwan   36
   HSUAN-YUN TED CHEN AND CHUNG-LI WU

4 **The China impact on Taiwan's elections: cross-Strait**
   economic integration through the lens of election
   advertising   53
   DAFYDD J. FELL

5 **The China impact on Taiwan's generational politics**   70
   SHELLEY RIGGER

 6 Facing the dragon and riding the tiger: assessing the
    mainland Taishang as an 'impact factor' in cross-Strait
    relations   91
    GUNTER SCHUBERT

 7 Signaling peace: a theory of the ECFA and a peace dividend
    beyond the Taiwan Strait   110
    HANS H. TUNG AND YUN-HAN CHU

 8 Political competition framed by the China factor? Looking
    beyond the 2012 presidential election   130
    NAI-TEH WU

PART II
The China impact on Taiwanese society   149

 9 The social basis of Taiwan's cross-Strait policies, 2008–2014   151
    CHIH-JOU JAY CHEN

10 Cross-Strait trade and class cleavages in Taiwan   174
    THUNG-HONG LIN

11 Escalator or merry-go-round? Taiwanese skilled migration
    to China   196
    YEN-FEN TSENG

12 Taiwan's immigration policy and the China impact: the case
    of cross-Strait families   215
    JIAN-BANG DENG

13 Taiwanese youth in mainland China: fragile identity in the
    shadow of China   239
    PING LIN

PART III
The China impact on Taiwan's security   259

14 The rise of China and its implications for US–Taiwan
    relations   261
    CHENG-YI LIN

15 Cross-Strait integration and Taiwan's new security challenges   282

JEAN-PIERRE CABESTAN

16 Conclusions: assessing the China impact   301

GUNTER SCHUBERT

Index   306

Figures

2.1	Support rates for the KMT and the DPP, 1995–2013	16
2.2	Patterns of cross-Strait interactions on Taiwan's statehood	22
5.1	Self-identification and attitude toward the ECFA by age	73
7.1	Return in the export sector	116
7.2	Return in the import-competing sector	117
10.1	Cross-Strait trade and poverty rate in Taiwan, 1992–2013	175
10.2	Changing geography of pan-blue- and pan-green-dominated cities/counties in Taiwan, 1998–2012	176
10.3	Causality among classes, trade and voting behaviour in Taiwan	182
10.4	Cross-Strait mobility and income inequality of social classes in Taiwan	187

Tables

2.1   Mean and variance of major indicators of cross-Strait relations, 1990–2012   24

3.1   Evidence rate of issue claims in Taiwanese presidential campaign ads   39

5.1   Patterns of attitudes across major issues by generation   76

5.2   Self-identification and generation   77

5.3   Independence/unification preference and generation   77

5.4   Partisan preference and generation   78

5.5   Consequences for Taiwan of opening cross-Strait economic exchanges   78

5.6   Are you worried about a military threat from the PRC?   78

5.7   Self-identification by five generations   81

5.8   Independence/unification preference by five generations   81

5.9   Partisan preference by five generations   85

5.10   Consequences for Taiwan of opening cross-Strait economic exchanges   85

5.11   Are you worried about a military threat from the PRC?   86

5.12   Patterns of attitudes across major issues by generation   87

8.1   Party identity and voting, 2013   133

8.2   National identity and voting: independent voters, 2013   135

8.3   Attitudes concerning the 1992 Consensus   138

8.4   1992 Consensus, support and awareness, 2013   140

8.5   The DPP's position on China: independent voters, 2013   142

8.6   The KMT's position on China: independent voters, 2013   143

8.7   Evaluation of cross-Strait economic relations: independent voters, 2013   144

A8.1   The national identity of Taiwan's general public, 1992–2013   146

A8.2   Logistic models predicting voting for Ma Ying-Jeou, 2013   147

9.1   Attitudes towards cross-Strait policies in Taiwan   154

9.2   Factors influencing support for signing the ECFA   157

9.3   Factors influencing support for allowing Chinese students into Taiwan   158

9.4   Factors influencing support for recognition of Chinese
       degrees   160
9.5   Factors supporting opening up Taiwan to Chinese
       individual tourists   161
9.6   Factors influencing increasing the number of Chinese group
       tourist quotas   162
9.7   Cross tables of personal characteristics and cross-Strait
       policies   164
9.8   Cross tables of gender, party and the ECFA   166
9.9   Cross tables of gender, party and allowing Chinese students
       into Taiwan   166
9.10   Cross tables of gender, party and recognition of Chinese
       degrees   167
9.11   Cross tables of gender, party and opening to individual
       tourists   167
9.12   Cross tables of gender, party and increasing Chinese group
       tourist quotas   168
A9.1   Descriptive statistics   171
10.1   Hypotheses from the literature of open economy politics   181
10.2   Descriptive statistics of selective variables in the
       2010–2013 surveys   184
10.3   Correlation matrix of selective variables in the 2010–2013
       China impact surveys   185
10.4   Class inequality related to cross-Strait mobility and income
       in Taiwan, 2010–2013   186
10.5   Subjective feelings of inequality connected to cross-Strait
       trade, 2010–2013   188
10.6   Trade policy and class voting in Taiwan, 2010–2013   190
12.1   Registered number of marriages according to nationality of
       spouses, 1998–2013   218
12.2   Registered number of foreign spouses and Chinese spouses,
       1987–2013   218
12.3   Registered number of Chinese spouses according to visa
       status, 1987–2013   219
12.4   Number of Chinese spouses remaining in Taiwan according
       to visa status in IONPA's White Paper   220
12.5   Percentage of Chinese spouses without household
       registration who stayed continuously in Taiwan   221
12.6.1 List of interviews with Taiwanese expatriates   224
12.6.2 List of interviews with Chinese spouses   225
12.7   Types of residence status of Chinese spouses of Taiwanese
       expatriates   226
14.1   GDP and projection of China, Japan and the US   262
14.2   US trade in goods with China   262
14.3   Taiwan's trade in goods with China   263

Contributors

Jean-Pierre Cabestan is Professor and Head of the Department of Government and International Studies at Hong Kong Baptist University. He is also an associate researcher at the Asia Centre, Paris, and a Senior Researcher at the French National Centre for Scientific Research. His most recent publications include *La politique internationale de la Chine. Entre intégration et volonté de puissance* (Presses de Sciences Po, 2010); *China and the Global Financial Crisis. A Comparison with Europe* (Routledge, 2012, co-edited with Jean-François Di Meglio and Xavier Richet); *Secessionism and Separatism in Europe and Asia. To Have a State of One's Own* (Routledge, 2013, co-edited with Aleksandar Pavkovic); *Le système politique chinois. Un nouvel équilibre autoritaire* (Presses de Sciences Po, 2014); and *Political Changes in Taiwan under Ma Ying-Jeou* (Routledge, 2014, co-edited with Jacques deLisle).

Chih-Jou Jay Chen, Ph.D., is an Associate Research Fellow at the Institute of Sociology at Academia Sinica, a jointly appointed Associate Professor at National Tsing-Hua University, and an adjunct Associate Professor at National Taiwan University. He served as Director of the Centre for Contemporary China, National Tsing Hua University, from 2007 to 2012, and was a visiting scholar at Harvard-Yenching Institute from 2014 to 2015. His current research focuses on popular protests and changing state-society relations in contemporary China and China's growing impacts on Taiwanese society. He is the author of *Transforming Rural China: How Local Institutions Shape Property Rights in China* (Routledge, 2004), and the co-editor of *Social Capital and Its Institutional Contingency: A Study of the United States, China and Taiwan* (Routledge, 2013).

Hsuan-Yun Ted Chen is a PhD candidate in the Department of Political Science at Pennsylvania State University. He is primarily interested in domestic audience costs and how this impacts on international interactions. His work has been published in the *Japanese Journal of Political Science* and the *Journal of Contingencies and Crisis Management*.

Yun-Han Chu is a Distinguished Research Fellow of the Institute of Political Science at Academia Sinica and Professor of Political Science at National Taiwan University. He is concurrently serving as President of the Chiang Ching-Kuo Foundation for International Scholarly Exchange. Professor Chu specializes in the politics of Greater China, East Asian political economy and democratization. He is the author, co-author, editor or co-editor of 15 books. Among his recent English publications are *How East Asians View Democracy* (Columbia University Press, 2008); *Citizens, Elections and Parties in East Asia* (Lynne Reinner, 2008); *Dynamics of Local Governance in China During the Reform Era* (Rowman and Littlefield, 2010); and *Democracy in East Asia: A New Century* (Johns Hopkins University Press, 2013).

Jian-Bang Deng is an Associate Professor at the Graduate Institute of Futures Studies, University of Tamkang, Taiwan. His current research focuses on the impact of mobility and cross-cultural interactions on transnational professionals as well as on the process of inward migration to inner China by Taiwanese manufacturers. Recent publications include 'Marginal Mobilities: Taiwanese Manufacturing Companies' Migration to Inner China', in *Border Crossing in Greater China: Production, Community and Identity* (Routledge, 2014, edited by Jenn-Hwan Wang); 'Citizenship Arrangement for Families of Taiwanese Expatriates with Chinese Spouses', *Taiwan: A Radical Quarterly in Social Studies* 87 (2012; in Chinese); and 'Family Firms and Generational Change: Taiwanese Manufacturing Businesses in the Pearl River Delta', *Mainland China Studies* 58(3) (2010, co-authored by Ming-Ju Wei; in Chinese).

Dafydd J. Fell is a Reader in Comparative Politics with special reference to Taiwan in the Department of Political and International Studies at the School of Oriental and African Studies (SOAS), University of London. He is also the Director of the SOAS Centre of Taiwan Studies. His first book was *Party Politics in Taiwan* (Routledge, 2005), which analysed party change in the first 15 years of multi-party competition in Taiwan. He has co-edited a volume examining the impact of the first change in ruling parties in Taiwan, *What has Changed? Taiwan's KMT and DPP Eras in Comparative Perspective* (Harrassowitz, 2006), and edited a four-volume reference collection of articles, *Politics of Modern Taiwan* (Routledge, 2008). His most recent publication is *Government and Politics in Taiwan* (Routledge, 2011) and he has also co-edited *Migration to and from Taiwan* (Routledge, 2013).

Cheng-Yi Lin is a Research Fellow at the Institute of European and American Studies, Academia Sinica, Taiwan. He received his PhD in Foreign Affairs from the University of Virginia in 1987. His papers have appeared in *American Foreign Policy Interests, Asian Survey, China Quarterly, Issues and Studies, Journal of Northeast Asian Studies*, and the Maryland Series in Contemporary Asian Studies. He co-edited, with Michael Hsiao, *Rise of China: Beijing's Strategies and Implications for the Asia-Pacific* (Routledge, 2009), and, with Denny Roy, *The Future of United States, China, and Taiwan Relations* (Palgrave Macmillan, 2011).

Jih-Wen Lin is a Research Fellow at the Institute of Political Science at Academia Sinica, Taiwan, and Professor of Political Science at National Chengchi University and National Taiwan University. He received his PhD in political science from the University of California, Los Angles (1996). His research interests include East Asian politics, comparative institutional design, and formal modeling, and he has had articles published in *Party Politics*, *Journal of Democracy*, *Electoral Studies*, *China Quarterly*, *Journal of East Asian Studies* and *Issues and Studies*, among others.

Ping Lin is an Associate Professor at the Department of Political Science, National Chung Cheng University, Taiwan. He specializes in migration studies, with a particular focus on issues concerning Taiwanese people in China. His works have been published in Chinese journals (*East Asian Studies*, *Taiwan Politicsl Science Review* and *Journal of Population Studies*) and in English-language journals (*China Review* and *China Information*). He co-edited *Migration To and From Taiwan* (Routledge, 2013, with Kuei-Fen Chiu and Dafydd Fell).

Thung-Hong Lin is an Assistant Research Fellow at the Institute of Sociology and a member of the Committee of the China Impact Survey, Academia Sinica. He is also an Assistant Professor at the Institute of Sociology and a member of the Executive Committee of Centre for Contemporary China, National Tsing Hua University, Taiwan. He specializes in social stratification and the sociology of disaster. His fieldwork research in both China and Taiwan has led to the publication of numerous journal articles (mainly in Chinese in the *Journal of Social Sciences and Philosophy*, *Taiwanese Sociological Review*, *East Asian Studies* and *Chinese Journal of Sociology*) on social stratification and the social impacts of earthquakes. He has also been working as a member of an NGO research team investigating the Foxconn workers' suicide events in China since 2010.

Shelley Rigger is the Brown Professor of East Asian Politics, Chair of Political Science, and Chair of Chinese Studies at Davidson College. She has a PhD in Government from Harvard University and a BA in Public and International Affairs from Princeton University. Rigger is the author of two books on Taiwan's domestic politics, *Politics in Taiwan: Voting for Democracy* (Routledge, 1999) and *From Opposition to Power: Taiwan's Democratic Progressive Party* (Lynne Rienner, 2001). In 2011, she published a book for general readers: *Why Taiwan Matters: Small Island, Global Powerhouse*. She has published articles on Taiwan's domestic politics, the national identity issue in Taiwan–China relations and related topics. Her monograph *Taiwan's Rising Rationalism: Generations, Politics and 'Taiwan Nationalism'* was published by the East West Center in Washington in 2006.

Gunter Schubert, PhD, is Professor of Greater China Studies at the Institute of Asian and Oriental Studies, University of Tübingen. He is also the founder and Director of the European Research Centre on Contemporary Taiwan at that university. His current research focuses on China's local political economy and local governance reforms, Taiwan's domestic politics, cross-Strait relations, Taiwanese entrepreneurs operating on the Chinese mainland

and the theoretical implications of research on regime legitimacy. Recent publications include *Participation and Empowerment at the Grassroots – Chinese Village Elections in Perspective* (Rowman and Littlefield, 2013, with Anna L. Ahlers), *Taiwanese Identity in the 21st Century: Domestic, Regional and Global Perspectives* (Routledge, 2011, co-edited with Jens Damm) and *Regime Legitimacy in Contemporary China: Institutional Change and Stability* (Routledge, 2009, co-edited with Thomas Heberer).

Yen-Fen Tseng is Professor of Sociology at National Taiwan University. Her research focuses on migration and the characteristics of places. She is currently studying Taiwanese cultural workers in China. Her recent publications include 'Reconfiguring Citizenship and Nationality: Dual Citizenship of Taiwanese Migrants in China' (with Wu Jieh-Min, *Citizenship Studies*) and 'Shanghai Rush: Skilled Migrants in a Fantasy City' (*Journal of Ethnic and Migration Studies*). She now holds a position as editor of *Taiwanese Journal of Sociology* and as corresponding editor to *International Journal of Urban and Regional Research*.

Hans H. Tung is an Assistant Professor in the Department of Political Science at National Taiwan University. He received his PhD in Government from Harvard University in 2011. His general research interests include international political economy, the political economy of authoritarianism, Chinese politics and the rise of China. In particular, his work seeks to uncover the political logic of authoritarian institutions in general and to explore its impacts on economic policy-making in China and on China's growing importance on the world stage. His dissertation dealt with the ways in which sectoral special interests influence trade policy outcomes in China's institutional context, where intra-elite political interactions are highly institutionalized. Some of the most important results will be published in the economics-oriented peer-reviewed journal *Emerging Markets Finance and Trade* and in other edited volumes.

Chung-Li Wu is a Research Fellow at the Institute of Political Science, Academia Sinica, Taiwan. His research interests are American politics, comparative politics, urban and minority politics, and electoral studies. He is the author of articles published in *Party Politics*, *China Quarterly*, *Parliamentary Affairs*, *Journal of Black Studies*, *Asian Survey*, *Issues and Studies* and *Japanese Journal of Political Science*, among others.

Nai-Teh Wu received a PhD in Political Science from the University of Chicago in 1987. He is a Research Fellow at the Institute of Sociology, Academia Sinica. He was a visiting Associate Professor in the Sociology Department at the University of Michigan, Ann Arbor, in 1996. He was also the founding president of the Taiwanese Political Science Association (1995–1997). He has published papers on topics related to democratic transition, ethnic politics, working class politics and transitional justice. His current research interest is the issue of national identity in Taiwan.

Foreword

Michael H.H. Hsiao

This edited volume is a product of the highly effective collaboration between the Institute of Sociology at Academia Sinica, Taiwan, and the European Research Centre on Contemporary Taiwan (ERCCT) at the University of Tübingen, Germany. It developed from a conference on 'Assessing the China Impact: Taiwan's Society and Politics in the Process of Intensifying and Multiplying Cross-Strait Interaction', jointly organized by the two institutions on 21–22 June 2012 in Tübingen. I had the pleasure of attending this conference and joining in the lively discussions about all the papers presented on that occasion. The authors who have contributed to this volume are indeed among the most highly qualified experts in their fields, and their contributions enhance our understanding of the emerging China impact in Taiwan as manifested in various aspects of domestic politics, society and security. In my best judgment, this is the first edited volume published in English or in Chinese to date that systematically explores the new frontier of the ever more complex relations across the Taiwan Strait.

The term 'China impact' was first officially coined on the occasion of the establishment of the Thematic Research Team on China Impact Study (CIS) at the Institute of Sociology in March 2011, which, since then, has been coordinated by Dr Mau-Kuei Chang. The CIS team members have taken serious note of the growing impacts resulting from increasing Taiwan–China interaction and integration. They have witnessed the expected and unexpected consequences of growing cross-Strait trade and investment, increasing cross-border immigration, tourism, academic and cultural exchanges, specially arranged high-level cross-Strait visits and meetings, and the signing of numerous related agreements between the two sides. The intellectual interest and policy implications of the concerns examined by the CIS have been enthusiastically taken on by Professor Gunter Schubert, ERCCT director, resulting in the jointly organized conference mentioned above and, eventually, in this volume.

The 16 chapters seek to answer crucial questions: What is the China impact on Taiwan? To what extent has Taiwan's 'space' been constrained or expanded by the China impact? What challenges or opportunities have arisen for Taiwan's future due to the China impact? And, finally, how should Taiwan respond to the China impact in order to sustain its national integrity and interests? The authors have tackled these issues with great care. I am sure that interested readers will find useful hints and clues for their own inquiries into the China impact.

After reading the manuscript of the book, I have been inspired to propose another set of perspectives that could be used to facilitate readers' appreciation of the various chapters. The first would be to map all the different China impacts described and analysed in the book. These could be direct or indirect, explicit or implicit, and short-term or long-term in nature. The second perspective would be to more systematically investigate the impact trajectories and mechanisms perceived in Taiwan's public life. These could be in the form of a direct military threat or brought about by pro-China connections – for instance, the activities of the Taishang (Taiwanese entrepreneurs with investments on the Chinese mainland) in trade and investment – or by cross-border marriage immigration, cross-Strait student exchange and skilled labour migration. The third perspective would then be to recognize the coping strategies adopted by Taiwan's civil society and political parties to deal with the China impact. How has the general public perceived and responded to the different impacts? Who has benefited and at whose cost? How have advocacy organizations within Taiwan's civil society as well as prominent intellectuals criticized and resisted these impacts? What are the crucial conflicting viewpoints held by different political parties in Taiwan, that is, the KMT, the DPP and the TSU?

Finally, I tend to agree with the impact assessments and policy recommendations proposed in the various chapters. In general terms, I am of the opinion that both the KMT and the DPP should come up with more responsible and sophisticated policies to accommodate and adapt to the China impact in order to protect Taiwan's interests. More specifically, I expect to witness more and more direct and influential counter-balancing and monitoring acts emerging from civil society to ensure that the China impact does not develop into an uncontrollable force and that the Taiwanese government pursues policies that constrain and restrict the actions of privileged political-economic interest groups in order to set future Taiwan–China relations on track towards a healthy course of development.

Taipei, December 2014
Michael Hsin-Huang Hsiao
Director, Institute of Sociology, Academia Sinica (Taiwan)

1 Introduction

Gunter Schubert

Relations between Taiwan and China have seen remarkable changes since 2008, when the Nationalist Party, or Kuomintang (KMT), regained power after eight years of Democratic Progressive Party (DPP) minority rule under the former independence activist and president, Chen Shui-Bian. The new KMT administration led by Ma Ying-Jiu immediately embarked on a new proactive China policy, which had been carefully prepared during informal talks with the Chinese leadership since the mid-2000s, by establishing an informal Economic Trade and Cultural Forum of the KMT and the Chinese Communist Party (CCP) to discuss practical matters of mutual concern and future cross-Strait policies.[1] New cross-Strait negotiations were set on track that have produced, to date, 20 bilateral agreements (*xieyi*) with far-reaching significance for the evolution of the cross-Strait relationship.[2] Most importantly, direct transportation, communication and trade links were established in late 2008, and in June 2010, the two sides signed an Economic Cooperation Framework Agreement (ECFA) to spur cross-Strait trade liberalization and economic integration (Chow 2013). Although Taiwan's new China approach was sternly opposed by the DPP at first, the results of the presidential and legislative elections in January 2012 showed that the incumbent Ma administration had a fairly solid public mandate. After the defeat of the presidential hopeful, Tsai Ying-Wen, in that year, the DPP was forced to undertake some serious soul-searching concerning the question of whether, and to what extent, it would have to adjust its own China policy in order to stand a fair chance of winning important national elections again in the future (Schubert 2012a).

More than two years into the second Ma administration, as this introduction is being written, cross-Strait relations seem to have arrived at a crossroads. The Sunflower movement (*Taiyanghua yundong*), which paralysed political life in Taiwan between 18 March and 10 April 2014, put an end to the relatively smooth process of rapprochement between Taipei and Beijing that had been developing during the previous few years. On the surface, the demonstrations and public debates were targeting the Trade in Services Agreement (*fumao xieyi*), which was suddenly pushed through the legislative process by the KMT and signed in June 2013 by representatives of China and Taiwan after months of uncompromising bickering in committee deliberations between the ruling party and the opposition.[3] There was, however, a more fundamental reason for the stand-off between the students and the government: to demonstrate open resistance to the China policy of the Ma administration, which was aimed at further liberalizing cross-Strait economic relations, allowing Chinese capital to enter Taiwan on a broad scale and, arguably, paving the way for cross-Strait 'political talks' to the detriment of Taiwan's sovereignty and freedom. In fact, after the new leadership had been established under Xi Jinping in late November 2012, the Chinese government alluded to a necessary shift from 'functional' to political talks on various occasions, highlighting their unfulfilled desire to settle the 'Taiwan issue' once and for all. Today, the Ma administration is being forced to walk a political tightrope, since it has repeatedly declared that there is no alternative to further cross-Strait economic liberalization if Taiwan's future well-being and solid integration in East Asian free trade regimes are to be ensured (see also Lin 2011). The critical question is how the government can reassure the Taiwan people that increasing exposure to Chinese trade competition, investment and labour migration, combined with political pressure reinforced by thousands of Chinese missiles targeting the island, will not pose a threat to Taiwan's security in the middle and long term.

There can be no doubt that China's economic and political rise is having a stronger effect on Taiwan than on any other country, given the Chinese government's claim to sovereignty over Taiwan and Taiwan's quest to maintain its democratic achievements and political identity as a sovereign state, however that state might be named.[4] Against this background, this volume deals with the 'bigger picture' of evolving relations across the Taiwan Strait, taking as a starting point the observation that China's impact on Taiwan has become continuously stronger over the last 20 years. This relates not only to the economy but also to Taiwan's domestic politics, society and so-called international space, i.e. Taiwan's leeway for becoming a recognized entity that is allowed to play a respected and effective role in regional and global politics.

A survey of the scholarly field reveals that numerous studies have dealt with the economic consequences of the China impact by examining Taiwanese capital flows and the relocation of Taiwanese factories to the Chinese mainland that started in the late 1980s and continued to intensify thereafter. This has triggered a long-standing debate on Taiwan's rising trade dependency on China and the 'hollowing out' of the Taiwanese economy (Tanner 2007; Fuller 2008) as well as, more recently, on the impact of Chinese capital gaining access to Taiwan's domestic markets – allegedly leading, among other things, to soaring prices in the real-estate sector, a depressed labour market and declining food security (Cheng and Mo 2006). From a different perspective, many studies have also gauged the China impact on Taiwan's economic security in more general terms, coming to different conclusions that have often been informed by a more fundamental stance on the opportunities and dangers of cross-Strait integration and globalization for Taiwan (Dent 2001; Ho and Leng 2004; Lee 2008). Taiwan's military security 'in the shadow of China' has been an issue of constant concern for Taiwan scholars observing the modernization of China's armed forces and

US–Taiwan relations (Zhang 2011; Gelsing 2012; Bush 2013). In this context, an alarming debate has arisen in the US in recent years on the proposal to launch a new policy that would eventually lead to Taiwan's being abandoned in order to remove the most difficult obstacle to amicable US–China relations (Mearsheimer 2014). Interestingly enough, this debate was triggered by the post-2008 détente in the Taiwan Strait, because some US scholars and politicians felt that Washington was no longer bound to support Taiwan and that the China policy premises should be redefined. At the same time, China has been exerting pressure on other states not to accommodate Taiwan's quest for more international space and persistently limits Taiwan's room for manoeuvre in those international organizations where Taiwan has already gained representation of some kind (Lindemann 2014).

Fewer studies, at least in Western languages, have discussed the China impact in terms of the long-term consequences for Taiwan's society. The useful volume edited by Kuei-Fen Chiu, Dafydd Fell and Ping Lin (2014) gives a good overview of the state of the field and includes some chapters that consider the consequences of Chinese migration to Taiwan, discussing, among other topics, the impact on official immigration policies, the formation of a mainland spouses' rights movement, and changing family patterns under the influence of cross-Strait marriages. In terms of party politics, a few Taiwan scholars have discussed the China policy dilemma that is facing the DPP as a result of the China impact, i.e. the search for a new approach to reconcile the quest for Taiwan's independence with the goal of winning elections, reflecting the pressure placed on the DPP to accommodate Taiwan's inevitable escape from the 'Chinese orbit' (Schubert 2012b). Many more studies could be cited which, to different degrees, have touched on the China impact on Taiwan's politics and society, but this topic has not yet been studied systematically or even considered from a comparative perspective. This volume is intended to fill this gap in the field of Taiwan studies.

As a joint undertaking by the European Research Centre on Contemporary Taiwan and the Institute of Sociology at Academia Sinica in Taipei,[5] political scientists and sociologists, including many from Taiwan, were invited to a conference held in Tübingen in July 2012 to examine and discuss the China impact on Taiwan in both empirical and conceptual terms.[6] More precisely, the participants in this conference were asked to respond to the following research questions:

- What precisely is the 'China impact' on Taiwan in the research area they are concerned with? How can this impact be measured?
- To what extent is Taiwan's political and social space constrained and/or enlarged by the 'China impact'?
- What kinds of challenges and/or opportunities arise from the 'China impact' for Taiwan's future, and how should Taiwan respond to them?

One thorny issue, of course, is measurement. With regard to economic relations between Taiwan and China, impact can be measured fairly accurately by, for example, Taiwan's evolving trade dependency on China or the changes in the relative percentage of Taiwanese investment flowing into China. The measuring process is much trickier, however, for political and social relations across the Taiwan Strait. For instance, the purely numeric increases in the number of mainland Chinese tourists who visit Taiwan every year and in the number of Taiwanese citizens who migrate to China to work and reside there more or less permanently does not tell us much about the long-term economic, social and political consequences in Taiwan proper. There is no authoritative methodology for measuring political and social impact, but – as the chapters in this volume show – there are a number of routes to impact assessment, based on quantitative survey data and/or qualitative interviews, and, most importantly, informed interpretation. This issue will be addressed again in the concluding chapter, where the general insights provided by the contributors to the volume will be discussed and the direction of future research will be laid out. First of all, however, brief summaries of the different chapters will give the reader a general idea of the direction in which this research is heading.

Starting with China's impact on Taiwan's domestic politics, Jih-Wen Lin draws on a modified version of Putnam's 'two-level game' model to explain how the Chinese government has become an important player in Taiwanese domestic politics by employing material incentives to influence the voting behaviour and change the ideological beliefs of the general public in Taiwan, primarily among the crucial constituency of 'undecided voters'. At the same time, the author shows how economic payoffs impact on the political alternatives of negotiators on both sides under specific circumstances: Beijing would offer the Taiwanese people more if there were an independence-leaning president who was facing increasing trade dependence on China. However, economic incentives – such as the ECFA, signed in mid-2010 – could negatively rebound on Beijing because any extra benefits for Taiwanese voters would be levelled off by market forces in Taiwan in the long term and this could have the effect of enhancing support for independence. On the other hand, Taipei is constrained by the consequences of increasing economic integration across the Taiwan Strait and the threat of military conflict if the issue of independence is pushed too far. An independence-leaning government would thus safely be able to allow more cross-Strait trade liberalization and hold Beijing hostage to its economic promises to Taiwan, but this would incur the risk of increasing dependency and political pressure. In the end, Beijing has to consider the possibility that the DPP may regain power in Taiwan, even if overall support for the 'pan-green' camp (those parties favouring a Chinese identity and links with China) is lower than that for the 'pan-blue' parties (those leaning towards independence from China). Only with a non-independence government in power is there a chance that the negative long-term effects on Taiwanese voters of the levelling off of material benefits by cross-Strait trade liberalization will not translate into even stronger support for the pro-independence camp. For this reason, Beijing has every reason to do what it can to keep the KMT in power.

Hsuan-Yun Ted Chen and Chung-Li Wu discuss the China impact on negative campaigning in Taiwan politics. They find that 'China' is an 'easy issue' because

China-related claims provoke 'gut responses' from the Taiwanese public; political opponents can therefore deploy such claims to attack each other without having to concern themselves with providing evidence in support of the claims being made. Relying on a dataset of television and newspaper campaign advertisements from four Taiwanese presidential elections, the authors show that the evidence rate for issues related to China is significantly lower than that for all other issues. This quantitative finding is buttressed by three qualitative case studies, in which anti-China sentiments were incited by politicians who attacked opponents and were then taken to court. In each of the cases, the supporting evidence was weak or even nonexistent. Unsubstantiated negative campaigning illustrates the high level of mistrust that exists in Taiwan's society with respect to 'China' and poses the question of the extent to which Taiwan's democratic political culture is compromised by invoking 'China' as a threat (or as an opportunity).

Dafydd J. Fell deals with the China impact on Taiwan's electoral politics and the significance of cross-Strait economic relations as a campaign issue after Taiwan's democratic transition. He finds that the political parties have been paying increasing attention to economic interaction across the Taiwan Strait since the early 1990s, which reflects the growing importance of China's market transformation for Taiwan's economic well-being. Whereas the New Party (NP) and the Taiwan Solidarity Union (TSU) have remained consistent in their treatment of the issue, the KMT and the DPP, for their part, vacillated considerably before starting to converge on cross-Strait economic issues after the ECFA debate came to a temporary halt in 2012. Today, the DPP no longer opposes the ECFA and cross-Strait economic integration, and the KMT has taken a firm pro-integration stance in accordance with much earlier NP campaign rhetoric. The author holds that Taiwan's political parties have generally been responsive to, and have learned from, the challenges stemming from China's economic rise, making Taiwan's democracy appear in much better shape than is usually suggested.

Shelley Rigger presents an analysis of the distinctive attitudinal patterns of Taiwanese citizens that reflect the influence of formative events in the island republic's post-war history on the mindsets of the Taiwanese people, including their thinking on China and cross-Strait relations. She distinguishes between five generations which have been shaped by such events: those born before 1932, who were born during the Japanese colonial era and witnessed the KMT arriving in Taiwan and installing its regime; those born between 1932 and 1953, who were socialized at a time when ideological rigidity, ethnic tension and political repression were at a peak; those born between 1954 and 1968, who grew up during the years when authoritarianism was increasingly being challenged; those born between 1968 and 1982, who lived through an era of rapid political change; and finally those born after 1982, who experienced the first coming to power of a DPP government and a new phase of democratic politics in Taiwan, as well as a changing cross-Strait relationship against the background of China's rise. Rigger is particularly interested in this latter generation of young Taiwanese, who were most intensely exposed to the China impact, and finds that their attitudes defy the 'established wisdom' that Taiwanese identity correlates with scepticism, if not outright hostility, towards China. On the contrary, fifth-generation Taiwan-ese easily identify themselves as Taiwanese but are ready to engage with China at the same time. They are optimistic about future economic integration and seldom express concern about military tensions across the Taiwan Strait – find-ings that are, however, challenged by the recent Sunflower movement with its China-sceptical outlook.

Gunter Schubert investigates the capacity of Taiwanese entrepreneurs with investments on the Chinese mainland (Taishang) to influence Taiwan's domestic politics and China policy-making. His analysis focuses on the Taishang's influ-ence as a voter bloc in important national elections; as a lobby group that spon-sors Taiwanese politicians and political parties, working through business associations in both China and Taiwan as well as through informal networks which have links to Taiwanese policy-makers at local and national levels; and as manipulators of public opinion, most notably through the acquisition of substan-tial commercial stakes in the Taiwanese media market. Schubert finds that the Taishang with investments on the Chinese mainland do not really have sufficient organizational power to exert strong influence within Taiwan, although their informal power is substantial. In addition to this, since the Taishang have not yet developed a collective identity, more coordinated action is required for them to realize their common interests, which converge in continuous market liberaliza-tion and economic integration across the Taiwan Strait. As a Chinese 'impact factor' they are much less effective than is generally perceived in Taiwan, although a number of powerful 'tycoons' suggest otherwise.

Hans H. Tung and Yun-Han Chu, in their theoretical chapter, propose a political-economy model to explain the conditions under which the Ma govern-ment would be able to send out a credible message to the international com-munity to the effect that it has adopted a conciliatory approach towards mainland China. The signing of the ECFA, the authors argue, was a 'costly signal' that indeed generated this credibility, informing China that Taiwan was ready for increasing mainland investment and informing the world that it was determined to restore its economic and political relations beyond China. By arguing that the ECFA has the potential to succeed in gaining international trust in Taiwan's policy agenda, the authors underline the possibility that the ECFA can impact positively on Taiwan's economy and further world market integration. Although they do not take sides in the debate between the protagonists and critics of the ECFA, which has been ongoing since the negotiations started in 2009, they clearly underline the potential of trade agreements with China to strengthen Tai-wan's global economic appeal.

In his survey analysis of China's impact on the 2012 presidential elections, Nai-Teh Wu focuses on the group of 'independent voters' as a core constituency that is decisive for the outcome of all national-level elections. He finds that inde-pendent voters who held positive views on cross-Strait economic integration supported the KMT. More interesting is his finding that those independent voters who thought that the KMT was overly inclined towards China did not necessarily show stronger support for the DPP. Even if independent voters held the opinion that both parties were overly inclined towards China, they would still support the KMT by a ratio of 60:40 against the DPP. Obviously, independent voters (and most Taiwanese, for that matter) judged that the economic benefits resulting from cross-Strait interaction outweighed the danger of Taiwan's becoming too dependent on the Chinese economy and too exposed to China's long-term political pressure. This suggests a rough ride ahead for the DPP and its hopes of regaining power.

Turning to the China impact on Taiwan's social fabric, Chih-Jou Jay Chen draws on comprehensive survey data to investigate the Taiwanese people's attitudes towards the various China-related policies that have been implemented by the KMT government since 2008: the signing of the ECFA; recognizing Chinese diplomas and degrees; allowing Chinese students to study in Taiwan; permitting individual Chinese tourists to enter Taiwan; and increasing the daily quota of Chinese tourists on group tours entering Taiwan. The author finds that individual stances towards these policies vary depending on the diverging social-political backgrounds of the respondents. Generally speaking, older Taiwanese, males, pan-blue supporters, and people enjoying higher incomes are more likely to support these policies than younger Taiwanese, females, non-pan-blue supporters, and people with lower incomes and socio-economic status. Interesting additional findings in Chen's study include the fact that middle-of-the road voters show less support for China-related policies than pan-blue supporters, and that Taiwanese women show less support for them than men. The latter phenomenon may be related, as Chen argues, to the consequences of the increasing social interaction across the Taiwan Strait for marriage and family patterns in Taiwan, which are perceived as widely negative by Taiwanese women.

Thung-Hong Lin discusses the impact of cross-Strait trade on class formation and class-based voting in present-day Taiwan. Drawing on open economy politics (OEP) theory, he shows how increasing economic integration and cross-Strait policies are changing Taiwan's income distribution and the voting behaviour of different social groups, categorized in neo-Marxist class terms as capitalists, the self-employed, the new middle classes and the working class. Increasing cross-Strait economic interaction, the author finds, strengthens the income and assets of the capitalists and the new middle classes in comparison to the self-employed and unskilled workers. The latter therefore prefer to vote for the pan-green camp, which is expected to be critical of economic integration across the Taiwan Strait, whereas the former vote for the pan-blue parties precisely because of their pro-integration stance. Class voting is mainly determined by the voters' attitudes towards cross-Strait trade and their assessment of Taiwan's (deteriorating) income distribution. The Taiwan case thus confirms the return of class voting in times of accelerating globalization of which China's economic rise and impact is a consequence that Taiwan has to face.

Yen-Fen Tseng investigates China's attraction for Taiwanese skilled workers, who are labelled by the author as 'independent movers', a rather new phenomenon of cross-Strait migration resulting from specific career expectations and aspirations that can no longer be satisfied in Taiwan. Tseng is particularly interested in the attitudes and life circumstances of these individuals in their host country, China, and the ways in which the Taiwanese state deals with their citizenship. Today's professional white-collar workers and managers from Taiwan who look for jobs in China differ substantially from the first generation of migrants. These were usually assigned to positions by their home companies, which had shifted all or many of their operations to the mainland market. By contrast, a merry-go-round attitude prevails among these new migrants, who switch easily between companies and geographical locations, have strong faith in the opportunities that can be found in China's global cities, but also feel the growing pressure of the competition from the local workforce. Tseng describes 'woman warriors' who enjoy more equality and respect in China than they had experienced in Taiwan, and young Taiwanese graduates who courageously plunge into the mainland market to make a career, against all odds. Interestingly enough, the Taiwanese state's reaction to skilled labour migration is conservative: dual citizenship for Taiwanese citizens residing long-term in China is impossible, and the mandatory linking of their Taiwanese nationality with universal health coverage back at home ensures that migrants do not switch to Chinese nationality. This approach gives rise to tensions among the migrant community and raises the question of how these Taiwanese citizens are going to integrate into their host society over time – an intriguing issue in the context of assessing the China impact on both the national identity and the social status of Taiwan's 'compatriots' living on the mainland.

Jian-Bang Deng analyses an interesting new pattern of cross-Strait marriages in which Chinese spouses increasingly opt to retain their PRC citizenship and do not apply for permanent residence in Taiwan. According to the author's findings, the main reason for this phenomenon is that Chinese spouses prefer to obtain an urban Chinese household registration (*hukou*) rather than Taiwanese citizenship, since they want to live their lives in urban China and do not wish to move to a country where they will be socially isolated and may not be able to find appropriate jobs. Being married to a Taiwanese citizen enables them to move upward in Chinese society; cross-Strait couples nowadays apply for Taiwanese citizenship for their children only. Against this background, the author identifies a 'family-based dual citizenship' arrangement according to which cross-Strait couples decide to reside in urban China but secure Taiwanese citizenship for their offspring in order to ensure that the latter enjoy more strategic options in the future. He argues that the present immigration policies in Taiwan must respond to this trend, since Taiwan is gradually changing from being an emigrant country into being both an emigrant and immigrant country.

Ping Lin is concerned with the formation and changes in identity of young Taiwanese people attending two Taishang Schools (schools established by Taiwanese business people) in Dongguan and Shanghai in the mid-2000s, and after their graduation some years later. He found that during their years at the TBSs, these teenagers developed a bifurcated identity: within the schools they constituted themselves as a non-Chinese community, while outside the schools they learned to mimic their Chinese compatriots' speech and body language. Lin identifies a sense of anxiety in these young people. It results from a feeling of distance that they perceive between themselves and Taiwan which has, arguably, intensified over time. When the author met his respondents again after they had graduated, he found that those who had stayed on in China were still living in this state of anxiety and longing to return to their 'lost' home. Nevertheless, they told him that they could not imagine living permanently in Taiwan. Those who had returned to Taiwan, on the other hand, felt socially marginalized, if not excluded, and found it difficult to communicate with their compatriots in Taiwan. With respect to their future career planning, almost all the respondents intended to work and live in China. Lin suggests that the China impact had made them develop a 'Taiwanese Overseas' identity based on their real life experiences as a Taiwanese community detached from Taiwan proper and therefore different from the Taiwanese people who had not lived on the mainland.

Turning to the dimension of foreign politics and regional security, Cheng-Yi Lin looks at changing US–Taiwan relations in the context of China's economic and military rise on the one hand, and improving cross-Strait relations on the other. The triangular relationship between Taipei, Beijing and Washington has certainly become more complex during recent years. For instance, in the South China and East China Sea island disputes, Taiwan (as the Republic of China) maintains its sovereignty claims against all other claimants. At the same time, Taiwan has been urged by Beijing to support a 'China' stance, a position which Taipei cannot adopt without alienating the US and Japan. As a matter of fact, Taiwan needs the latters' support to protect itself against the continuous threat of Chinese military intervention. Given the tensions between the US and China as well as between China and Japan, Taiwan is being forced to walk a political tightrope, trying not to tilt towards China or the US. However, this is becoming increasingly difficult because China expects Taiwan to engage in political negotiations to deepen the cross-Strait détente; at the same time, the US is displaying an ambivalent attitude towards the rapprochement between Taipei and Beijing, which may not ultimately serve its geostrategic interests in East and Southeast Asia. This chapter shows quite clearly that the China impact is multifaceted with regard to Taiwan's security and that sophisticated policies are required to accommodate all the major players in the region: the US and Japan, but first and foremost China.

Jean-Pierre Cabestan highlights Taiwan's many security challenges from both external and domestic perspectives: the military threat of a modernizing PLA which is all the more serious given Taiwan's shrinking defence budget; the lack of a security dialogue and the structural impediments to implementing meaningful CBMs; the more critical stance towards the political and military value of Taiwan that has been adopted by the US as a result of the PLA's increasing combat capabilities and of the overall geostrategic considerations in Washington which attribute paramount importance to the US–China relationship; the new KMT nationalism that is accompanying the Ma administration's pro-China policies; the DPP's obvious dilemma stemming from being forced to come to terms with the '1992 Consensus' if it ever intends to become the ruling party again; the activities of cross-Strait lobbying groups, such as the Taiwanese business people, who are in favour of more interaction across the Taiwan Strait and actively shape the China discourse in Taiwan; and finally, Beijing's United Front Strategy that targets not only Taiwanese migrants to the Chinese mainland but also the political elites back in Taiwan. As a matter of fact, Taiwan's quest for sovereignty seems to be becoming less and less tenable as the island is slowly dragged into the Chinese orbit. It is therefore of critical importance for Taiwan to revitalize and strengthen the four factors that have so far secured its de facto independence: a meaningful military defence system, US support, democracy, and an overarching 'sovereignist consensus'.

The selection of the chapters in this volume is certainly not comprehensive, as the focus is on the political and social dimensions of the China impact on Taiwan. China's impact on Taiwan's 'international space', with reference to participation in international organizations and East Asia's protracted process of gradual economic and political integration, are also important topics. In addition, studies to assess the impact of the changing Chinese economy on Taiwan's industry and service sectors both at home and in mainland China would also have served to complement this volume. However, in view of the limited space, as well as the aim of achieving a high level of disciplinary coherence, the compilation of the chapters presented here seems plausible enough to the editor and, it is hoped, to the reader as well.

Finally, this volume would not have been possible without the committed support of Dr Michael Hsin Huang Hsiao and Dr Chang Mau-kuei from Academia Sinica's Institute of Sociology (ISO). Michael set the 'China Impact Studies Research Team' (CISRT) of ISO on track and, in this context, wholeheartedly supported the ISO-ERCCT joint conference in Tübingen. Mau-kuei, as responsible CISRT coordinator, was of critical importance in integrating this group of scholars into the project. He also secured a major part of the Tübingen conference's funding and was of great help in the initial phase of the editorial process. I extend my special gratitude to him.

Notes

1 These annual meetings were first held in 2006. See also Beckershoff (2014).
2 The Chinese and English texts of these agreements, including the current status of legislative deliberation, can be found on the government's Mainland Affairs Council website (n.d.).
3 As a direct result of the Sunflower movement, a final reading of the Trade in Services Agreement (TSA) has been stalled in the Legislative Yuan. The government has promised to draft a new law to ensure more legislative oversight and transparency in cross-Strait negotiations, but the opposing camps are contesting whether this law could be applied to the TSA. The Ma administration has maintained its stance that the TSA could not be modified by the Legislative Yuan since this would entail new negotiations with the Chinese government. It is quite probable that the accord will not be ratified before the next presidential elections in early 2016. At a more ideological level, the leaders of the Sunflower movement have promised to continue the struggle, not only by keeping a watchful eye on the Ma administration's China policy but also

by rejuvenating Taiwan's civil society and strengthening the people's national consciousness.

4 The borderline for all political parties in Taiwan and the overall majority of Taiwanese is the undisputable sovereignty of the Taiwan state, whether this be called the Republic of China – its official designation – or the Republic of Taiwan, which is the title of a still unfulfilled project being pursued by the Taiwan independence movement.

5 The Institute of Sociology at Academia Sinica launched a research project in 2012 which gathers survey data to assess the China impact on Taiwan; this has already led to a number of conferences. The outcome of this ongoing research is partly reflected in the chapters in this volume.

6 I would like to thank my colleague and friend of almost 25 years, Dr Chang Mau-Kui, for helping to organize the conference in Tübingen and to express my regret that sudden illness prevented him from attending.

References

Beckershoff, André (2014) 'The KMT-CCP Forum: Securing Consent for Cross-Strait Rapprochement', *Journal of Current Chinese Affairs*, 43, 1: 213–241.

Bush, Richard C. (2013) *Unchartered Street. The Future of China–Taiwan Relations*, Washington DC: Brookings Institution Press.

Cheng, Joseph Y. S., and Mo, Shixiang (2006) 'The Entry of Mainland Chinese Investment into Taiwan. Considerations and Measures Adopted by the Taiwan Government', *China Information*, 22, 1: 91–118.

Chiu, Kuei-Fen, Fell, Dafydd, and Lin, Ping (eds) (2014) *Migration To and From Taiwan*, Abingdon: Routledge.

Chow, Peter C. Y. (ed.) (2013) *Economic Integration Across the Taiwan Strait*, Cheltenham: Edward Elgar.

Dent, Christopher M. (2001) 'Being Pulled into China's Orbit: Navigating Taiwan's Foreign Economic Policy', *Issues and Studies*, 37, 5: 1–34.

Fuller, Douglas B. (2008) 'The Cross-Strait Economic Relationship's Impact on Development in Taiwan and China', *Asian Survey*, 48, 2: 239–264.

Gelsing, Jeroen (2012) 'Taiwan's Growing Security Vulnerability: From Chen Shui-Bian to Ma Ying-Jiu', *Asian Affairs*, 43, 2: 253–267.

Ho, Szu-Yin, and Leng, Tse-Kang (2004) 'Accounting for Taiwan's Economic Policy toward China', *Journal of Contemporary China*, 13, 41: 733–746.

Lee, Chun-Yi (2008) 'When Private Capital Becomes a Security Asset: Challenging Conventional Government/Business Interaction', *East Asia*, 25, 2: 145–165.

Lin, Tsu-Jia (ed.) (2011) *ECFA yu dongya jingjin zhenghe ji chanye hezuo* [ECFA and East Asian Economic Integration and Industrial Cooperation], Taipei: National Policy Foundation.

Lindemann, Bjoern (2014) *Cross-Strait Relations and International Organizations. Taiwan's Participation in IGOs in the Context of its Relationship with China*, Wiesbaden: VS Springer.

Mainland Affairs Council website (n.d.) www.mac.gov.tw/ct.asp?xItem=67145&CtNode=5710&mp=1 (in Chinese) (accessed 24 October 2013).

Mearsheimer, John J. (2014) 'Say Goodbye to Taiwan', *National Interest*, March–April.

Schubert, Gunter (2012a) 'Between Strategic Change and Ideological Adjustment: The DPP's China Policy Debate in the Aftermath of the 2012 National Elections', *Taiwan Zhengzhi Xuekan* [Taiwanese Political Science Review], 16, 2: 233–270.

Schubert, Gunter (2012b) 'No Winds of Change: Taiwan's 2012 National Elections and the Post-Election Fallout', *Journal of Current Chinese Affairs*, 41, 3: 143–161.

Tanner, Murray S. (2007) *Chinese Economic Coercion Against Taiwan*, Santa Monica CA: Rand Corporation.

Zhang, Baohui (2011) 'Taiwan's New Grand Strategy', *Journal of Contemporary China*, 20, 69: 269–285.

Part I

The China impact on Taiwan's domestic politics

2 The PRC as a player in Taiwan's domestic politics

A two-level game analysis

Jih-Wen Lin

In Taiwan's domestic politics, the People's Republic of China (PRC) is not only a significant factor but also a major player. The PRC's central government in Beijing[1] has a clear agenda on Taiwan: to use whatever means necessary to eradicate the 'Taiwan independence force'. For example, in Taiwan's 2012 presidential election, the top business leaders' endorsement of the '1992 Consensus' on the existence of only one China was critical for Ma Ying-Jeou's victory; most likely, Beijing's implicit agreement was required for these tycoons to make this claim.[2] The government in Beijing, being sensitive to the fact that China's economic growth had the capacity not only to attract the interested parties but also to remind them of the cost of running away, was clearly employing a cautious strategic approach. How would Beijng fulfill this goal? Beijing's catchall strategy toward Taiwan says little about whether any specific group will be treated differently, especially when resources are limited. Taiwan's presidential election is a good example. The outcome of the presidential election is determined not only by the popularity of the two camps, but also by the 'floating' voters between them. In this chapter, a two-level game model will demonstrate how Beijing's strategy plays a decisive role by affecting the vote choices of Taiwan's nonpartisan voters – it would be inefficient to spend resources on the deep green or deep blue voters, whose vote choices are unlikely to be modified by material interests.

The key issue is cross-Strait exchanges. The pro-independence camp wishes to protect their constituencies from being infiltrated by Chinese capital precisely because Beijing has a strong incentive to import goods produced by Taiwan's primary sector, in which many potential pan-green supporters work. Alternatively, free trade promoted by an anti-independence leader would expose undecided voters employed in vulnerable industries to a greater risk. Nevertheless, Beijing hopes to increase the dependence of Taiwan's nonpartisan voters on the mainland economy and, by this means, to minimize their support for Taiwan's independence. The success of Beijing's strategy depends on the partisanship of Taiwan's president, which is strongly affected by the structure of Taiwan's national identity.

In the next section, I will review the relevant literature and explain why a revised two-level game model is helpful. A two-level game model will then be constructed in order to demonstrate the political significance of Beijing's eco-nomic strategy. This will be followed by an empirical test of the propositions. The three case studies presented thereafter will show that the theoretical proposi-tions are, in fact, reflections of reality.

Cross-Strait relations: why is a two-level game needed?

The deep impact of cross-Strait relations on practical politics has inspired many policy-oriented studies on current issues. Inevitably, a gap exists between what we know and how we know it.[3] In particular, an important but not frequently discussed issue is how the strategic interaction between government leaders on the two sides of the Taiwan Strait is correlated with their domestic constituents.[4] These people are situated in a peculiar dyad constituted by the PRC and Taiwan: the two sides are economically interdependent but, at the same time, politically competitive. So the key question with regard to cross-Strait relations is how the two governments and their constituents view and affect each other. One plausible way of answering this question is to examine how the PRC, as an authoritarian regime, can build an economic structure to incorporate Taiwan, and how the resultant policies might affect the survival of Taiwan's leaders.[5] Some further points need to be clarified, however, before a theory can be presented that satisfies these requirements.

First, we need to identify the vital actors. Although the Kuomintang (KMT) has always been the dominant party, it is only one part of the pan-blue alliance.[6] The Democratic Progressive Party (DPP) of the pan-green camp has only once received more than 50 per cent of the votes in a presidential election, but the KMT was not the outright favourite in the 2012 race (Figure 2.1 compares the

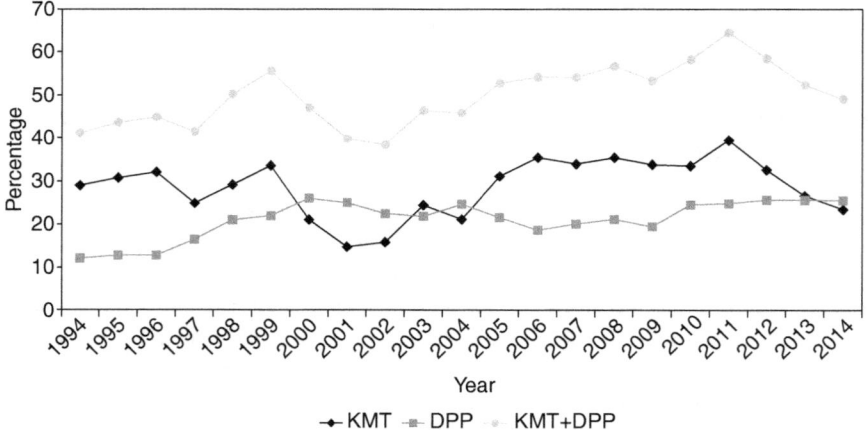

Figure 2.1 Support rates for the KMT and the DPP, 1995–2013 (source: Election Study Center (ESC) at National Chengchi University, see http://esc.nccu.edu.tw/course/news.php?Sn=165#, accessed 19 May 2014; the ESC is the only insti-tution that provides longitudinal data covering the past two decades).

support rates of the two parties). The winner of a presidential election may not be from the most popular party, if there are more than two candidates or if the percentage of non-partisan voters is high. Later in this chapter, we will see from Taiwan's presidential elections how these short-term factors affect the results and how the new president shapes cross-Strait relations.

It is reasonable to assume that Beijing's short-term objective should be to prevent the pro-independence contenders from winning the presidency; in the long term, however, the focus should be on cultivating a Taiwanese economy that is reliant on the PRC for its survival. It should be noted that Beijing, as a powerful authoritarian government, is more capable of achieving these goals than other types of regimes. A follow-up question concerns the precise relationship between Beijing's political objective and its economic policy: does a tough response to sovereignty disputes imply a more stringent economic policy, or is it the other way around?

The answer depends on Beijing's ability to subdue Taiwanese voters and how this affects the electoral chances of the pan-green and pan-blue camps. Since multiple players are involved at the international and domestic levels, the two-level game theory developed by Robert Putnam offers an appropriate approach.[7] In Putnam's model, the consensus shared by a group of players is depicted as the win-sets, that is, the options preferred by these players to the status quo. The model is two-level because domestic thresholds of decision-making or veto points have a strong impact on the results of negotiations.[8] For example, a domestic ratification requiring a qualified majority approval is almost certain to produce smaller win-sets than if a simple majority rule is used, and this is sometimes advantageous for the country with the greater constraints because the reduced win-set may be closer to the ideal position of its negotiators. Domestic institutions thus change the consensus of negotiating countries even if the preferences of the negotiators remain unchanged.

The second question concerns the limits of Putnam's model. When Putnam contends that large win-sets make negotiations more likely, the underlying presumption is of a multidimensional space where the issues exist independently.[9] If the issue space is one-dimensional, the win-sets over the status quo located between the negotiators will always be empty no matter how the domestic conditions change. The one-dimensional issue space with regard to cross-Strait relations is discussed by Lin (2000), who demonstrates the importance of dimensionality. It is also possible that there may be no dimension at all if preferences are not single-peaked.[10]

Lastly, negotiators in Putnam's model cannot change each other's payoffs, which differs from what is going on between the two sides of the Strait. The economic leverage that Beijing enjoys has become stronger than that of Taipei, giving it the capacity to shape the preferences of Taiwanese voters. In contrast, Taiwan's strategic set is dominated by the intensity of pro-independence claims.

A refined two-level game model can provide answers to these questions by demonstrating how Beijing's strategy is correlated with Taiwan's economic dependence and the pro- (or anti-) independence tendency of Taiwan's presidents.

In this game, Beijing's strategy includes the toughness of its attitude toward statehood problems and the extra benefits that it can deliver to the Taiwanese. On the other hand, Taipei can only choose the intensity with which it reveals its pro- (anti-)independence inclinations. Taiwan's statehood options can be represented by a unidimensional space with 'immediate unification' and 'immediate independence' at the two extremes. Beijing hopes to modify the material gains of Taiwanese voters and change their preferences in the statehood dimension. In the following section, I will show how this model can be built and how it can yield testable hypotheses.

The two-level game model reconstructed

Seemingly abstract, the two-level game has perceptible implications: when Taiwan is led by a pro-independence president but does not depend on cross-Strait exchanges to survive, a vicious circle of pro-independence versus retaliation will follow; when Taiwan relies on cross-Strait exchanges to grow, the benefits to undecided voters are intentionally increased (by Beijing) when Taiwan's leader is pro-independence, but otherwise Beijing will allow free trade to even out their benefits unless a backlash seems likely to affect the electoral chances of the anti-independence camp.[11] This section focuses on introducing the assumptions underlying the causal relationship among these variables.

The first assumption is related to the players of the game. In the past two decades, competition among the political parties in Taiwan has intensified, resulting in two changes of regime. We can thus assume that Taiwan's players are the main electoral contenders and that their goal is to maximize their votes. For the Beijing leadership, preventing a DPP candidate from gaining majority support is a top priority. To achieve this goal, Beijing should discourage Taiwan's voters from voting for the DPP. Since a military threat is likely to scare these people away, Beijing should consider the potential effects of economic incentives. The weight placed on economic factors is therefore another important variable. The second assumption is that Beijing's major target should be the voters who are neither pan-green nor pan-blue; in Taiwan, these voters also form the critical minority for any contender who is serious about winning the presidential election.

The undecided voters deserve special attention due to their decisiveness in Taiwan's electoral competitions. The results of most of the research in this area have shown that, notwithstanding a few highly informed people, the bulk of the undecided voters have high efficacy but low political interest;[12] they are predominantly ethnic Taiwanese living outside northern Taiwan;[13] they are more likely to be labourers, farmers or fishermen and usually have 'dual identities' (both Taiwanese and Chinese);[14] their backgrounds are similar to those of DPP supporters except that the latter have a strong Taiwanese and pan-green identity.[15] One implication is that if a group of voters satisfies all these conditions with the exception of pan-green identification, the likelihood of their endorsing the expansion of cross-Strait exchanges is higher, although they are also potential supporters of the DPP. To sum up, most undecided voters have little interest in politics and are economically vulnerable; given their sub-ethnic background as Taiwanese, the threat from the PRC may encourage them to vote for the DPP, but economic concerns may prompt them to support peaceful cross-Strait relations. In the spatial model, the undecided voters and the median voters look alike, since both groups stand in the middle of the spectrum. The median voters serve as the pivot in a two-candidate race, but the ballots in the hands of undecided voters are what the major candidates want to garner.

The third assumption is that Beijing's interest in the undecided voters should by no means be seen as implying that Beijing will always try to please them. To understand the reasons for this, consider Beijing's decision-making body. No matter how opaque Beijing's decision-making structure is, the president of the PRC is ultimately responsible for Taiwan policy. The Taiwan Affairs Office (TAO) of the State Council (whose membership is the same as that of the Taiwan Office of the Chinese Communist Party Central Committee) is an agency in charge of economic, trade and cultural relations with Taiwan. The TAO, known for its flexible approach to Taiwan, has extensive connections with the Taiwanese people. In contrast, the People's Liberation Army may have an interest in seeing the intensification of the security dilemma in East Asia. Over all these agencies is the Central Leading Group for Taiwan Affairs (CLGTA), which, established in 1979 and led by the General Secretary of the Chinese Communist Party (CCP), is responsible to the CCP politburo.[16] With this structure in place, the PRC president must seek a consensus before he finalizes the Taiwan policy. To build this consensus, Beijing's top leader has two alternatives: get tough or buy off. It is evident that the benefits of persuading Taiwan's undecided voters to support an anti-independence candidate are greater than those of getting tough with them unless the economic card fails to work out.

To sum up, the model depicts the fundamental dispute between the two sides of the Strait over Taiwan's statehood, in which Taiwan's undecided voters play a crucial role in determining the result of the collective choice. Meanwhile, issue positions on Taiwan's statehood are correlated with the economic cards held by Beijing. At one extreme, Beijing can place all the emphasis on sovereignty, which will antagonize the DPP's potential supporters but appease the PRC's hardliners; at the other extreme, Beijing will only consider economic incentives, gambling on the victory of the anti-independence camp. A follow-up question here concerns the way in which the Taiwan leader's stance on the statehood issue is associated with the gains of the undecided voters.

Based on these assumptions, four propositions will now be derived from the two-level game model and the empirical implications of these propositions will be addressed.

Proposition 1: If Taiwan's economic dependence on the PRC is low and the Taiwan leader is anti-independence, then the governments on the two sides of the Strait will coexist peacefully.

This is the simplest outcome the model can imply: low dependence makes it difficult for Beijing to win over Taiwan's voters by economic means, but the two governments are both opposed to Taiwan independence. No conflict exists across the Strait with this result, which can be seen as the baseline of the model. The other propositions will demonstrate how changes in economic factors and stances on Taiwan's statehood affect the equilibrium.

Proposition 2: When Taiwan's economic dependence on the PRC is low but its leader is pro-independence, Beijing will get tough even if this strategy is likely to increase the pro-independence inclination of the Taiwan populace.

Proposition 1 no longer holds if Beijing finds Taiwan's leader to be pro-independence. If the PRC's capacity to provide economic benefits for Taiwan is still constrained, the PRC's decision-maker will be pressured by the hardliners to play tough. Under threat from Beijing, the most likely response in Taiwan will be a shift among undecided voters toward the pro-independence side, an outcome that might lead to the formation of a vicious circle across the Strait.[17]

Proposition 3: If Taiwan is highly dependent on the PRC and the government is anti-independence, the two sides can promote a free trade agreement through which the extra benefits of undecided voters will be levelled out unless the consequences undermine the winning odds of the anti-independence camp.

If the conditions of this proposition are fulfilled, Beijing can adjust Taiwan's payoff structure in several ways. The most effective method is free trade, which tends to level out the benefits of some undecided voters who work in traditional industries or the primary sector. As will be described in more detail later, Beijing's strategy may vary according to the sectors in which the undecided voters work, as well as the responses of these voters. Free trade across the Strait may encounter a barrier if the victims no longer support the anti-independence regime in the coming elections.

Proposition 4: If Taiwan's dependence on the PRC is high but the pro-independence camp controls the government, Beijing is likely to work out a plan to increase the net benefits for Taiwan's undecided voters.

The logic of this proposition is the reverse of the preceding one. In Taiwan's presidential race, the winner should have received the ballots of the undecided voters. For Beijing, giving these voters extra benefits is a convenient means of changing their choices, as they are more sensitive to economic incentives than to ideological mobilization.

In the next section, I will turn the propositions into hypotheses by specifying their initial conditions. Three case studies on Taiwan's presidents will follow. We will see that economic dependence on the mainland is indeed a long-term trend for Taiwan, but the positive or negative payoffs received by the undecided voters in cross-Strait exchanges still vary according to the president's stance on national identity.

The hypotheses

In this section, I will examine the extent to which the propositions capture the reality. According to the codebook (see Appendix 2), the larger the number on the Taiwan statehood dimension the stronger the pro-independence proclivity is signified. Coded from eight sources, the data contain 478 events related to Taiwan's statehood.[18] The time period starts from the first presidential term of Lee Teng-Hui, since this marks the starting point of Taiwan's democratization. The authoritarian period under Chiang Ching-Kuo's leadership, although excluded from the dataset, satisfies proposition 1 and can be seen as the baseline of change. The data are sequenced by date, and the unit of analysis of the longitudinal data is the time period. The data to be analysed will use the broadest time period – the term served by a president – because Beijing has differentiated qualitatively among Taiwan's presidents. The presidents are compared by the mean and variance of their positions on Taiwan's statehood. For the economic variables, economic dependence is measured by the percentage of Taiwan's trade that is conducted with the PRC, with trade dependence approximated by the percentage of its exports that are shipped to the PRC.

The PRC, as an authoritarian regime, can modify the payoff structure of Taiwan's undecided voters in different ways:

1   It can increase their benefits by purchasing their products, restraining the export of substitute goods and encouraging investments that facilitate their employment or increase their incomes.
2   It can decrease their costs by limiting investments that may promote inflation and restricting the inflow of capital that may increase the unemployment rate or housing costs.

Such efforts can be seen in the trade between Taiwan and the PRC. Accordingly, negotiations over cross-Strait exchanges play a critical role in determining Beijing's strategy. Note that Beijing's strategy may differ across sectors. While Beijing may continue to purchase agricultural or fishery products during the terms of office of different presidents of Taiwan, free trade may aggravate pressure on labourers working in traditional industries because their employers may be encouraged to move their companies to the mainland. These aspects will be discussed in the case studies.

As illustrated in Figure 2.2, we begin by ordering the data according to the previously mentioned model and refer to this order as 'the prediction'. Then we compare the actual order with the prediction. The closer the actual order fits the prediction, the stronger is our belief that the model is valid. The following are the hypotheses to be verified.

H1: The sequence of the scores on Taiwan's statehood is Chen 2 > Chen 1 > Lee 2 > Lee 1 > Ma 1 > Ma 2; Beijing's positions should go in the opposite direction.

The number attached to a president's name refers to his term of office. This hypothesis is derived from the assumption that the DPP and the KMT espouse opposing proposals to resolve Taiwan's statehood problem and the proposition that electoral competition forces the contenders to converge on the median voters when they are seeking reelection. It is more difficult to tell whether Lee's 'true colour' (Lee 2) is less pro-independence than Chen's is, but we do know that his sub-ethnic background draws him closer to the Taiwanese identity than does Ma's.

H2: For the Taiwan presidents, the variance of the positions on Taiwan's statehood is term 1 > term 2 and DPP > KMT.

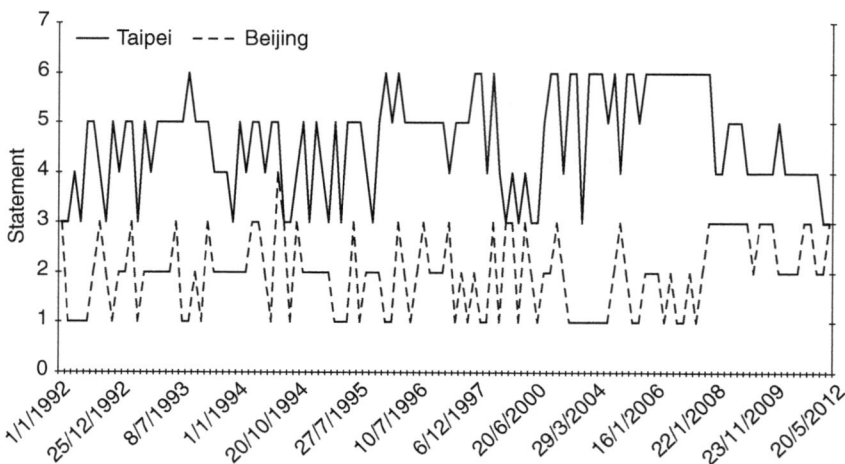

Figure 2.2 Patterns of cross-Strait interactions on Taiwan's statehood (see Appendix 2 for the coding scheme).

The variance reveals the consistency of the actors, the constraint of their presidential terms and their distance from the median position. H2 and H1 share the same assumptions. That is, if the presidents had been hoping to attract the support of the undecided voters during their first terms, Chen would have been more likely to swing between the DPP's ideal point and the median than his counterparts from the KMT.

H3: The variance of Beijing's positions on Taiwan's statehood claims should be Lee > Chen > Ma.

The two-level game implies an interactive dynamic between the two sides of the Strait. H3 predicts the consistency of the cross-Strait messages: there should be a synchronized variance across the Strait indicating that Beijing and Taipei respond quickly to the claims of the other side.

H4: Taiwan's exports to the PRC increased most rapidly after Chen was elected.

The PRC's huge market is an obvious inducement for Taiwan's business owners to endorse a more conciliatory cross-Strait policy. When Chen, known for his pro-independence background, was elected president, Beijing should have been strongly motivated to attract Chen's potential supporters by expanding Taiwanese exports to the mainland.

H5: Taiwan's unemployment rate will rise after Beijing and Taipei have negotiated a free trade agreement.

The proponents of the Economic Cooperation Framework Agreement (ECFA) and the associated agreements claim that free trade can boost Taiwan's economic growth and hence the employment rate. Whether this is true or not, free trade will most likely cause a structural unemployment in the short term, due to mismatched supply and demand in the labour market. In particular, the undecided voters who work in vulnerable sectors are exposed to a greater risk: primary sector products imported from the mainland may intensify market competition, and employees may lose their jobs because business owners have an incentive to shift their investment to the other side of the Strait and cause a slow-down in Taiwan's industrial upgrading (Lin and Hu 2011).

Now is the time to examine how well the data fits the hypotheses. Table 2.1 presents the mean and variance of the code of positions of different regimes and the accompanying economic indicators. Note that some of the indices may have

Table 2.1 Mean and variance of major indicators of cross-Strait relations, 1990–2012

Indicators	Lee 1	Lee 2	Chen 1	Chen 2	Ma 1	Ma 2
Taiwan government's position on Taiwan's statehood	4.10 (0.79)	4.67 (0.63)	4.32 (1.82)	5.31 (0.98)	3.88 (0.46)	3.40 (0.48)
Taiwan leader's position on Taiwan's statehood	4.01 (0.76)	4.66 (0.71)	4.56 (1.91)	5.39 (0.91)	3.97 (0.50)	3.67 (0.49)
PRC government's position on Taiwan's statehood	1.91 (0.60)	1.84 (0.65)	1.95 (0.68)	1.50 (0.45)	2.61 (0.25)	2.60 (0.52)
PRC leader's position on Taiwan's statehood	1.96 (0.47)	2.30 (0.41)	2.50 (0.25)	2.23 (0.49)	2.69 (0.23)	2.50 (0.59)
% of Taiwan's trade with the PRC	1.03 (0.00)	2.42 (0.00)	8.06 (0.16)	17.85 (0.03)	21.22 (0.00)	21.45 (0.00)
% of Taiwan's exports to the PRC	0.19 (0.00)	1.20 (0.00)	9.09 (0.36)	23.37 (0.06)	27.12 (0.00)	26.70 (0.00)
% unemployment	1.63 (0.00)	2.80 (0.00)	4.60 (0.01)	4.03 (0.00)	5.03 (0.00)	4.19 (0.00)

Sources: Directorate-General of Budget, Accounting and Statistics, Executive Yuan (ROC); Department of Statistics, Ministry of Finance (ROC); MOEA, Evaluating the Impact of Cross-Strait Trade and Investment (ROC).

Note
The data of Ma 2 ends on 31 March 2014; variances are in parentheses; Taiwan began to record exports to the PRC in August 1992 and imports from the PRC in August 1991.

a long-term cause, but the sudden change between regimes reveals the short-term political impacts.

For the most part, the data validates H1 (the sequence of positions). With one exception, the two indicators of positions on Taiwan's statehood are ordered as hypothesized. Note that Lee 1 already departs from peaceful coexistence (proposition 1). What H1 fails to predict accurately is the transition from Lee 2 to Chen 1: during his second term, Lee's remark about 'special state-to-state' relations across the Taiwan Strait gives him a high score; in contrast, Chen's 'five nos' inaugural speech delivered on 20 May 2000, is more moderate than the DPP's claims for cross-Strait relations. H2, the variance of positions on Taiwan's statehood, is mostly verified by the data – for Lee and Chen, the scores during their second terms are closer to independence than those during their first terms. H3 is also confirmed: in both Taipei and Beijing, the variances in claims related to Taiwan's statehood change synchronously no matter whether we use data on leaders or on the government. On the whole, H1 and H3 reflect the interactive nature of the cross-Strait messages.

The other two hypotheses posit how cross-Strait economic exchanges are related to the backgrounds of the Taiwan leaders. The test for H4 can be measured by the growth rates of the five transitions between presidential terms, which are 5.32, 6.58, 1.57, 0.16, and –0.02. Clearly, the power transition between Lee and Chen marks the greatest expansion in Taiwanese exports to the PRC. The demand for Taiwan's exports is unlikely to grow at such a rate if the market is the major driving force. The underlying cause is most probably political.

The last hypothesis concerns the unemployment rate under different regimes. It appears that, in the long term, Taiwan's unemployment rates correspond with exports to the PRC, suggesting the impact of dependence on the number of available jobs. In the short term, the comparison between Chen and Ma is most interesting. In Chen 2, when the president became an open advocate of Taiwan independence, the unemployment rate dropped, but it went up after Ma was elected president and began advocating an ECFA. The difference can be explained by the causes of unemployment: the average number of employees who lost their jobs because they were laid off or their companies were closed down is 201.46 in Chen 1, 129.60 in Chen 2, 218.92 in Ma 1, and 138.24 in Ma 2.[19] As will be discussed later, these figures are related to the economic policies of the two presidents in the context of cross-Strait interactions.

Although the hypotheses are largely confirmed, case studies are still needed to flesh out the actual policy-making process. The next section will explain how Beijing mades a qualitative differentiation among the three Taiwanese presidents and will also show the outcomes.

Case studies

The following case studies will discuss the ways in which the Taiwan presidents declared their positions on Taiwan's statehood, Beijing's responses, and the economic relationship between the two sides. Of particular importance is whether the presidents revealed their true preferences during their second terms and how Beijing dealt with the re-elected presidents. We can gain a better understanding of cross-Strait relations by matching the quantitative analyses with the case studies.

Lee Teng-Hui

The first presidential term of Lee Teng-Hui was marked by Taiwan's first direct presidential election. When Lee came to power after Chiang Ching-Kuo passed away in 1988, the status quo was peaceful coexistence (proposition 1), but the direct presidential election brought about a fundamental change. As a native Taiwanese, Lee stood a good chance of attracting support beyond the group of KMT loyalists. As suggested by the data in Table 2.1, the PRC accounted for only a tiny percentage of Taiwan's total trade when Lee was in power. Being assertive was probably the only strategy Beijing could adopt in response to Lee's pro-independence moves (proposition 2).

Lee Teng-Hui began his presidency by re-legitimizing his leadership. At that time, mainlanders were disproportionately represented in the state apparatus, a pattern that Lee had to overcome when he succeeded Chiang Ching-Kuo. Requesting that the president be elected by the people of Taiwan, Peng-Hu, Kinmen and Matsu was a tactic designed to expand the president's power base.

This move had a strong impact on cross-Strait relations because Beijing may have seen it as a de facto step toward Taiwan's achieving independence. During his second term (1996–2000), the most important event was Lee's claim that the two sides of the Taiwan Strait shared a 'special state-to-state' relationship. Judging by the pro-unification stance adopted by Lee in the early phase of his presidency, he had significantly transformed his interpretation of Taiwan's statehood.

The chronology tells a more detailed story. At the beginning of Lee's presidency, he and Jiang Zemin, his counterpart in the PRC, were both consolidating their power bases within their respective parties. Lee was the first Taiwan-born president, but he was, at first, a proponent of the reunification of China. Jiang became General Secretary of the CCP at the Thirteenth Party Congress on 23 June 1989 and chairman of the PRC's Military Commission on 1 January 1990. The organizations that were set up in Taipei and Beijing to handle relations between the two sides, Taiwan's Straits Exchange Foundation (SEF) and the PRC's Association for Relations Across the Taiwan Straits (ARATS), held their first meeting on 26 March 1992. Taiwan's Legislative Yuan passed the Act Governing Relations between the People of Taiwan and the Mainland on 16 July 1992. The establishment of the National Unification Council (NUC) on July 29 was a sign that Taipei acknowledged that there was only one China, although it was currently separated into two political entities. In this way, Lee demonstrated that he accepted the 'one China' principle, and the talks held in Singapore between the heads of the SEF and ARATS, Koo Chen-Fu and Wang Daohan, were based on this consensus.

The trust between the two sides of the Strait was soon disrupted by Taiwan's presidential election and the implicit U.S. support for Taiwan. After Lee was granted permission by Washington to visit Cornell University, his alma mater, in June 1995, the PRC launched a series of three missile tests in July 1995 and March 1996 which were only constrained by the deployment of U.S. aircraft carriers in the Taiwan Strait.

In the meantime, economic growth in China had gradually enlarged the mainland market for Taiwan's business people, compelling Lee to announce the 'no haste, be patient' policy on 14 September 1996. Lee's stance, then, was a rehearsal for the confrontation that developed during his second term. Lacking effective means to curb Lee's pro-independence behaviour, Beijing turned to Washington. On 30 June 1998, President Bill Clinton of the United States announced the 'three nos' policy. In response, Lee initiated a new discourse on Taiwan's statehood. On 9 July 1999, Lee made his statement on special state-to-state relations. In the months that followed, officials in the PRC issued a series of strong statements blaming Lee for destroying the 'one China' principle and warning Taiwan that force would be used if Taiwan refused to negotiate.

During Lee's presidencies, cross-Strait exchanges expanded but Taiwan's dependence on the PRC was limited. Partly due to Lee's 'no haste, be patient' policy, Taiwan's trade with the PRC was kept below 4 per cent of total trade – it would be as high as 12.15 per cent in 2003 after the DPP came to power – and the unemployment rate was always below 3 per cent. This may explain why Beijing chose assertive strategies to circumvent Lee.

Chen Shui-Bian

The Chen Shui-Bian presidencies (2000–2008) fit proposition 4: cross-Strait exchanges increased rapidly after Chen came to power, although Taipei and Beijing were still antagonistic toward each other on the matter of Taiwan's statehood. In this section, I will explain why political rivals may establish economic cooperation.

Three candidates stood for the presidency in Taiwan in 2000, and Chen was elected with 39.3 per cent of the votes. At that time, Chen was not yet a diehard advocate of Taiwan independence. His party, the DPP, was known for the Taiwan Independence Party Platform that was adopted in 1991 and called for the founding of a Republic of Taiwan. A more moderate DPP proposal was contained in the Resolution on Taiwan's Future (ratified in 1999), stating that an independent Taiwan could call itself the Republic of China. These documents gave Chen space to interpret the status of Taiwan's sovereignty.

Chen began his presidency with some gestures toward moderation. Immediately after he was elected, Chen declared that there was room for negotiation on the 'one China' principle. In his inauguration speech on 20 May 2000, he underscored the five nos: no declaration of Taiwan independence, no change of state name, no independence referendum, no mention of special state-to-state relations in the Constitution, and no abolition of the NUC. Regarding the sovereignty issue, Chen proposed that the two sides of the Taiwan Strait should be integrated in a European Union (EU)-style confederation. In response to Chen's conciliatory signals, Beijing decided to 'wait and see'.

But the lack of trust soon forced both sides to adjust their policies. According to proposition 2, a tough stance on Beijing's part would have increased the distrust of the Taiwanese voters, and pro-independence leaders would have been able to rely on this tension to consolidate their political bases. This is what actually happened. On 16 October 2000 the PRC released its White Paper on National Defence, which denounced the separatist forces in Taiwan. On 23 March 2001, Jiang rejected Chen's EU-style integration proposal. Chen rejected Beijing's claims and made his 'one country on each side across the Strait' statement on 3 August 2002. Beijing strongly criticized Chen's remark, and the confrontations continued.

This kind of clash makes the expansion of cross-Strait exchanges all the more noteworthy. If Beijing had really wanted to 'place its hope on the Taiwan people', the payoff of cross-Strait interactions could have been manipulated to achieve this goal. Chen would have been marginalized if Beijing had unilaterally decided on the package that the Taiwanese were going to receive. Beijing's bargaining power rested on Taiwan's economic dependence, which was determined not only by the division of labour between the two sides of the Strait but also by

Beijing's policies. Beijing should take a particular interest in the welfare of the nonpartisan voters, especially those working in the primary sector. A good example of this kind of behaviour is the announcement made by Beijing on 1 August 2005, to the effect that 15 types of fruits purchased from Taiwan would be exempt from import taxes.[20] In fact, Chen had already suggested that Beijing should enter into negotiations with him over imports of Taiwan's fruit (and other functional issues).

In addition to the procurement of agricultural and fishery products, labourers in Taiwan also benefited from the asymmetry in cross-Strait economic relations – as long as Beijing kept turning down Chen's requests for functional negotiations, the existence of trade barriers would ward off the threat to jobs posed by imports of low-priced goods from the mainland. An intriguing consequence follows: if trade barriers are removed by an anti-independence president, the extra benefits of the undecided voters may be levelled out by market forces. This is the topic we turn to now.

Ma Ying-Jeou

Ma Ying-Jeou of the KMT won two presidential terms, in 2008 and 2012, and his party also gained a majority of seats in the legislature on both occasions. According to proposition 3, an anti-independence president during a period of high dependence on the PRC has a good reason to offer free trade, under which the extra benefits of the undecided voters will gradually be balanced out by market forces, in exchange for peace.

Ma's position on Taiwan's statehood has been quite consistent (see Table 2.1 for the small variations), because he is neither in favour of Taiwan' achieving independence nor an ardent advocate of reunification. In Ma's view, Taiwan cannot be prosperous unless there is peace between the two sides of the Taiwan Strait. He held that the first step toward galvanizing Taiwan's economy was the establishment of a cross-Strait FTA, thus facilitating the negotiation of similar agreements with other countries. That explains why Ma's key policy was the negotiation of the ECFA, which was eventually signed by Taiwan and the PRC on 29 June 2010.

Whether the ECFA will be as advantageous as was promised depends on many conditions. If tariffs are to be abrogated and trade barriers removed, the ECFA will benefit Taiwan if Taiwanese exports to the PRC are increased and the cost of living on the island is reduced by allowing imports of cheap goods from the PRC. Anyone who loses their job as a result of this should be able to receive help from a welfare system financed by increased tax revenues. But free trade can also be risky – it can drive jobs away to places with lower labour costs or discourage enterprises from upgrading their products if wage drift is halted. If this is the case, the more effective the ECFA is in removing trade barriers across the Strait, the more likely it is that Taiwan's business owners will make money from cheap labour; if so, they will either relocate their businesses to the mainland or keep wages in Taiwan from rising.

Critics of the ECFA have drawn attention to several of its possible side effects.[21] The first of these is that although capital can be moved quickly from one side of the Strait to the other, unskilled labour is almost immobile. The combination of these two factors makes an increase in the unemployment rate in Taiwan almost inevitable. Second, the ECFA may increase Taiwan's economic dependence on the mainland; it may also delay industrial upgrading if overseas enterprises find it easier to accumulate profits by cutting labour cost than by making long-term investments in research and development. Third, the ECFA is in line with World Trade Organization rules in spirit, but not in practice. It is a bilateral agreement signed and negotiated by two parties that do not recognize each other as states. Lacking an arbitration mechanism above the two governments, the ECFA is highly political.

It should be noted that although the PRC is still purchasing agricultural and fishery products from Taiwan, the farmers and fishermen are now facing tougher competition from similar products from the mainland, imports of substitute products and the export of Taiwan's technologies. Even more worrying is what is happening to Taiwan's traditional industries – there is a high chance that their owners will move their investment to the mainland and sell their products back to Taiwan at a cheaper price. Unemployment rates during Ma's first term and Chen Shui-Bian's two terms as president were compared in the previous section, and it was found that, under Ma, more labourers were laid off because they were no longer needed.

In Ma's second term, the Cross-Strait Trades in Services Agreement (CSTSA, a follow-up agreement of the ECFA) was intended to liberalize the investment of service industries across the Strait. Critics claim that the CSTSA will create some undesirable consequences. Taiwan's wealth distribution will become more unequal because the government is underprepared to look after the likely victims of the agreement, while the benefits are to be monopolized by a few. Meanwhile, national security may be threatened because Taiwan can hardly guard against Chinese capital infiltrating the island, whereas some Taiwanese businesses (such as the publishing industry) may face Beijing's censorship.

Taiwan's growing social grievances converged in the outbreak of the 'sunflower student movement'. Participants of this movement occupied the Legislative Yuan from 18 March until 10 April 2014 to protest against the KMT's sloppiness in the deliberation of the CSTSA. The subsequent delay in the passage of the CSTSA may have further reduced the credibility of the Ma government. Indeed, Ma's plummeting popularity has sent Beijing a signal that Taiwan's undecided voters (including many young people) may shift their support to the DPP in the upcoming elections.

Conclusion

Beijing is an important player in Taiwan's domestic politics and has sought to change the ideological beliefs of the Taiwan people by reshaping their material interests. The two-level game model developed by Putnam was refined to examine the ways in which economic payoffs constrain the political alternatives of negotiators, which is especially useful for the study of cross-Strait relations. People in Taiwan are free to select their president, but their choices are conditioned by the economic incentives that are devised by Beijing.

According to this logic, the refined two-level game suggests several hypotheses. The central argument is that when Taiwan is dependent on the PRC for its survival, the need to 'place hope on the Taiwan people' increases in urgency as pro-independence opinion intensifies. One way to attract these undecided voters is to expand their net benefits from cross-Strait exchanges. Still, the effectiveness of Beijing's policy by no means suggests that it will end calls for Taiwan's independence, much less the upsurge in the Taiwanese identity. No matter how Taiwan's political map changes in the future, one thing is for sure: the number of Taiwan's nonpartisan voters is increasing, and so is the importance of the role they play in the election results.

Appendix 1: the game

A two-level game is played by Beijing, the KMT and the DPP, each having a particular preference with regard to the options available for solving Taiwan's statehood problem. To maximize their domestic popularity, players in Taiwan announce their positions on Taiwan's statehood, even though these may differ from their true preferences. Beijing seeks to win the support of Taiwan's voters while placating hardliners at home. Taiwan's players face the dilemma of whether or not to converge on the median voters, and Beijing's choices are limited by the views of domestic hardliners and Taiwan's voters. The cross-Strait exchanges are more complex. Taiwan's economic dependence on the PRC gives Beijing particular leverage with regard to adjusting the net benefit of Taiwan's voters.

To put it formally, the players have a single-peaked preference over the alternatives on the Taiwan statehood issue. Below, B, K and D represent the ideal points of Beijing, the KMT and the DPP, respectively. PRC hardliners are represented by H and Taiwan's median voters are M. H and M are parameters, but they play an essential role in the strategies chosen by the other players. Taiwan's economic dependence on the PRC is $w \geq 0$, b (c) is the pure benefit (cost) of the median voters in cross-Strait exchanges, and $-d \leq 0$ is the default distance between B and M in Taiwan's statehood spectrum when b and c are not counted. Also, $-t \leq 0$ is the distance between H and B.

Assumptions

A1 Whoever receives the vote of M wins the presidential election.
A2 In equilibrium, the sequence of $H \geq B \geq K \geq M \geq D$ will not be changed.
A3 The net benefit M receives from B shortens $-d$. Thus, the complete description of the distance between B and M is $-d + w(b-c)$.

A4 d/w is the upper limit of $b-c$ because $-d+w(b-c)\leq0$.

A5   B chooses $max[-t, -d+w(b-c)]$ and offers $b-c$ to M only if $-t<-d+w(b-c)$. It says that if B shifts to B' in equilibrium, then (1) B'=H if $-t\geq-d+w(b-c)$, meaning that B will not offer $b-c$ to M; (2) B'=B if $-t<-d+w(b-c)$, suggesting that B will offer $b-c$ to M.

Theorem 1: In equilibrium, B'=H if $w\leq(d-t)/(b-c)$.
Proof: A5 implies that B'=H if and only if $w\leq(d-t)/(b-c)$. Note that A5 describes the strictly dominant strategy of B – although B seeks to help K win the presidential election by adjusting the payoff of M, we have no reason to exclude the possibility of D being the winner.

Theorem 2: In equilibrium, B'=B if $w>(d-t)/(b-c)$.
Proof: A corollary of Theorem 1.

These theorems constitute the foundation of the propositions. One implication of Theorem 1 is that when Taiwan's dependence on the mainland is limited, the ideological distance between Beijing and Taiwan's median voters will be trapped in a vicious circle – Beijing may find it rewarding to stand by its hardliners, which will further alienate Taiwan's median voters. Theorem 2 suggests that when w is fixed at a high level, $d-t$ increases (decreases) as the pro-independence inclination of the Taiwan leader increases (decreases). Accordingly, the baseline for $b-c$ to pass is high (low) when the Taiwan leader is pro-independence (anti-independence).

Appendix 2: the coding scheme

6 = Taiwan is not a part of China; its country name should be Taiwan.

*   Promote Taiwan's independence or a new constitution.
*   Taiwan is not a part of China (including the ROC).

5 = Taiwan, called the ROC, is independent of the PRC.

*   The ROC is an independent country/state that is different from the PRC.

4 = Taiwan is willing to talk with the PRC with backup from its military.

*   The PRC should drop its military threat against Taiwan and stop limiting the ROC's diplomatic space.
*   Taiwan should issue official documents concerning how it will defend itself against the threat from the mainland.

3 = Taiwan is willing to set sovereignty issues aside in order to talk with the mainland.

- Unification can be considered if the two sides have similar political and social systems.
- Neither unification nor independence; sometimes other forms of unity are suggested, such as confederation and regional integration.
- The governments on the two sides of the Strait share the 1992 Consensus.

3 = The PRC is willing to engage in conciliatory talks with Taiwan; it allows Taiwan some international space.

- The governments on the two sides of the Strait share the 1992 Consensus.
- Beijing allows Taipei/Taiwan to participate in or even join international organizations.

2 = Declaration of 'one country, two systems' without mentioning the use of force.

- Peaceful unification under 'one country, two systems'.
- Allowing Taiwan to have its own armed forces after unification.

1 = Assertive claim for unification; violation will result in armed conflict.

- Beijing insists that non-peaceful means will be used if Taiwan refuses unification.

Notes

1 'The PRC' refers to the name of the country and 'Beijing' to its government. In a similar fashion, 'Taiwan' denotes the territory under the jurisdiction of the Republic of China (ROC) with 'Taipei' as its government.
2 Another issue is the date of the election, which was one week before the eve of the Lunar New Year. This date dissuaded some Taiwanese employees who were working on the mainland from coming home to vote, because they would have had to take a long leave of absence. In contrast, employers had greater freedom to decide their schedules. For details of this presidential election, see the Central Election Commission: www.cec.gov.tw (accessed 20 May 2014).
3 For theoretical discussions on cross-Strait relations, see Kuan 2009; Wu 2000a, 2000b, 2009.
4 For the interaction between domestic politics and cross-Strait relations, see Cheng and Tam 2005; Chu 2003, 2004; Gilley 2010; Goldstein 1999; Holmes 2008; Tsai 1997; Tucker 2002; Wu 1999, 2006, Wu 2005.
5 Chan (2006) discusses the political implications of cross-Strait economic exchanges. Keng (2009) analyses the political impacts of PRC policies that favour the Taiwanese business community. Chuang and Liu (2012) show that although economic integration and political conflicts follow different logics, the two variables are highly interdependent.
6 The most typical way of assessing the political landscape is to ask respondents which is their favourite political party (or candidate).
7 See Putnam 1988. Only a few of the existing works focus on Taiwan's quest for international space, such as Wang and Liu 2004; Wang *et al.* 2011. For a thorough

discussion of Taiwanese identity and its dilemma, see Wu 1995, 1996, 2002, 2005; Liu and Ho 1999; Ho and Liu 2003.

8 See Putnam 1988; Mo 1994, 1995.
9 See Putnam 1988: 437–441.
10 Issue-space refers to the space constituted by different policy issues. Dimensionality, the number of linearly independent vectors in the space, can be smaller than the number of issues. A player has a single-peaked preference over a group of options if one of them is his/her best choice.
11 For the formal analysis, see Appendix 1.
12 Hu *et al.* 2007.
13 Wu and Hsu 2003.
14 Chuang 2001.
15 Chen *et al.* 2009: 104–112.
16 Changes in the composition of the CLGTA indicate adjustments to Beijing's Taiwan policy. See Chu 2003.
17 From 1996 to 1999, the percentage of 'Taiwanese identifiers' rose from 24.1 to 39.6; in 2014, the percentage surged to 60.4. See http://esc.nccu.edu.tw/course/news.php?Sn=166# (accessed 9 November 2014).
18 In alphabetical order, these sources are the Central News Agency, the Centre for Strategic and International Studies, the Centre for Studies in Communism, the Mainland Affairs Council, the Ministry of Foreign Affairs, the National Policy Foundation, the Taiwan Affairs Office, and the *United Daily*.
19 See www.stat.gov.tw/ct.asp?xItem=17144&ctNode=517&mp=4 (accessed 9 November 2014).
20 See www.customs.gov.cn/publish/portal0/tab518/info11148.htm (accessed 10 November 2014).
21 See Tung 2011 for a detailed analysis.

References

Chan, S. (2006) 'The Politics of Economic Exchange: Carrots and Sticks in Taiwan–China–U.S. Relations', *Issues and Studies*, 42, 2: 1–22.

Chen, L. H., Keng, S., Tu, P. L., and Huang, K. B. (2009) 'Lixing zili huo ganxing rentong? Yingxiang Taiwan minzhong liangan jingmao lichang yinsu de fenxi' [Interest-driven or Identity-based? An Analysis of Taiwanese People's Positions on Cross-Strait Economic Exchanges], *Soochow Journal of Political Science*, 27, 2: 87–125.

Cheng, Y. S., and Tam, C. K. (2005) 'The Taiwan Presidential Election and its Implications for Cross-Strait Relations: A Political Cleavage Perspective', *Asian Affairs: An American Review*, 32, 1: 3–24.

Chu, Y. H. (2003) 'Power Transition and the Making of Beijing's Policy Toward Taiwan', *China Quarterly*, 176: 960–980.

Chu, Y. H. (2004) 'Taiwan's National Identity Politics and the Prospect of Cross-Strait Relations', *Asian Survey*, 44, 4: 484–512.

Chuang, T. L. (2001) 'Woguo 'duli xuanmin' de fazhan yu bianqian (1989–1999)' [The Development and Changing Situation of Independent Voters in Taiwan (1989–1999)], *Journal of Electoral Studies*, 8, 1: 71–115.

Chuang, Y. C., and Liu, D. W. (2012) 'Jingji zhenghe yu zhengzhi chongtu de guanlianxing: yi liangan guanxi weili' [The Nexus between Economic Integration and Political Conflicts: The Case of Taiwan and China], *Mainland China Studies*, 55, 1: 23–39.

Gilley, B. (2010) 'Not So Dire Strait', *Foreign Affairs*, 89, 1: 44–60.

Goldstein, S. (1999) 'The Cross-Strait Talks of 1993 – The Rest of the Story: Domestic Politics and Taiwan's Mainland Policy', in Zhao, S. (ed.) *Across the Taiwan Strait: Mainland, China, Taiwan, and the 1995–1996 Crisis*, London: Routledge.

Ho, S. Y., and Liu, I. C. (2003) 'The Taiwanese/Chinese Identity of the Taiwan People in the 1990s', in Lee, W.C., and Wang, Y. T. (eds) *Sayonara to the Lee Teng-Hui Era*, Lanham MD: University Press of America.

Holmes, J. R. (2008) 'A Clausewitzian Appraisal of Cross-Strait Relations', *Issues and Studies*, 44, 4: 29–70.

Hu, Y. W., Lin, P. N., and Lin, C. K. (2007) 'Taiwan zhongjian xuanmin shehui beijing, xinli tezhi yu chuanbo xingwei fenxi' [The Demographic, Psychological and Communication Behavioural Characteristics of Taiwan's Independent Voters], *Journal of Election Review*, 2: 39–56.

Keng, S. (2009) 'Limitations on China's Economic Statecraft: China's Favour-Granting Policies and their Political Implications', *Issues and Studies*, 48, 3: 1–32.

Kuan, H. C. (2009) 'Taiwan guonei xuanju dui qi dalu zhengce zhi yingxiang' [The Impact of Taiwan's Domestic Elections on its Mainland Policy], in Bao, T. H., and Wu, Y. S. (eds) *Chongxin jianshi zhengbian zhong de liang'an guanxi lilun* [Revisiting Theories on Cross-Strait Relations], Taipei: Wunan.

Lin, J. W. (2000) 'Two-level Games Between Rival Regimes: Domestic Politics and the Remaking of Cross-Strait Relations', *Issues and Studies*, 36, 6: 1–26.

Lin, T. H., and Hu, K. W. (2011) 'Aihen ECFA, liang'an maoyi yu Taiwan de jieji zhengzhi' [Cross-Strait Trade and Class Politics in Taiwan], *Thought and Words*, 49, 3: 95–134.

Liu, I. C., and Ho, S. Y. (1999) 'The Taiwanese/Chinese Identity of the Taiwan People', *Issues and Studies*, 35, 3: 29–74.

Mo, J. (1994) 'The Logic of Two-level Games with Endogenous Domestic Coalitions', *Journal of Conflict Resolution*, 38, 3: 402–422.

Mo, J. (1995) 'Domestic Institutions and International Bargaining: The Role of Agent Veto in Two-level Games', *American Political Science Review*, 89, 4: 914–924.

Ministry of Economic Affairs (2007) *Evaluating the Impact of Cross-Strait Trade and Investment*, Taipei: Ministry of Economic Affairs.

Putnam, R. D. (1988) 'Diplomacy and Domestic Politics: The Logic of Two-level Games', *International Organization*, 42, 3: 427–460.

Tsai, W. (1997) 'The Making of Taiwan Policy in Mainland China: Structure and Process', *Issues and Studies*, 33, 9: 1–30.

Tucker, B. (2002) 'More of the Same: The Impact of Taiwan's Elections on the U.S.–China–Taiwan Triangle', *American Foreign Policy Interests*, 24, 3: 237–241.

Tung, C. Y. (2011) *Taiwan de zhongguo zhanlue: cong hucong dao pingheng* [Taiwan's Strategy toward China, from Bandwagoning to Balancing], Taipei: Independent and Unique.

Wang, T. Y., and Liu, I. C. (2004) 'Contending Identities in Taiwan: Implications for Cross-Strait Relations', *Asian Survey*, 44, 4: 568–590.

Wang, T. Y., Lee, W. C., and Yu, C. H. (2011) 'Taiwan's Expansion of International Space: Opportunities and Challenges', *Journal of Contemporary China*, 20, 69: 249–267.

Wu, C. L., and Hsu, W. P. (2003) 'Shei shi zhengdang rentong zhe yu duli xuanmin? Yi 2001 nian Taiwan diqu xuanmin zhengdang rentong de jueding yinsu weili' [Who are Partisans and Independents? Determinants of Party Identifications of Taiwan's Voters in 2001], *Taiwanese Political Science Review*, 18: 101–140.

Wu, N. T. (1995) 'Ethnic Consciousness, Political Support, and National Identity', *Taiwan Studies*, 1, 2: 45–66.

Wu, N. T. (1996) 'Ziyou zhuyi yu zuqun rentong: souxun Taiwan minzu zhuyi de yishi xingtai jichu' [Liberalism, Ethnic Identity and Taiwanese Nationalism], *Taiwanese Political Science Review*, 1: 5–40.

Wu, N. T. (2002) 'Rentong chongtu han zhengzhi xinren: xian jieduan Taiwan zuqun zhengzhi de hexin nanti' [The Conflict of Identities and Political Trust: The Core Dilemmas of Taiwan's Contemporary Identity Politics], *Taiwanese Sociology*, 4: 75–118.

Wu, N. T. (2005) 'Aiqing yu mianbao: chutan Taiwan minzhong minzu rentong de biandong' [Romance and Bread: A Preliminary Study of the Identity Change in Taiwan], *Taiwanese Political Science Review*, 9, 2: 5–39.

Wu, Y. S. (1999) 'Taiwanese Elections and Cross-Strait Relations: Mainland Policy in Flux', *Asian Survey*, 39, 4: 565–587.

Wu, Y. S. (2000a) 'Taiwan zongtong daxuan duiyu liangan guanxi chansheng de yingxiang: xuanpiao jidahua moshi yu zhanlue sanjiao tujing' [The Impact of Taiwan's Presidential Elections on Cross-Strait Relations: Vote-maximizing Model and Strategic Triangle Approach], *Prospect Quarterly*, 1, 3: 1–33.

Wu, Y. S. (2000b) 'Theorizing on Relations Across the Taiwan Strait: Nine Contending Approaches', *Journal of Contemporary China*, 9, 25: 407–428.

Wu, Y. S. (2006) 'Domestic Political Competition and Triangular Interaction among Washington, Beijing, and Taipei: The U.S. China policy', *Issues and Studies*, 42, 1: 1–46.

Wu, Y. S. (2009) 'Chongxin jianshi zhengbian zhong de liangan guanxi lilun' [Revisiting Theories on Cross-Strait Relations], in Bao, T. H., and Wu, Y. S. (eds) *Chongxin jianshi zhengbian zhong de liangan guanxi lilun* [Revisiting Theories on Cross-Strait Relations], Taipei: Wunan.

3 Cross-Strait relations as an 'easy' issue

China's impact on evidence provision in negative political campaigning in Taiwan

Hsuan-Yun Ted Chen and Chung-Li Wu

Negative campaigning has traditionally been considered 'bad' for democracy. In addition to the research associated with the demobilization hypothesis, there is the argument that over-negativity in political campaigning decreases voter turnout and, more generally, suppresses enthusiasm for the political process (Ansolabehere and Iyengar 1995; Ansolabehere *et al.* 1994; Ansolabehere *et al.* 1999; Buchanan 2000; Patterson 2002). Pundits, practitioners and academics alike have denounced attack advertisements for their detrimental effects on the information environment (Jamieson 1992; Kamber 1997; Mark 2007). As the argument goes, elections are one of the primary means of communication between potential representatives and the constituency. Campaign advertisements are supposed to function as proposals from candidates on which the citizenry base their decisions when choosing their representative (Riker 1996). A common claim is that attack advertisements are designed to mislead voters or, at least, are more likely to contain misinformation that misleads voters. Another claim can be made on the basis of limited resource allocation. If candidates are allocating funding to criticize their opponents, then they are not spending as much on communicating from their own platforms. Likewise, a voter's information processing ability is finite, and attention paid to negative advertisements is attention diverted away from positive, supposedly more informative sources. If the above points are valid, and assuming that information and dialogue between representatives and constituents form the basis of a healthy democracy, then the reasonable prescription would be to curtail negative campaigning for the sake of democracy.

Recent research from US politics, however, suggests that such concerns may be exaggerated or even misplaced, and that negative campaign advertisements in fact contain a higher degree of information than positive advertisements because of the perceived need to support criticism with evidence (Geer 2006). Furthermore, contrary to the initial studies supporting the demobilization hypothesis, recent studies tend to suggest that although negativity affects the voters' perception of the fairness and efficacy of the overall political process in complex ways (Brooks and Geer 2007; Jackson *et al.* 2009; Lau *et al.* 2007; Sides *et al.* 2010) and may affect the voters' perception of the targeted candidate, depending on each voter's characteristics (Fridkin and Kenney 2011), it does not decrease voter turnout (Freedman *et al.* 2004; Freedman and Goldstein 1999; Garramone *et al.* 1990) and, in some cases, may even result in a slight increase (Brooks and Geer 2007).

Similarly, the findings from US politics have been upheld by the quantitative research on negative campaigning in Taiwan (Sullivan 2008, 2009, 2010), contrary to what might be suggested by the qualitative observations of Taiwanese elections made by both the popular media and academic sources (Rawnsley 2000; Schafferer 2006). Using data obtained from the four presidential elections between 1996–2008, Sullivan found that, in general, negative claims, defined as a candidate's statements about an opponent, are much more likely to be supported by evidence than are positive claims, defined as a candidate's statement about herself/himself. In the four presidential elections, while the evidence rate of negative claims is admittedly low at 9.3 per cent for newspaper advertisements and 6.8 per cent for television advertisements, it is considerably higher than the 0.9 per cent and 0.8 per cent evidence rate of positive claims.

Our defence of negativity is not to do with the argument that negative campaigning is necessarily good or bad; our intention is to consider its benefit or detriment to the information environment *relative to positive campaigning*. In line with Geer's analysis of US politics, Sullivan's findings clearly support the claim that, on the whole, negative claims are much more likely to be supported with evidence.

How can we explain the discrepancy between qualitative and quantitative observations? Is there something else at play other than our senses being inherently unsuited to qualitatively assessing campaign advertisements, something specifically designed to manipulate our perception? Drawing upon Carmines and Stimson's distinction between 'easy' and 'hard' issues (1980), we contend that the discrepancy is due to the high salience of a subset of negative advertisements specific to Taiwan: that is, attack advertisements based on the prevalent anti-China sentiment in Taiwan. Because the cross-Strait relations issue is a very 'easy' one that evokes immediate 'gut responses' from the Taiwanese population, candidates and their campaign managers tend to disregard the traditionally perceived need to buttress criticism with evidence.

In order to better understand the impact of 'China' on negative campaigning in Taiwan, we tested our hypothesis in two stages. First, using the same sample of campaign advertisement as Sullivan (2010), we examined whether introducing the China factor negatively impacts on the evidence rate of campaign advertisements, especially negative ones. We found that there is a significant difference in the evidence rate between China and non-China attack advertisements. In order to assess whether the easiness of 'China' or 'cross-Strait relations' is the factor contributing to this phenomenon, we reviewed three significant instances of politicians inciting anti-China sentiments for political purposes. While it is difficult to conclusively test this mechanism, we observed that the discourse in these instances supports our contention that the easiness of the China issue is encouraging candidates not to provide evidence for their claims.

Quantitative analysis: evidence rate of issue claims regarding China

Our quantitative analysis follows an established method found in the literature on the evidence rate in negative campaigning (Geer 2006; Sullivan 2010). To assess the evidence rate, we consider the number of claims made versus the number of pieces of evidence provided. A single claim is operationalized as 'a word or phrase that contains a claim about the sponsor of the ad, i.e. a positive claim, or about an opponent, i.e. a negative claim' (Sullivan 2010, 108). Evidence is defined as a piece of 'information that is used as a substantive basis for a directly related claim', and operationalized as 'sourced statistics or official reports, or direct quotation or visual confirmation of directly related claims' (Sullivan 2010, 122). The data used includes television and newspaper advertisements paid for by the Kuomintang (KMT) and Democratic Progressive Party (DPP) candidates or by their respective parties during the 1996, 2000, 2004 and 2008 presidential election campaigns.[1]

The advertisements are limited to those that appeared during the official 28-day campaign period. Television advertisements include all unique spots and, further, exclude those that differ only in the language in which they are broadcast. Newspaper advertisements include all those that appeared in the *Liberty Times*, *China Times* and *United Daily News*, excluding duplicates based on advertisement title, date printed, and claim and evidence numbers. In total, the dataset is exhaustive of all campaign advertisements broadcast on television and published in three major Taiwanese newspapers during the officially stipulated campaign periods.

Each claim, and when applicable its corresponding evidence, is coded as either positive, when the claim is about the candidate sponsoring the advertisement, or negative, when it is about an opponent of the sponsor. This operationalization provides the most basic and least subjective way of differentiating between negative and positive claims (Geer 2006). More recent examinations of negativity in campaign advertisements have begun to consider the degree of incivility as a more precise measure of what is meant when 'negativity' is discussed (Brooks and Geer 2007; Mutz 2007; Mutz and Reeves 2005; Sobieraj and Berry 2011). However, this approach introduces a certain degree of subjectivity into the analysis. Although there are ways to mitigate this problem (e.g. Sobieraj and Berry 2011, 25–26), we have elected to completely exclude this concept from our quantitative analysis: although it is an interesting topic of examination, it does not necessarily add much to our ability to answer our research question. However, as will be discussed below, we do keep this factor in mind for exploratory purposes when conducting our qualitative examination.

Claims, both positive and negative, are further refined into categories according to their content. For the purposes of our examination, we focus on issue claims, which are still further refined into the issue areas of cross-Strait relations, the economy, governance, social issues, ethnic policy and democratic reform. The other categories are value, trait and strategy. The only other category of claims for which 'China' is a possible variable is that of value claims. We exclude this category from our examination in consideration of our posited mechanism. If the easiness of an issue is the variable that decides whether evidence is provided for a claim, then we should limit our examination to issue claims only. Adding value claims, which are probably made following a system of logic than differs from that of issue claims, would only serve to confound the examination. Given the above considerations, we compare, with 'China' as our primary variable of interest, the evidence rate of all cross-Strait issue claims to that of all other issue claims.

The results of this examination, presented in Table 3.1, are as we expected. Out of 154 negative cross-Strait issue claims, evidence was provided for eleven, giving a 7.1 per cent evidence rate. For all 974 other negative claims, 119 were supported with evidence, giving a considerably higher rate of 12.2 per cent. In other words, for the advertisements in our dataset, negative issue claims pertaining to cross-Strait relations are 0.58 times as likely to be supported with evidence as are all other negative issue claims. A negligible difference was observed in the evidence rate of the two groups' positive claims, both of which, as expected from Sullivan's findings (2010), were virtually devoid of evidentiary support. These results support our hypothesis. To examine whether the discrepancy in the evidence rate is attributable to our posited causal mechanism, we proceed to review three instances of strategic use of the anti-China sentiment by Taiwanese politicians.

Qualitative analysis: three instances of strategic discourse based on anti-China sentiments

As noted above, it is difficult to prove our posited causal mechanism, that the easiness of the cross-Strait issue induces and allows candidates to disregard the traditionally perceived need to buttress criticism with evidence. However, observations in terms of expectations derived from Carmines and Stimson's characterization of 'easy issues' (1980) should shed light on our hypothesis. As Carmines and Stimson claim, compared with hard issues, which are generally the type referred to in discussions on the virtues of issue voting, easy issues require less conceptual sophistication. They elicit a 'gut response' from all types of voters, in contrast to hard issues that only resonate with more sophisticated voters.

Table 3.1 Evidence rate of issue claims in Taiwanese presidential campaign ads (number of claims)

	Negative tone	*Positive tone*	*Both tones*
China issue	0.071 (154)	0.016 (307)	0.035 (461)
Other issues	0.122 (974)	0.014 (1,312)	0.060 (2,286)
All issues	0.115 (1,128)	0.014 (1,619)	0.056 (2,747)

This ability of easy issues to evoke a visceral response from all voters, we contend, is the reason why candidates do not bother to support with evidence negative claims based on such issues. Our mechanism, then, is candidate behaviour. Recognizing this, we can derive a set of expected observations from Carmines and Stimson's discussion. Assuming candidates and their campaign teams prefer not to provide evidence when they can get away with it, whether or not evidence is provided depends on whether they think they can get away with not providing it. In other words, whether evidence is provided depends on how easy, or how gut-response-evoking, candidates perceive the given issue to be. Easiness, as Carmines and Stimson argue, is based on three factors: (1) the easy issue would be symbolic rather than technical; (2) it would more likely deal with policy ends than means; and (3) it would be an issue that has long been included on the political agenda (1980, 74). These criteria are conceptually intuitive; policy means are almost inevitably technical issues and are too complex to be understood at gut level, while a new issue probably needs more time to reach all audiences.

An issue of the magnitude of 'China' encompasses both symbolic and technical aspects, and can be discussed in terms of ends or means. It therefore offers candidates a choice of going easy or going hard. This is where we focus our examination. Our assumption outlined above is that if candidates perceive the China issue to be easy, all other factors being equal, they prefer not providing evidence over providing evidence. This means that if our posited mechanism is correct, then candidates, in accordance with the first two criteria,[2] (1a) will choose to make claims based on the symbolic aspects rather than the technical aspects of an issue, or (1b) will choose to make claims regarding policy ends rather than policy means, and, logically, (2) will not provide evidence for these claims.

In arriving at our expected observations, we have, quite evidently, made many assumptions about candidate preferences and expectations in the contexts of costs and benefits. While there is only a low likelihood that all our assumptions will prove to be valid, a set of clearly stipulated assumptions are necessary guidelines for our examination. In the following examination, observations that are in line with our expectations are considered to be in support of our hypothesis.

To examine our posited mechanism, we reviewed in detail three significant instances of politicians inciting anti-China sentiments for political purposes. Our three cases are not drawn from the same set of data as our quantitative analysis, and, strictly speaking, they are not campaign advertisements. They are, instead, examples of negative strategic political statements in Taiwan's 'year-round campaign' that have been made the subject of a court case by the individuals attacked. We selected our cases by searching the *Law and Regulations Retrieving System of the Judicial Yuan of the Republic of China* database using the keywords 'elections' (*xuanju*), 'Chinese Communists' (*zhonggong*) and 'slander' (*huibang*). Our cases are exhaustive of those satisfying these three criteria. Our rationale for taking this approach instead of selecting an approach based on a different metric, such as political salience measured by amount of press coverage, which most likely would have led to our rejecting the third case for the purposes of this study, was that court decisions that are reached through the judicial process probably afford a relatively objective standard to assess whether evidence was provided. Our initial review showed, however, that court decisions are based on more than whether evidence exists, especially since the three cases were all procedurally different and based on different laws, and are therefore incommensurable. We therefore decided against using official court decisions as a standard indicator of evidence, and instead considered, holistically, the evidence collected for the court cases.

Despite this, all things considered, these three cases are still appropriate for our purpose. First, while the official court decisions are not useful, the data entries are still richly documented with whatever evidence is available for the given case. Second, the fact that these are court cases makes it likely that the accused publicly responded to the charges, which provides us with another opportunity to observe their attitudes toward their initial claims. Third, the three cases cover a range of contextual variables including the time period, the level of election and the political prominence of the actors involved. Finally, as protracted events that played out over the course of a relatively long period of time, these cases allow us to better examine (1) the content of the claims made, (2) the evidence that was or was not provided and (3) the tone in which the initial claims and the responses to charges were made.

For each of the three cases below, we begin by summarizing the event. We then state the court decision and present the relevant findings. At the end of our summaries, we discuss the findings as they relate to our research expectations.

Chen Shui-Bian charges China with giving clandestine support to the KMT and People First Party

On 6 October 2003, Chen Shui-Bian, then President, gave an interview to the *Washington Post*'s Beijing correspondent, John Pomfret. The article was published on 10 October. At one point during the interview, Pomfret asked:

> I would like to know your opinions about China. It has been more than three years since you took office. China has not been friendly toward Taiwan on many issues, especially during the outbreak of SARS and the legislation of Hong Kong's Article 23 of the Basic Law, although the latter has no direct relations with Taiwan. Mr President, were you disappointed with China because they were not willing to assist or coordinate with Taiwan on preventing SARS and hold talks with Taiwan on topics such as the three links?

Chen responded:

> The Chinese government does not want to give credit to our government. Thus, they think only of their own interests in every matter while neglecting

the ideals and the greater interests pursued by the 23 million people of Taiwan. China has never recognized our country, nor do they accept the results of the democratic election in 2000 as decided by the 23 million people of Taiwan. Therefore, they have never been able to accept the reality that I am the head of state. In 2000, they mistakenly thought that I would be subject to recall. They even believed that the DPP would suffer a crushing defeat in the legislative elections of 2001. In the end, not only did I not face a recall, but the DPP won the 2001 legislative elections and became the largest party in the Legislative Yuan. In the two years since, China has taken heart at the cooperation between the KMT and the PFP [People First Party] in obstructing the DPP government's policies. They have even given clandestine assistance. Even more, China believes that Mr Lien Chan and Mr James Soong, by cooperating, can win the presidential election in 2004, and that it has only to wait for the results of the presidential election on 20 March 2004 to make contact with the current government of Taiwan unnecessary. Any exchanges would give credit to the current government. We must make it clear that, in fact, China is wrong and the Chinese leadership is wrong. In other words, over the past two to three years, the Chinese communists, the KMT, and the PFP have devoted considerable thought to overthrowing the DPP government and dragging down President Chen Shui-Bian. Even now, they haven't yet given up. Once we are re-elected on 20 March next year, then the leaders of the KMT and the PFP will give up. The Chinese Communist Party and its leadership will give up. Over the past three or four years, we have slowly grown accustomed to China's boycotts, suppression, opposition, and even negation. However, we have faith in Taiwan. We have faith in our people and ourselves. Everything will change when we win the presidential election on 20 March 2004.

This response drew a considerable amount of attention in Taiwan. The media quickly treated this as Chen's insinuating that the KMT and PFP are colluding with the Beijing government against the DPP. The statement 'they [China] have even given clandestine assistance [to the KMT and the DPP]' was especially salient. Over the course of the following week, DPP and KMT officials traded exchanges through the media.

- On 12 October, Joseph Chao-Hsieh Wu, the deputy secretary general of the Presidential Office, stated at an unofficial function that Chen's statements mean that the two pan-blue parties have been 'exchanging feelings with China through their glances', a Chinese phrase meaning tacit flirting. He further stated that such interactions had begun after the DPP had been elected in 2000, citing instances of KMT and PFP legislators travelling to China to attending scholarly conferences on different integration models as evidence.
- On the same day, both Lien Chan and James Soong, running mates in the upcoming presidential elections and the leaders of the KMT and the PFP

respectively, asked Chen to provide evidence. Lien further stated that Chen was making false claims for the purpose of slandering him and that Chen should apologize to the Taiwanese citizens for his actions.

- On 13 October, the presidential office released a Chinese translation of the question and response from the *Washington Post* interview.[3]
- On the same day, Lee Ying-Yuan, deputy secretary general of the DPP, and Yeh Yi-Jin, director of the DPP's Department of Women's Development, held a press conference at DPP headquarters. They stated that Chen's statements were actually very reserved and that China was actually openly aiding Lien and Soong. They claimed that Chen simply stated the truth and did not commit slander. As evidence, they cited (1) Zhu Rongji, who, at that time, was the Chinese Premier, warning the Taiwanese to not vote for Chen in 2000, (2) the alleged case of KMT legislator Kao Ming-Chien, who attended the World Health Organization's SARS conference as a representative of the People's Republic of China, (3) invitations to Lien-Soong's election support group being handed out at an official function in China.
- Also on the same day, the KMT spokesperson, Tsai Cheng-Yuan, stated that the party would be forming a team of lawyers to keep track of Chen's slandering activities, and would be pressing charges at the end of his presidential term.
- On 16 October, Chiou I-Jen, secretary general of the presidential office, stated at a press conference at the presidential office that Chen's statements were based on a report, 'China's Taiwan Policy: Still Listening and Watching', by Bonnie Glaser, presented at the Centre for Strategic and International Studies, Pacific Forum. He stated that Chen only claimed that China clandestinely assisted the pan-blue, and never accused the pan-blue of accepting such assistance, but that such implications were not without basis.
- On the same day, Li Chia-Chin and Chow His-Wei (KMT and PFP legislative whips respectively) challenged Chiou's reading of Glaser's report. They stated that the article discussed only the meetings between KMT legislators and Chinese leaders without mention of clandestine assistance, and that the PFP was not even mentioned. They questioned whether Chen's misrepresentation and Chiou's misquoting of Glaser was the result of their subpar English language abilities or of malicious intent.

Following this sequence in the media, Lien, on behalf of the KMT, pressed charges against Joseph Wu, Lee Ying-Yuan, Yeh Yi-Jin and Chiou I-Jen on the grounds of public humiliation and slander. In the decision handed down on 25 April 2005, the judge found the accused not guilty on both counts. The context of the situation was factored strongly into the court's decision. As the decision report states, the comments by the four accused were made during the presidential election period, and were on issues related to party conduct and of national importance. Given the importance of information during this period for a healthy election, unless firm evidence exists that the statements were made to defame, they shall be considered to be made with the good intention of providing citizens with the information necessary to make an informed choice. The statements were made in response to Chen's *Washington Post* interview. They are interpretations or opinions regarding an issue already in existence, and they were not intended to be slanderous, especially given that these issues, candidate conduct and attitude in the context of relations with the Chinese government, are considered to be of national importance. It is therefore imperative that statements raising public awareness and enabling public discussion of these issues be protected. Given these considerations, the court found the four accused to be innocent.

Chen Shui-Bian accuses James Soong of conducting backroom deals with China

On 8 May 2005, Chen took part in a televised interview on the Taiwanese broadcasting station SET with Cheng Hong-Yi. At one point, Chen stated that he had information that James Soong, during a trip to Washington DC in February, met with Chen Yun-Lin from the Chinese Taiwan Affairs Office. He claimed that China was seeking to block the constitutional amendments and intended to constitutionalize the public's right to a referendum taking place in Taiwan later that month, on 14 May. He then insinuated that Soong had made a deal with the Chinese leaders, agreeing to oppose the upcoming amendments in exchange for a high-profile trip to China. When Cheng asked for confirmation that this is what Chen meant, Chen nodded, and cited the fact that both Soong and Lien Chan had changed the dates of their respective trips to China from the originally scheduled June to before 14 May. He stated that the 14 May National Assembly elections were no longer a Taiwanese domestic matter concerning its constitution but that there had been heavy interference by China. Once again, this episode played out through the media.

- On 9 May, the PFP legislator Hwang Yih-Jiau denied Chen's claims. He stated that the PFP's opposition to the constitutional amendment was the result of party consensus that resulted from an intra-party debate and that it had nothing to do with whether or not Soong had met with Chen Yun-Lin.
- On 10 May, a number of PFP officials rejected Chen's claims. Liao Wen-Chang, the PFP's deputy director of public affairs, stated that Chen's information was completely erroneous and questioned the provenance of his sources. Lee Yung-Ping, the PFP legislative whip, noted that Soong and Chen Yun-Lin's respective schedules did not overlap at all while they were in the US; by the time Soong arrived in the US, Chen Yun-Lin had already left. She also questioned the provenance of of Chen's source. Lee Hung-Chun, PFP legislator, questioned the logic of Chen's argument: if the PFP had used opposition to the constitutional amendment to barter for Soong's China trip, then why can Lien Chan go to China while the KMT is in support of the amendment?
- On 15 May, Soong rejected Chen's claims and questioned his sources.

- On 20 May, Yu Shyi-Kun, secretary general of the Presidential Office, stated while on a visit to Washington DC that the president would not make such claims without having proper evidence.
- On 27 May, Soong, along with his advisors and a team of lawyers, requested that Chen provide evidence for his statements regarding Soong's meeting with Chen Yun-Lin. They threatened to take legal action if their requests were not met. Chang Hsien-Yao, the director of the PFP's Policy Research Centre, stated that Chen should make a public apology if his claims were fabricated or should provide the relevant information if he had received inaccurate intelligence.
- On 3 June, Soong filed a civil claim against Chen for damages to his public image. He asked for compensation as follows: (1) one New Taiwan Dollar, (2) Chen was to hold a press conference where he would clear Soong's name, and (3) Chen was to release a statement for publication on the front pages of *Liberty Times*, *China Times*, *United Daily News* and *Taiwan Daily*, clearing Soong's name, for three consecutive days.
- On the same day, Yu Shyi-Kun, responding to Soong's charge that Chen's 8 May claims lacked evidence, stated that Chen had many sources of information.

With this, the situation fell out of the media spotlight for the following four months, until Chen gave another interview to SET on 17 October. During this interview, Chen restated his claim regarding Soong's meeting with Chen Yun-Lin in Washington DC. He then reemphasized the fact that he had solid evidence to back up his claims. He also claimed that he had shown the evidence to a 'heavy-weight pan-blue leader'. He stated that, if summoned by the court, he would present the evidence to the court and would ask whoever provided the information to him to appear as his witness. These statements correspond to the statement of defence that he submitted to the court.

On 19 October, the PFP legislators responded. Citing a conversation between the AIT director, Douglas Paal, and Soong, during which Paal assured Soong that the US did not have any information regarding the meeting of Soong and Chen Yun-Lin in the US, Hwang Yih-Jiau argued that given American intelligence capabilities, if they did not have any information about this occurrence then it could not have happened. Chang Hsien-Yao stated that during Soong's meeting with Hu Jintao, on which occasion Chen Yun-Lin was also present, Chen Yun-Lin responded with a 'no' when Hu asked him whether he had met Soong in the US. Lee Ching-An asked Chen to provide the evidence that he claimed he had. She stated that if Chen's evidence was found to be valid, the party would ask Soong to resign his post as PFP chairperson and to leave politics forever. If the evidence was found to be unreliable, Chen should take responsibility and step down from his position.

On the same day, Soong raised his demand for compensation to: (1) NT$50,000,000, and (2) Chen was to release a statement for publication on the front pages of *Liberty Times*, *China Times*, *United Daily News*, *New York Times*,

The Times and *Le Figaro* clearing Soong's name, for three consecutive days. The court decision, dated 15 Febuary 2007, ordered Chen to pay Soong NT$3,000,000 in damages and to release a statement for publication on the front page of the three Taiwanese newspapers requested by Soong. Two concerns were factored into the decision. First, the court deemed Chen's statements damaging to Soong, given the domestic sensitivities surrounding relations with China. Second, the information Chen claimed as his evidence turned out to be two pieces of letter-sized paper without any formal documentation, provided for him by Yeh Sheng-Mao, director of the Investigation Bureau.

The KMT and the DPP mutually accuse each other of selling Budai Harbour to China

In June 2009, Zheng Lizhong, the deputy director of the Taiwan Affairs Office, visited Chiayi. While he was there, Zheng had meetings with several officials and discussed various issues, such as agriculture and development. He was a flashpoint between the KMT and DPP officials. On 19 October a legion of 200 KMT supporters, led by four KMT legislators, protested in front of the Chiayi County Hall, which at that time was under the control of the DPP. They charged the Chiayi County magistrate, Chen Ming-Wen, with 'selling Taiwan' at his meeting with Zheng on the night of 14 October. Chen Ming-Wen had already publicly responded to this issue two days previously. He acknowledged meeting Zheng, stating that Zheng had invited him to discuss agricultural matters and that other relevant officials were present as well.

Facing the KMT protestors, Chen Ming-Wen, along with approximately 20 supporters including DPP councilors, held up signs showing a photograph of Zheng and Wong Chung-Chun, a KMT legislator from Chiayi, while chanting 'Do not be a modern Wu Sangui', referring toa reviled collaborationist from Chinese history whose name was synonymous with 'traitor'. The photograph shows Wong pointing to something not visible in the frame while Zheng, standing beside him, looks on. The signs also include the statement being chanted, and 'Taiwan opens its doors wide for Chinese investment to develop Budai Harbour'. The situation quietened down without much else happening. Later the same day, Chen Ming-Wen stated that he and Wong had had separate meetings with Zheng. He claimed that he had spent most of his meeting communicating the Taiwanese perspective on its pursuit of sovereignty and expressed regret that Wong, instead, had discussed plans to develop Budai Harbour using Chinese funds.

On 23 October of the same year, during an interpellation at the Chiayi County Council, the KMT councilor Chen Chun-Hung, one of the councilors who had led the protest on 19 October, addressed Chen Ming-Wen:

> Zheng Lizhong came to Budai Harbour as our guest. They have played host to us many times [when we went to China]. I felt that as a councillor I was not important enough to receive him, so I asked [legislator] Wong Chung-Chun to act as host. The next day, you chanted phrases, such as 'Chinese investments

in Taiwan', '[they are] selling Budai Harbour to China', and 'modern Wu Sangui'. Magistrate, is this how you treat your guests?

Chen Ming-Wen responded,

> The photograph clearly shows Wong giving Zheng a briefing. Am I wrong? ... You are opening the doors of Budai Harbour to investment from an enemy state; how are you different from Wu Sangui? ... When we invest in China, we are making money from them. If you open our doors to let them in, you are crazy.... Taiwan is a sovereign country. Our harbors and airports are our gates; is it right for us to open our gates to enemy states so they can help us develop? ... The Taiwanese will not accept this.

For this statement, Wong took Chen Ming-Wen to court, accusing him of slander. He argued that Chen Ming-Wen was aware that there was no project being planned for Budai Harbour and that Chen's statement during the interpellation amounted to mud-slinging and was intended to undermine his magisterial campaign. The court decision handed down on 19 March 2010 sided with Chen Ming-Wen, deciding that Chen's statement was a response to Wong's questioning, not intentional slander.

Summary of cases

In the question that sparked Chen's accusation that China gave clandestine support to the pan-blue, Pomfret began by asking for Chen's opinion of China in general, but then specifically mentioned potential talking points, the SARS incident and the Three Links. Chen therefore had the opportunity to take the question as he wished. His response was on topic, but it was vague and did not address specific issues. While not all his claims could have been backed up with evidence, those that could have been, such as the 'clandestine assistance' claim, were not. Many of these claims that lacked evidence, although symbolic, would probably require evidence before they found general acceptance. And although Chen did not directly claim that the KMT and PFP had colluded with the Chinese government, it was heavily insinuated, especially considering the way he grouped the three sides together when discussing how they 'devoted considerable thought to overthrowing the DPP government and dragging down President Chen Shui-Bian'.

In the ensuing media hubbub, prior to the case being taken to court, four DPP officials (those who were later sued by the KMT) clarified and confirmed Chen's interview response that the Chinese government had indeed been assisting the pan-blue camp. In one instance, China was said to be offering outright assistance. In all three instances, the DPP officials attempted to provide evidence of Chinese assistance in one way or another, meaning that (1) at least one event or source was cited and that (2a) the cited event can be taken as an example of Chinese assistance without being dismissed as completely absurd, at least as the event exists in the public's knowledge, or (2b) that the public is likely to deem the source as valid. For example, Chiou I-Jen cited an article by Bonnie Glaser as the supposed source of Chen's claims. Although the KMT later disputed the validity of this claim, this does not change the fact that Chiou cited a specific source.

Chen's claim that Soong met with Chen Yun-Lin in Washington DC was similar to the 'clandestine assistance' claim in the way it publicly played out in the media, but it was more narrowly focused. Chen's initial statement concerned a very specific and very serious issue which definitely required evidence. Chen did not provide any evidence during the interview but presented instead some factual information and explained how he had arrived at his conclusions. These facts were based on incomplete information regarding the schedules of Soong and Chen Yun-Lin. The connection between the information presented and Chen's conclusion is tenuous at best, and by almost any standard it sounds more like a conspiracy theory. Within two days, PFP officials presented more information regarding Soong and Chen Yun-Lin's respective schedules to the media as evidence to refute Chen's claims. The DPP did not respond for over a week, until Yu Shyi-Kun, without attempting to provide evidence for Chen's claims, stated that Chen would not make any accusations without providing evidence. Four months later, in a televised interview, once again without attempting to provide evidence, Chen claimed that he had solid evidence and would make it available to the court if requested to do so. The court asked to see the evidence and found that it consisted of an informal intelligence report, written on two pieces of paper without any official documentation, that had been provided for Chen by Yeh Sheng-Mao, Director of the Investigation Bureau. Yeh testified that the document was compiled from various sources by intelligence agents, but that he was unable to verify the content because the meeting took place overseas.

The final case, which consists of two parts, differed from Chen's two claims in that it was much less politically salient. The first instance involved a local standoff between the KMT and the DPP during which the two sides accused each other of 'selling Taiwan' to China. The KMT's claim was based on the public knowledge that the DPP magistrate, Chen Ming-Wen, had met with a Chinese official. Since Chen Ming-Wen had already acknowledged the meeting, whether or not the KMT provided evidence is a moot point. The DPP's counter-claim was based on the fact that a KMT legislator, Wong Chung-Chun, met with the same Chinese official. As evidence, the DPP side held up signs showing the two men standing together looking at something, supposedly Budai Harbour, off in the distance. Both sides' claims could have been discussed as specific policy matters, but were instead framed as symbolic issues.

The second instance occurred during a Chiayi Council interpellation, when the magistrate, Chen Ming-Wen, was questioned about his supposedly inhospitable conduct in criticizing the KMT legislator for selling Taiwan and hosting the Chinese official. The member of the council who conducted the interpellation was the same one who led the KMT protesters in criticizing Chen Ming-Wen for meeting with the same official. During the interpellation, Chen Ming-Wen's response was partially substantive, when he explained how the benefits of Taiwanese investment in China differ from the dangers of allowing Chinese investment in Taiwan, and partially symbolic, when he evoked the historical image of Wu Sangui.

Discussion of qualitative findings

As discussed above, we expected to observe, if our posited mechanism is correct, politicians (1a) discussing the symbolic aspects of the China issue, or (1b) discussing the issues in terms of policy ends, and (2) not providing evidence for their claims. Our three cases present mixed results. None of the claims were purely symbolic or purely technical, but on balance they leaned toward the former. Chen, for example, avoided discussing specific instances of Chinese assistance being granted to the KMT and PFP, choosing instead to frame the issue in terms of broad claims. In the third case, both KMT and DPP camps, when faced with the opportunity to discuss an issue that was potentially very technical, chose to evoke the highly symbolic 'selling Taiwan' frame. Chen's claim regarding Soong and Chen Yun-Lin's meeting certainly focused on a very specific issue, that is, the national assembly elections and the constitutional amendment, but it still also appealed to the 'selling Taiwan' frame.

Both of Chen's claims played out in the media and offer us insights into how these claims were subsequently challenged and defended. In both cases, the one who was attacked called for evidence and either questioned the attacker's motive for making such a claim or questioned the credibility of the attacker's sources. In the first case, ample attempts were made to provide evidence. Without judging the veracity of the evidence provided, we deem them to have been acceptable in the view of the general public because they were not dismissed immediately. The second case is harder to assess. No evidence was provided at all until the court demanded it, but Chen had publicly made the offer to reveal his evidence in court before being requested to do so. Regardless of whether Chen truly believed his intelligence to be accurate or whether he was bluffing, the fact that he chose to make the claim that he had evidence suggests that he had perceived that there would be a need to provide it.

The high rate of attempted evidence provision in the first two cases runs contrary to our expectations, but we believe this is a result of our case selection rather than evidence against our posited mechanism. Both of these cases were of the highest political salience possible, given that they were accusations made by the president against his main opposition. The combination of media attention, the well-played defence that called for evidence and then scrutinized whatever was provided, and the high-salience court cases all contributed to the heightened need for the attacker to provide evidence. Evidence was finally provided, but judged from an informed, non-layperson perspective, the body of evidence, on the whole, appeared to be hastily put together and uncharacteristic of what might be expected from a well-planned campaign. This conjecture regarding our case selection is also supported by the third case. Evidence was not much of an issue in this case because all the events were already public knowledge, but the disregard for campaign propriety – the KMT council member, Chen Chun-Hung, acted hypocritically in chastising the magistrate, Chen Ming-Wen, for something that Chen Chun-Hung himself had done at exactly the same time – is suggestive of what the easiness of the China issue affords politicians if it is not reined in by the highest level of public scrutiny.

Ultimately, the expected observations can be seen as guidelines toward answering our research question. In our three cases, we wanted to determine whether the easiness of the China issue and its likelihood of evoking gut responses allowed and induced candidates to disregard the traditionally perceived need to provide evidence for their claims. After considering the evidence holistically, we believe that the three cases support our posited mechanism. In both of Chen's cases, it appears that Chen and his team were thinking that he could gain from making claims about his opposition, only to be surprised by the unexpectedly bright spotlight placed on him owing to his presidential status. In contrast, the standoff between the KMT and the DPP over Budai Harbour demonstrates the politicians' perception of the China issue under normal circumstances.

Conclusion

At the beginning of this chapter, we asked why there is a discrepancy between the qualitative and quantitative assessments of negative campaigning in Taiwan. We put forward the hypothesis that the 'easiness' of the China issue made it less likely to be supported by evidence when compared to other issues. Our quantitative examination showed that negative 'China' issue claims were only 0.58 times as likely to be supported by evidence as are negative claims for all other issues. While our case selection required us to qualify our findings, the evidence from the qualitative examination still supports our posited mechanism. Our examination of the three cases revealed that politicians considered the China issue to be an easy issue that evoked gut responses from the audience, which in turn encouraged them to provide less evidence for their claims.

Notes

1 We would like to express our thanks to Jon Sullivan for providing this data, which he collected and coded for his doctoral dissertation (2010).
2 The China question, as has been discussed extensively, satisfies the third criterion, length of existence. However, because significant variations in this factor cannot be readily observed – candidates have no control over this matter as they do for the other two criteria, and the China issue had long been entrenched in Taiwanese politics by the time elections started, so that we do not expect variations to exist between our four election periods – we do not pay particular attention to it.
3 We deem the translation accurate.

References

Ansolabehere, Stephen D., and Iyengar, Shanto (1995) *Going Negative: How Political Advertisements Shrink and Polarize the Electorate*, New York: Free Press.

Ansolabehere, Stephen D., Iyengar, Shanto, and Simon, Adam (1999) 'Replicating Experiments Using Aggregate and Survey Data: The Case of Negative Advertising and Turnout', *American Political Science Review*, 93: 901–909.

Ansolabehere, Stephen D., Iyengar, Shanto, Simon, Adam, and Valentino, Nicholas (1994) 'Does Attack Advertising Demobilize the Electorate?' *American Political Science Review*, 88: 829–838.

Brooks, Deborah J., and Geer, John G. (2007) 'Beyond Negativity: The Effects of Incivility on the Electorate', *American Journal of Political Science*, 51: 1–16.

Buchanan, Bruce (2000) 'Regime Support and Campaign Reform', in Bartels, L., and Vavreck, L. (eds) *Campaign Reform*, Ann Arbor: University of Michigan Press.

Carmines, Edward G., and Stimson, James A. (1980) 'The Two Faces of Issue Voting', *American Political Science Review*, 74: 78–91.

Freedman, Paul, and Goldstein, Ken (1999) 'Measuring Media Exposure and the Effects of Negative Campaign Ads', *American Journal of Political Science*, 43: 1189–1208.

Freedman, Paul, Franz, Michael, and Goldstein, Kenneth (2004) 'Campaign Advertising and Democratic Citizenship', *American Journal of Political Science*, 48: 723–741.

Fridkin, Kim L., and Kenney, Patrick J. (2011) 'Variability in Citizens' Reactions to Different Types of Negative Campaigns', *American Journal of Political Science*, 55: 307–325.

Garramone, Gina G., Atkin, Charles K., Pinkleton, Bruce E., and Cole, Richard T. (1990) 'Effects of Negative Political Advertising on the Political Process', *Journal of Broadcasting and Electronic Media*, 34: 299–311.

Geer, John G. (2006) *In Defense of Negativity*, Chicago: University of Chicago Press.

Jackson, Robert A., Mondak, Jeffery J., and Huckfeldt, Robert (2009) 'Examining the Possible Corrosive Impact of Negative Advertising on Citizens' Attitudes toward Politics', *Political Research Quarterly*, 62: 55–69.

Jamieson, Kathleen H. (1992) *Dirty Politics: Deception, Distraction, and Democracy*, Cambridge, UK: Oxford University Press.

Kamber, Victor (1997) *Poison Politics: Are Negative Campaigns Destroying Democracy?* New York: Insight Books.

Lau, Richard R., Sigelman, Lee, and Rovner, Ivy B. (2007) 'The Effects of Negative Political Campaigns: A Meta-Analytic Reassessment', *Journal of Politics*, 69: 1176–1209.

Mark, David (2007) *Going Dirty: The Art of Negative Campaigning*, Lanham, MD: Rowman and Littlefield.

Mutz, Diana C. (2007) 'Effects of 'In-Your-Face' Television Discourse on Perceptions of a Legitimate Opposition', *American Political Science Review*, 101: 621–635.

Mutz, Diana C., and Reeves, Bryon (2005) 'The New Videomalaise: Effects of Televised Incivility on Political Trust', *American Political Science Review*, 99: 1–15.

Patterson, Thomas E. (2002) *The Vanishing Voter*, New York: Knopf.

Rawnsley, Gary D. (2000) ' 'Where's the Beef?' The 1998 Mayoral Elections in Taiwan', *American Journal of Chinese Studies*, 7: 147–169.

Riker, William (1996) *The Strategy of Rhetoric*, New Haven: Yale University Press.

Schafferer, Christian (2006) *Election Campaigning in East and South-East Asia*, Aldershot: Ashgate.

Sides, John, Lipsitz, Keena, and Grossmann, Matthew (2010) 'Do Voters Perceive Negative Campaigns as Informative Campaigns?' *American Politics Research*, 38: 502–530.

Sobieraj, Sarah, and Berry, Jeffery M. (2011) 'From Incivility to Outrage: Political Discourse and Blogs, Talk Radio, and Cable News', *Political Communication*, 28: 19–41.

Sullivan, Jonathan (2008) 'Campaign Advertising and Democracy in Taiwan', *The China Quarterly*, 196: 900–911.

Sullivan, Jonathan (2009) 'Defending Negativity? Evidence from Presidential Campaigns in Taiwan', *East Asia*, 26: 305–320.

Sullivan, Jonathan (2010) *Negativity and Information in Campaign Advertising*, PhD thesis, University of Nottingham.

4 The China impact on Taiwan's elections

Cross-Strait economic integration through the lens of election advertising

Dafydd J. Fell

Since the lifting of martial law in 1987, there has been a transformation in Taiwan's trade and investment patterns. In that year, Taiwan's dominant trade partners were still the United States and Japan, while trade and investment with China remained outlawed and only limited indirect flows were possible. It was not until 1987 that the Taiwanese were permitted to visit China, and it would be another two decades before there was genuine liberalization in the form of Chinese visitors coming to Taiwan for tourism and study.[1]

The shift towards increasing trade relations with China began in the early 1990s, although it was largely registered as trade with Hong Kong. Similarly, much of the initial China-bound Taiwanese investment was routed via Caribbean tax havens, such as the British Virgin Islands and the Cayman Islands. However, between the mid-1990s and the fall of the Democratic Progressive Party (DPP) government in 2008, a political stalemate featured prominently in cross-Strait relations, while rapid integration or convergence was the dominant trend in the economic sphere. The return to power of the Kuomintang (KMT) in 2008 resulted in much closer economic integration and warmer political relations. By the time Taiwan signed the Economic Cooperation Framework Agreement (ECFA) with China in 2010, China (including Hong Kong) had become by far Taiwan's leading trading partner and destination for outward investment. The fact that Taiwan still enjoys a healthy trade surplus with China is critical for the country's capacity to maintain an overall balance of payments surplus.

Over the last two decades, Taiwan's governments have fluctuated between liberalizing and attempting to control levels of cross-Strait trade and investment. Key elements in its attempts to prevent trade dependence in the 1990s were the 'go south' (南向政策) policy that encouraged Taiwanese companies to invest in South East Asia rather than in China, and the 'go slow, be patient' (戒急用忍) guidelines that aimed to monitor and limit the level of Taiwanese investment in China. Such measures were primarily motivated by political concerns, such as expanding Taiwan's international relations and also preventing China from exploiting trade dependence in its bid to achieve its ultimate goal of Chinese unification. Under both the DPP (2000–2008) and KMT (2008–present) administrations there has been a progressive trend towards trade and investment liberalization. Nevertheless, the question of whether the economic benefits of

cross-Strait economic integration outweigh the potential national security consequences has been a hotly debated political issue since Taiwan's democratic
transition. The centrality of the Cross-Strait Services Trade Agreement in the
Sunflower social movement protests in 2014 reflects the fact that Taiwan's
society remains deeply divided on the issue of economic integration.

This study considers the China impact on Taiwan's electoral politics. The
China impact is conceptualized here by looking at how growing economic integration has affected the way that Taiwan's economic relations with China have
been debated in electoral propaganda. The relationship has been two-way, since
the increase in economic links has made cross-Strait trade an increasingly salient
electoral issue and, at the same time, electoral debate has had a growing effect
on how cross-Strait policy is developed on the Taiwan side. As with other policy
areas, there has been a shift from top-down decision-making to a situation in
which cross-Strait economic policy has to take into account public opinion and
lobbying by societal actors.[2]

Using an approach that employs political communications data to analyse
changing patterns in the economic relations debate has a number of advantages.
First, election advertising represents one of the most accessible forms of political
communication in Taiwan. Such messages are impossible to avoid because of
the vast quantity of election advertising in newspapers, on television and online.
In comparison, voter exposure to election policy white papers (generally the
closest thing to manifestoes in the Taiwan context) or even to the presidential
debates is far lower.[3] Second, since political advertising tends to be designed for
the ordinary voter, complex policy issues have to be simplified and more
informal reader-/viewer-friendly language has to be employed. By adopting
another perspective, we can distinguish between what Carmines and Stimson
call 'hard' and 'easy' issues.[4] They argue that easy issues tend to be symbolic,
not requiring great factual knowledge, and are easily understood at gut level.
Effective political advertising will always frame an issue as an easy issue. Third,
as I have shown in a number of previous studies, political advertising can tell us
much about the state of political competition.[5] Content analysis of political
advertisements can reveal the issues on which the parties are competing and
whether the parties are adopting radical or moderate stances. This can contribute
to the debate on whether parties are moving towards the centre or becoming
polarized.[6] Lastly, such a study can contribute to the arguments about the state of
Taiwan's democracy. Jean Grugel defines democracies as 'political systems
comprising institutions that translate citizens' preferences into policy'.[7] To
achieve this condition, it is essential for parties to offer voters a clear picture of
their positions and, ideally, there should be a degree of choice between the
parties. Parties therefore also need to go beyond just adopting slogans; they have
to try to educate the voters on their policy preferences as well as persuade them
to vote accordingly.

For the purposes of this chapter, I have examined the content of a range of
political advertising data to find out how proponents and opponents of closer
economic integration with China have tried to sell their ideas over the last 20

years. The two main data sources examined are TV election advertisements and newspaper election advertisements.[8] I aim to show how the quantity and quality of issue emphasis has changed over time, using an approach based on time series analysis. In this era of growing economic ties between China and Taiwan, the central research questions are:

1   How have the parties altered their treatment of the cross-Strait economic integration issue in their propaganda?
2   What are the implications of these changes for Taiwan's party system?

In this chapter, I argue that Taiwan's parties moved from largely ignoring the issue at the outset of multi-party elections to participating in quite heated election debates on the pros and cons of economic integration with China. There have also been significant changes in terms of party emphasis and positions over time. Although there have been some similarities to the trends in changes in party positions on the issue of unification versus independence (*tong du* 統獨), there are also significant differences. The *tong du* issue is often conceptualized as a spectrum in which the far right advocates rapid unification and the promotion of Chinese nationalism while the far left calls for a declaration of Taiwan independence. Likewise, we can think of the cross-Strait economic issue as a spectrum in which the far right represents complete economic integration while the far left prioritizes national security and thus maintains strict controls over economic ties with China. The main parties have shown considerable movement in their positions on this issue, although the overall trend has been towards the acceptance of greater economic liberalization with regard to China. My research also reveals how the issue agenda is changing over time, for while during much of the 1990s contestation over China–Taiwan relations was focused on the abstract debate on unification versus independence, there has since been a genuine shift towards debates on more practical economic cross-Strait issues.

Early election treatment of cross-Strait economic issues

Despite the sudden initial explosion in cross-Strait economic ties in the early 1990s, the issue received surprisingly little attention in campaign propaganda. Instead, the focus of the debate on cross-Strait relations was both highly political and abstract. The parties were extremely polarized in their visions in the first two full democratic elections in 1991 and, to a lesser extent, in 1992.[9] The DPP and its candidates tended to call for an independent Republic of Taiwan and warned of the dangers of political unification with China.[10] In contrast, while the KMT spoke positively about its proposal for unification under the National Unification Guidelines, it focused its attacks on the costs and dangers of Taiwan independence.[11] The KMT, in particular, employed what I have described as its terror formula of 'DPP = Taiwan Independence = CCP invasion' in numerous advertisements.[12] Similarly, the DPP tried to scare voters by warning of the terrifying consequences of unification with China. For instance, a DPP candidate asked,

'Are you willing to see the five star red flag flying over Taiwan?'[13] One of the few exceptions to the avoidance of cross-Strait economic ties in elections came in an advertisement placed by the KMT candidate in Taipei City, Chen An-bang (陳安邦), in the 1991 campaign for the National Assembly. One of his three core slogans was 'direct cross-Strait trade'.[14] This featured in his newspaper advertisements and also on his street posters.[15] However, this should not be taken as reflecting the official KMT positions since, in fact, Chen's other two core slogans were borrowed from the DPP. These were 'direct presidential election' (總統直選) and 'welfare state' (福利國家). At this point, however, the two main parties adopted similarly cautious positions on economic links with China.

In the mid-1990s, the Taiwan government attempted to reduce economic dependence on China with various initiatives such as the 'go south' policy. However, the issue still seemed to be mainly off the electoral agenda. Both the leading parties continued to use their terror messages, but they also largely steered clear of the ultimate solutions for cross-Strait relations that they had promoted in 1991.[16] With the cross-Strait crisis of 1995–1996 ongoing, it was not surprising that much propaganda was related to the risks of conflict breaking out.[17] The KMT tended to stress its strength in standing up to China, while the New Party preferred to blame the KMT's gradual independence policies for taking Taiwan to the brink of war.

One element of economic integration that the DPP did try to bring into the electoral debate was the prospect of uncontrolled Chinese labour migration if Taiwan were to be unified with China; to this effect, two migration-themed TV advertisements were launched in 1995. Nevertheless, the DPP's treatment of the issue of economic integration was not yet at the policy level. It was highly symbolic and emotionally charged, showing images of crowds of homeless Chinese migrants in major Chinese cities and dehumanizing the migrants by portraying them as almost zombie-like figures with blank eyes. Moreover, neither of the DPP's competitors were making proposals to open up Taiwan to Chinese labour migration.

The first instance of a party coming up with specific policies in its election advertising to promote cross-Strait economic integration was the New Party (NP). The NP had been established in 1993 by former KMT politicians who were dissatisfied with their party's ties with political corruption and its national identity positions under Lee Teng-Hui (李登輝). In 1995, the NP issued a full-page newspaper advertisement entitled 'All New Beef, Wisdom of the Highest Quality' (全新牛肉, 智慧極品).[18] In this advertisement, the NP called for 'special economic trade zones' (經貿特區) to be established in Taiwan that could engage in direct trade with China and thus promote cross-Strait economic and trade relations. In addition, it called for the protection of the rights of the Taiwanese business people or Taishang (台商) in China. This was therefore one of the first election appeals to the growing Taiwanese community living and working in China; it also set a precedent for the detailed manifesto-style advertisements that other parties would later produce to give voters the necessary information on party policy positions for issue voting.

In 1995–1996, at least in its propaganda, the KMT had not yet warned voters that it planned to urge business restraint in Chinese trade and investment. There were not yet open calls for what would become the 'go slow, be patient' policies. For instance, the 1996 advertisement entitled 'The Beef is Here' (牛肉在 這裡) touted the KMT's success in achieving gradual economic liberalization with China and cited the 1995 cross-Strait trade figures as evidence of this success.[19] In the same advertisement, the KMT also called for an expansion of the 'go south' project. However, the related project on which the KMT placed most emphasis in 1995–1996 was the concept of turning Taiwan into an Asia-Pacific Regional Operations Hub (亞太營運中心) for businesses in the region.[20] The concept was open to interpretation either as a bid for closer economic ties with China or as a tool to strengthen Taiwan's economic diplomacy with Southeast Asian and Western countries.

In short, the review of the campaigns up until the first direct presidential election suggests that the China impact had not yet fully come into play. In other words, despite closer cross-Strait economic ties, such issues were not viewed as salient by the major parties as a means of winning voters' support. The NP represented a lone voice openly calling for closer economic integration. The pattern on the cross-Strait issue seemed to overlap with that of the changes in the positions of the parties on national identity, with the KMT and DPP converging in the mid-1990s on a position that prioritized national security in economic relations with China, leaving the NP isolated in its more orthodox Chinese nationalist stance.[21]

Debates of the late 1990s

Despite the KMT government's 'go slow, be patient' guidelines, Taiwan was becoming increasingly economically dependent on China, as Taiwanese companies found ways to expand their trade and investment in China. In this context, there were signs that the parties were starting to take the issue more seriously by the late 1990s. In the 1997 local elections, while the main parties were focused on domestic issues such as welfare systems and political corruption in their campaign advertising, the NP was actually trumpeting its success in winning the debate on closer cross-Strait economic ties. One such advertisement pointed out that the NP had advocated direct links since its formation four years earlier and had argued that the Asia-Pacific Operations Hub would not be able to succeed without such links. The same advertisement also mentioned the fact that other parties had previously labelled the NP as a 'spokesperson for the CCP' (中共代 言人) for advocating direct transport links to China, but now the DPP chairperson, Hsu Hsin-Liang (許信良), and leading entrepreneurs, such as Chang Yung-Fa (張榮發) (President of Evergreen), had come out in support of the three links.[22]

In 1998, the DPP held the China Policy Conference at which the party chairman, Hsu Hsin-Liang, and allies spoke in favour of boldly going west. In other words, Hsu was calling for a policy of economic liberalization with China that was similar to the NP's policy. Nevertheless, Hsu's vision faced considerable opposition within the party from factions that held a position similar to that of Lee Teng-Hui. In the event, a compromise formula was reached under the heading of 'strengthen the base and go west' (強本西進), which attempted to locate the party between the NP's full liberalization and the KMT's 'go slow, be patient' guidelines. Nevertheless, perhaps due to the DPP's internal divisions over the issue, the decision was made to not test this new formula by using it as an election appeal in the December national elections. In contrast, it was only the KMT that paid greater attention to economic issues in its propaganda. A number of the KMT advertisements trumpeted the party's success in guiding Taiwan through the Asian financial crisis, which had had such a detrimental impact on its neighbours such as South Korea.[23] Moreover, for the first time the KMT started to emphasize in its TV advertisements that the promotion of 'go slow, be patient' policies was vital for defending Taiwan's national security.[24]

After the decisive presidential election of 2000 and the political turnover of power, both continuity and change could be observed in the way that the main parties addressed the issue of economic integration. The DPP's Resolution on Taiwan's Future (台灣前途決議文) and China Policy Conference demonstrated moderation in its cross-Strait and *tong du* positions. However, because the DPP again preferred to keep such topics off the election agenda they therefore did not feature prominently in its campaign advertising. This was the last time that the KMT used a heavy anti-independence appeal at the core of its campaign with frequent use of the terror message. Since the KMT candidate, Lien Chan (連戰), was the handpicked successor to Lee Teng-Hui, there were still no signs of a change of stance on cross-Strait economic liberalization. Other than repeating Lien's 'success' in promoting Taiwan as an Asia-Pacific Operations Hub, the KMT instead preferred to concentrate on attacking what it saw as the change-ability and danger of the DPP's China policies. For instance, one KMT TV advertisement under the slogan 'changeable, contradictory, dangerous' (搖擺, 矛盾, 危險) contrasted Chen Shui-Bian's (陳水扁) claim of promoting a New Middle Way (新中間路線) with his slogan of 'Long live Taiwan independence' (台灣獨立萬歲) and the dangers of his calls to open Taiwan up to Chinese investment. A similar newspaper advertisement also questioned the 'dangerous and contradictory' nature of Chen's China policy. This time, in addition to Chinese investment, Chen was criticized for promoting direct links with China.[25] The advertisement went on to cite survey data showing that the public had greater trust in Lien to handle cross-Strait relations.

In short, the elections in the late 1990s suggested that the main parties were finally taking the economic integration issue seriously: they were beginning to move the debate on how to interact on economic issues with China on to the electoral agenda. On the policy spectrum, the DPP was gradually moving towards the NP's position of accepting economic liberalization with China, while the KMT remained the most conservative on this topic. The DPP was still clearly divided on the issue, however, and was therefore cautious about openly advocating liberalization in its propaganda.

Debates on cross-Strait integration under the DPP government, 2000–2008

Although the DPP era also featured the continuation of economic convergence and political divergence, it differed strongly from the final Lee administration (1996–2000) in that the DPP government was more willing to allow economic liberalization in China relations. A key moment in this process was the consensus reached at the Economic Development Advisory Conference (經發會), in August 2001, to lift the 'go slow, be patient' limits on cross-Strait investment.[26] Despite the economic consensus and Taiwan's economic recession at the time, the 2001 elections featured quite limited discussions on economic integration with China. Although the KMT repeatedly blamed the DPP for the economic recession, it was not yet ready to openly repudiate its anti-integration policies of the 1990s. Once again, the only party attempting to make the case for real change was the NP, which was moving towards its most extreme national identity position to date under the leadership of Hsieh Chi-Ta (謝啟大).[27] In an advertisement placed in major newspapers on 25 July 2001, the NP used the slogan, 'idiot, the problem is cross-Strait' (笨蛋, 問題在兩岸).[28] The advertisement called for peaceful unification under what it called the 'One Country, Three Systems' (一國三制) model.[29] From the NP's perspective, the solution to the crisis facing Taiwan was not purely economic but lay in the need for real cross-Strait integration. The advertisement argued, 'Everyone knows that only if a greater Chinese economic community can be established by the three cross-Strait places will they be able to be mutually complementary and share common prosperity. Only in this way will Taiwan be able to avoid the effect of economic flight'. (誰都知道，唯有兩岸三地建構起一個大中華經濟圈，互補互利、共存共榮，才是台灣經濟化解磁吸效應。)

By 2004, it had become clear that a new pattern was developing in the party spectrum on cross-Strait economic ties. The KMT came out strongly in support of closer economic integration. Its proposals were quite similar to those of the NP in the mid-1990s and late 1990s, positions that it would previously have condemned as endangering Taiwan's security. For instance, one of the KMT's 2004 presidential advertisements called for direct transport links with China and the creation of air safety corridors.[30] In addition, it advocated the establishment of free trade ports to promote closer cross-Strait trade relations.

The DPP government had come to power with quite a positive view on cross-Strait economic ties that did not rule out establishing direct links. In its first two years in power, the DPP made some conciliatory gestures towards the PRC. Nevertheless, the PRC did not view the DPP conciliatory gestures as sufficient, since the DPP had not been willing to fulfil the preconditions of accepting the 1992 Consensus or the one China principle. Thus the only progress that the DPP was able to make with regard to establishing direct transport links took the form of the three mini-links, which involved direct shipping between the islands of Kinmen and Mazu and China's Fujian Province. This meant that, despite the continued economic integration, the DPP had little to gain from placing the issue on the election agenda. It could not gain anything from opposing integration and highlighting the costs of integration, as it was responsible for the lifting of the 'go slow, be patient' restrictions. The DPP therefore largely steered clear of the topic in the 2004 national election campaigns for the president and parliamentary seats.

Instead, it was the DPP's ally, the Taiwan Solidarity Union (TSU), that led the voices of caution on the dangers of economic integration with China. In this way, the party adopted a similar position to that of Lee's KMT in the 1995–2000 period. A representative TSU TV advertisement was the 2004 football advertisement (足球篇). In this spot, the TSU was represented as a goalkeeper saving repeated penalty kicks in which each shot symbolized an element of political or economic integration with China. The blocked shots included eight-inch wafer production going to China, the liberalizing of stock-market-listed company investment in China, and the unequal three links (八吋晶圓西進, 放寬上市集資投資中國, 不對等三通). The Taiwanese being protected from such dangers were represented in the advertisement as infants playing inside the goal, a mother bottle-feeding her child and an old lady knitting behind the goal.

The elections which saw perhaps the greatest attention being paid to economic integration, however, were the final elections of the DPP era, those for the Legislative Yuan in January 2008 and the presidential election in March. Landslide victories brought the KMT back to power and, with it, a degree of political domination that Taiwan had not experienced since the democratic transition period of the late 1980s to early 1990s.

Once again, the party taking the strongest line against economic integration with China was the TSU. Instead of the abstract approach it had taken 2004, it tried to convince the public of what it saw as the negative consequences of the China impact, thus attempting to move voters by telling the true stories of how the Taiwanese people were becoming victims of cross-Strait integration. The Tea Farmer TV advertisement (茶農篇) showed how, because of competition from Chinese tea imports, a tea picker had been forced to leave the fields and face the hardship of becoming a trainee hairdresser in the city. She appealed to the audience, saying 'I would rather go back to picking tea leaves. Can you help me?' The advertisement ends by explaining how the TSU protects local industries by successfully gaining significant subsidies for Taiwanese tea producers to cope with Chinese imports. The second such advertisement tells the story of a towel factory producer that has now been reduced to distributing towels in his friend's KTV club. We see images of the factory closing down and are told that most towels are now imported from China but that the quality of Taiwanese towels is much better. The advertisement ends by pointing out how the TSU has protected local industry by promoting an anti-dumping tax for Chinese towel imports. What is special about these two advertisements is that they not only warn against the impact of trade integration but also promote policies to deal with the consequences.

Particularly in the 2008 presidential election, one of the DPP's most emphatic appeals was against the KMT's proposal for a Cross-Strait Common Market

(兩岸共同市場) or what the DPP often preferred to call the One China Common Market (一中共同市場). For instance, the 'Taiwanese labour friends, are you ready?' TV advertisement (台灣勞工朋友你準備好了嗎?) claimed that Ma Ying-Jeou (馬英九) supported a One China Common Market and the recognition of Chinese education qualifications. The narrator talked of the 200 million unemployed people in China and images were shown of huge crowds of homeless migrants in major Chinese cities (last seen in the DPP's 1995 advertisements). Viewers were told that 'Chinese labour is coming' (中國勞工要來了). Another advertisement warned that Chinese salaries were a fifth of those in Taiwan and asked whether (if Ma were to win the election) viewers would want to compete against 200 million people. A number of advertisements stressed the dangers of recognizing Chinese education qualifications under Ma's One China Common Market. The narrator asked whether 'with the streets full of fake diplomas will you still be able to make a living?' (滿街的假學歷, 你能夠保住你的飯碗嗎?). A similar advertisement showed a teacher, a nurse and a civil engineer all voicing concern about fake diplomas and the future careers of professionals trained in Taiwan.

The DPP also warned of the potential consequences of the One China Common Market for Taiwan's farmers, with a number of advertisements that visualized how Taiwan would be swamped by Chinese agricultural products. These were designed to challenge the KMT's argument that Taiwanese farmers would be able to profit from the Chinese market. In the Banana TV advertisement (香蕉篇), a cartoon showed a Taiwanese banana farmer cheerfully receiving payment for his crops at the Cross-Strait Agricultural Product Market (兩岸農產市場), but then moments later being buried under a mountain of bananas coming from China. The advertisement ends with the slogan 'Under Ma Ying-Jeou's One China Common Market, Taiwan will not come to a good end' (馬英九的一中共同市場, 台灣沒有好下場). Another DPP strategy was to warn of the dangers of 'evil Chinese products' (黑心中國產品): we hear the US presidential candidate, Barack Obama, saying that he will ban imports of Chinese toys and the Japanese PM (after the poisoned dumpling incident) saying that he will strengthen the testing system for imported Chinese products. This is contrasted with Ma's advocacy of a One China Common Market which would allow Chinese products and people to freely enter Taiwan. We then hear Hu Jintao (胡錦濤) calling for the strengthening of cross-Strait trade and other forms of exchanges under the One China principle, and the advertisement ends by asking Ma 'Which country's side are you on?' (你到底站在哪一國?) In this way, the advertisement ties in well with the DPP's questioning of the loyalty of KMT politicians to Taiwan in a number of campaigns, insinuating that they are going to sell out Taiwan to China.

The KMT's promotion of a Cross-Strait Common Market in 2008 reveals how the party had shifted towards policies promoted by the NP in earlier campaigns. However, in that year the KMT actually had far more advertisements on its goal of promoting Taiwan's international space than on new China policies. Some of the advertisements were quite reminiscent of those showing Lee on the international stage during the 1996 presidential campaign. The difference was that the leading actor in the show was now Ma. In one TV advertisement, we see Ma calling for UN membership as well as direct cross-Strait transport and trade normalization. The idea of a balance between international and cross-Strait economic relations is visible in the concluding slogans for making Taiwan into (1) the Global Innovation Centre (全球創新中心), (2) the Asia-Pacific Economic Trade Pivot (亞太經貿樞紐) and (3) the Taishang Operations Headquarters (台商營運總部). However, the KMT did try to defend its cross-Strait policies and to refute the DPP's terror message regarding the dire consequences of Ma's Cross-Strait Common Market. For instance, in one 50-second TV advertisement, the KMT's vice presidential candidate, Vincent Siew (蕭萬長), criticized the DPP government for its economic failures and election tricks. He then defended his Cross-Strait Common Market proposal, claiming that it was Taiwan-centred and that it offered a solution to Taiwan's economic problems. The screen showed multiple newspaper reports in which Chen Shui-Bian, the premier Chang Chun-Hsiung (張俊雄) and the economics minister Lin Hsin-Yi (林信義) all praised the idea of a Cross-Strait Common Market. Another advertisement tried to challenge the DPP's warning that Taiwan risked being flooded by Chinese labour. Here the slogan was, 'The DPP slanders the Cross-Strait Common Market, the people can see through this' (民進黨抹黑兩岸共同市場, 人民看的清). A voice is heard asking, 'How can the Chinese come to work here without ROC ID cards?' And a lawyer asks, since people with Chinese diplomas will not be able to take licence examinations, will they be able to gain licenses? A teacher even asks 'how can they come here to teach if they cannot read complex characters?' And a doctor explains that the KMT is 'talking about opening up to Chinese tourists, not to Chinese labour'. This last advertisement follows a line that often appeared in the KMT's propaganda during the last years of the DPP era, warning voters not to be taken in by what it terms 'DPP lies and dirty tricks'.

In 2008, therefore, the parties were far apart when it came to economic relations with China and the issue received far more election-advertising attention than had any earlier election. The KMT had replaced the NP in trying to convince voters that cross-Strait economic integration would act as a tonic for Taiwan's economic crisis. In contrast, the DPP and TSU, although critical of Ma's Cross-Strait Common Market concept, were not able to offer an alternative policy package. Thus, just as Taiwan's parties became polarized on national identity issues during Chen's second term, we saw similar trends in their treatment of cross-Strait economic issues.[31] Although election results are dependent on multiple variables, the 2008 elections did offer voters a real choice on how to handle cross-Strait relations, and the KMT's resounding victories could be interpreted as giving Ma the legitimacy to put his Cross-Strait Common Market pledges into practice.

Electoral debates over cross-Strait ties in the Ma Ying-Jeou era

On coming to power, Ma and his KMT administration moved quickly to transform cross-Strait economic and political relations. Meetings between the Straits Exchange Foundation (SEF) and the Association for Relations Across the Taiwan Strait (ARATS), which had last been held in 1998, were revived and became a regular feature during Ma's first term in office. A total of 16 agreements emerged from these meetings under the first Ma administration (2008–2012), many of which have had substantive impacts. Key developments include (1) direct shipping and scheduled flights, (2) allowing Chinese students to study in Taiwan, (3) large numbers of Chinese tour groups and limited opening up to independent Chinese tourists wishing to visit Taiwan, (4) liberalization of Chinese investment in Taiwan, and (5) food safety agreements. However, from the perspective of the KMT (and the CCP) the jewel in the crown of their cross-Strait agreements was the signing of the Economic Cooperation Framework Agreement (ECFA) in 2010. This large-scale agreement allowed for significant tariff reductions on a large number of items of cross-Strait trade and was an agreement which many economic analysts view as being of greater economic benefit for Taiwan. Naturally, the CCP is trying to use closer economic ties to achieve its political goals of preventing Taiwan independence and promoting unification. A key means of doing this is keeping the DPP out of power. Therefore, the CCP has attempted to use economic incentives to convince voters of the benefits of closer ties. One feature of this has been large Chinese provincial procurement groups coming to Taiwan as well as highly targeted economic procurement aimed at locations with strong DPP voting support. One such case that received much publicity has been promotion of exports of milkfish from the DPP's stronghold of Xuejia (學甲) in Tainan to China.[32]

The new cross-Strait economic agreements left the DPP facing a severe dilemma. Many of these cross-Strait developments were actually quite popular and benefited Taiwan economically. Moreover, many of these policies had been initially developed under the DPP and it was the PRC that had prevented them from being fully implemented earlier in order not to allow the DPP government to claim the credit.[33] It did, however, together with the TSU put up a strong campaign against the ECFA. These parties tried in vain to promote a national referendum on the ECFA.[34] In the run-up to the signing of the EFCA, the two major parties tried to influence voters with a series of advertisements focused on the ECFA. The DPP once more stressed the dangers of the ECFA for Taiwan's labour market. In the 'Who will benefit from the ECFA?' advertisement (ECFA 對誰有利?篇), the DPP warned voters that after Hong Kong signed an economic agreement with China, the gap between rich and poor had become the worst in the world. The advertisement then ended with the slogan, 'we do not want an ECFA where the rich get richer and the poor get poorer', (我們不要讓富者越富 窮者越窮的ECFA). In response, a number of KMT government ministries launched TV advertisements extolling the potential benefits for Taiwan's business people that would accrue from increasing economic competitiveness. The highlight of the ECFA campaign came in the form of the televised debate on the proposal between Ma Ying-Jeou and the DPP chairwoman Tsai Ing-Wen (蔡英文). Many observers argued that Ma performed better than Tsai in the debate.[35] It is debatable whether the DPP really wanted to see a referendum over the ECFA because public opinion in Taiwan generally tends to adopt an 'economics first' position on controversial issues.[36]

In January 2012, combined legislative and presidential elections were held in Taiwan. These represented the first real opportunity for voters to offer their verdict on the full package of Ma's cross-Strait policies in national level elections.

The KMT employed a number of strategies to address the issue. First of all, attention was drawn to the positive consequences of integration for Taiwan's fruit farmers by showing a number of KMT advertisements that explained how Taiwan had exported more fruit in the three years under the KMT than during the eight under the DPP, and that certain fruits had sold especially well in China, Japan and even America. One such advertisement visualized these exports by means of images of people with fruit-shaped heads being widely acclaimed abroad. Similarly, an advertisement was issued on 12 December 2011 that praised the role played by the ECFA in increasing Taiwan's economic growth rate and in increasing agricultural exports (including tea and fish) along with growth in consumer spending.

Second, action was taken to convince the Taishang that only the KMT government could protect the interests of the Taishang through its cross-Strait policies. On 27 November 2011, the KMT issued a TV advertisement which was designed to look like a TV news interview in which Ma praised the role that the Taishang play in improving cross-Strait relations and promoting Taiwan's economic growth. This was part of a concerted KMT attempt to appeal to the Taishang to come back to vote and to help to ensure that Ma was re-elected.

Third, the KMT's cross-Strait record was compared with that of the DPP. On 3 January 2012, a KMT advertisement started with images of economic prosperity in 2011, and then, by means of a 'flash-back', displayed some poor economic figures from the DPP era. This was intended to urge voters not to let everything go back to the starting point (別讓一切退回原點). Next came a 'fast forward' to positive economic statistics, including the 10.72 per cent growth rate in 2010 and the 65 per cent increase in tourists coming to Taiwan. The advertisement did not specifically refer to tourists from China, and tourist numbers have increased from a range of other tourist-issuing markets.[37] However, any viewer that has recently been through a Taiwanese airport, to one of Taiwan's tourist hotspots or to one of the large hotels will be aware that the fastest-growing source of new tourists is China. Another of the comparative style advertisements accused the previous DPP government of locking up the nation's economy, which was visualized in the form of a *Gulliver's Travels*-style giant tied down by hundreds of tiny ropes. The advertisement shows that, under the KMT, these ropes are broken by policies such as the ECFA and the expansion of visa-free travel.

Finally, Ma and his running mate Wu Den-Yih (吳敦義) call on the Taiwanese giants that created the Taiwan miracle to stand up again for the next ten golden years. This advertisement again reflects the KMT message used in both 2008 and 2012 that, under their management, Taiwan will profit from international space, harmonious cross-Strait relations and strong economic growth.

Although Taiwanese businesses in China had already begun to issue pro-KMT advertisements in earlier post-2000 elections, the scale of such advertisements was unprecedented in 2012. This element of the China impact on Taiwan's electoral politics and, in particular, the debate on cross-Strait links was visible in both Taishang-sponsored advertisements and the ways in which key business leaders with operations in China publicly announced their support for Ma and his China policies.[38] The KMT tended to leave its attacks against the cross-Strait policies of the DPP presidential candidate, Tsai, to such sponsored newspaper advertisements. For instance, an advertisement carrying the slogan 'supporting Ma' (挺馬) was sponsored by the Mainland Taishang Ma Wu Campaign Support Association (大陸台商馬吳競選後援總會).[39] This advertisement first outlined the benefits for Taiwan under Ma's continued presidency. These included (1) how Taiwan would benefit from stable cross-Strait relations under the 1992 Consensus and Ma's 'three nos';[40] (2) how, under Ma, commercial opportunities for Taiwanese business had rapidly expanded, emphasizing the benefits of cross-Strait agreements such as the ECFA and proposed investor protection agreement for Taiwanese business; (3) Taiwan's expanded international space under Ma; and (4) how cross-Strait cooperation would be the best way for Taiwan to avoid being dragged into the effects of the European debt crisis. The advertisement then continued with a list of what its sponsors believed would happen if Tsai were to win. First, it was argued that, without the 1992 Consensus and by supporting one country on each side (一邊一國), the mainland would not have contacts with a DPP government. This would reduce Chinese tourist groups and Taiwanese exports to China, which would have a damaging impact on Taiwan's economy. It also claimed that this would prevent further SEF-ARATS talks and create obstacles for the implementation of the existing 16 cross-Strait agreements. This would severely damage the interests of Taiwanese people. A further argument was that Taiwan would have reduced international space. Lastly, the advertisement stated that a Tsai government with limited government experience and lacking support in the huge Chinese market would lead Taiwan into recession, which would result in reduced household income, a stock market crash and increased unemployment. This was just one of a large number of supposedly Taishang-sponsored advertisements in support of Ma, his contribution to improving cross-Strait relations and the associated economic benefits.

In 2012, the DPP aimed to portray itself as both more moderate and more pragmatic on China than had been the case under Chen Shui-Bian. In contrast to the 2009–2010 period, the DPP was no longer openly opposing the ECFA. However, its advertisements largely avoided the topic of China. In fact, apart from the call for a nuclear-free Taiwan and the slogan of 'Fairness, Justice, Change, Taiwan' (公平, 正義, 改變, 台灣), the DPP advertisements were generally very vague on policy. Tsai's candidate image and attacks on Ma's government performance were the main themes of most of the advertisements. Considering this vagueness, it is actually surprising how little the KMT attacked Tsai's cross-Strait policies in its advertisements. In one KMT TV advertisement, the former health minister Yang Zhi-Liang (楊志良) comments that 'I really have not heard or seen what her [Tsai's] actual policies are'. While the analysis of the advertisements seems to confirm this, the same could also be said about Ma's plans regarding China for his second term. In 2008, the KMT had offered a clear vision on what it hoped to do about China, but this changed in 2012, when the KMT seemed to prefer to concentrate on contrasting its record in power with the alleged failures of the DPP era. However, one lesson that can be drawn from the 2012 campaign is that if the DPP wishes to return to national office, it will need to convince a wider voter constituency, including the Taishang, that it has the ability to develop a workable set of policies to handle cross-Strait economic relations.

The 2008 and 2012 election defeats have left the DPP facing a severe dilemma over how to deal with economic ties with China. It has tended to fiercely oppose the economic agreements introduced by the Ma administration in parliament, but once passed and put into operation, it has not called for them to be repealed. As the former DPP legislator Julian Kuo (郭正亮) notes with regard to the new services industry agreement with China, 'the DPP is very likely to slip once again into the negative cycle of saying a big "no" to the agreement before it is signed, but agreeing to abide by it once it is in force'.[41] The dilemma the party faces is that it is struggling to reach an acceptable balance on China policy between its two core component groups. In other words, the challenge is quite similar to the situation discussed earlier during its 1998 China policy debate. As Kuo again notes, 'One group firmly believes that Taiwanese independence should be placed above all else, while the other group feels that gaining political power should be the top priority'.[42] Whether the party is able to develop a workable China policy will depend on the latter group winning the inner party debate.

Conclusions

This study represents a preliminary attempt to examine the China impact on Taiwan's electoral politics. The way this was operationalized was to examine how, in an era of growing economic integration with China, Taiwan's parties have debated economic ties with China. This was achieved by tracking down how Taiwan's major parties have dealt with questions related to Taiwan's economic relations with China in their election political communications. The parties moved from largely ignoring the issue to gradually giving it greater attention by the turn of the century. In the last two presidential elections, it has become one of the most salient issues in Taiwan's electoral politics. The patterns that have been revealed offer a new angle on the story of party and party system change in Taiwan. While the NP and TSU have been quite consistent in their treatment of the issue, the KMT and DPP positions have fluctuated over time. However, it would appear that after the partisan divergence on the issue during the late DPP era through to the ECFA debate in 2010, a trend towards partisan convergence had developed by 2012, as the DPP no longer seemed to oppose the cross-Strait agreements from Ma's first term. In many respects, it appears that although the NP has ceased to be an electorally viable party, many of the cross-Strait economic proposals put forward during the 1990s have finally become implemented government policy under Ma. A NP politician would probably feel vindicated after reading this chapter.

This study has also shown that cross-Strait policy-making can no longer be insulated from public opinion. In the 1990s, Lee imposed the 'go south' and 'go slow, be patient' policies without any real democratic debate. However, since 2000, Taiwan's parties have actually increasingly offered voters clearer policy options in their political communications on cross-Strait economic relations. In 2008, the parties presented voters with a genuine debate on how they would handle cross-Strait economic issues; four years later, the KMT asked voters to judge the party on its cross-Strait record. As has been the case with the *tong du* spectrum, public opinion places severe constraints on how parties deal with cross-Strait economic relations. Greater economic integration has placed political parties under pressure to develop viable economic policies to allow Taiwan to take advantage of the China market. On the other hand, public opinion is not prepared to tolerate the complete liberalization of economic relations. On the issue of economic ties with China, Taiwan's parties have proved to be adaptable in responding to their political environment. They have been responsive to perceived pressures of public opinion, election results and the changing international context. From the ways in which the KMT and the DPP handle cross-Strait economic issues, we can see how both parties have attempted to implement the lessons learned from their electoral successes and defeats. In the light of the Sunflower movement of 2014, it is likely that the issue of cross-Strait economic ties will be high on the agenda in the next rounds of election campaigns. It is, however, unclear how the main political parties will respond to the growing reservations within society over the potential risks of increased economic integration with China. In contrast, political parties face pressures from China and big business to accelerate integration. Such conflicting pressures will pose a severe challenge to Taiwan's political system for the foreseeable future.

Notes

1 Chinese tourist groups and short-term student visits did begin in the DPP era but were not yet significant in economic terms.
2 The trends seen on cross-Strait policy show significant parallels to those seen in the design of welfare systems. For discussion of this issue, see Wong (2004).
3 The viewing figures for Taiwan's presidential debates are actually quite impressive: for instance, 35 per cent of respondents stated that they watched the second 2012 presidential debate. See www1.tvbs.com.tw/tvbs2011/pch/tvbs_poll_center.aspx (accessed 13 June 2013).

4 Carmines and Stimson (1990|).
5 For instance, see Fell (2005).
6 On this topic, see Tan and Clark (2012).
7 Grugel (2002: 36). His other core criteria are 'effective states that act to protect and deepen democratic rights and count on a strong participatory and critical civil society'.
8 I should point out here that although I have examined a very extensive range of advertisements over the last 20 years, there are some gaps in my dataset and, for this chapter, I was not able to examine every single advertisement since 1991.
9 See Fell (2005: Chapter 6).
10 See DPP advertisement (1991).
11 See KMT advertisement (1991).
12 See KMT advertisement (1995).
13 See *Liberty Times*, 23 November 1991, 4.
14 See *Liberty Times*, 9 December 1991, 4.
15 See Digital Archives Taiwan (n.d.).
16 The KMT, for the most part, stopped mentioning the National Unification Guidelines and the DPP ceased campaigning on the Republic of Taiwan. The exception to this pattern was, of course, the DPP's presidential candidate, Peng Ming-Min, who made calls for Taiwanese independence that were similar to the DPP's position in 1991.
17 See Zhao (1999).
18 *United Daily News*, 18 November 1995, 32. The term 'beef' here is borrowed from American campaign language and refers to the idea that there is substance in a party's proposals.
19 *China Times*, 4 March 1996, 28.
20 See *United Daily News*, 24 February 1996, 1.
21 See Fell (2005: 102–108).
22 *United Daily News*, 15 November 1997, 13. The term 'three links' refers to direct postal, transportation and trade links between China and Taiwan.
23 See KMT advertisement (1998).
24 For instance, see the 1998 Guaranteeing Taiwan's Security TV advertisement (*baozhang Taiwan anquan pian*).
25 KMT advertisement (2000).
26 See *Taipei Times* (2001).
27 For more on the NP's shift towards extremism, see Fell (2006).
28 This is a variation on Bill Clinton's 1992 slogan, 'It's the economy, stupid'.
29 This was the NP's variation on China's proposal for unification under the 'One Country, Two Systems' model that has been used for Hong Kong and Macau. According to the NP, a third system is required for Taiwan due to the fact it clearly differs from the former European colonies.
30 *Liberty Times*, 1 March 2004, 11.
31 See Fell (2011).
32 Huang (2012).
33 For example, significant numbers of Chinese tourist cross-Strait charter flights began under the DPP.
34 Loa and Chao (2010).
35 Hsu (2010).
36 It could also be questioned whether the DPP really supported a referendum on the fourth nuclear power station back in 2000–2001.
37 The numbers of tourists from Japan and South East Asia have continued to increase, but China has replaced Japan as the top source of Taiwan's inbound tourists. See Tourist Bureau data, http://admin.taiwan.net.tw/statistics/year_en.aspx?no=15 (accessed 13 June 2013).
38 For instance, the founder of the Evergreen Group, Chang Jung-Fa, publicly announced his support for the 1992 Consensus during the campaign.

39 KMT support advertisement (2011).
40 Ma's 'three nos': a reference to his inaugural address pledge of no unification, no independence, and no use of force against China.
41 Kuo (2013a).
42 Kuo (2013b).

References

Carmines, Edward, and Stimson, James (1990) *Issue Evolution: Race and the Transformation of American Politics*, Princeton: Princeton University Press.
Digital Archives Taiwan (n.d.) http://catalog.digitalarchives.tw/item/00/3a/7e/7b.html (accessed 13 June 2013).
DPP advertisement (1991) *Liberty Times*, 11 December, 2.
Fell, Dafydd (2005) *Party Politics in Taiwan*, London: Routledge.
Fell, Dafydd (2006) 'The Rise and Decline of the New Party: Ideology, Resources and the Political Opportunity Structure', *East Asia: An International Quarterly*, 23, 1: 47–67.
Fell, Dafydd (2011) 'The Polarization of Party Competition in the DPP Era', in Ash, Robert, Garver, John W., and Prime, Penelope (eds) *Taiwan's Democracy: Economic and Political Challenges*, London: Routledge, 75–98.
Grugel, Jean (2002) *Democratization*, London: Sage.
Hsu, Yu-Fang (2010) 'Debate gives Ma a Short-term Win', *Taipei Times*, 30 April, 16, available at www.taipeitimes.com/News/editorials/archives/2010/04/30/2003471801 (accessed 13 June 2013).
Huang, Annie (2012) 'China Uses Trade to Influence Taiwan Election', *Guardian*, 9 January, available at www.guardian.co.uk/world/feedarticle/10031754 (accessed 13 June 2013).
KMT advertisement (1991) *Liberty Times*, 25 November, 1.
KMT advertisement (1995) *China Times*, 30 November, 1.
KMT advertisement (1998) *China Times*, 28 November, 32.
KMT advertisement (2000) *China Times*, 18 February, 7.
KMT support advertisement (2011) *China Times*, 22 December, A1.
Kuo, Julian (2013a) 'DPP is All Talk and No Action', *Taipei Times*, 30 June, 8.
Kuo, Julian (2013b) 'DPP Must Reach China Consensus', *Taipei Times*, 13 July, 8.
Loa, Iok-Sin, and Chao, Vincent Y. (2010) 'ECFA Referendum Proposal Rejected', *Taipei Times*, 4 June, 1.
Taipei Times (2001) 'Business Lauds End of No Haste Curbs', 28 August, 1.
Tan, Alexander, and Clark, Cal (2012) *Taiwan's Political Economy: Meeting Challenges and Pursuing Progress*, Boulder: Lynne Rienner.
Wong, Joseph (2004) *Healthy Democracies: Welfare Politics in Taiwan and South Korea*, Ithaca: Cornell University Press.
Zhao, Suisheng (ed.) (1999) *Across the Taiwan Strait: Mainland China, Taiwan and the 1995–1996 Crisis*, London: Routledge.

5 The China impact on Taiwan's generational politics

Shelley Rigger

The chapters in this volume emphasize the ways in which Taiwan's deepening engagement with mainland China since the late 1980s has affected the island. As important as that trend has been, it is but one of the forces that helped transform Taiwan at the end of the twentieth century. Taiwan's society also experienced accelerated economic development and, perhaps most importantly, democratization. These three trends' roots are intertwined; each helped drive the others in complex ways, and together they reshaped the island's ideological and institutional landscapes. The Taiwan that today's young adults inhabit is utterly different from the one in which their parents grew up. Where their parents endured privation, they enjoy prosperity. Where their parents experienced political repression, they participate in democracy. And where their parents saw danger across the Strait, they see opportunity (and also risk). As result, today's young people constitute a distinct political generation. But theirs is not the only identifiable political generation in Taiwan.

In a 2006 publication, I described four political generations in Taiwan. Now, seven years later, it is possible to describe a fifth (Rigger 2006). This chapter uses data drawn from the Taiwan Elections and Democratization Surveys from 2012 and 2008 to reveal the distinctive attitudinal patterns that characterize each of these five generations.[1] It pays particular attention to the fifth generation, the group shaped most strongly by the cross-cutting influences of democratization and the China impact.

The 'national identity' conundrum

Students of Taiwan's democratic politics have identified national identity as the primary cleavage shaping public opinion and driving political allegiances. Definitions and measures of 'national identity' differ, but most focus on a set of traits that appear – based on history, logic and some empirical evidence – to align in consistent ways. According to conventional wisdom about Taiwan politics, five traits – provincial origin; self-identification as Taiwanese, Chinese, or both; preference regarding unification and independence; partisan leanings; and attitudes toward mainland China – constitute a complex of attitudes that are associated with different national identities.

Provincial origin is the foundation of this complex – it is an objective characteristic that social scientists have found useful for explaining the subjective preferences that constitute national identity. Provincial origin is not an attitude; it is a demographic label that describes how an individual's family fits into the linguistic and historical landscape of Taiwanese society. It differentiates between *benshengren* – Taiwanese whose families arrived on the island before the Japanese colonial era – and *waishengren* – islanders who arrived with the Nationalists after the Japanese surrender, between 1945 and 1949.

Until the early 1990s, provincial origin was an official demographic datum defined and policed by the Taiwanese government. Taiwanese were categorized according to where their paternal family was living in 1945. *Benshengren* used identification documents that listed their province of origin as Taiwan. Each *waishengren* carried a document identifying him or her as a native of one of China's mainland provinces. Ironically, while the official categories disaggregated *waishengren* into their respective provinces, they merged Taiwan's indigenous cultural and linguistic groups – Hakka, Minnan and Aborigines – into a single category – *benshengren*.[2] Although this information is no longer printed on identification cards, most Taiwanese know whether they are *waishengren* or *benshengren*.

Research on public opinion in Taiwan has found that the remaining traits that constitute 'national identity' are correlated (albeit loosely) with provincial origin. While individual variation is substantial, by and large *benshengren* are more likely than *waishengren* to self-identify as Taiwanese, prefer independence as Taiwan's ultimate status, support the Democratic Progressive Party or other 'green camp' parties, and hold Sino-sceptical (or even Sinophobic) attitudes. Those whose provincial origin places them in the mainlander (*waishengren*) demographic are more likely than *benshengren* to self-identify as Chinese, prefer unification with the mainland, support the Kuomintang or other 'blue camp' parties, and support engagement with mainland China (Lin 2004).

Linking these individual dimensions in order to construct competing Taiwanese and Chinese national identities allows scholars and pundits to simplify their measurements. For example, some scholars use respondents' preferences for independence or unification to measure national identity, while others measure that concept by recording respondents' self-identification as Taiwanese, Chinese or both (Hsieh 2004). However, assuming that these two phenomena are reflections of a single underlying preference is problematic. For one thing, the correlations among these traits are weak and growing weaker. Provincial origin, the presumed basis on which the attitudinal distinctions are constructed, is far less relevant today than it was 60 – or even 20 – years ago.[3] Also, while carefully-designed academic studies explain their assumptions, methodologies and limitations, such precautions are regrettably rare in popular discourse.

Many journalists and policy-makers have extrapolated from the correlations in the scholarly literature and take self-identification and the independence/unification preference as two sides of a single coin, which leads them to view an increase in Taiwanese self-identification as evidence that Taiwan is moving toward a pro-independence position (Johnson 2005, Carpenter 2005). A further inference that is often made is that increases in Taiwanese self-identification benefit the DPP. A single sentence in a 2000 report to the Australian parliament perfectly captured the cascade of assumptions that constitute this multidimensional national identity logic:

> The [2000] elections boiled down to a race between the Kuomintang or affiliated movements representing the status quo in Taiwan politics and, on the other hand, the pro-independence DPP [Democratic Progressive Party] which represented the aspirations of a growing number of young people who identified themselves as Taiwanese, not Chinese.
>
> (Klintworth 2000)

Prior to 2008, observers who worried about the potential for trouble between Taiwan and the PRC, which could be sparked by a rise in pro-independence sentiment, took solace in the fact that none of the national identity indicators seemed to be moving strongly in that direction. Support for independence was flat, and equal numbers of survey respondents identified as Taiwanese and 'both'. However, since 2008, the percentage of Taiwanese identifying themselves as Taiwanese has surpassed the percentage identifying as 'both', with the most recent surveys showing 'Taiwanese' leading 'both' by approximately 20 percentage points (Election Study Centre 2014). This finding alarms those who assume that self-identification as 'Taiwanese' is equivalent to support for independence, despite the fact that the percentage of Taiwanese expressing support for independence has barely risen. In short, in an atmosphere where policymakers and security planners are constantly scanning for trends that could destabilize the Taiwan Strait, the assumption that each of these attitudes can act as a proxy for the others contributes to alarming – albeit erroneous – conclusions. A more nuanced approach to these trends is therefore urgently needed.

Generational politics and national identity

Upon reaching middle age, human beings across time and space have cherished the conviction that young people nowadays are *different*. This idea has a firm hold in democratic Taiwan, but in this case the evidence suggests it may be true, and measurable. When it comes to the island's central political debates, the attitudinal patterns observed in Taiwanese people of different ages *are* different, in important ways. These patterns are far more complex than simply young-versus-old, and they raise interesting questions. What explains the differing attitudinal patterns across age groups? Do they reflect generational shifts, or secular changes associated with the life cycle? Can we use them to anticipate future voters' political preferences? In addition to these questions, this chapter also considers the question raised by the mandate of the China Impact Study: how does interaction with mainland China affect the views of Taiwanese citizens and how it will affect them in the future?

Generational politics theory holds that historical experiences can bond an age cohort in ways that distinguish it from others over time. A competing theory holds that attitudinal differences across age cohorts reflect the stages that each cohort passes through in turn. Generational politics theory envisions each generation as a surfer, riding its particular wave to the beach. Life cycle theory sees age cohorts as a line of buoys, all tethered to the ocean floor, bouncing up and down in succession as time's swells pass beneath them.

The attitudinal patterns we observe in Taiwan incline us toward a generational politics model rather than a life cycle approach because the correlations between age and attitudes are not consistent across different attitudinal measures. For example, as Figure 5.1 shows, neither self-identification nor attitudes toward cross-Strait economic cooperation have a linear relationship with age. Moreover, while the relationship between Taiwanese identity and age curves upward for the youngest and oldest Taiwanese, like a smile, the relationship between age and optimism about cross-Strait economic cooperation looks more like a frown. A life cycle approach would predict that 'matching' values should vary in synch across age groups; a generational model is better able to explain the non-linear and contradictory patterns in Figure 5.1.[4]

Karl Mannheim first introduced the idea of political generations in his 1928 essay entitled 'The Problem of Generations'. He blended ideas drawn from a number of disciplines into an analytical framework that has proven persuasive and durable. According to Mannheim, generations form when individuals born close together in time and space (an age cohort) pass through events and experiences that destabilize the norms in a society just at the time when the political views of these individuals are being formed – between the ages of 18 and 25. Destabilizing events bond these similarly-aged individuals into a political

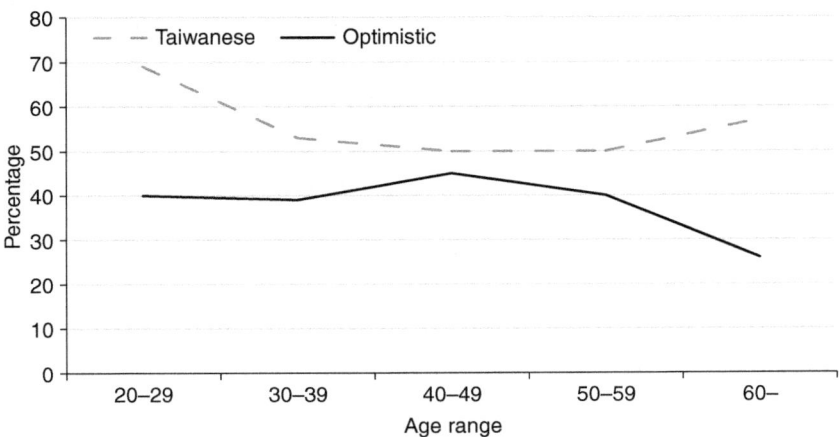

Figure 5.1 Self-identification and attitude toward the Economic Cooperation Framework Agreement (ECFA) by age, $N = 1,826$ (source: TEDS 2012). 'Optimistic' refers to respondents who said that Taiwan's economy had gotten better since the signing of the cross-Strait ECFA.

generation. In Mannheim's words, it is through 'participation in the common destiny' of their society during their 'formative years' that generations are born (Mannheim 1952: 303, 283). Mannheim did not claim that all members of a generation would think alike, only that the distribution of attitudes within a political generation would differ from the distribution of attitudes in other age cohorts.

Eventful politics thus can be expected to encourage generational formation, and Taiwan's politics over the past seven decades has been nothing if not eventful. Modern Taiwan hit its first historical inflection point in 1949 when the island settled into a 'new normal' after the brutal disruptions of the 1940s. The stable Japanese colonial rule that had defined *benshengren* life for half a century was over, while *waishengren* faced violent displacement from their homeland. For the next 20 years, the Kuomintang-led ROC government devoted itself to solidifying its monopoly on power through a concerted programme of authoritarian governance and state-led economic development. Its policies toward the outside world focused on resisting the PRC's claim to represent China internationally and building sufficient military strength to 'recover' the mainland. The generation that came of age in the cauldron of ideological rigidity, ethnic tension, political repression and forcible mobilization that characterized those first two decades – Taiwanese born between 1932 and 1953 – developed a political outlook that differed from that of their parents, whether *bensheng* or *waisheng.*

The early 1970s were a second turning point in Taiwan's history. After the United States president visited Beijing, and Taiwan lost the Chinese seat in the United Nations, the KMT could no longer ignore the global momentum that was building towards recognizing the PRC. Once the PRC emerged intact from the Cultural Revolution, the KMT could no longer make a persuasive claim to legitimacy based on its promise to unify China under the ROC flag. These external challenges shook the ruling party's confidence and emboldened its opponents. The result was a struggle for political reform that lasted from the first internal KMT party reforms in 1972 until the creation of an opposition party in 1986. The Taiwanese people who reached their formative years during this period – those born between 1954 and 1968 – thus came to political awareness at a time when the established verities of Taiwan's political life were being challenged and contested from many directions.

After 1986, Taiwan's democratization proceeded relatively smoothly. In 1987, the regime lifted martial law, a move which opened the political system to multi-party competition and extended civil rights to the entire population. In 1991 and 1992, the Taiwanese elected their national representative bodies and, in 1996, they directly elected their president for the first time. In 2000, the opposition Democratic Progressive Party won the presidency, marking the first time in Chinese history that a challenger party captured executive authority through a democratic process. Changes in cross-Strait relations paralleled Taiwan's domestic transformation. In 1987 Taipei lifted restrictions on travel to the mainland, and by the early 1990s the two governments were communicating regularly through quasi-official emissaries. Unfortunately, interaction did not guarantee better relations: the mid-1990s saw some of the tensest moments between the two sides since the civil war.

These three turning points – the late 1940s, the early 1970s and the mid-1980s – constitute precisely the kind of destabilizing moments Mannheim said could create a generational 'break'. They divided Taiwan society into four generations (for a statistical justification for this periodization, see Chang and Wang 2005a). Taiwanese who were born before 1932 were past their formative years when the KMT settled on Taiwan; they constitute the first generation. Those who were born between 1932 and 1953 experienced their formative years when the authoritarian regime was at its height (between 1949 and 1971); they are the second generation. The third generation includes the Taiwanese whose political formation occurred during the period of rapid political change, both domestic and external (1972 to 1986), that is, those born between 1954 and 1968. The fourth generation – Taiwanese born after 1968 – grew to political maturity in a democratic Taiwan.

Table 5.1 shows how broad attitudinal trends are distributed across generations. For each generation, the distribution of attitudes on each issue area is compared with the overall distribution of attitudes on that issue in the sample. Where preferences are distributed roughly equally in the entire sample and a particular generation, that generation is 'neutral' on that issue. Where a particular generation's responses differ notably from the sample, the direction of that difference is recorded. For example, first-generation Taiwanese tend to self-identify as 'Taiwanese' in relatively high numbers, express preferences on the independence/unification issue similar to those of Taiwanese overall, prefer the KMT in greater numbers than other generations, express relatively sceptical views about the effect of cross-Strait economic engagement on Taiwan's economic prospects, and perceive the PRC's military threat to Taiwan as benign, compared with the sample as a whole.

The table is heuristic rather than quantitatively precise, but it reveals two interesting phenomena. First, Taiwan's generations cannot be divided into blue and green. Most generations show a mixture of blue and green attitudes, especially if we observe that the sample overall is more blue than green, so that 'neutral' views tend to reflect that overall blue inclination. Second, there is one exception to the previous observation: the second generation – Taiwanese born between 1931 and 1953, those who reached their formative years during the era of deep authoritarianism – show a distinct green colouration. In fact, one could reasonably describe the second generation, unlike the others, as possessing precisely the complex of traits analysts typically have in mind when they talk about Taiwanese national identity.

Provincial origin introduces an additional dimension into this analysis. Because *benshengren* and *waishengren* experienced many historical events from different sides, attitudes within generations differ across the two groups – especially in the older generations, for which provincial origin was an especially salient force shaping their experience of historical events. Mannheim's theory accounts for this development. When history delivers destabilizing events, he

Table 5.1 Patterns of attitudes across major issues by generation

Generation	Self-identification	Independence/unification	Party	Cross-Strait economic ties	Cross-Strait military threat
First	Taiwanese	Neutral	KMT	Pessimistic	Optimistic
Second	Taiwanese	Independence	DPP	Pessimistic	Neutral
Third	Both	Neutral	KMT	Neutral	Neutral
Fourth	Both	SQ	Neutral	Optimistic	Neutral

Source: TEDS 2008. Light shading indicates that the generation has a green tilt on a particular issue, relative to the sample as a whole. Dark shading indicates a blue leaning. The absence of shading indicates a neutral position relative to the sample.

observes, members of newly-forming generations will 'take sides' (Mannheim 1952: 301). He calls the resulting subgroups 'generation units':

> Youth experiencing the same concrete historical problems may be said to be part of the same actual generation; while those groups within the same actual generation which work up the material of their common experiences in different specific ways constitute separate generation units.
>
> (Mannheim 1952: 304)

As Mannheim reminds us, because provincial origin is an important factor determining *how* Taiwanese 'work up the material of their common experiences', we should expect *benshengren* and *waishengren* within a generation to differ in their views.

The China impact on generational politics

Taiwan's political generations coalesced in response to developments in domestic politics and external relations; inevitably, the China impact on each generation has been significant. Tables 5.2 through 5.6 detail the attitudinal

Table 5.2 Self-identification and generation (*N* = 1,238)

Generation	Taiwanese	Both	Chinese
First	57.45	25.53	6.38
Second	53.89	36.14	6.54
Third	43.08	49.49	2.82
Fourth	45.83	47.08	4.38
Total	47.5	44.18	4.52

Source: TEDS 2008. Cells contain row percentages. 'Don't know' and other non-responses are omitted.

Table 5.3 Independence/unification preference and generation (*N* = 1,238)

Generation	Leans independence*	Status quo**	Leans unification***
First	14.89	46.8	14.9
Second	20.56	44.54	11.83
Third	18.2	57.95	16.15
Fourth	19.37	63.75	14.17
Total	19.14	56.3	14.21

Source: TEDS 2008. Cells contain row percentages. 'Don't know' and other non-responses are omitted.

Notes
* Combines 'immediate independence' and 'status quo now, independence later'.
** Combines 'status quo now, decide later' and 'status quo forever'.
*** Combines 'immediate unification' and 'status quo now, unification later'.

Table 5.4 Partisan preference and generation (*N*=1,238)

Generation	KMT	DPP	NP	PFP	TSU	None
First	38.3	17.02	0	0	0	44.68
Second	28.04	24.3	1.56	0	0.31	44.55
Third	42.05	22.05	1.79	0.26	0.51	32.31
Fourth	36.25	24.58	0.83	0	1.67	35.63
Total	36.03	23.42	1.29	0.08	0.89	37.24

Source: TEDS 2008. Cells contain row percentages. 'Don't know' and other non-responses are omitted.

Table 5.5 Consequences for Taiwan of opening cross-Strait economic exchanges (*N*=755)

Generation	Better	Worse	Same	Don't know
First	29.63	25.94	11.11	18.52
Second	29.3	30.23	12.56	16.28
Third	42.98	24.38	16.94	7.44
Fourth	51.66	18.08	22.51	2.21
Total	41.72	23.84	17.48	8.48

Source: TEDS 2008. Cells contain row percentages.

Table 5.6 Are you worried about a military threat from the PRC? (*N*=755)

Generation	Very	A little	Not too much	Not at all
First	7.41	29.63	40.74	14.81
Second	11.63	30.23	41.4	10.23
Third	9.5	34.3	42.98	11.16
Fourth	6.27	38.75	47.97	5.9
Total	8.87	34.57	44.24	9.14

Source: TEDS 2008. Cells contain row percentages. 'Don't know' and other non-responses are omitted.

profiles of each generation on five individual measures: self-identification, independence/unification preference, partisanship, outlook toward economic cooperation with the mainland, and concern about the PRC military threat. Based on these tables, I construct a profile of each generation and explain how that generation's make-up reveals the impact of China.

The first generation

Asked to self-identify, the first generation is more likely to choose either Taiwanese or Chinese, and it embraces 'Taiwanese' identity more enthusiastically than any other generation. At the same time, the most elderly Taiwanese are the least likely of any age group to express a preference for independence. These findings seem contradictory if we accept the logic that Taiwanese identity and support for independence 'go together', but if we consider the historical circumstances that shaped this generation, they are anything but surprising.

The Taiwanese in this age group formed their political identities before the confusing circumstances of the post-war era set in. The *Benshengren* in this generation experienced less indoctrination in Chinese identity than those educated later, under the Kuomintang, while the *waishengren* (who came to Taiwan as adults) clearly perceived themselves as Chinese. While their sense of themselves as Taiwanese or Chinese is stable, these elderly men and women show little appetite for the risks and dangers associated with a formal change in Taiwan's status.

On the political question of partisanship, a plurality of elderly Taiwanese rejects all parties, but they are twice as likely to lean toward the KMT as the DPP. These trends, too, are consistent with the generation's historical background and experience. While the necessities of business (and the blandishments of land reform) did win the KMT some support in this generation, most *benshengren* in this age group avoided active political engagement, especially on the opposition side, thanks to the 1947 political purge and subsequent White Terror. The first generation also includes surviving members of the nationalist government and military who moved to Taiwan in the 1940s, a highly KMT-identified group. Still, preferring the KMT and leaning in its direction on the independence/unification issue does not mean that this is a Sinophilic generation. Their attitudes toward mainland China are mixed. Asked whether increasing cross-Strait economic interactions are likely to benefit Taiwan's economy, they are relatively pessimistic, but they are no more worried about China's military threat than other age groups.

There is no question that 'China' has influenced the first generation's attitudes on a range of issues. The *benshengren* in this group passed through their formative years under Japanese colonial rule; for them, China was a distant abstraction until their early adulthood, at which point 'China' – in the form of the Republic of China government, its Nationalist (KMT) ruling party and its *waishengren* elite – dropped onto Taiwan like an alien spacecraft. That alien China imposed itself on Taiwan by force, completely displacing the political leaders and institutions under which the *benshengren* had grown up.

Because they were adults in the 1940s, the first generation also received relatively little of the Chinese-identity-reinforcing education and indoctrination to which Taiwanese born later were subjected. It is not surprising, then, that the most elderly Taiwanese are likely to view self-identify based on their provincial origin. In the 2008 Taiwan's Election and Democratization Study (TEDS) survey, 70 per cent of first-generation *benshengren* identified as Taiwanese; only 14 per cent identified as both Taiwanese and Chinese. That is a sharp contrast to the younger generations, especially the third and fourth, in which the *benshengren* were equally likely to self-identify as Taiwanese or 'Both'.

Elderly Taiwanese, especially the *benshengren*, also are less likely than others to interact with mainland China today. More than 87 per cent of first-generation respondents in the 2008 TEDS survey had not visited the mainland in the previous five years, compared with 76 per cent in the sample overall. It is not surprising that this group is less willing than the other generations to give answers to questions about cross-Strait engagement. Nor is it surprising to find their responses less consistent across the two dimensions, economic and military. In short, the most elderly Taiwanese are, fundamentally, the product of pre-war socialization and a post-war adulthood spent adjusting to life in the Republic of China on Taiwan, experiences that meant very different things to the *benshengren* and the *waishengren*.

The second generation

The second generation – the Taiwanese who grew up during the 'high tide' of KMT single-party authoritarianism – conforms the most closely to the stereotype associated with Taiwanese nationalism. It has a strong Taiwanese self-identification, especially compared with the younger generations. It is more pro-independence than other generations, and the gap between independence-leaning and unification-leaning individuals is wide. Competition between the KMT and DPP for support in this generation is tight; it is the only generation that is more pro-DPP than Taiwanese overall. It also is the most Sino-sceptical generation; for example, it is the only one in which more respondents believed that increased economic interactions harm Taiwan's economy.

The second generation's 'green tilt' is consistent with the cohort's formative experiences. The generation came of age when KMT authoritarianism was at its most rigid and repressive. For the *benshengren*, the 1950s and 1960s were decades of fear and humiliation. Schoolchildren were punished for speaking their mother tongue and prevented from learning about their homeland; their childhood was suffused with Chinese nationalist propaganda that denigrated Taiwan and exalted the mainland. The *waishengren* in this generation were raised in an atmosphere of tragedy, charged with a sacred mission that they were incapable of accomplishing, and living, in most cases, isolated and segregated from the *benshengren* community.

Mainland China had little direct impact on the second generation's political formation, because during its formative years (the 1950s and 1960s) Taiwan was entirely cut off from the mainland; there was no economic or social exchange across the Strait. Interactions between the two sides were hostile, even militarized. The KMT government constructed the Chinese Communist Party and the PRC state as enemies of the Chinese nation that would have to be destroyed for the ROC's destiny to be fulfilled. Mainland China as a socio-economic reality – as opposed to a political symbol – was entirely absent from Taiwan people's lives. Even abroad, Taiwanese rarely encountered 'the other China', thanks to the PRC's autarkic policies in those decades.

In short, when the second generation was growing up in Taiwan, 'China' meant the China inside Taiwan – the ROC. For the *benshengren*, the anger and wounded pride created by the KMT's repressive policies was directed at that China. For the *waishengren*, China was the longed-for China of the past – and an imagined future. For both groups, the mainland was both the source and the target of fear and hostility. As Taiwan opened itself to interactions with the PRC, the suspicion and negativity with which the second-generation Taiwanese viewed China – both the China within and the China on the other side of the Strait – diminished but did not disappear, leaving this cohort Sino-sceptical overall, and some of its members deeply Sinophobic.

The stereotypical view of Taiwanese national identity as a complex of attitudes that 'go together' is popular in part because it seems logical, and it conveniently compresses a complex reality. Another reason it is influential, however, is that it characterizes well some of contemporary Taiwan's best-known political personalities. The second generation includes the two most recent presidents, Chen Shui-Bian and Ma Ying-Jeou. The core leaders of the democratic movement and its successor, the DPP, are in this group, as are the KMT leaders (with the exception of the first generation member, Lee Teng-Hui) who have governed Taiwan in the democratic age. The contrasting viewpoints offered by these leaders and captured in the party platforms they have crafted reflect patterns of attitudes that are characteristic of their generation. One of the challenges they face, however, is that those viewpoints do not align as well with those of other Taiwanese – especially younger voters.

The China impact on the second generation is complex. As Tables 5.7 and 5.8 show, it is nearly as polarized as the first generation when it comes to identity

Table 5.7 Self-identification by five generations ($N=1,826$)

Generation	Taiwanese	Both	Chinese	Don't know
First*	60.00	22.86	8.57	8.57
Second	60.64	29.79	5.32	2.98
Third	51.19	40.04	5.67	1.65
Fourth	49.66	46.22	2.52	0.23
Fifth	68.25	29.67	0.89	0.59
Total	56.57	36.64	4.00	1.59

Source: TEDS 2012. Cells contain row percentages.

Note
* First-generation respondents formed less than 2% of the sample.

Table 5.8 Independence/unification preference by five generations ($N=1,826$)

Generation	Unification	Status quo	Independence	No response
First	14.29	37.14	25.71	22.86
Second	13.62	50.00	23.4	12.98
Third	15.17	64.53	16.64	3.66
Fourth	13.04	62.47	22.65	1.83
Fifth	6.82	59.94	31.45	1.78
Total	12.71	58.93	22.73	5.64

Source: TEDS 2012. Cells contain row percentages.

and the independence/unification debate – despite the fact that its members are among the most active participants in cross-Strait economic interactions. In 2008, 71 per cent of second-generation TEDS respondents said they had never been to mainland China – the lowest percentage of any generation.[5] This generation also included the largest percentage of respondents reporting three or more visits to mainland China in the previous five years: 16.5 per cent.[6] The explosion in cross-Strait economic ties coincided with the second generation's moment of greatest professional productivity and influence, so it makes sense that the second generation would constitute a substantial proportion of the Taiwanese working and living in the PRC.

The expectation that familiarity makes Taiwanese feel more favourable toward China is an important part of Beijing's strategy for winning hearts and minds on the island. The hope is that a sense of connection and shared interest with the mainland will gradually erode the Taiwanese people's feeling of separateness, opening the door to political unification. However, the attitudes of second-generation Taiwanese (at least those who live in Taiwan, within reach of TEDS pollsters) provide little evidence to support that logic. Instead, they are consistent with studies by Keng Shu and others which argue that engagement with the mainland does not diminish the sense of a separate identity held by Taiwanese – even among those with very close interactions with the mainland (Keng and Lin 2013). It seems, then, that the impressions of China that second-generation Taiwanese developed during their formative years have changed very little in the decades since.

The third generation

The contrasts between the second and third generations are sharp. While the second generation grew up in an era of authoritarian hegemony, the third reached political maturity in the midst of rapid change, in an unprecedented atmosphere of freedom and possibility. As a result, the rigidity and ideological tendencies of the second generation are replaced in the third by flexibility and pragmatism. The changes that began in the early 1970s were not uniformly positive; on the contrary, the 1970s and 1980s were decades of deep instability and insecurity. Nonetheless, these changes enabled – and in fact required – Taiwan to confront the reality of its unsustainable global role and to reform its political institutions and social practices.

Moderation, flexibility and pragmatism are hallmarks of the third generation. They choose a dual identity by the widest margin of any generation. They are more willing than other generations to commit to a political party, and they prefer the KMT by a wide margin – which is not surprising if we recall that this generation has no memory of the White Terror but does remember the economic boom and political decompression that the KMT engineered in the 1970s and 1980s. Their relatively moderate views also help to explain why, although they share other generations' preference for the status quo on the independence/ unification issue, they are slightly more willing than other generations to entertain unification as an option for Taiwan. Even many who support the DPP tend toward moderation on these issues. The Democratic Progressive Party's fundamentalist wing is peopled largely with second-generation politicians, while its pragmatic, election-oriented politicians – people such as Chen Chi-Mai, Bi-Khim Hsiao, Duan Yi-Kang and Su Chia-Chuan – are disproportionately from the third generation.

The China factor plays a very different role for the third generation than for the second. Chinese nationalist propaganda was a central theme in the third generation's education, but it was not unchallenged. In the 1970s and 1980s, new ideas began to compete with KMT ideology just at the time the ruling party's certainty and confidence were beginning to flag. The speed with which the democratization movement gathered momentum testifies to the readiness of Taiwan society for new political institutions, and the ease with which third-generation Taiwanese seized opportunities in the mainland after 1987 reflects their openness to China. During their youth, the idea of the 'Communist bandits' as implacable enemies to be destroyed was replaced by a more realistic image of the mainland as a neighbouring country whose global stature and domestic development were on the rise. Even on Taiwan, it was impossible to ignore a global trend away from 'Taiwan-as-China' in favour of the idea that 'China equals the PRC'.

The fourth generation

The fourth-generation Taiwanese grew up with democratization and reached political maturity in a democratic Taiwan. They have never voted in an election without multi-party competition, and they have been able to travel freely to the mainland, in most cases since childhood. Neither Taiwan independence nor any other idea has ever been declared off-limits to them by the government; the only presidents they have known are elected ones. In contrast to the third generation, which was taught to be ashamed of *benshengren* identity, the fourth generation has grown up thinking of Taiwanese cultures and languages as fashionable and cool. The openness of Taiwan's society during the formative years of these young people has allowed them more scope for self-definition and the opportunity to develop hybridized identities.

Democratization altered profoundly the way Taiwanese could talk and think. It thus gave rise to a generation of young people who identify with the homeland in which they were born and grew up. The confusion over how to define that homeland – as Taiwan or as the Republic of China – that plagued earlier generations was much less acute for the fourth generation, not because it was resolved (it was not) but because it was openly discussed, and an important choice – Taiwanese – was for the first time one of the options under discussion. Many members of this generation experienced a Chinese nationalist education, so they are not immune to the claim that Taiwan is Chinese. Nonetheless, they were exposed to a wider range of views on the identity issue than previous generations; those views are reflected in the high proportion in this generation whose responses to questions about self-identification and the independence/unification debate are moderate (that is, they identify as both Taiwanese and Chinese, and they prefer the status quo).

On political issues, too, the fourth generation is more pragmatic than ideological or emotional. Its support for the status quo in cross-Strait relations is the strongest of any age group. When it comes to unification and independence, it is more pro-unification than the Sinophobic second generation and more pro-independence than the stability-conscious third generation. Fourth-generation Taiwanese are more willing than other age groups to express a preference for a political party, and while they prefer the KMT, they are not nearly as pro-KMT as the third generation: they are more willing than the third generation to give the DPP a chance. They are also more optimistic about China than the other generations. In 2008, more than half the TEDS survey participants in this age group said they thought cross-Strait economic ties were beneficial to Taiwan's economy.

A fifth generation?

Generational politics theory suggests we should expect to see new political generations form in response to major political changes. Few political changes are as significant as the first exchange of executive power in 50 years, so it is reasonable to hypothesize that Chen Shui-Bian's election to the presidency in 2000 would be a generation-making event. Not only was his the first national victory for the opposition, but the positions he took differed profoundly from those of his predecessors. His presidency initiated a sea change in political rhetoric, and his administration introduced new educational curricula that emphasized Taiwan's subjectivity. Assuming that Chen's presidency represented a large enough rupture with the past to spark a new political generation, Mannheim's 'formative years' rule of thumb advises us that the members of that fifth generation would be the Taiwanese people born after 1982 – the eldest of whom were entering their formative years when Chen was elected in 2000.

If it is true that the politics of the Chen Shui-Bian era shaped a new political generation, how would we expect this generation to look, compared to the others? Under President Chen, being Taiwanese was more than fashionable; it was encouraged by the state. So we can expect the fifth generation to identify more strongly as Taiwanese. During the Chen years, there was also more open talk of Taiwan independence as an option, so we would expect young people reaching political maturity during his presidency to lean more toward independence than older Taiwanese, most of whom grew up with tight restrictions on pro-independence speech. Given Chen's success, the Taiwanese choosing partisan attachments in the early 2000s would have recognized the DPP as a viable contender in a way that previous generations would not, which we can expect to lead to an increase in support rates for the party among this group. Finally, the first eight years of the twenty-first century saw extremely rapid growth in cross-Strait economic ties but also an increase in military tensions. Those trends, too, should be reflected in the fifth generation's attitudes.

The 2008 TEDS survey included very few members of a potential fifth generation (just under five per cent of the survey respondents), so in Tables 5.1 through 5.6, individuals born since 1982 are included in the fourth generation. Tables 5.7 through 5.12 break out these potential fifth-generation respondents and test the propositions in the previous paragraph.[7] Table 5.7 shows that the first proposition is supported: while the percentage of respondents claiming a Taiwanese identity increased in all groups between 2008 and 2012, those whose formative years coincided with the Chen presidency are substantially more likely than those in any other age group to identify as Taiwanese; the biggest gap is between the fourth and fifth generations. Table 5.8 shows similar results: as expected, the fifth generation favours independence far more strongly (and is more sceptical of unification) than the others. Likewise, Table 5.9 offers support for the expectation that growing up with a DPP president would make 'Gen Fivers' more willing to express support for the DPP than previous generations.

The data presented in Tables 5.7, 5.8 and 5.9 reveal the fifth generation to be relatively green: Taiwanese in identity, open to independence, and more pro-DPP than other generations. However, as Tables 5.10 and 5.11 show, this green outlook does not imply hostility toward mainland China. Unlike the similarly-green second generation, which was evenly divided over whether cross-Strait economic exchanges would make things better or worse for Taiwan, respondents

Table 5.9 Partisan preference by five generations (*N* = 1,826)

Generation	KMT	DPP	New party	PFP	TSU	None
First	51.4	22.9	0.0	0.0	0.0	25.7
Second	33.2	26.6	0.9	0.6	1.5	37.2
Third	46.4	25.6	1.0	1.1	0.9	24.9
Fourth	39.6	30.9	0.7	1.1	0.7	27.0
Fifth	37.1	32.3	0	1.5	0.3	28.8

Source: TEDS 2012. Cells contain row percentages.

Table 5.10 Consequences for Taiwan of opening cross-Strait economic exchanges (*N* = 755)

Generation	Better	Worse	Same	DK
First	29.63	25.94	11.11	18.52
Second	29.3	30.23	12.56	16.28
Third	42.98	24.38	16.94	7.44
Fourth	57.89	17.89	16.84	2.11
Fifth	49.46	17.93	25.00	2.17
Total	41.72	23.84	17.48	8.48

Source: TEDS 2008. Cells contain row percentages.

Table 5.11 Are you worried about a military threat from the PRC? (*N*=755)

Generation	Very	A little	Not too much	Not at all
First	7.41	29.63	40.74	14.81
Second	11.63	30.23	41.4	10.23
Third	9.5	34.3	42.98	11.16
Fourth	6.32	33.68	50.53	9.47
Fifth	5.98	41.30	45.65	5.43
Total	8.87	34.57	44.24	9.14

Source: TEDS 2008. Cells contain row percentages. 'Don't know' and other non-responses are omitted.

in the fifth generation were far more favourable, with 50 per cent saying exchanges would have positive consequences for Taiwan, and less than half that number (18 per cent) predicting a negative outcome. The fifth generation reported a moderate feeling of threat from the mainland; the percentage reporting feeling 'very worried' about the PRC military threat was half that of the second generation, but a higher percentage reported feeling worried (either 'very worried' or 'a little worried') than in the survey overall.

The fifth generation defies the stereotype that Taiwanese identity and Sino-scepticism 'go together'. Among the youngest Taiwanese, attitudes toward Taiwan's domestic issues are largely decoupled from feelings toward the mainland. Generational politics logic can help to explain why. Unlike earlier generations, the youngest Taiwanese did not grow up confused by the gap between government rhetoric and day-to-day reality. 'Republic of China' was (and is) still heard, of course, but much less frequently than in the past. Taiwan's junior high schools adopted the textbook *Renshi Taiwan* (*Get to Know Taiwan*) in 1997, displacing 'China' from the centre of school curricula and giving Taiwanese youth permission to focus on their homeland. This generation also grew up in a Taiwan that interacted continuously with a PRC that had come to define 'China' in the international community. It is hardly surprising that they think of 'China' as mainland China – the China on the other side of the Strait – and therefore of themselves as Taiwanese.

The fifth generation's attitudes toward independence, unification and partisanship reflect the influence of a DPP presidency. The proportion supporting unification is the lowest by far of any generation, and the percentage supporting independence is the highest. Unlike many older Taiwanese, who remember when pro-independence activism was a crime, 'Gen Fivers' do not hesitate to express an opinion on the issue. Still, their preference for independence does not reflect a desire to wholly reject the PRC, as Table 5.10 shows.

To sum up, separating out a fifth generation allows us to observe interesting and meaningful differences between those who came of age under President Lee Teng-Hui and those who came of age under Chen Shui-Bian. But as Table 5.12 summarizes, the youngest Taiwanese – like all generations except the second – are neither consistently green nor consistently blue. One example of the fifth

Table 5.12 Patterns of attitudes across major issues by generation

Generation	Self-identification	Independence/unification	Party	Cross-Strait economic ties	Cross-Strait military threat
First	Taiwanese	Neutral	KMT	Pessimistic	Optimistic
Second	Taiwanese	Independence	DPP	Pessimistic	Neutral
Third	Both	Neutral	KMT	Neutral	Neutral
Fourth	Both	Neutral	Neutral	Optimistic	Optimistic
Fifth	Taiwanese	Independence	DPP	Optimistic	Pessimistic

Source: TEDS 2012 (Self-ID, Independenc/Unification and Party) and 2008 (cross-Strait economic ties and military threat).

generation's approach to politics is the Sunflower movement that erupted into the headlines in spring 2014. The Sunflower activists who occupied Taiwan's legislative chamber for a month were not affiliated with any political party, nor did they take a position on the question of whether Taiwan should deepen its economic engagement with China. Instead, they advocated a more transparent and democratic decision-making process and called on leaders to protect the economic interests of Taiwan's middle class.

Conclusion

Generational politics is less a statistical phenomenon than a heuristic device for understanding differences in political behaviour across time. Thus my goal in this chapter is not to prove that modern Taiwan has four or five political generations, but to use Mannheim's theory to illuminate two mysteries in Taiwan politics. The first is the tendency of Taiwanese attitudes to seem inconsistent, even contradictory. What does it mean, for example, when the percentage of islanders claiming a strictly Taiwanese identity grows steadily while the percentage preferring independence remains flat? A generational approach allows us to see the relationship between these two preferences in new ways. The link between identity and independence may be strong for those who grew up convinced that the only way for Taiwan to become the subject of its own history was to reject the idea that Taiwan is part of China. It may not be strong for those whose life experiences teach them that Taiwan is already the subject of its own history, a history in which 'China' is part of 'Taiwan'.

The second mystery that a generational analysis can help to unravel concerns the origins of political preferences. About 85 per cent of Taiwanese *benshengren*, yet only a little over half call themselves 'Taiwanese' and fewer than 20 per cent support formal independence. Clearly, provincial origin alone does not explain Taiwan politics. But filtered through the specific experiences of particular Taiwanese – both *benshengren* and *waishengren* – unfolding over time, political preferences can be rendered coherent.

Taiwanese who came of age in authoritarian Taiwan were forced to choose between identifying with Taiwan or with China. 'Gen Fivers' have never been asked to make that choice. For them, identifying with Taiwanese is natural. But so too is engaging with China. For their second-generation grandparents, 'China' – the China within Taiwan even more than the China on the other side of the Strait – was a cauldron of confusion and regret, hope and humiliation, anger and fear. To the 'Gen Fivers', China is just a nearby country that offers both opportunities and risks, ones they are free to explore from the secure platform of Taiwan, their home.

Notes

1 The chapter uses data from both surveys because while the 2008 survey included questions about attitudes toward mainland China that are critically important to my analysis, the 2012 survey included a much larger number of fifth-generation respondents.

2 The Aboriginal community is comprised of more than a dozen linguistically and cultur-ally distinct groups, most of which enjoy state recognition.
3 For example, among the older respondents in the Taiwan's Election and Democrat-ization Study (TEDS) 2012 survey (those born between 1932 and 1953), 55 per cent of Hakka, 85 per cent of Minnan and 37 per cent of *waishengren* said that their spouses were from the same background as they were. Among younger respondents, those born between 1969 and 1981, the corresponding percentages were 23 per cent, 52 per cent and 9 per cent, suggesting a much higher incidence of intermarriage.
4 Panel studies provide the most persuasive evidence for political generations, because they allow researchers to compare the same individuals over time. They can determine which is predominant: attitudinal changes over the life cycle or persistent differences between age cohorts over time. We do not currently have data that would allow us to conduct such a study in Taiwan.
5 Percentage of each generation reporting zero visits to mainland China (excluding Hong Kong and Macao): first, 87 per cent; second, 72 per cent; third, 75 per cent; fourth, 78 per cent; fifth, 90 per cent (TEDS 2008).
6 The third generation came in second on this measure, with 14.5 per cent reporting three or more visits.
7 Tables 5.7, 5.8 and 5.9 use TEDS 2012 data in order to maximize the number of fifth-generation respondents. Tables 5.10 and 5.11 use TEDS 2008 survey, which has fewer fifth-generation respondents but included valuable questions that were not in the 2012 questionnaire.

References

Carpenter, Ted Galen (2006) *America's Coming War with China: A Collision Course over Taiwan*, New York: Palgrave Macmillan.

Chang, G. Andy, and Wang, T. Y. (2005) 'Taiwanese or Chinese? Independence or Unifi-cation? An Analysis of Generational Differences in Taiwan', *Journal of Asian and African Studies*, 40, 1/2: 29–49.

Chang, Yu-Shan (1991) 'Waisheng dierdai shengji yishi yanjiu' [Research on the Provin-cial Origin Consciousness of Second-generation Mainlanders], MA thesis, Taipei: National Chengchi University.

Chen, Wen-Chun (1998) 'Taiwan diqu xuesheng de zhengzhi wenhua: Zhong, daxuesh-eng de zhengzhi taidu yu Taiwan minzhuhua de qianjing' [Political Culture of Taiwan Students] *Guoli Zhongshan Daxue Shehui Kexue Jikan*, 1, 3: 23–60.

Chen, Yi-Yan (1996) 'Butong zuqun zhengzhi wenhua de shidai fenxi' [A Generational Analysis of Different Groups' Political Culture], *Zhengzhi Xuebao*, 27: 83–121.

Dalton, Russell J. (1987) 'Generational Change in Elite Political Beliefs: The Growth of Ideological Polarization', *Journal of Politics*, 49, 4: 976–997.

Election Study Centre of National Chengchi University (2014) 'Important Political Atti-tude Trend Distribution', available at www.esc.nccu.edu.tw/course/news.php?Sn=166# (accessed 21 July 2014).

He, Rongxing (2001) *Xueyun shidai* [The Student Movement Era], Taipei: Shibao Wenhua.

Hsieh, John Fuh-Sheng (2004) 'National Identity and Taiwan's Mainland Policy', *Journal of Contemporary China*, 13, 40: 479–490.

Jennings, M. Kent (2002) 'Generation Units and the Student Protest Movement in the United States: An Intra- and Intergenerational Analysis', *Political Psychology*, 23, 2: 303–324.

Jennings, M. Kent, and Stoker, Laura (2004) 'Social Trust and Civic Engagement Across Time and Generations', *Acta Politica*, 39: 342–379.

Johnson, Larry (2005) 'Independent-minded Youth Hold the Future of Taiwan in their Hands', *Seattle Post-Intelligencer*, 27 November.

Keng, Shu, and Lin, Emmy Ruihua (2013) 'Bidding for Taiwanese Hearts: Evaluating the Achievement of China's Economic Statecraft Against Taiwan', in Hu, Richard Weixing (ed.) *New Dynamics in Cross-Taiwan Straits Relations: How Far Can the Rapprochement Go?* London: Routledge.

Klintworth, Gary (2000) 'China and Taiwan – from Flashpoint to Redefining One China', Research Paper 15, Parliamentary Library, Parliament of Australia.

Kryshtanovskaya, Olga, and White, Stephen (2002) 'Generations and the Conversion of Power in Postcommunist Russia', *Perspectives on European Politics and Society*, 3, 2: 229–244.

Kuo, Cheng-Liang (1998) *Minjindang zhuanxing zhi tong* [The DPP's Painful Transition], Taipei: Tianhsia.

Leach, Michael (2003) ' 'Privileged Ties': Young People Debating Language, Heritage, and National Identity in East Timor', *Portuguese Studies Review*, 11, 1: 137–150.

Li, Shu-Liang (2014) 'Taiwan qingnian shidai xinxiang Zhongguo?' [What Does Taiwan's Young Generation Think of China?], *Shengjia*, 1 November, 76–80.

Lin, Chia-Lung (2004) 'The Political Formation of Taiwanese Nationalism', in Liew, Leong H., and Wang, Shaoguang (eds) *Nationalism, Democracy and National Integration in China*, London: Routledge, 122–144.

Lin, Eric (2004) 'Sketches of Dreams amid Generational Change', *Sinorama*, 29, 1: 13–15.

Liu, I-Chou (1993) 'Taiwan de zhengzhi shidai' [Taiwan's Political Generations], *Zhengzhi Xuebao*, 21: 99–120.

Liu, I-Chou (1994) 'Taiwan xuanmin zhengdang xingxiang de shidai chayi' [Generational Differences in Taiwan Voters' Party Images], *Xuanju yanjiu*, 5: 53–73.

Liu, I-Chou (1996) 'Generational Discrepancies in Public Attitude on Taiwan's Unification Issue', *Issues and Studies*, 32, 9: 103–121.

Mannheim, Karl (1952) 'The Problem of Generations', in Kecskemeti, Paul (ed.) *Essays on the Sociology of Knowledge*, London: Routledge and Kegan Paul, Ltd.

Rigger, Shelley (2006) *Taiwan's Rising Rationalism: Generations, Politics and 'Taiwanese Nationalism'*, Washington: East West Center.

Schubert, Gunter (2004) 'Taiwan's Political Parties and National Identity: The Rise of an Overarching Consensus', *Asian Survey*, 44, 4: 534–554.

Schuman, Howard, and Scott, Jacqueline (1989) 'Generations and Collective Memories', *American Sociological Review*, 54, 3: 359–381.

Sears, David O., and Valentino, Nicholas A. (1997) 'Politics Matters: Political Events as Catalysts for Preadult Socialization', *American Political Science Review*, 91, 1: 45–65.

Tessler, Mark, Konold, Carrie, and Reif, Megan (2004) 'Political Generations in Developing Countries: Evidence and Insights from Algeria', *Public Opinion Quarterly*, 68, 2: 184–216.

Tranter, Bruce, and Western, Mark (2003) 'Postmaterial Values and Age: The Case of Australia', *Australian Journal of Political Science*, 38, 2: 239–257.

Wu, Nai-Teh (1999) 'Jiating shehuihua he yishixingtai: Taiwan xuanmin zhengdang rentong de shidai chayi' [Family Socialization and Ideology: Generational Differences in Taiwan Voters' Party Identification], *Taiwan Shehui Yanjiu* [Taiwan Social Research], 3: 53–85.

6 Facing the dragon and riding the tiger

Assessing the mainland Taishang as an 'impact factor' in cross-Strait relations

Gunter Schubert

Cross-Strait relations have seen remarkable change over the last 20 years.[1] With the intensification of economic interaction between China and Taiwan and an increasing number of Taiwanese entrepreneurs (Taishang) investing in labour-intensive and, subsequently, high-tech industries, cross-Strait migration in both directions has risen steadily as well. Since the late 1980s, a growing number of Taiwanese citizens, among whom entrepreneurs and factory managers with their families are the most visible 'Taiwanese compatriots', have taken up permanent residence on the Chinese mainland. In the more recent past, many Taiwanese students and young professionals went to China in pursuit of careers that were no longer believed to be available in Taiwan. China's dynamic economy, with its lower production costs and a plethora of well-paid jobs situated in what is perceived to be an attractive business environment, will certainly attract the Taiwanese work force for years to come, irrespective of noticeable structural changes in the Chinese economy, which may eventually cancel out China's current comparative advantages.[2] This sub-official dynamic obviously spurs economic and social integration across the Taiwan Strait.

At the same time, the political climate across the Taiwan Strait has remained tense during most of the past two decades. Only since the return to power of the well-entrenched Nationalist Party (Kuomintang, KMT) in mid-2008, after eight years of rule by the Democratic Progressive Party (DPP) under the former political activist Chen Shui-Bian, have cross-Strait relations witnessed a turn towards a more constructive dialogue that has substantially deflated tensions across the Taiwan Strait. A number of new bilateral agreements led to, among other issues, the reinstallation of the 'three links' of direct trade, transport and communication, and culminated in the signing of an Economic Cooperation Framework Agreement (ECFA), a quasi-FTA, in late June 2010.[3] However, competing sovereignty claims and a still vital independence movement in Taiwan, as partly highlighted by the Sunflower student movement in early 2014,[4] combined with the uncompromising demands issued by the Chinese government for eventual 'unification', still impede 'full-scale' cross-Strait rapprochement. Taiwan and China thus maintain a paradoxical relationship of accelerating economic and social integration set against ongoing political separation.

Against this background, little is known to date about the ways in which Taiwanese business people with mainland investments (the Taishang) have affected (and continue to affect) *high-level politics* in China and Taiwan, or more specifically, cross-Strait policy-making.[5] Recent studies have argued that their political significance has been limited from the outset, although they played a role in maintaining a minimum of official contact across the Taiwan Strait when the DPP government was in power between 2000 and 2008 and Sino-Taiwanese relations froze down to their lowest point ever. In addition, they exerted a fairly substantial influence on Chinese local politics during the early years of Taishang migration to the mainland, when local governments were competing for Taishang capital to spur economic development in their jurisdictions. However, this influence has been eroding since the mid-2000s, when the Chinese economy started to thrive. Gradually, the Taishang have lost their privileged position and preferential treatment in terms of tax reduction, access to land and labour, and political connections. Moreover, when the KMT regained the presidency in 2008, an event that was immediately followed by cross-Strait dialogue and rapprochement, Taiwanese entrepreneurs with mainland investments were no longer needed as middlemen between Beijing and Taipei, and this further reduced their political significance (Lee 2012, 2014).

However, the question of the extent to which Taiwanese business people with investments and operations on the Chinese mainland have attempted to influence or, indeed, have been successful in influencing China policy-making in Taiwan proper has not yet been subjected to systematic study. The potential danger posed by the Taishang has long been debated in Taiwan, with particular regard to the powerful tycoons who enjoy close relationships with the Chinese government. This danger finds expression in the fear that they will help 'the enemy' to penetrate Taiwan's economy in order to force the Taiwanese people into political surrender and imposed unification, or that they will buy off Taiwan's policy-makers for the same purpose, since there is a long tradition of lawmakers at both national and local levels being financially supported by entrepreneurs – particularly by those who have extensive business investments in China and expect China-friendly policies to be pursued by their clients. However, these 'established truths' are supported by astonishingly little empirical evidence.

This chapter draws on qualitative interview data obtained from fieldwork that has been conducted since 2006 in mainland China and in Taiwan,[6] relevant secondary literature, and journal and newspaper articles to provide a more comprehensive picture of the scope and limits of Taishang political agency in Taiwan proper. The starting point is the role played by the Taishang as a voting bloc in important domestic elections and their relationships with Taiwan's political parties. The chapter then turns to the Taishang's 'organizational power' by looking at the activities of the mainland-based Taiwanese business associations (TBAs, *Taixiehui*) and at the major *domestic* business associations that have been established to protect and advance the Taishang's commercial interests on the Chinese mainland. Then follows a brief analysis of the Taishang's 'informal power' as it materializes via network-building among the political elite, and the grip of powerful tycoons on the Taiwanese media market. Finally, there is an assessment, albeit rather tentative, of the influence of the Taishang on the content of important recent cross-Strait agreements. The chapter concludes with a summary of the main findings, arguing that more research is essential to further our understanding of the impact of the Taishang on Taiwan.

The Taishang as a voting bloc in domestic elections

The Taishang's political influence is most often associated with their voting power in important elections in Taiwan. It is well known that the ruling Kuomintang party (KMT) goes to great lengths to mobilize the electoral support of the Taishang and to persuade them to vote accordingly, since it is generally believed that most Taiwanese business people side with the Nationalists and the KMT's 'pro-Chinese' policies. Following the same logic, the Chinese authorities 'encourage' the 'Taiwan compatriots' to go home to vote in legislative or presidential elections, convinced that, out of mere economic interests, they will vote for the KMT rather than for the pro-independence DPP. TBAs all over the mainland regularly collect donations from their members to support the KMT. They also negotiate for cheap air travel tickets, which are offered to the Taiwanese by Chinese airlines: a meaningful incentive to make the trip to Taiwan when an important election is due.[7] Hence there is a widely shared conviction in Taiwan that the TBAs are politically biased or that they respond opportunistically to Chinese demands to rally behind the 'pro-China' camp.[8]

There is no question that the Taishang vote can be decisive. In the 2000 presidential election, Chen Shui-Bian won by a relatively small margin of only 313,000 votes; four years later, he secured victory in a very close call with just 30,000 votes. The Taishang, allegedly amounting to some 250,000 to 300,000 votes when company staff and family members are included,[9] can thus make an important difference, especially when an election race is tight, as it was in the presidential ballot in 2004. It is, however, far from clear whether the mainland Taishang are actually willing or able to constitute a collective voter bloc pursuing group-specific interests, or whether they are only concerned to make individual political choices – which may or may not support the 'pan-blue' camp.

Getting to the crux of the mainland Taishang's political attitudes and voting behaviour is not easy (see Schubert 2010 and 2013). As my interviews suggest, there may have been considerable changes over time. In the Pearl River Delta in the 1990s, many of the Taishang maintained strong anti-KMT and anti-PRC positions and supported the DPP. In the run-up to the 1996 presidential election, large numbers of Taishang in Dongguan, Shenzhen and Guangzhou organized 'teams' to go back to Taiwan, and many of them voted against the pro-unification KMT candidates, Lin Yang-Kang and Hao Po-Tsun. This was the early generation of Taiwanese entrepreneurs who invested in the mainland, overwhelmingly natives of Taiwan and inclined towards independence. However, from the late 1990s onwards, a new wave of Taishang started to arrive in China. This young and well-educated group primarily invested in high-tech industries and tended to settle in the Shanghai-Kunshan metropolitan area rather than in the Dongguan-Shenzhen axis, with its myriads of labour-intensive factories and millions of Chinese migrant workers. The general mindset of these Taishang varied from that of their predecessors: they were more focused on economic opportunities in China, more cosmopolitan, and ideologically less influenced by Taiwan's historic struggle for democratization and quest for sovereignty. Many of them, and many of those belonging to the 'first generation' of mainland Taishang as well, had become alienated from the DPP government under Chen Shui-Bian, which they accused of endangering the Taishang's mainland business operations, denying their contributions to the revitalization of the Taiwanese economy, and unfairly discrediting their loyalty to Taiwan.[10] Consequently, many of the Taishang became more supportive of the KMT's pro-integration stance over the years and welcomed the proactive China policy approach of the new government under Ma Ying-Jeou that was elected in 2008.

According to the information that was obtained during my interviews, it is reasonable to assume that some 25 to 35 per cent of the mainland Taishang constituency voted for the DPP in the 2004 and 2008 presidential elections, whereas 65 to 75 per cent supported the KMT. This conforms to the general estimates published in the Taiwanese media and produced by Taiwan scholars over the years (see Schubert and Keng 2012), and such estimates are held to have been valid for the 2012 presidential election as well.[11] However, it is difficult to establish how many of the Taishang actually voted in the end and much bespeaks the fact that the impact of the Taishang vote has actually been quite limited in past elections.[12] As a matter of fact, it is quite difficult today to mobilize Taiwanese business people to donate money and to make the trip back to Taiwan to vote in elections. Many of them are disillusioned and detached from Taiwan's domestic party politics and their never-ending ideological in-fighting. Although they generally consider the KMT's China policy approach to be much more helpful with regard to the protection of their entrepreneurial interests on the mainland, they believe that, first and foremost, they have to rely on themselves and their networks with local cadres and governments to survive economically. Those who are not personally involved in the work of a local TBA, in particular, find it hard to believe that Taiwan's government can do much for them or that elections back home are of any significance in this respect. Although they welcome bilateral trade and investment agreements as necessary means to promote their mainland businesses and identify them as overarching interests, the Taishang mindset has remained surprisingly parochial and self-centred over the years. Most of the Taishang think that taking collective action to defend or advocate common interests within their constituency is futile, simply a waste of time and money.

There are several reasons for this pessimistic outlook. To begin with, many of the Taishang are reluctant to declare allegiance to a political camp. Although voting is secret, they are concerned about showing that they are articulate in political matters because this could lead to their being identified with a party and this, in turn, could result in negative repercussions for their reputations at home and for their companies back in China, in the form of either bad press coverage in the DPP-leaning media in Taiwan or, even worse, 'technical' problems caused by the Chinese authorities as a result of openly demonstrated sympathy for the 'green camp'.[13] Consequently, not a few Taiwanese business people attempt to stay out of politics from the start and prefer to abstain from participating in any elections whatsoever. Added to this is the fact that many of the Taishang have undergone a gradual shift in their identities over the years that they have spent living and working on the Chinese mainland. Those who have stayed long enough and even plan to retire in China tend to become less preoccupied with Taiwan in the course of time and claim that Taiwan politics do not matter to them very much anymore. In fact, identity change and a mainland-centred outlook on their economic interests seem to be the main reasons for the indifference found among broad segments of the Taishang community as far as Taiwan's politics are concerned.

This sounds counterintuitive from a Taiwan-based perspective, according to which the Taishang are considered to be not only a critical voter constituency but also a powerful political broker. Although the latter assumption holds particularly true for a number of powerful tycoons and cannot be dismissed by the simple fact that the Taiwanese economy depends strongly on the business community (see below), it is equally true that the overall majority of mainland Taishang do not conceive of themselves as politically influential and do not act as if they are. To speak of politically active Taishang is to speak of a very small group of people indeed.

Assessing Taishang organizational power

Generally speaking, there are two avenues which Taiwanese entrepreneurs can take in organizational terms: first, via Taiwanese business associations in China, as far as they stretch across the Taiwan Strait to engage in political lobbying on the island; and second, via domestic business associations, most of the members of which have extensive mainland businesses.

Taiwanese business associations on the mainland

At the end of 2014 there were 138 TBAs operating all over China, loosely coordinated by the national-level Association of Taiwan Investment Enterprises on the Mainland (ATIEM, *Quanguo taiwan tongbao touzi qiye lianyihui*) located in Beijing.[14] As has been noted by a number of Taiwan scholars (Lin 2004; Keng and Lin 2007; Lin and Keng 2012; Lee 2013), local TBAs operate as service and information platforms for their members rather than as interest groups with a meaningful policy input. They negotiate with local governments to resolve problems of Taishang companies related to, for instance, access to scarce land, tax and fee reduction, labour conflicts, local infrastructure, government subsidies, etc. They also assume the function of transmission belts to provide information on government policies and to ensure good relations between the Taiwanese community and local authorities. Whereas the national-level ATIEM, for its part, at least attempts to bring the Taishang perspective into the national policy process, the activities of the local TBAs are strictly local.

However, they also report back to Taiwan's government on the overall situation of the mainland Taishang and on more specific policy problems that need to be addressed in cross-Strait negotiations. For that matter, the TBAs communicate regularly and closely with the Straits Exchange Foundation (*Haixia jiaoliu jijinhui*), a semi-official organization under the supervision of Taiwan's government-level Mainland Affairs Council that is responsible for managing all the practical issues concerning cross-Strait relations.[15] Moreover, the leaders of the most significant TBAs in economic terms, from Dongguan, Kunshan and Shanghai, and the leading officials of the ATIEM enjoy immediate access to the Mainland Affairs Council and other government ministries. These channels are obviously used to make the Taishang voice heard when the Taiwanese government is involved in negotiating important trade agreements with its mainland counterpart, and it is here, therefore, where the policy impact should be most effective (see below). The TBAs are also important for establishing communication links with Chinese local cadres and Taiwan's national and local authorities. For instance, if a local Chinese government intends to send a delegation of high-ranking cadres to Taiwan, it usually goes through the nearest TBA for help in approaching government ministries or local administrations, the Straits Exchange Foundation, party officials, business associations or individual enterprises, depending on their agenda for such talks. Visits by Chinese cadres to Taiwan are frequent, since almost each and every local government, at provincial, municipal and county levels, is interested in promoting economic development by attracting Taiwanese investment, learning from Taiwan's government system and sector-specific policies or, not to be underestimated, just having a good time in a different place. TBAs also organize trips to China for local governments from Taiwan, mostly delegations of county governments and assemblies. Finally, as has been explained above, TBAs are critical for mobilizing Taishang financial support for candidates in the run-up to important elections in Taiwan, and they negotiate with the local Taiwan Affairs Offices and Chinese airlines for cheap plane fares for Taiwanese citizens who are resident in China to return home and cast their ballots.

The TBAs therefore provide a great deal of help and assistance for the mainland Taishang, primarily in practical matters. However, they exert their political influence, in both China and Taiwan, mainly by making use of informal communication channels to government authorities. They usually maintain a low public profile. This is entirely comprehensible given the political environment on the Chinese mainland where organizational autonomy is highly sensitive, but it is less plausible in Taiwan, where the TBAs could pursue a strategy of formal political lobbying by establishing a separate Taiwan-based interest group structure. However, all my respondents, whether they had been active TBA officials or not, rejected any such an idea. They argued that Taiwan does not suffer from too little but too much interest representation by business associations of all kinds, and that public lobbying would only expose the Taishang to the futile quarrelling that goes on in Taiwan's domestic politics without any positive effects for their mainland-based businesses. They also reacted sceptically to my suggestion that the Taishang could stand for political office themselves, as party politicians or parliamentarians. The standard reply to this idea was that the Taishang lack the necessary group coherence and collective outlook to be able to rally behind candidates representing their constituency. The Taishang, as many of my respondents claimed, are individuals who 'bowl alone' and mainly rely on their own networks to get ahead. Only if this failed would they contact a TBA, and even then, only for the sake of their own enterprise and not to safeguard any collective interests.[16]

Domestic business associations

Taiwan certainly does not suffer from a lack of interest organizations to serve business people; there is a myriad of business associations covering the entire range of industry and trade that Taiwanese enterprises are involved in, with a number of well-known national organizations as well. Most of their members have commercial stakes in China, a fact that makes Taiwan's business associations a natural channel for approaching the government to give feedback on the situation of Taiwanese enterprises in China and to propose trade policies and advice on the content of cross-Strait economic agreements. Most important in this respect are the three national-level associations which represent different sectors of the Taiwanese economy, including its mainland 'offspring': the Chinese National Federation of Industries (*Zhonghua minguo quanguo gongye zonghui*, CNFI), the General Chamber of Commerce of the Republic of China (*Zhonghua minguo quanguo shangye zonghui*, ROCCOC) and the Chinese National Association of Industry and Commerce *Zhonghua minguo gongshang xiejinhui*, CNAIC).[17] As a result of their corporatist past, they all maintain cooperative relations with the government.[18] However, the same cooperative approach is employed by the sector-specific associations as well, most of which were established during the democratic era.

Judging by their websites and official publications and by my interviews with the leading personnel of all three organizations, it seems that working and lobbying on behalf of the Taishang constitute the major part of their activities today.[19] They carry out regular survey work on Taiwanese enterprises operating on the mainland and publish reports on their economic performance, their problems and their market challenges. They sponsor workshops and special lectures that provide information on trade policies which have been finalized in China and Taiwan. They host meetings with government officials for the specific purpose of addressing Taishang concerns, and they regularly invite Taiwanese entrepreneurs to give feedback on specific policy measures or to express their opinions on policies that are in the making. Finally, they invite official delegations from China to visit Taiwan or organize delegations of Taiwanese entrepreneurs and association officials to visit the mainland, for instance to take part in cross-Strait conference events.[20] In this sense, CNFI, ROCCOC and CNAIC have to be considered important transmission belts connecting the Taiwan government and the Taishang. Overall, they seem to be more policy-oriented than the TBAs, whose main objective is to serve individual enterprises and to solve practical problems in their respective localities. However, it is difficult to assess or measure precisely how effective the policy input of the domestic business associations actually is in Taiwan (see below). As in the case of the TBAs, much government-business communication is informal and mainly shaped by influential entrepreneurs or tycoons who often serve as leading officials in their business associations. And as much as the TBAs maintain a low profile vis-à-vis both the Chinese and the Taiwanese authorities, Taiwan's domestic business associations usually abstain from public lobbying or arguing with the government, and tend to support the latter's general policies.

Assessing the informal power of the Taishang

'Feeding' lawmakers

It is widely known in Taiwan that domestic politics are fuelled by money. Whenever possible, Party candidates standing for election at national and local levels cultivate close relations with wealthy entrepreneurs in order to gain their help as sponsors for their campaigns. The informal nexus between mainland Taishang interests and domestic politics can therefore safely be taken for granted and, in fact, forms part of an ongoing and controversial debate in Taiwan. Although there are laws and regulations that restrict donations to political parties and individuals, these are difficult to enforce.[21] Informal political lobbying beyond the business associations mentioned above is ubiquitous and is most noticeably undertaken by large-scale entrepreneurs who, unlike the owners of small and medium-sized businesses, can influence Taiwanese politics by several means, most notably substantial party and candidate sponsoring, direct access to leading government and party elites on both sides of the Taiwan Strait, and the power to make specific investment decisions which directly affect Taiwan's economy.[22] Although reports on political donations made by business people are legendary in Taiwan and few candidates standing for public office can afford to do without these donations, reliable information on the systematic sponsoring of political contenders by the mainland Taishang – as well as by Taiwan's business world in general – is hard to come by.[23] My interview data, however, proved to be quite revealing in terms of the Taishang's political agency in general: when entrepreneurs or enterprises decide to support a candidate or a party, they each pursue their own strategy, and there is no collective effort to lobby Taiwan's political elites by coordinating campaign support. This accords with the above-mentioned observation that Taiwanese business people keep away from the political institutions and proactive lobbying of business associations, and generally maintain a low political profile on both sides of the Taiwan Strait.[24] At the same time, political parties shy away from giving Taishang access to their party apparatus: among the reasons for this is the fear of being accused of corruption, which is a

powerful election issue notwithstanding the vote-buying and political favourit-
ism in Taiwan's politics.

Media influence

One important topic related to the informal power of the Taishang is their
alleged attempt to influence, if not to steer, domestic public opinion by acquiring
substantial financial stakes in Taiwan's print and electronic media. There have
been numerous rumours over the years (and there is also some evidence) that
business magnates or large companies with substantial commercial stakes in
China control, or at least attempt to control, Taiwan's media market. The most
notable case, and one that also attracted much public attention, was the purchase
in November 2008 of the China Times Group by the Want Want Group (*Wang
Wang jituan*), a Taiwanese food manufacturing company listed in Hong Kong
with some 100 manufacturing plants in China. With this move, the Want Want
Group gained control of the *China Times* (*Zhongguo Shibao*), one of Taiwan's
four major newspapers, and two TV channels: China Television/CTV (*Zhongguo dianshi gonsi*) and CTi Television (*Zhongtian dianshi*), among other acqui-
sitions. It was then renamed the Want Want China Times Group. The group's
chairman, Tsai Eng-Meng, an influential entrepreneur with good political connections in both China and Taiwan, was soon heavily criticized by the DPP-
leaning media for having enforced a new editorial policy within the *China Times*
to soften criticism of the KMT-led government, support closer cross-Strait ties
and intensify pro-China advertising. In 2011, the Want Want Group then
acquired China Network Systems, Taiwan's second-largest cable TV provider.
This was followed in 2012 by an attempt to purchase the Next Media Group,
which included the widely-read *Apple Daily*, in a joint bid with two other investors. This deal eventually failed, but due to the obvious link between Tsai's
'mainland connections' and media concentration in Taiwan, Taiwan's press
freedom became an issue of national and international debate.[25] At roughly the
same time, in 2012, an Anti-Media Monopoly Movement (*Fan meiti longduan
yundong*) was launched by various social groups, supported by many intellectuals from prestigious scholarly institutions such as Academia Sinica (Rawnsley
and Feng 2014; Hsu 2014).[26] This has increased public awareness of the link
between the financial power of the Taishang and commercial interests in China
on the one hand, and media concentration in Taiwan on the other.

The Want Want China Times Group's largest share of profits, by far, stems
from its business operations in China; the case has therefore become the most
prominent example for critical observers of the way in which 'big business'
attempts to manipulate public opinion in Taiwan, allegedly encouraged and
backed up with money from China.[27] The Taiwanese media, for instance,
reported that Tsai Eng-Men interfered with the *China Times*' editing process to
influence news coverage of China, exerted pressure on journalists and used his
media outlets to promote the KMT's China policies.[28] As a matter of fact, during
the last decade business magnates have repeatedly and publicly demanded that

the Taiwan government lift its restrictions on cross-Strait trade and promote more economic interaction. This echoes the viewpoints of all the Taishang with whom I have spoken, no matter what kind of industry they are involved in or how big their operations on the mainland are. The assumption that this increasingly translates into substantial media influence cannot be easily dismissed in Taiwan in the light of the Want Want China Times Group case and the apparent 'taming' – or self-censorship – of a number of television channels during recent years with respect to their critical reporting on China (Hsu 2014: 524–530).

This topic certainly merits more systematic research, particularly in the context of the accelerating opening up of Taiwan for Chinese investment, but also because of the mounting pressure on Taiwanese mainland businesses due to structural changes in the Chinese economy. Privileged and protected access to China accompanied by Chinese 'monetary assistance' to spur the commercialization and concentration of the Taiwanese media market to ensure positive reporting on China – or to sideline critical voices – may act as powerful incentives for many of the Taishang to follow Tsai Eng-Meng's line. For the time being, however, the Taishang are not making any large-scale or coordinated attempt to shape public opinion in favour of a 'pro-China outlook' by 'conquering' the media in Taiwan. Moreover, the chances of success for any such strategy is rather doubtful, since the reputation of the China Times Group's media outlets has been seriously damaged by Tsai's actions. Also, there is still a lively media market that allows for alternative and critical reporting on Taiwan, and the Anti-Media Monopoly has been quite successful in forcing regulators in Taiwan into having a closer look at media concentration.[29] But since cross-Strait relations are a moving target, increasing influence and control over the Taiwanese media will remain an attractive avenue for Taishang informal power to make itself felt in domestic politics over time and will have to be closely observed in the future.

Assessing impact on policy-making

It is always difficult to measure the extent by which a specific social constituency or interest group has shaped policy outcomes, even more so in the sensitive area of China policy-making in present-day Taiwan. Obviously, there is a small group of Taishang, mostly well-connected tycoons and successful business leaders, who advise the government on a more or less regular basis.[30] These 'frontrunners' are also the driving force of the TBAs and domestic business associations who lobby the government to ensure some degree of policy impact. At the same time, however, I have been told by many Taishang, including those with regular access to government officials, that business people usually do not play much of a role in determining the content of important cross-Strait accords, such as the Cross-Strait Economic Cooperation Agreement (*Liang'an jingji hezuo jiagou xieyi*) signed on 29 June 2010; the Cross-Strait Bilateral Investment Protection and Promotion Agreement (*Haixia liang'an touzi baozhang he cujin xieyi*) signed on 16 August 2012; the Cross-Strait Trade in Services Agreement (*Liang'an fuyu maoyi xieyi*) signed on 6 June 2013; and the Cross-Strait Trade in

Goods Agreement (*Liang'an huowu maoyi xieyi*), which is still under negotiation at the time of writing.[31] Many of my respondents complained that the Taishang are sidelined by the government when it comes to important policy formulation and negotiations, and even when the government asks for feedback on certain policy proposals by inviting influential entrepreneurs to meetings of experts or by working through the SEF, TBAs and domestic business associations, the Taishang often feel that their viewpoints and advice are not taken sufficiently into account.

This may be a strategic understatement, since there is certainly a fair amount of government–business dialogue on cross-Strait policies as indicated above, even if much of it seems to remain informal or is limited to a number of gatherings that are usually initiated by the government. However, the consistency of my respondents' comments on this issue over time still suggests that the Taishang have only a limited policy impact. There is a general rationale in Taiwan's politics that can help to explain this: while entrepreneurs with businesses in China certainly welcome policies that protect their mainland investments and urge the government to push ahead with cross-Strait liberalization and increasing integration, even a so-called 'pro-China' government has to exercise caution when following this course. In addition to considerations of national security in their own right, the threat of the next election forces any ruling party in Taiwan to constantly calibrate its China policy approach to respond to public sentiments and opposition tactics. As the Sunflower movement in early 2014 has shown, there is widespread opposition to the way in which cross-Strait policies have been designed, introduced to the public and implemented by the Ma administration, and there has been outright rejection of further liberalization and integration across the Taiwan Strait by at least a part of the populace. In such a situation, the government may not be able to respond fully to demands linked with 'capitalist interests' for further cross-Strait liberalization. At the very least, the government has to proceed carefully in order not to evoke the image of an elitist clique selling out Taiwan to 'big business' under the guidance of the Chinese government. Consequently, there is much tension between the Taiwanese government and the business community with its mainland operations. The latter is overwhelmingly disappointed with the Ma administration's recent hesitant and defensive stance on cross-Strait economic relations. Many Taishang complain bitterly that Taiwan's tragedy is a foolhardy blend of politics and economics, to the detriment of the island's long-term prosperity.[32]

The 2012 *CNFI White Book* (CNFI 2012) provides a good overview of the Taishang policy demands directed at the Taiwan government which widely correspond to the mindset of my respondents. Since 2008, the CNFI has conducted an annual survey among its members to identify the most pressing issues to be raised with the Taiwan government. In the 2012 survey, the following issues were the most prominent:

- authorising non-government organizations (for example, the CNFI) to sign trade agreements with their non-official mainland Chinese counterparts;

- officially acknowledging the Taishang as members of local Chinese Political Consultative Conferences, which are official advisory bodies to local governments;
- expanding the liberalization of market access in Taiwan for Chinese investments including those sectors currently considered 'sensitive', although this process should be properly supervised;
- liberalizing Chinese advertising in Taiwan as a complementary measure to the attraction of investment from the mainland;
- liberalizing the conditions for mainlanders entering Taiwan to explore business opportunities;
- liberalizing Renminbi transactions and clearing in Taiwan;
- signing an agreement to allow for the mutual exemption of social insurance contributions (particularly for pension and unemployment insurance).[33]

All these issues are indeed on the agenda of the Taiwanese government, and the high degree of congruence between the cross-Strait negotiation content and Taishang demands suggests a significant policy impact on the part of business. However, as has been indicated above, this impact is limited by Taiwan's domestic politics and, as has been pointed out by most of my respondents who expressed an opinion on the issue, by a Taiwan government that prefers to leave negotiations to professional bureaucrats and to collect feedback only for policy decisions that have already been taken – instead of asking for Taishang input before and during negotiations. This results, it seems, in much frustration on the part of many Taiwanese entrepreneurs who often express deep pessimism about Taiwan's economic future and who lament their lack of power and influence to change it for the better.

Conclusion

The analysis of the Taishang who have investments in mainland China and the extent to which they are able to influence Taiwan's domestic politics and governmental policy-making paints a mixed picture. To begin with, these entrepreneurs are critical for the vitality of Taiwan's export economy. They operate through a solid structure of business associations in both China and Taiwan, which suggests that there is considerable policy impact. They also enjoy a considerable degree of informal power: first, because their networks and social capital give them access to government bureaucrats and decision-makers; second, because they have the financial means to support politicians campaigning for office; and third, at least in the case of affluent tycoons, because they have the capacity to penetrate Taiwan's media market. They therefore form a mighty constituency that no political party can afford to ignore. At the same time, the Taishang usually maintain a low political profile. In Taiwan, with the exception of tycoons such as Kuo Tai-Ming, the president of the Hon Hai Precision (Foxconn) Group, and Tsai Eng-Meng, they usually abstain from openly lobbying the government and from adopting a public stance on cross-Strait policies. The ability of Taiwanese entrepreneurs to shape politics and policies in Taiwan may therefore be quite limited. Although many of the Taishang effectively engage in informal lobbying and 'money politics' on a large scale, they do so as individuals – and mainly out of purely personal motives. Hence, the Taishang's informal power is primarily used to realize parochial rather than overarching interests. To put it differently: although Taiwan's prominent capitalists are certainly influential in Taiwan politics, the Taishang as a collective actor, i.e. as a visible and coherently acting interest group, are not. As my respondents stated almost unanimously, they do not feel, as entrepreneurs, any sense of belonging to a social constituency that is capable of coordinated action and pushing through a policy agenda.

This astounding observation may be partly explained by the diverse social backgrounds and economic interests of Taiwanese business people in general: they belong to different generations, have been to China at different times, and differ in educational levels, professional experience and political affiliation. In addition, they face different market challenges depending on the scale of their businesses and the industrial sector in which they are working. The Taishang on the Chinese mainland are used to 'bowling alone' and do not (yet) believe in the value of autonomous political agency in Taiwan – a fact that is related, at least to some extent, to their precarious political exposure to Taiwan's domestic politics, where a good proportion of the Taiwanese populace quickly and willingly buys the argument that the Taishang with investments in mainland China are traitors to Taiwan.[34]

Although it is difficult to shed light on the business–political complex, future research concerned with the impact of China on Taiwan should continue to investigate the strategies employed by the Taishang, who are mainland-based or invest in the mainland, to shape political discourse and policy-making in Taiwan. We need more knowledge on how the mainland TBAs operate in Taiwan proper; on the extent to which domestic business organizations have become engaged in political lobbying on behalf of mainland-oriented economic interests; on how strongly and to what effect the Taishang have penetrated the Taiwanese media market; and on the kinds of strategic alliances that have formed between, on the one hand, big business and the domestic political elite, and on the other, the Taishang and the mainland capitalists who are coming to Taiwan and investing there in ever increasing numbers. Further research is also required on the political mindset of Taiwanese business people in order to gain an understanding of their outlook on cross-Strait relations and on the role that they wish to play in this respect. Only then will it be possible to determine the scope and limits of Taishang political agency and the long-term consequences for Taiwan's struggle for sovereignty, democracy and prosperity 'in the shadow of China'.

My research has revealed a picture of the Taishang with investments on the mainland as a cautious species that supports continuous cross-Strait liberalization and integration but not necessarily political integration or even unification. Their earlier significance as a cross-Strait 'linkage group' (Keng 2011) bringing vital capital and expertise to China and mediating in cross-Strait dialogue has declined considerably since the late 2000s, due to the changing Chinese economy and the political rapprochement between Taipei and Beijing since 2008. However, they will remain an important factor in shaping the future of cross-Strait relations, since the dynamics of these relations will be driven by economic concerns for years to come. The Taishang face the Chinese dragon by riding the Taiwanese tiger – a fate which, no question, they share with each and every Taiwanese citizen.

Notes

1 Cross-Strait bilateral trade stood at US$125 billion at the end of 2013, according to official Taiwanese figures (mainland customs statistics reported US$197 billion), amounting to 21.6 per cent of Taiwan's total foreign trade. Between 1991 and mid-2014, Taiwanese entrepreneurs invested some US$140 billion in the mainland, although this official figure certainly does not match the reality: much Taiwanese capital has entered China illegally or has been hidden by complex sending routes. See *Cross-Straits Economics Statistics Monthly* (n.d.). To date, some 90,000 Taiwan companies are operating in China and more than one million Taiwanese live there permanently. See www.stormmediagroup.com/opencms/news/detail/62b90b1a-3574–11e4–87d0-ef2804cba5a1/?uuid=62b90b1a-3574–11e4–87d0-ef2804cba5a1 (accessed 7 October 2014).

2 China's economy has been undergoing a process of structural change, supported by national and local governments, with rising labour and capital costs, a dramatic shortage of land and increasing anti-pollution requirements for some years now. This has placed many labour-intensive enterprises under great pressure to upgrade their product lines, shift their production facilities further inland or move to other countries altogether, most notably in Southeast Asia, to make a reasonable profit. For a systematic overview of the recent challenges faced by the Taishang, see Tung and Cao (2014).

3 All 20 bilateral agreements (October 2014) signed up to now – although they have not been ratified in all cases by Taiwan's legislature – by the representatives of the two semi-official organizations responsible for cross-Strait negotiations, Taiwan's 'Straits Exchange Foundation' (SEF) and China's 'Association for Relations Across the Taiwan Strait' (ARATS), are listed on the official website of the ROC Mainland Affairs Council; see www.mac.gov.tw/ct.asp?xItem=67145&CtNode=5710&mp=1 (accessed 7 October 2014).

4 The Sunflower student movement (*Taiyang hua xuesheng yundong*), which occupied the Legislative Yuan and its surrounding streets for three weeks between 18 March and 10 April 2014, targeted a controversial Trade in Services Agreement (*fumao xieyi*) pushed through the legislative process by the ruling KMT for a final vote on 17 March – which, in the end, did not materialize. On the surface, the students were objecting to a technical issue related to a policy measure which was considered to lack public support and democratic legitimacy. At the core of the movement, however, was much more general opposition to the government's 'pro-China' policies and a commitment to Taiwanese nationalism.

5 Leng Tse-Kang has been one of the few who have dealt with the policy impact of big business in Taiwan in the early period of Taishang mainland investment, assigning them 'some bargaining power with both sides of the Taiwan Strait' (1998: 509). See also Leng 1995 for a more descriptive approach to business strategies to influence policy-making in Taiwan.

6 I conducted interviews with some 100 entrepreneurs and factory managers in China's Pearl River and Changjiang River Deltas in 2007, 2008, 2009 and 2014,

complemented by fieldwork of several weeks during each stay in Taiwan in 2012, 2013 and 2014. The sample contains a wide array of labour-intensive and high-tech industries of varying sizes, from small and medium to large and multinational. I mainly spoke either to the company head (as individual owner, major shareholder or president of the board of directors) or the CEO, although this was not always possible and sometimes I was only able to talk to an individual at the lower management level. In total, the sample is quite representative of Taiwanese businesses operating on the Chinese mainland. The chapter summarizes the preliminary findings of an ongoing research project on Taishang political agency jointly conducted with Professor Wang Jenn-Hwan of National Chengchi University, Taipei, and sponsored by the German Research Foundation (DFG) and Taiwan's National Science Council.

7 Most often, the TBAs receive assistance from local Taiwan Affairs Office branches in negotiating cheaper two-way tickets with Chinese airlines for return flights to Taiwan. However, this practice is not officially acknowledged.

8 TBA-initiated campaign rallies and 'donor conventions' garner a good deal of attention from both the Chinese and Taiwanese media. Quite obviously, most of these events support KMT or 'pan-blue' candidates.

9 Figures according to estimates by TBA officials in Dongguan and Shanghai, given to the author on various occasions.

10 During the DPP's rule (2000–2008), party politicians and the DPP-leaning media often claimed more or less explicitly that the Taishang were being manipulated by China to exert pressure on the Taiwanese government (*yishang bizheng*), that they were responsible for hollowing out Taiwan's economy by diverting most of their investments to mainland China and, consequently, that they were working against Taiwan's national interests.

11 It has been estimated that some 200,000 Taiwanese citizens returned to Taiwan to cast their ballots in the 2012 national elections. See *New York Times* (2012). The numbers of the Taiwanese returning to vote can be roughly calculated from the number of air tickets sold by Chinese and Taiwanese airlines and the increase in entries to Taiwan registered by the Taiwanese immigration authorities in the days and weeks before important elections.

12 According to sources in the local TBAs of Dongguan and Shanghai, it was estimated that in the highly contested 2004 presidential election, the total number of Taiwanese returning home to cast their ballots did not exceed 30,000 to 40,000. The *China Times* predicted, in early March 2008, that no more than some 70,000 mainland Taishang would vote in the 2008 presidential election – far fewer than the 250,000 votes that the Mainland Association of Taiwan Investment Enterprises and its subordinate TBAs had aimed to mobilize in that year. See 'Buru zhengzhi renwu guji gao' (n.d.).

13 One example of these 'technical problems' that was often cited by my respondents was the sudden appearance of local tax officials at the company's gates, armed with the intention of checking the books. And, as is common knowledge all over China, no tax declaration is good enough to escape serious punishment by local governments once such an investigation has been launched.

14 The ATIEM maintains a website with information on its activities and links to all regional TBAs (www.qgtql.com).

15 SEF officials are quick to point out that their relations with the TBAs are very close (*hen miqie*) and that both sides do everything possible to support the mainland Taishang, by helping them to solve problems on the ground, informing the Taishang about new Chinese policies and organizing meetings in China and Taiwan to gather first-hand information from the Taishang to be funnelled into the cross-Strait policy process. Moreover, there are three big banquets each year – around Chinese New Year, the Dragon Boat Festival and the Mid-Autumn festival – organized by the SEF on behalf of the Taiwan government, when all TBA heads are invited to gather in Taipei and meet government and KMT leaders.

16 To date, the Legislative Yuan has only seen one parliamentarian specifically representing the mainland Taishang: Huang Liang-Hua, who took the seat of a KMT supplementary member in November 2007. See *Xinxinwen* [The Journalist] (2007).

17 The CNFI is a non-profit organization representing 155 member associations and
some 100,000 registered companies in the manufacturing industry. It was founded in
1947 in Nanjing. The ROCCOC was originally established in 1946 in Nanjing and,
like the CNFI, reinvigorated in the early 1950s after the Nationalist government had
been firmly installed in Taiwan. Today, it represents 2,400 member associations with
some 1.5 million registered companies from services and trade. The CNAIC was
founded in Taiwan in 1952 and extends across the industrial and commercial sectors.
It has some 1,400 members, comprising big business conglomerates and large companies as well as small and medium-sized enterprises.

18 The Taiwanese government no longer directly sponsors these national-level organizations. However, all organizations can apply for government projects. This money
seems less important in the case of the CNFI (some 7 per cent of the total annual
budget), but more so in the case of the CNAIC (between 20 per cent and 50 per cent)
according to my sources. In any case, membership fees constitute the backbone of
each association's finance.

19 It is worth noting that many leading TBA officials simultaneously hold positions in
the steering bodies of Taiwan's sector-specific and national business associations.
According to information from the CNFI, some 70 per cent of the companies represented by CNFI associations have business in mainland China.

20 As I was told, 'delegation traffic' has become so intensive that the headquarters of
Taiwan's national business associations are now almost paralyzed. In many cases,
mainland delegations 'drop by' only to prove that they have attended an official
meeting, this being necessary to legitimize their travel expenses claims back home.
These delegations are not specifically issued with invitations, but 'invite themselves'.

21 Donations are subject to a number of legal restrictions, most notably the Political
Donations Law, promulgated in 2004 and amended in 2010, which caps annual donations to the same political party or political association by individuals (NT$300,000),
a profit-seeking business (NT$3,000,000) or a civil association (NT$2,000,000) (Art.
17). For a single candidate, donations are limited to NT$100,000, NT$1,000,000 and
NT$500,000, respectively (Art. 18).

22 Capital can be sent to the Chinese mainland instead of being invested in Taiwan and
thus figures as a major bargaining chip for negotiating special privileges granted by
the Taiwan government. Although these negotiations are limited to backstage manoeuvring and seldom, if ever, become public knowledge, there is no doubt that they
happen all the time.

23 However, Taiwan's government watchdog, the Control Yuan, regularly publishes lists
of officeholders and companies that have come under scrutiny for suspected violations
of the Political Donations Act. These lists provide a good picture, not only of the
scope of private donations exceeding the legally accepted level, but also of the
number of private enterprises with China-related business involved in these cases. See
Control Yuan Bulletin (*Jianchayuan gongbao*), (n.d.).

24 Some of my respondents made the point that they would rather support several candidates than only one; they always ensure that they have candidates from both the
'blue' and the 'green' camps on their 'payroll'. For them, this is a strategy for 'risk
diversification' or 'investment optimization' in times of quickly changing political
tides. In any case, campaign support by the Taishang is much more dependent on personal relationships with individual politicians than on ideological inclinations towards
a particular party.

25 Freedom House confirmed that Taiwan's drop in ranking for freedom of the press, to
forty-eighth in 2011, was directly linked to the Want Want Group's apparent suppression of KMT-critical reporting. See *Taipei Times* (2011).

26　See *Taipei Times* (2013). See also Want Want Group (n.d.) for a response of the Want Want Group to its critics.

27　For instance, Want Want China received US$47 million in subsidies from the Chinese government in 2011, amounting to 11.3 per cent of its annual profit in that year: *The Economist* (2013).

28　In November 2008, some weeks after he had finalized the China Times Group deal, Tsai was said to have given three orders to the group's leading managers: support strongly the Ma administration; improve cross-Strait relations; do not discuss unification or independence in the group's media (Hsu 2014: 520–21).

29　Taiwan's main regulatory bodies for the media sector are the National Communications Commission (NCC) and the Fair Trade Commission, although the latter is responsible for monopoly control in all economic sectors.

30　I have had discussions, on many occasions, with one Taishang individual who has acted as a presidential advisor to the Ma administration.

31　For the full texts of the first three agreements, see www.ecfa.org.tw (accessed 21 October 2014). Note that the Investment Protection and Promotion Agreement and the Trade in Services Agreement have not yet been ratified by Taiwan's legislature.

32　This criticism is shared by many of the 'green' Taishang with whom I have spoken over the years. They are in an awkward position, which further reinforces their preference for remaining politically low-key: 'green' Taishang reject the KMT for ideological reasons but find it difficult to support the DPP because of the party's reservations on cross-Strait trade liberalization – although most of them, I assume, nevertheless eventually vote for the DPP.

33　The ROC Chamber of Commerce, for its part, also publishes a catalogue of policy recommendations annually. In its 2012 *Suggestions on the Mainland Taishang Service Sector* (ROCCOC 2012), the organization issued specific demands from the Taiwan government to liberalize access to Taiwanese banks and credit institutions, insurance companies and security firms for the mainland market; and to negotiate with the Chinese authorities on better and fairer market access in China for Taiwanese companies belonging to sectors ranging from real estate, high technology and innovative industries, wholesale and retail, logistics and the medical industry to tourism.

34　The Taishang's apparent lack of a collective identity and their scepticism about the value of public action may also have much to do with Taiwan's post-war political economy and the specific circumstances of the rise in private entrepreneurship during the 1950s and 1960s. As is well known, Taiwan's entrepreneurs grew up in the shadow of the authoritarian developmental state and have never played a significant political role, not even during the *Dangwai* period in the 1970s and 1980s, when Taiwan's democratization was set on track. For a recent study on the history of Taiwanese entrepreneurs and their complex position in the struggle for Taiwanese nationalism and identity, see Mengin (2013).

References

'Buru zhengzhi renwu guji gao: Taishang zuozou xuanqing zuiduo jin 7 wan piao' (n.d.) [Despite politicians' highest predictions: Taiwanese business people to command no more than 70,000 ballots], http://big5.huaxia.com/tw/sdbd/zq/2008/00774839.html (accessed 9 October 2014).

CNFI (Chinese National Federation of Industries) (2012) *2012 Quanguo gongye zonghui baipishu. Dui zhengfu zhengce de jianyan* [2012 CNFI White Book. Suggestions for the Government's Policies], Taipei: CNFI.

Control Yuan Bulletin (*Jianchayuan gongbao*) (n.d.) Honest Politics Special Issue

(*Lianzheng zhuankan*), http://sunshine.cy.gov.tw/GipOpenWeb/wSite/lp?ctNode=442 (accessed 10 October 2014).

Cross-Straits Economics Statistics Monthly (n.d.) 255, published by the Mainland Affairs Council, www.mac.gov.tw/ct.asp?xItem=109630&ctNode=5934&mp=3 (accessed 7 October 2014).

Hsu, Chien-Jung (2014) 'China's Influence on Taiwan's Media', *Asian Survey*, 54, 3: 515–539.

Keng, Shu (2011) 'Understanding Integration and 'Spillover' Across the Taiwan Strait: Towards an Analytical Framework', in Schubert, Gunter, and Damm, Jens (eds) *Taiwanese Identity in the 21st Century: Domestic, Regional and Global Perspectives*, London and New York: Routledge, 155–175.

Keng, Shu, and Lin, Rui-Hwa (2007) 'Zhidu huanjing yu xiehui xiaoneng: talu taishang xiehui de ge'an yanjiu' [Institutional Environment and Organizational Effectiveness: A Case Study on Taiwanese Business Associations on the Mainland], *Taiwan Zhengzhi Xuekan*, 11, 2: 93–171.

Lee, Chun-Yi (2012) *Taiwanese Business or Chinese Security Asset? A Changing Pattern of Interaction between Taiwanese Businesses and Chinese Governments*, London and New York: Routledge.

Lee, Chun-Yi (2013) 'Social Dimensions of the Changing Cross-Strait Relations in the Case of Taishangs', in Hu, Weixing (ed.) *New Dynamics in Cross-Taiwan Strait Relations*, London and New York: Routledge, 190–201.

Lee, Chun-Yi (2014) 'From Being Privileged to Being Localized. Taiwanese Businessmen in China', in Chui, Kuei-Fen, Fell, Dafydd, and Lin, Ping (eds) *Migration to and from Taiwan*, London and New York: Routledge, 57–72.

Leng, Tse-Kang (1995) 'State, Business, and Economic Interaction across the Taiwan Strait', *Issues and Studies*, 31, 11: 40–58.

Leng, Tse-Kang (1998) 'Dynamics of Taiwan–Mainland China Economic Relations', *Asian Survey*, 38, 5: 494–509.

Lin, Rui-Hwa (2004) 'Ba wangluo daihuilai: taishang canyu taizi qiye xiehui zhi dongli fenxi' [Bringing the Network Back In: Analysis of the Dynamics of Taishang Participation in Taiwanese Business Associations], Graduate Institute of East Asian Studies, Taipei: National Chengchi-University.

Lin, Rui-Hwa, and Keng, Shu (2012) 'Zhongguo dalude zifa xiehui yu gongminshehui: Kunshan yu Dongguan taixiede ge'an yanjiu' [China's Spontaneous Associations and Civil Society: Case Studies on the Kunshan and Dongguan TBAs], in Keng, Shu, Shu, Keng-The, and Lin, Rui-Hwa (eds) *Taishang Yanjiu* [Taishang Studies], Taipei: Wunan, 189–241.

Mengin, Françoise (2013) *Fragments d'une guerre inachevée. Les entrepreneurs taiwanais et la partition de la Chine* [Fragments of an Unfinished War. Taiwan's Entrepreneurs and the Partition of China], Paris: Karthala.

New York Times (2012) 'Taiwan Vote Lures Back Expatriates in China', 11 January, www.nytimes.com/2012/01/12/world/asia/taiwan-vote-lures-back-expatriates-in-china.html?pagewanted=all&_r=0 (accessed 10 October 2014).

Rawnsley, Ming-Yeh T., and Feng, Chien-Yan (2014) 'Anti-Media Monopoly Policies and Further Democratisation in Taiwan', *Journal of Current Chinese Affairs*, 43, 3: 105–128.

ROCCOC (Republic of China Chamber of Commerce) (2012) *Dalu taishang fuwuyu jianyanshu* [Suggestions on the Mainland Taishang Service Sector], Taipei: ROCCOC.

Schubert, Gunter (2010) 'The Political Thinking of the Mainland Taishang. Some Preliminary Observations from the Field', *Journal of Current Chinese Affairs*, 1: 73–110.

Schubert, Gunter (2013) 'Assessing Political Agency Across the Taiwan Strait: The Case of the Taishang', *China Information*, 27, 1: 51–79.

Schubert, Gunter, and Keng, Shu (2012) 'Taishang as a Factor Shaping Taiwan's Domestic Politics', in Tsang, Steve (ed.) *The Vitality of Taiwan. Politics, Economics, Society and Culture*, London and New York: Palgrave Macmillan, 139–163.

Taipei Times (2011) 'Drop in Free Press Needs to be Addressed', 13 July.

Taipei Times (2013) 'Anti-media Monopoly Explained', 4 February.

The Economist (2013) 'China's Economy: Perverse Advantage', 27 April.

Tung, Chen-Yuan, and Cao, Hsiao-Heng (eds) (2014) *Liang'an jingji guanxide jiyu zu tiaozhan* [Challenges and Opportunities For Cross-Strait Economic Relations], Taipei: Hsin-jui wen-chuang.

Want Want Group (n.d.) 'Taiwan Anti-media Monopoly BIASED in treatment of Certain Media Groups', www.wantchinatimes.com/news-subclass-cnt.aspx?id=20130622000 010&cid=1701 (accessed 14 October 2014).

Xinxinwen [The Journalist] (2007) 'Taishang yong jiao toupiao, Huang Liang-Hua shi tuishou' [The Taishang vote with their feet, Huang Liang-Hua is a helping hand], 1078: 66–69.

7   Signaling peace

A theory of the ECFA and a peace dividend beyond the Taiwan Strait

Hans H. Tung and Yun-Han Chu

This chapter adopts a signaling game approach to examine the way in which Taipei created a 'peace dividend'[1] by signing the Economic Cooperation Framework Agreement (ECFA) with mainland China as a signal to reveal its conciliatory mainland policy preference to other countries. The cross-Strait relationship between mainland China and Taiwan has been fundamentally changed since the Kuomintang (Chinese Nationalist Party, KMT) was returned to power in 2008. Not only has Taipei adopted far more conciliatory policies towards Beijing, but the latter has also responded positively by reducing diplomatic tensions and offering more opportunities for economic cooperation. On the Taiwanese side, this development has given rise to many new economic opportunities that were nearly impossible when both sides were engaged in confrontations over various strategic issues ranging from Taipei's memberships in international organizations to US arms sales to Taipei. These new opportunities come in two main forms. First, as an economic inducement to cultivate more pro-unification constituencies, Beijing has launched a series of government procurement projects to increase imports from Taiwan. Second, the reduction in cross-Strait conflicts has also had the positive effect of inducing new private investment and trade from other countries.

While both of these are important sources of a 'peace dividend' in this new era of the cross-Strait relationship, they actually work on very different principles in terms of how they are generated. The first type of peace dividend, generated by newly created investments and trade from mainland China, mingles both politically-driven purchases by government and state-owned enterprises and economically-incentivized private investments. As far as the former are concerned, an economic cost–benefit analysis is unnecessary, because the government agencies, both central and local, that are behind these purchases care for nothing but the spillover effects and their potential to create closer economic and political ties across the Taiwan Strait.

Compared with the first type of peace dividend, however, the generation of the second type faces an *information* problem that has to be resolved in order for Taipei to improve (or mend) its economic relationship with the rest of the world beyond mainland China. That is, while the political tension[2] between Beijing and Taipei has indeed been reduced to a great extent, it does not necessarily follow that the business communities in the other countries were *well-informed* about this new development or convinced that the two governments on each side of the Strait were serious about it. As far as Taipei is concerned, this information problem is especially critical. On the one hand, Taipei's international space in both economic and political affairs has long been squeezed by Beijing, and therefore the tools for the Ma administration to publicize its conciliatory approach internationally have also been limited. On the other hand, the confrontational approach adopted by the former Democratic Progressive Party (DPP) administration under Chen Shui-Bian's presidency was also very likely to leave legacies behind that would not simply disappear after the power turnover in 2008 and would continue to affect the perception of the cross-Strait relationship around the world. For instance, on 30 August 2008, immediately after the KMT's presidential candidate Ma Ying-Jeou had completed 100 days in office, various pro-independence activist groups, in collaboration with the DPP, marched through Taipei to protest President Ma's mainland China policy, which in their view was going to damage Taiwan's political sovereignty and economic security.[3] In other words, given the continuing political pressures exerted by Taiwan's pan-green coalition on cross-Strait issues, foreign business communities might receive mixed signals regarding the sustainability of the détente across the Strait. As a result, the extent to which Taipei can resolve this information problem will have a profound influence on foreign investors' political risk assessments and therefore also on how big a peace dividend can be created.

We focus on the creation of the second type of peace dividend.[4] We propose a theoretical political-economy model that identifies the conditions under which Taipei would send out a costly signal to reveal its mainland policy preference, so that its trading partners, except for mainland China, could be able to assess Taipei's policy resolve (i.e. a separating equilibrium). More specifically, we view the signing of the ECFA as a costly signal, for Taipei, to convey a credible message internationally that it would adopt a conciliatory approach towards mainland China. The chapter is structured as follows. We first elaborate on how the ECFA can be regarded as a costly signal. We then develop a signaling model with political-economy characteristics that can identify conditions under which a separating equilibrium is possible in settings of both deterministic and stochastic signals. We conclude with some thoughts on possible policy implications.

ECFA as a costly signal

This section offers a justification for considering (international) signaling to be an appropriate framework for analysing the signing of the ECFA and why this preferential trade agreement between Beijing and Taipei can be a costly and credible signal for the latter to reveal its mainland policy preference.

Upon their return to power, one of the key issues at the top of the KMT's policy agenda was to restore Taipei's relationship with Beijing and change the image of the Taiwan Strait from that of a hotspot to that of a peaceful place welcoming international business. There were two potential targets. One target was to increase investment and trade from mainland China. This was not only because mainland China was the third largest economy globally in 2008 but also because there was so much Taiwanese investment in mainland China that could be tapped into.

The other target was to improve or restore Taipei's economic and political relationships with the rest of the world beyond China, which had been substantially undermined both by cross-Strait tensions during the Chen administration and the resulting uncertainties. For instance, Taipei's representative in India, Wen-Chi Ong, contributed an article, 'Reaping Cross-Strait Peace Dividend', to *Uday India*, noting that 'the Taiwan Strait is now morphing into a gateway not only for lasting reconciliation between Taiwan and mainland China, but also a conduit for regional peace and prosperity' (Ong 2010). Moreover, President Ma himself, at press conferences, has also repeatedly emphasized the fact that his administration had constructed an environment for cashing in a cross-Strait peace dividend and had removed the Taiwan Strait as a flashpoint from Asia's security landscape.[5]

The economic effect can also go beyond new investments and trade from mainland China. Sensing that the tension across the Strait has been reduced, business communities in other countries might have more incentives to invest in and trade with Taiwan. More importantly, Taipei's long-term objective in signing this agreement with Beijing is to gain access to the economic integration that has been going on in Asia for a long time. As a consequence, to avoid being marginalized in the new East Asian regionalism (Dent 2009), the Ma administration pinned their hopes to the signing of the ECFA as a way of reassuring other countries that Beijing will not be upset if they sign similar free trade agreements with Taipei.

However, for a signal to be considered credible, rather than just cheap talk, it has to be *costly*. In the literature of (international) signaling, a signaling cost can either arise *ex ante* (e.g. bids for hosting the Olympics as in Rose and Spiegel 2011), or *ex post* (e.g. signing bilateral investment treaties as in Elkins *et al.* 2006). From this perspective, Ong's article in *Uday India* and President Ma's announcements at press conferences are costless and hence unconvincing; the signing of the ECFA, however, is very different.

The cost structure of the ECFA contains both *ex ante* and *ex post* parts. Regarding the latter, the fact that the ECFA was ratified by Taiwan's highest legislative organ, the Legislative Yuan, has made it very costly for this bilateral trade agreement to be nullified even if the DPP were to return to power in the next presidential election.[6]

In other words, this sends a very strong message to Taipei's trading partners that Taiwan's government will not adopt the sort of confrontational foreign policy approach that was seen under the Chen administration.

As far as the *ex ante* costs are concerned, they are chiefly political in nature. From the very beginning of President Ma's first term, Beijing made it quite clear that the 1992 Consensus was the bedrock on which a peaceful cross-Strait relationship had to be based. In addition to accepting the 1992 Consensus, President

Ma himself had also made quite a few U-turns in his personal attitudes towards China's political dissidents. For instance, while he was still the mayor of Taipei City, he gave the Dalai Lama a warm welcome and even issued a press release to publicize his visit. However, in 2008, after the Dalai Lama had openly expressed his wish to visit Taiwan several times, President Ma made an open remark at an international press conference that the timing of the Dalai Lama's visit was not appropriate.[7] In 2009, the Dalai Lama was again invited by the DDP mayors of Taiwan's southern cities and counties to come to Taiwan to give his blessing to those who had suffered from the typhoon Morakot. Although the Ma administration allowed him to come this time, President Ma neither attended the event featuring the Dalai Lama nor met with him in Taipei. He has also substantially toned down his remarks in support of overseas Chinese democratic movement activists.[8]

In other words, the growing dependence on Beijing for economic benefits has led to Taipei's losing some of its space for diplomatic politicking.

What has to be noted here is that the signing of the ECFA can hardly be interpreted as announcing Taiwan's intention to liberalize its trade regime. This is because the signing of the ECFA was very closely linked with Beijing's political move of making concessions (*rangli*)[9] to Taipei. For instance, during the negotiations over the specific terms to be included in the ECFA, Beijing deliberately did not include agriculture on the agenda and this saved Taipei from having to face thorny issues regarding the opening of Taiwan's agricultural market.[10] In other words, the ECFA is not quite a *bona fide* 'free trade' agreement with reciprocity, but a *political* agreement in economic disguise predicated on Beijing's intention to create its local constituency in Taiwan.[11] In the following section, we develop a signaling model for the political dynamics discussed above.

A political-economy signaling model

The brief discussion of Taipei's approach to the cross-Strait relationship under the Ma administration suggests that one of this government's primary goals is to send an international signal containing the message that, in contrast to the previous administration, it has adopted a conciliatory approach to the cross-Strait relationship and the resulting reduction in the tension across the Taiwan Strait has made the region a safe place for investment and trade. In this part of the chapter, we develop a signaling model with political-economy features (i.e. the distributional effects of investment and trade expansion resulting from the signing of the ECFA) that explores both the conditions under which a separating equilibrium is possible, and the differences in country receivers' responses to Taipei's signal (i.e. whether they view the signal as credible). In contrast to signaling models that have either 'tying hands' or 'sinking costs/burning money' (Fearon 1997) as costs, our model has both features. That is, while signing a bilateral agreement such as the ECFA to signal foreign policy intent generally involves *ex post* costs if the agreement is binding (i.e. tying hands), the ECFA also entails *ex ante* costs. This is because, before the agreement was signed in Chongqing, Taipei had paid the costs of being diplomatically self-constrained with regard to entering into any possible conflict with Beijing (i.e. sinking costs).

Taipei's costly activity – sending a signal of rapprochement across the Strait by means of signing the ECFA – pays off when Taiwan gains more investment and trade from countries that receive the signal and expect Taipei to continue to employ a conciliatory approach.[12]

Generally speaking, our results show that, under certain parameter conditions, a separating equilibrium exists when countries that prefer to maintain long-term peace also choose to sign an agreement with their conflicting parties and those that are unwilling to be reconciled do not send any signals.

To incorporate political-economy features, our model is specified as a two-sector model (export, *x*, and import-competing, *m*, sectors) with the specific factors of a small open economy in political/military conflict with another economy. The tension between them afflicts this small economy with high business risks that discourage foreigners from investing in or trading with it.[13] The political-economy features of this setting arise from two important facts. First of all, when the political tension between these two economies is reduced, the increase in the economic activities of investment and trade in this small economy has different effects on the export and import-competing sectors. A simple analysis based on international economics shows that, given a certain level of economic openness, the increase in investment and trade leads to price increases in the export sector, and to lower prices in the import-competing sector.

In the context of Taiwanese politics, the political dynamic between the export and the import-competing sectors is fairly close to what Kastner (2007) documented in his analysis of Taipei's cross-Strait economic policy under Chen Shui-Bian's presidency. Even during this confrontational period of the cross-Strait relationship, the export sector, or the internationalist economic interests (those actors that support and gain from integration in global markets; Kastner 2007: 665) still exerted some degree of influence on Chen's decision to liberalize.[14] Second, what makes *signaling* an appropriate framework for analysis in the current case of interest is that, given Taipei's previous record under the DPP regime, it was very difficult for the Ma administration to credibly reveal its foreign policy preference for rapprochement across the Strait without engaging in some costly activities to show its resolve.

In order to highlight the effect exercised by price changes owing to the signing of the ECFA, we assume that the domestic factor (capital) used by both the export and the import-competing sectors is fixed and sector-specific. In contrast, international capital, κ, is assumed to be mobile across sectors and its international market rate of return is π^* (assumed to be fixed). We then specify the real output levels in both sectors to satisfy $y_i(\kappa)$, where $y_i' > 0$ and $y_i'' < 0$, $i = x, m$. In other words, since the domestic factor is assumed to be constant, the real output is set to be merely a function of international capital. We denote prices for both sectors when the tension is high (*h*) by p_x^h and p_m^h, and when the tension is low (*l*), by p_x^l and p_m^l ($p_x^l > pp_x^h$ and $p_m^h > p_m^l$).

As for the timing of the game:

1 the government decides whether or not to sign the ECFA with mainland China;
2 the private agents make their investment decisions, based on their expectations of the type of the government (i.e. whether it is confrontational or conciliatory);
3 finally, the government makes its mainland China policy and reveals its type.

The game is solved backwards to ensure sub-game perfection. We first write both sectors' pre- and post-ECFA payoffs:

$$v_i^h = p_i^h y_i(\kappa_i^*) - (1 + \pi^*)\kappa_i^* \tag{1}$$

and

$$v_i^l = p_i^l y_i(\kappa_i^*) - (1 + \pi^*)\kappa_i^* \tag{2}$$

These two expressions allow us to know how capital reallocation is determined across the export and import-competing sectors. Differentiating between both of them with respect to κ_j^* yields

$$p_i^l y_i'(\kappa_i^*) = 1 + \pi^* \qquad i = x, m; t = h, l \tag{3}$$

Since $\dfrac{\partial \kappa_i^*}{\partial p_i} = \dfrac{-y'}{p_i y''} > 0$,[15] we know that $\kappa_x^{*l} > \kappa_x^{*h}$ and $\kappa_m^{*h} > \kappa_m^{*l}$.

To derive the difference in return between high and low political tension, $v_i^l - v_i^h$ *i=x, m* for both sectors, we first notice that the value of κ_i^{*h} is a continuous variable that varies within the range between κ_i^{*h} and κ_i^{*h}. Graphically, $v_x^l - v_x^h$ is basically the shaded area in Figure 7.1.

Formally, the derivation of an expression for $v_x^l - v_x^h$ where we compare its value to that of $v_m^l - v_m^h$ takes two steps. We first consider the situation $\kappa_x^* = \kappa_x^{*h}$ (i.e. the border condition when the price has changed but the capital allocation remains the same)

$$\left. \left(v_x^l - v_x^h \right) \right|_{\kappa_x^* = \kappa_x^{*h}} = \left(p_x^l - p_x^h \right) y_x \left(\kappa_x^{*h} \right) \tag{7}$$

Second, when $\kappa_x^* \in (\kappa_x^{*h}, \kappa_x^{*l})$

$$\left. \left(v_x^l - v_x^h \right) \right|_{\kappa_x^* \in \left(\kappa_x^{*h}, \kappa_x^{*l} \right)} = \int_{\kappa_x^{*h}}^{\kappa_x^{*l}} \left[p_x^l y_x \left(\kappa_x^* \right) - \left(1 + \pi^* \right) \kappa_x^{*h} \right] d\kappa_x^* \tag{8}$$

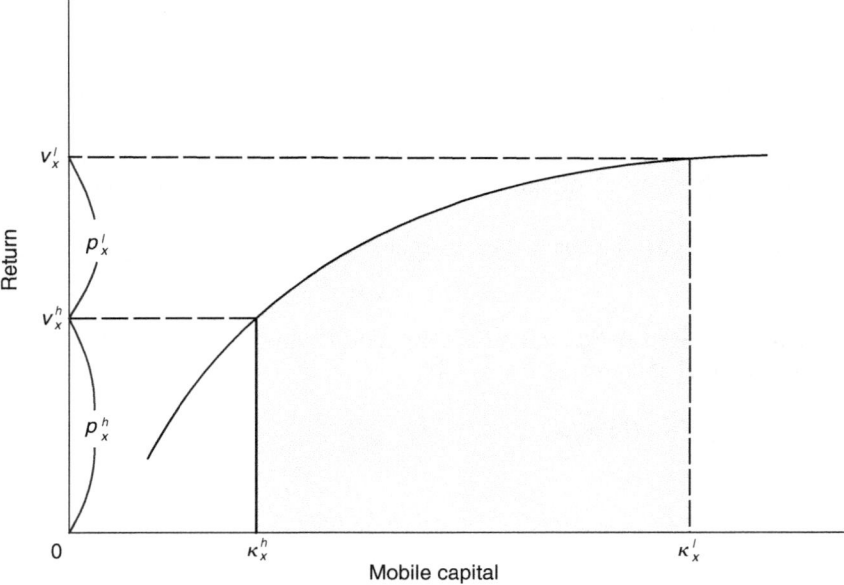

Figure 7.1 Return in the export sector.

Combining (7) and (8) yields

$$\left(v_x^l - v_x^h\right)\Big|_{\kappa_x^* \in [\kappa_x^{*h}, \kappa_x^{*l})} = \left(p_x^l - p_x^h\right)y_x\left(\kappa_x^{*h}\right) + \int_{\kappa_x^{*h}}^{\kappa_x^{*l}}\left[p_x^l y_x\left(\kappa_x^*\right) - \left(1 + \pi^*\right)\kappa_x^{*h}\right]dk_x^* > 0 \quad (9)$$

which, given $p_x^* > p_x^h$, is strictly positive.

As for $v_m^l - v_m^h$, its graphical presentation is given in Figure 7.2.

Given the previous result, $\kappa_m^l - \kappa_m^h$, Figure 7.2 has shown that the value of its shaded area is negative. To formally derive the result, we follow the same steps in the case of the export sector and obtain

$$\left(v_x^l - v_x^h\right)\Big|_{\kappa_x^* \in [\kappa_x^{*h}, \kappa_x^{*l})} = \left(p_x^l - p_x^h\right)y_x\left(\kappa_x^{*h}\right) + \int_{\kappa_x^{*h}}^{\kappa_x^{*l}}\left[p_x^l y_x\left(\kappa_x^*\right) - \left(1 + \pi^*\right)\kappa_x^{*h}\right]dk_x^* > 0 \quad (10)$$

In other words, we have shown that the return in the export sector is greater when the political tension is lower and the relationship is just the opposite in the import-competing sector.

After specifying the distribution of benefits in both sectors, we proceed to elaborate on the cost structure of this model: this will shed light on two of its critical political-economy features. First of all, while the signing of the ECFA consolidates the economic benefits derived from a more peaceful cross-Strait relationship, it nonetheless entails more *ex post* political costs in Taipei's

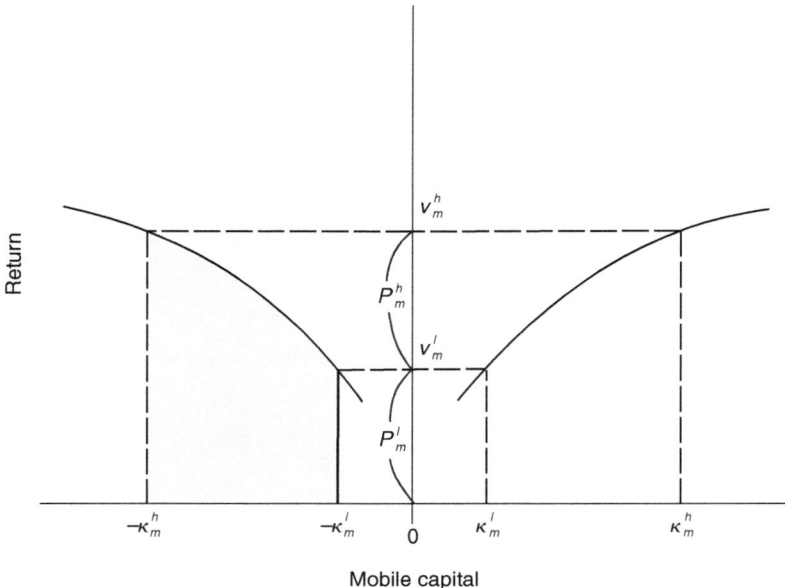

Figure 7.2 Return in the import-competing sector.

diplomacy (denoted by C_D in the model). On the one hand, Taipei's foreign policy of diplomatic truce (*waijiao xiubing*) or flexible diplomacy (*huolu waijiao*), while saving money from being spent on countries threatening to break diplomatic relationships with Taiwan, has greatly restrained Taipei from engaging in any diplomatic politicking. On the other hand, as conveyed by the political mantra repeated by both Beijing and Taipei, 'Economy First, Politics Later' ['*xianjing houzheng*'], after the signing of the ECFA, which can be seen as a milestone in cross-Strait economic cooperation, politics lie awaiting. After all, the political coalition behind the current cross-Strait policy regime is also under enormous pressure from its political rivals (e.g. the DPP and other more pro-independent political groups) to show that this regime is working towards the goal of preventing Taiwan from being marginalized in the unfolding process of regional economic integration.[16]

In contrast to the bulk of signaling models in the literature, where the decision to signal is exogenously given, our two-sector setting allows our model to endogenize the signaling decision with the parameter α_i denoting the weight of sector i in the government's objective function. The parameter of α_i captures information, such as sector i's ability to solve its collective action problem or its strategic importance to Taiwan's economy that can potentially affect how much it is valued by the government.[17]

Now we turn to the specification of the government's objective function, which is the weighted average of each sector's utility, $u(v_i)$, $i=x, m$.

$$U_G = \sum_i \alpha_i u(v_i), \quad i = x, m \tag{11}$$

where U_G is assumed to be concave in $u(v_i)$, and $u' \geq 0$ and $u'' \leq 0$. What is worth noting here is that the specification of the government objective function is more structural and simplified than the standard 'Protection for Sale' model in Grossman and Helpman (1994). The main reason for this simplification is that, in contrast to the 'Protection for Sale' literature that focuses on industry-specific protection measures (e.g. tariffs or non-tariff barriers), the economic consequences of lowered political tension tend to be sector-wide.

To further simplify the model without loss of generality, we normalize the weight attached to the import-competing sector to unity, $\alpha_m = 1$ and therefore the weight to the export sector becomes $\dfrac{\alpha_x}{\alpha_m}$. To avoid abusing the use of notations, we replace $\dfrac{\alpha_x}{\alpha_m}$ with α.

Before the signal (i.e. ECFA) is sent, U_G then satisfies

$$U_G = \alpha u(v_x^h) + u(v_m^h) \tag{12}$$

The post-ECFA government utility is denoted by $\tilde{U}_G$

$$\tilde{U}_G = \alpha u(v_x^l) + u(v_m^l) - C_D \tag{13}$$

Equilibria with deterministic and stochastic signals

When certain conditions are met, we derive a separating equilibrium in which a government that chooses to adopt a conciliatory rather than a confrontational foreign policy also chooses to sign a free trade agreement, such as the ECFA. In contrast, a government that prefers to prioritize Taiwan's autonomy over mainland China's economic influence does not send the signal nor does it adopt more conciliatory policies.[18] This equilibrium maximizes the government's utility in tandem with investment decisions, maximizing returns to both sectors conditional on the signal sent by the government.

Deterministic setting

To derive a separating equilibrium, we first consider two off-the-path outcomes, both of which lead to discrepancies between the signal sent and the mainland policy decision that follows. The first off-equilibrium path outcome to be considered is *false signaling*, where the government sends the signal but subsequently adopts a confrontational policy. Denote as $\bar{U}_G$ the government's expected utility when it sends a credible signal while failing to adopt a conciliatory policy; $\bar{U}_G$ satisfies the condition specified by the equation:

$$\bar{U}_G^h = \alpha u(\tilde{v}_x^h) + u(\tilde{v}_m^h) - C_D \tag{14}$$

where

$$\tilde{v}_i^h \equiv v_i^h(\kappa_i^{*l}) = p_i^h y_i(\kappa_i^{*l}) - (1+\pi^*)\kappa_i^{*l}, \ i = x, m \tag{15}$$

$\tilde{v}_i^h$ is the return to sector i when the government sends a false signal. The level of mobile capital has changed from κ_i^{*h} to κ_i^{*l}, but, since a conciliatory policy does not follow suit, the prices remain the same as those when the cross-Strait tension is high.

The second off-the-path outcome occurs when the government adopts a conciliatory policy towards mainland China without sending any signal. We have to exclude this possibility because, in this case, receivers would not be able to make a correct inference about the type of the government. Define $\bar{U}_G^l$ as the government's utility when it turns propitiatory without sending a signal like the ECFA, and it satisfies

$$\bar{U}_G^l = \alpha u(\tilde{v}_x^l) + u(\tilde{v}_m^l) \tag{16}$$

where

$$\tilde{v}_i^l \equiv v_i^l(\kappa_i^{*h}) = p_i^l y_i(\kappa_i^{*h}) - (1+\pi^*)\kappa_i^{*h}, \ i = x, m \tag{17}$$

$\tilde{v}_i^l$ is sector i's revenue when prices change to p_i^l owing to the cross-Strait rapprochement while the amount of mobile capital in sector i remains at κ_i^{*h} in the absence of a signal. In a nutshell, in both of the off-the-equilibrium cases, no correct inferences can be made regarding the correspondence between signal and policy.

To exclude these two off-the-path outcomes, we first derive the welfare differences (i.e. the differences in the government utilities in different scenarios) in both cases. First of all, given that the signal has been sent out, the welfare difference between lowering and maintaining the level of political tension can be given by

$$\tilde{U}_G - \bar{U}_G^h = \alpha\left[u(v_x^l) - u(\tilde{v}_x^h)\right] + \left[u(v_m^l) - u(\tilde{v}_m^h)\right] \tag{18}$$

and for $\bar{U}_G^h$ to be excluded from the path to the equilibrium, (18) has to be non-negative. Moreover, it is also easy to see that $\tilde{U}_G - \bar{U}_G^h$ is monotonically increasing in α.[19] That is, the increase in the government's utility when it adopts a conciliatory policy is monotonically increasing in the government's preference for the export sector. This property allows us to derive the lower bound for the outcome of a false signal to be excluded:

$$\alpha \geq \frac{u(\tilde{v}_m^h) - u(v_m^l)}{u(v_x^l) - u(\tilde{v}_x^h)} \tag{21}$$

To exclude the other off-the-equilibrium outcome, costless rapprochement, we compute the welfare difference between lowering and maintaining the level of political tension given that no signal is sent.

$$\bar{U}_G^l - U_G = a\left[u(\tilde{v}_x^l) - u(v_x^h)\right] + \left[u(\tilde{v}_m^l) - u(v_m^h)\right] \tag{22}$$

Similarly, $\bar{U}_G^l - U_G$ is also monotonically increasing in a.[20] However, for the cost-less rapprochement to be excluded, (23) has to be negative and this result allows us to derive the upper bound of a

$$a < \frac{u(v_m^h) - u(\tilde{v}_m^l)}{u(\tilde{v}_x^l) - u(v_x^h)} \tag{25}$$

When (21) and (25) are satisfied simultaneously, both false signaling and cost-less rapprochement can be excluded.

For the government to adopt an indifferent position between adopting a conciliatory approach after sending a signal and doing nothing, $\tilde{U}_G - U_G$ must be zero,

$$\tilde{U}_G - U_G = a\left[u(v_x^l) - u(v_x^h)\right] + \left[u(v_m^l) - u(v_m^h)\right] - C_D = 0 \tag{26}$$

and since the government's utility is monotonically increasing in a, (26) allows us to derive a threshold below which the government does not have any incentive to send a signal,

$$a^* = \frac{C_D - \left[u(v_m^l) - u(v_m^h)\right]}{u(v_x^l) - u(v_x^h)} \tag{27}$$

Moreover, combining (21) and (27) yields a *sufficient* condition for a^* to satisfy (21):

$$v_x^h \geq \tilde{v}_x^h \tag{28}$$

This condition[21] says that, under the condition that the tension is high, the payoffs to the export sector are greater than the payoffs when a false signal is sent. Alternatively, combining (25) and (27) gives us the other *sufficient* condition from a's upper bound:

$$v_x^l > \tilde{v}_x^l \tag{30}$$

which implies that, under the opposite condition of low tension, the returns to the export sector should be higher than the returns when no signal has been sent. Together, both conditions, (28) and (30), clearly show that the export sector will be worse off as a result of the two off-the-path strategies.

Moreover, (28) and (30) allow us to derive a not only separating equilibrium but also a more general interpretation that facilitates a cross-country comparison. That is, these two conditions lead to a proposition that a separating equilibrium exists in which governments with $a^g \geq a^*$ send the signal and adopt conciliatory policies and those with $a^g < a^*$ do not send the signal and do not adopt conciliatory policies.

Stochastic setting

In the deterministic setting, the signal is assumed to have been sent without any noise, which allows the receiver to make a correct inference about its meaning (while not necessarily being sure about the sender's type). Hence, in the previous section, when the ECFA was signed, the countries that were informed of the event did not have any difficulty in perceiving this agreement to be a sign of peace and adjusting their trade and investment decisions (i.e. from κ_i^h to κ_i^l). They were, however, uncertain as to whether Taipei was really being sincere. In fact, however, a deterministic signal does not always fit the reality. For instance, in October 2010, only four months after the ECFA had been signed, the head of the delegation from mainland China to the Tokyo International Film Festival, Jiang Ping, asked the Taipei delegation to change its name from 'Taiwan' to 'Taiwan Province' or 'Taiwan, China'. This unfriendly gesture soon stirred up popular anger against mainland China in Taiwanese society, and President Ma himself quickly made a public statement warning Beijing that political bickering of this kind could destroy the mutual trust that both sides were just starting to establish. While the 'Jiang Ping affair' did not escalate to such a degree that it caused Beijing and Taipei to make a U-turn in their cross-Strait policies, it obviously represented a *noise* in the process of signal transmission, since the ECFA had been signed only one month previously.

In addition, noises can also arise from the signal-receiving countries. For example, the political characteristics of receiving countries can also have an effect on how the signal is received. Countries with higher media freedom obviously keep their private investors better informed about the changes in the cross-Strait relationship than those with less media freedom. Given the presence of noises, the original assumption of correct inference no longer holds, and the nature of the signaling process is better characterized as stochastic with uncertainties than as deterministic. To generalize the signaling model to the stochastic setting, we formalize the idea of noise as uncertainties in the post-ECFA *expected returns* to the export and import-competing sectors. From a game-theoretical perspective, since the government's signaling decision precedes investors' decisions in capital reallocation, the former is made on the basis of the government's expectation of the latter. In other words, given the modeling structure that was presented in the previous section, the model below formalizes the *effect* of the stochastic signal rather than the signal itself.[22]

First of all, we rewrite the government's utility after the signal is sent as:

$$\tilde{U}_G^s = \alpha u(v_x) + u(v_m) - C_D$$
$$= \alpha u\left[\sum_j\left(v_{xj}^h - r_{xj}\Delta_{xj}\right)\right] + u\left[\sum_j\left(v_{mj}^h - r_{mj}\Delta_{mj}\right)\right] - C_D \tag{31}$$

where $r_{ij} \in \{0, 1\}$, $i = x, m$, is country j's decision to respond to the signal. When $r_{ij} = 1$, country j responds positively to the signal and the amount of trade and investment therefore changes correspondingly by Δ_{ij}.[23]

In contrast, if $r_{ij}=0$, country j basically ignores the signal because of the noises; the reallocation of capital across the two sectors does not take place and the level of economic activities between Taiwan and country j remains at v_{ij}^h when political tension is high.

In order to know the government's strategic choice under this setting, we need to calculate the stochastic process to show how the decision regarding r_{ij} is made by country j.[24]

Given the symmetry between the export and the import-competing sectors, we drop the subscripts x and m from the following analysis. Moreover, since this decision is highly correlated with how the signal is received, we introduce a continuous measure of country j's signal-receiving mechanism S_j^* to satisfy

$$r_j = \begin{cases} 1 & \text{iff } S_j^* > 0 \\ 0 & \text{iff } S_j^* \le 0 \end{cases} \tag{32}$$

and it is linearly modelled by

$$S_j^* = W_j \gamma - \delta_j \tag{33}$$

where W_j is a vector of factors affecting the reception of the signal by country j, γ is a parameter (to be estimated by data) defining how sensitive the signal receiving process is to W_j, and δ_j a stochastic noise that is (standard) normally distributed, $\delta_j \sim N(0, 1)$.

Finally, according to the value r_j takes, country j's revenue from either sector can be given respectively by

$$\begin{cases} v_j^l = X_j^l \beta^l + \varepsilon_j^l & \text{When } r_j = 1 \\ v_j^h = X_j^h \beta^h + \varepsilon_j^h & \text{When } r_j = 0 \end{cases} \tag{34}$$

where $v_j^l = v_j^h + \Delta_j$, X_j^k ($k=l$, h) is the vector of factors affecting the economic relationship between Taiwan and country j under either low or high political tensions across the Taiwan Strait,[25] β^k is the parameter capturing how sensitive country j is to Taiwan's economic fundamentals and new political developments in the Taiwan Strait, and $\varepsilon_j^k \sim N(0,(\sigma_j^k)^2)$ represents the stochastic errors. In addition, since the tension across the Strait is either low or high, it is further assumed that the co-variance between their economic outcomes is zero, i.e. $\sigma_{lh}=0$. More importantly, consistent with the basic modeling setup of the economy, the model here captures the distributional effect between the export and the import-competing sectors by setting $\beta^h < \beta^l$ for the former and $\beta^h > \beta^l$ for the latter. In other words, the model captures the positive price effect in the export sector by making country j more sensitive to the rapprochement across the Strait, and the opposite effect in the import-competing sector by making it less sensitive to the new development.

Having completed the setup for our model in the stochastic setting, we are now ready to derive the government's expectation regarding the low-tension returns to both sectors given country j's national characteristics and its choice to positively respond to the signal, $E[v_j^{*l}|X_j^l, r_j = 1]$.[26]

The expectation is conditioned on $r_j = 1$, since this condition is what really changes the government's payoffs between the different states of the cross-Strait relationship. Furthermore, it also has to be noted here that our model allows the reception of the signal by country j to be endogenous to its level of investment and trade with Taiwan. In other words, the covariance between the former and latter is non-zero, i.e. $\sigma_{l\delta}, \sigma_{h\delta} \neq 0$.

Utilizing the normality assumption of and the law of iterated expectations (i.e. Adam's Law), we obtain

$$
\begin{aligned}
E\left[v_j^{*l}\left|X_j^l, r_j = 1\right.\right] &= X_j^l \beta^l + E\left[\varepsilon_j^l \left|\delta_j < W_j \gamma\right.\right] \\
&= X_j^l \beta^l + \sigma_{l\delta} E\left[\delta_i \left|\delta_i < W_j \gamma\right.\right]
\end{aligned}
\tag{35}
$$

Again, given $\delta_j \sim N(0, 1)$, it is easy to see that $E[\delta_i|\delta_i < W_j \gamma]$ is simply what has been known as the inverse Mills ratio. As a result, we obtain

$$
E\left[v_j^{*l}\left|X_j^l, r_j = 1\right.\right] = X_j^l \beta^l - \sigma_{l\delta} \frac{\varphi\left(W_j \gamma\right)}{\Phi\left(W_j \gamma\right)}
\tag{36}
$$

Given the normality assumption of ε_j^l, it is clear that the second term in (36),

$-\sigma_{l\delta} \dfrac{\varphi\left(W_j \gamma\right)}{\Phi\left(W_j \gamma\right)}$, captures the effect owing to country j's signal-receiving bias and

the difference between deterministic and stochastic signals.[27] Moreover, by symmetry, we can also derive the expression when $r_j = 0$

$$
E[v_j^{*h}|X_j^h, r_j = 0] = X_j^h \beta^h + \sigma_{h\delta} \frac{\varphi(W_j \gamma)}{1 - \Phi(W_j \gamma)}
\tag{37}
$$

Now we go back to the government's utility under the stochastic setting. The expected value of (31) can be given as

$$
\begin{aligned}
E\left[\tilde{U}_G^s\right] = \alpha u &\left\{\sum_j \left[P\left(S_j^* > 0\right) E\left[v_{xj}^{*l}\left|X_{xj}^l, r_j = 1\right.\right] + P\left(S_j^* \leq 0\right) E\left[v_{xj}^{*h}\left|X_{xj}^h, r_j = 0\right.\right]\right]\right\} \\
+ u &\left\{\sum_j \left[P\left(S_j^* > 0\right) E\left[v_{mj}^{*l}\left|X_{mj}^l, r_j = 1\right.\right] + P\left(S_j^* \leq 0\right) E\left[v_{mj}^{*h}\left|X_{mj}^h, r_j = 0\right.\right]\right]\right\} - C_D
\end{aligned}
\tag{38}
$$

where we use the property of linearity of expectations. Moreover, as we have mentioned above, since what really matters is the changes, i.e. Δ_j, the expression is further simplified to be

$$E\left[\tilde{U}_G^s\right] \propto \alpha u\left\{\sum_j E\left[v_{xj}^{*l}\,|\,X_{xj}^l\,,r_j=1\right]\right\} + u\left\{\sum_j E\left[v_{mj}^{*l}\,|\,X_{mj}^l\,,r_j=1\right]\right\} - C_D$$

(39)

$$= \alpha u\left\{\sum_j \left(X_{xj}^l \beta_x^l - \sigma_{l\delta}^x \mu\right)\right\} + u\left\{\sum_j \left(X_{mj}^l \beta_m^l - \sigma_{l\delta}^m \mu\right)\right\} - C_D$$

where $\mu = \dfrac{\varphi(W_j\gamma)}{\Phi(W_j\gamma)}$. We should also notice that $\Sigma_j X_{ij}^l$ can be replaced by $E[v_i^l]$.

We then repeat the process we have gone through in the deterministic case and find that tthe two off-the-path equilibria can both be excluded given certain parameter conditions, and α to satisfy

$$\alpha_{stochastic}^* = \frac{u(v_m^h)u\left(E[v_m^l]-\sigma_{l\delta}^m \mu\right)}{u\left(E[v_x^l]-\sigma_{l\delta}^x \mu\right)-u(v_x^h)}$$

(40)

which gives rise to a similar proposition that, in a stochastic setting, a separating equilibrium also exists in which governments with $\alpha_{stochastic}^* \geq \alpha^*$ send the signal and adopt conciliatory policies and those with $\alpha_{stochastic}^* < \alpha^*$ do not send the signal and do not adopt conciliatory policies. The stochastic version of the threshold differs from the deterministic version chiefly in the addition of the biases owing to countries' signal-receiving mechanisms. The empirical implication of this addition is that future studies that test the hypotheses derived from our theoretical argument should be able to include a covariate controlling for countries' abilities to receive Taipei's signal when it is possible that noises are present.

Conclusion

In this chapter, we have offered a formal explanation of the reasons underlying the Ma administration's decision to sign a trade agreement, the ECFA, with mainland China. The idea emerged in early 2009, less than a year after President Ma's presidential inauguration, and Beijing and Taipei soon signed the agreement in Chongqing in June 2010. This theoretical exercise shows not only that the signing had much to do with Taipei's attempt to revive its economy by bringing in more foreign investment and trade, but that it might also introduce a new perspective for considering what the ECFA really means for Taiwan's economic relationship with the world.

Although the signing of the ECFA was well-received among the Taiwanese business community across the Taiwan Strait, some sceptics nonetheless take an opposite view: for example, given the fact that Taipei has been slow in signing free trade agreements (FTAs) with other economies, concern has been voiced that the ECFA might have a *lock-in* effect that makes Taiwan even more reliant on economic relations with mainland China. Moreover, what is more unsettling is that as the Taiwanese economy integrates more profoundly with the Chinese economy, Beijing will be able strengthen its leverage against Taipei and push forward with its political agenda. In other words, for sceptics, having closer economic ties with mainland China entails both distancing the Taiwanese economy from the world and undermining Taipei's ability to engage in diplomatic politicking[28] due to security externalities (Gowa and Mansfield 1993) of the ECFA.

Deciding the outcome of the debate between the anti-ECFA and pro-ECFA camps does not fall within the scope of this chapter, but a contribution has been made towards furthering the understanding of the issue by exploring, from a theoretical perspective, one of the possible positive effects of the signing of the ECFA.

More specifically, this debate boils down to one critical question: does the ECFA make it easier or more difficult for Taipei to maintain economic relations with its trading partners beyond mainland China? The anti-ECFA camp obviously regards the ECFA as having driven a wedge between Taiwan and the world economy.[29] However, in an era when mainland China has emerged as one of the major trading powers and its role in the global economy is becoming more prominent (e.g. 'Chimerica' in Ferguson and Schularick 2007), this dichotomous view between China and the world seems to have overlooked an important part of the global economic landscape. In other words, the real effect of the ECFA on Taiwan's economic relationship with the rest of the world beyond mainland China may well be diametrically opposed to the predictions of the anti-ECFA camp. Signing the ECFA could actually, as the pro-ECFA camp has expected, help Taiwan ride the global trend of China fever and also reduce the business risks that have emerged as a result of the military and political tension across the Taiwan Strait.

Notes

1 It should be noted that the way in which the concept of 'peace dividend' is used in this chapter differs slightly from the way in which it is used in the literature, where the term 'peace dividend' is typically used to refer to the reduction in the defence budget due to the termination of military conflicts. However, despite the political bickering and military manoeuvring that has gone on between Beijing and Taipei, there has never been any real fighting between the two sides of the Taiwan Strait in recent years. As a consequence, we stretch the concept here to include the increase in investment and trade that has resulted from the decrease in political tensions. See Lee and Vedder (1996) for recent theoretical developments.

2 Militarily speaking, however, the potential tension has not eased very much. As a matter of fact, according to some reports, the number of missiles targeting Taiwan has even increased. See *Taipei Times* (2012).

3 The event, '100-Days Outcry from the People', was organized mainly by pro-independence groups, such as the Taiwan Society and the Taiwan Association of University Professors. See www.taiwansociety. org.tw/en/article.php?articleid=192 (accessed 25 July 2014) for the press release about this event that was issued by the Taiwan Society.

4 Of course, mainland China's private investors, compared with its government counterparts, might also suffer from the same information problem. Although, relatively speaking, they are much more informed about cross-Strait affairs than business communities in other countries, given the long history of confrontations between Beijing and Taipei and the authoritarian nature of the mainland Chinese government, they might not necessarily know how serious both governments are about creating a more

peaceful environment across the Taiwan Strait. Our chapter basically sets aside this issue, and focuses only on the second type because Taiwan's over-dependence on mainland China's market has long been at the centre of Taiwan's political debates; the possibility of attracting more trade and investment from non-Chinese sources by reducing the political tension across the Strait was therefore, arguably, the ultimate concern of the Ma administration.

5 In addition, to attract more Taiwanese capital from abroad, the Taiwanese government also lowered the inheritance tax from 50 per cent to 10 per cent in 2008. See *China Post* (2008).

6 This prediction was partly verified by a remark made by the DPP's candidate for the 2012 presidential election, Tsai Ing-Wen. Tsai said that she would not rescind the ECFA even if she won the election. See *Taipei Times* (2011).

7 *Liberty Times*, 10 December 2008, available at www.libertytimes. com.tw/2008/new/dec/10/today-fo6–2.htm (accessed 25 July 2014).

8 President Ma's approach differed greatly from the approach employed by the Chen administration, since the latter actually funded these overseas groups as a way of undermining Beijing's international reputation, while the former has maintained a relatively lukewarm attitude towards these groups since 2008.

9 The Chinese Premier, Wen Jiabao, in his response to a question raised by a netizen in an online interview, stated that

> We will take the differences in economic scale and market conditions between the two sides across the Taiwan Strait into consideration. In order to take good care of the interests of small and medium Taiwanese enterprises as well as the grass roots of Taiwanese society, farmers in particular, we can make concessions in this regard. The reason is simple. The compatriots in Taiwan are our brothers.

Wen's interview is available at http://big5.xinhuanet.com/gate/big5/news.xinhuanet.com/politics/2010–02/27/content_13063169.htm (accessed 25 July 2014).

10 As a matter of fact, President Ma has openly said a couple of times that the agreement with Beijing would not allow more agricultural goods to be imported from mainland China (*Liberty Times*, 4 April 2010, available at www.libertytimes.com.tw/2010/new/apr/4/today-fo1.htm) (accessed 25 July 2014). In other words, although Beijing did not explain what exactly Wen Jiabao meant by *rangli* in his online interview, Taipei had actually sent a clear message (e.g. no increase in agricultural imports) to Beijing about the concessions that were wanted.

11 However, this strategy does not work out uniformly across Taiwan. Take milkfish as an example. To fulfill Wen's *rangli* promise and create more pro-unification supporters, milkfish was included in the ECFA's early harvest list, on which the included products were able to enjoy lower tariff barriers before the negotiations over all the products had been concluded. Moreover, Beijing signed a 0.13 billion (TWD) contract with milkfish farmers in a small town in southern Taiwan, Xuejia, which has been a stronghold for the DPP. Nonetheless, according to a report by *Business Weekly* [*Shangye Zhoukan*] in October 2011, the milkfish farmers in Xuejia did not seem to change their political attitudes and, as far as the 2012 presidential election in Taiwan was concerned, the DPP's presidential candidate obtained 68 per cent of Xuejia's votes against the 29 per cent gained by the KMT. Obviously, Beijing's strategy for converting the DPP supporters' political attitudes by means of economic inducements did not seem to work in this particular case.

12 This increase in investment and trade, however, has a distributional effect between different sectors. This effect will be discussed after the idea has been formalized.

13 We are not implying that foreign investments or trade are the only source of economic growth in this economy, but there is little doubt about the detrimental effect of political/economic conflicts on international economic activities (Keshk *et al.* 2004).

14 For instance, when Chen announced his new cross-Strait policy guideline, 'Aggressive Opening, Effective Management', the administration also lifted the $50 million dollar limit on individual investments and relaxed restrictions on bank transfers (Kastner 2007: 678).

15 This result can be obtained by deriving an expression for p_i from (3)

$$p_i^t = \frac{1+\pi^*}{y_i'(\kappa_i^*)} \tag{4}$$

Differentiating it with respect to κ_i^* yields

$$\frac{\partial p_i^t}{\partial \kappa_i^*} = -y_i'(\kappa_i^*)^{-1} p_i^t y_i'(\kappa_i^*) \tag{5}$$

Alternatively,

$$\frac{\partial \kappa_i^*}{\partial p_i^t} = \frac{-y_i'(\kappa_i^*)}{p_i^t y_i''(\kappa_i^*)} > 0 \tag{6}$$

16 The inclusion of this term renders our model different from that provided in Rose and Spiegel (2011), where the costs are completely absorbed by sectoral actors.

17 The assumption that the strength of interest groups is exogenously determined is often found in endogenous-policy literature (e.g. Grossman and Helpman 1994). Mitra (1999) is an exception in this regard.

18 The Taiwan Solidarity Union, an extremist pro-independence political party, called the ECFA a 'suicidal policy'. See *Liberty Times*, 22 March 2010, available at www.libertytimes.com.tw/2010/new/mar/22/today-t1.htm (accessed 25 July 2014). Moreover, the former Chairwoman of the Democratic Progressive Party, Tsai Ing-Wen, in the early phase of her presidential campaign, also opposed the signing of the ECFA, viewing it as a policy that undermined Taiwan's competitiveness. See *Liberty Times*, 30 April 2009, available at www.libertytimes.com.tw/2009/new/apr/30/today-fo2–2.htm (accessed 25 July 2014). However, Tsai modified her stance later on during the presidential campaign.

19 This can be easily proven by differentiating (18) with respect to

$$\frac{\partial(\tilde{U}_G - \bar{U}_G^h)}{\partial a} = u(v_x^l) - u(\tilde{v}_x^h) = u[p_x^l y_x(\kappa_x^{*l}) - (1-\pi^*)\kappa_x^{*l}] - u[p_x^h y_x(\kappa_x^{*l}) - (1-\pi^*)\kappa_x^{*l}] \tag{19}$$

Since $p_x^l > p_x^h =$ and $u' \geq 0$, it is clear that

$$\frac{\partial(\tilde{U}_G - \bar{U}_G^h)}{\partial a} \geq 0 \tag{20}$$

and $\tilde{U}_G - \bar{U}_G^h$ is monotonically increasing in a.

20 This can be easily shown by differentiating (22) with respect to a

$$\frac{\partial(\tilde{U}_G^l - U_G)}{\partial a} = u(\tilde{v}_x^l) - u(v_x^h) = u[p_x^l y_x(\kappa_x^{*h}) - (1-\pi^*)\kappa_x^{*h}] - u[p_x^h y_x(\kappa_x^{*h}) - (1-\pi^*)\kappa_x^{*h}] \tag{23}$$

For the same reasons as those stated in the previous case, it is clear that

$$\frac{\partial(\tilde{U}_G^l - U_G)}{\partial a} \geq 0 \tag{24}$$

and $\vec{U}_G^l - U_G$ is also monotonically increasing in a.

21 It can be easily seen from the following inequality

$$\frac{C_D - [u(v_m^l) - u(v_m^h)]}{u(v_x^l) - u(v_x^h)} \geq \frac{u(\tilde{v}_m^h) - u(v_m^l)}{u(v_x^l) - u(\tilde{v}_x^h)}, \tag{29}$$

which holds when $u(v_x^h) \geq u(\tilde{v}_x^h)$. Moreover, according to the assumption that $u' \geq 0$, (28) follows.

22 Jeitschko and Normann (2012), in contrast, offer a model with a stochastic signal.
23 The sign of the change differs between the export and the import-competing sectors.
24 What should be noted here is that we assume all private agents in country j face the same strategic situation. In other words, they are homogeneous in facing uncertainties in Taipei's signals when making their investment decisions.
25 For example, they must include all the essential factors of the gravity equation.
26 Given the property of linearity, $E[\Sigma_j v_j^{*l}|X_j^l, r_j = 1]$ can be broken down to the summation of the expectation of return in individual countries, $\Sigma_j E[v_j^{*l}|X_j^l, r_j = 1]$.
27 If the bias is absent, there is no difference between deterministic and stochastic signals since the expected values of v_j^{*l} will be identical.
28 The period under the DPP administration between 2000 and 2008 was filled with examples of diplomatic politicking. For instance, the former president, Chen Shui-Bian, used to take advantage of layovers in the US to meet with US politicians. This is what people call 'transit diplomacy'. See *United Daily*, 9 May 2008, available at http:// mag.udn.com/mag/abian/storypage.jsp?f_ART_ID=37005 (accessed 25 July 2014).
29 If the economic argument is correct, then the political argument based on the concept of security externalities will simply follow. That is, if signing the ECFA means higher economic integration with mainland China at the price of Taiwan's economic connections with the rest of the world, the resulting gains in trade will be mainly harvested by Beijing, which will increase Beijing's resources and leverage against Taipei.

References

China Post (2008) 'Inheritance, Gift Tax Rate Cut to 10 per cent', *The China Post*, 4 December available at www.chinapost. com.tw/taiwan/business/2008/12/04/186065/ Inheritance-gift.htm (accessed 25 July 2014).

Dent, Christopher M. (2009) 'Taiwan and the New East Asian Regionalism', *Issues and Studies*, 45, 4: 107–158.

Elkins, Zachary, Guzman, Andrew T., and Simmons, Beth A. (2006) 'Competing for Capital: The Diffusion of Bilateral Investment Treaties, 1960–2000', *International Organization*, 60: 811–846.

Fearon, James D. (1997) 'Signaling Foreign Policy Interests: Tying Hands versus Sinking Costs', *Journal of Conflict Resolution*, 41, 1: 68–90.

Ferguson, Niall, and Schularick, Moritz (2007) ' 'Chimerica' and the Global Asset Market Boom', *International Finance*, 10, 3: 215–239.

Gilley, Bruce (2010) 'Not So Dire Straits: How the Finlandization of Taiwan Benefits U.S. Security', *Foreign Affairs*, 89, 1: 44–60.

Gowa, J., and Mansfield, Edward D. (1993) 'Power-Politics and International Trade', *American Political Science Review*, 87, 2: 408–420.

Grossman, Gene M., and Helpman, Elhanan (1994) 'Protection for Sale', *American Economic Review*, 84, 4: 833–850.

Jeitschko, Thomas D., and Normann, Hans-Theo (2012) 'Signaling in Deterministic and Stochastic Settings', *Journal of Economic Behaviour and Organization*, 82: 39–55.

Kastner, Scott L. (2007) 'When Do Conflicting Political Relations Affect International Trade?' *Journal of Conflict Resolution*, 51, 4: 664–668.

Keshk, Omar M. G., Pollins, Brian M., and Reuveny, Rafael (2004) 'Trade Still Follows the Flag: The Primacy of Politics in a Simultaneous Model of Interdependence and Armed Conflict', *Journal of Politics*, 66, 4: 1155–1179.

Lee, Dwight R., and Vedder, Richard (1996) 'The Political Economy of the Peace Dividend', *Public Choice*, 88, 1/2: 29–42.

Mitra, Devashish (1999) 'Endogenous Lobby Formation and Endogenous Protection: A Long-Run Model of Trade Policy Determination', *American Economic Review*, 89, 5: 1116–1134.

Ong, Wenchi (2010) 'Reaping Cross-Strait Peace Dividend', *Uday India*, 22 May.

Rose, Andrew K., and Spiegel, Mark M. (2011) 'The Olympic Effect', *The Economic Journal*, 121: 652–677.

Taipei Times (2011) '2012 Elections: Tsai Says she is "Open-minded" on China Visit', 26 November, available at www.taipeitimes.com/News/front/archives/2011/11/26/2003519237 (accessed 25 July 2014).

Taipei Times (2012) 'China Aiming 200 More Missiles at Taiwan: MND', 4 September, available at www.taipeitimes.com/News/front/archives/2012/09/04/2003541913 (accessed 25 July 2014).

8 Political competition framed by the China factor?

Looking beyond the 2012 presidential election

Nai-Teh Wu

Ever since Taiwan's democratic transition in the late 1980s, one of its most important political issues has been the question of how to handle relations with China. The salience of this issue in Taiwan's politics also manifests itself in the fact that national identity has become the only dividing line between Taiwan's two main political parties. In recent years, as economic ties between Taiwan and China have strengthened and the two economies have integrated, the impact of the China factor on Taiwanese politics has also been growing. If China's economic development does not halt or radically change course, the impact of this factor is likely to persist into the foreseeable future. What will become of cross-Strait relations if on one side, Taiwan starts to experience a growing desire for independence, while on the other, China continues to claim sovereignty over Taiwan? To be sure, the answer to this question still lies in the future. An examination of the present situation, however, may help to shed light on the impact of the China factor on Taiwanese politics after more than a decade of cross-Strait economic integration.

The China factor has affected Taiwanese politics in at least two ways. First of all, there is the influence of the China factor on the national identity of the general public, which has been leaning towards Taiwanese nationalism since the democratic transition of Taiwan in the late 1980s. In this context, the question to be considered is this: have the developments that have taken place in recent years, such as Taiwan's heavy reliance on the Chinese economy, China's rising influence in international politics and the expansion of the Chinese military, weakened 'Taiwanese identity' and even increased the Taiwanese people's 'Chinese identity?' I focused on this important question in a previous study, using the data from a survey conducted in 2011. This previous study revealed that the developments mentioned above did not impact on national identity trends. Taiwanese identity continued to grow stronger, while Chinese identity continued to weaken (Wu 2012). The findings from the 2013 survey, on which this chapter is based, did not differ much from those obtained two years previously: a mere 21 per cent of respondents said that they would be willing to unite with China, even if China were to become a democratic country with sound economic and social development. Within this same group, 8.2 per cent would also accept an independent Taiwan. The 'true Chinese nationalists' therefore constituted only 12.9 per cent of the group. This figure was almost the same in 2011 (see Appendix 1).

The second impact of the China factor on Taiwan's politics is likely to be on the electoral competition for ruling power. Although the China factor appears to have had little influence with regard to shaping the national identity of Taiwan's people, it might still be assumed to wield significant influence on the political competition in Taiwan, as witnessed by both the campaigns and the turnouts for national elections in recent years. Taiwan's electorate seems to take into serious consideration the benefits of economic integration with China and hence tends to favour the political party that adopts a position inclined towards active engagement with China. The China factor was indeed the most salient, if not the only, issue during the 2012 presidential election. This issue took the form of whether Taiwan should accept the 1992 Consensus, which Beijing claimed as the bottom line for its dealings with Taiwan. The tenets of the Consensus are the principle that there is only one China and that Taiwan is part of China. Taiwan's Kuomintang (KMT) administration has honoured the Consensus in order to achieve active engagement with China but has also added another condition, that the two sides define 'China' differently. The opposition Democratic Progressive Party (DPP), however, has bluntly rejected the existence of any such consensus. Since the official position of the DPP is pro-independence, it is obliged to assert Taiwan's claim to sovereignty and the right to full self-determination.

This difference in the parties' positions on the 1992 Consensus became the most salient issue in the presidential campaign for the 2012 election. Close to the end of the campaign, some renowned business figures, presumably by arrangement with the ruling KMT, publicly questioned the DPP's position on the 1992 Consensus. These prominent personalities included the HTC chairwoman, Cher Wang, the Evergreen chairman, Chang Yung-Fa, the Foxconn founder, Terry Gou, and the Ruentex chairman, Samuel Yin. HTC's Cher Wang even repeated, in both Taiwanese dialect and Mandarin, that 'it's hard to imagine [what] bilateral relations [would be like] without the 1992 Consensus'.[1] Ms Wang's comment was broadcast repeatedly by all television news agencies in the final days of the presidential campaign. It became possibly the most famous phrase of the election.

After the ruling KMT won the presidential election (51.60 per cent against 45.63 per cent for the DPP), many pundits and influential figures among the DPP attributed the party's defeat to its rejection of the 1992 Consensus. Some prominent DPP members were quoted as saying that 'Praying to Matsu [Goddess of the Sea] and taking care of the stomach are both necessary'. In other words, although the DPP has to honour the core value of national sovereignty in its political ideals, it also needs to face the reality of China's impact on the Taiwanese economy. The discussions and sometimes disputes over whether the DPP should change its official position on Taiwan independence were still ongoing at the end of 2013, when this chapter was written. Some powerful figures in the party, including the Legislative Yuan caucus leader Ke Jian-Ming, even advocated 'freezing' or suspending the clause referring to Taiwan's independence in the party's platform.

But did the China factor and, more specifically, the 1992 Consensus contribute to the defeat of the DPP and the victory of the ruling KMT? If so, then how significantly? And more importantly, will the China factor continue to wield influence on, or even frame, Taiwan's political competition? This chapter aims to assess the effects of the China factor on the 2012 presidential election. To be sure, the electoral outcome was influenced by various factors, including party identification, candidates' image, performance and leadership abilities, the economy, and the effect of social networks or mobilization. The telephone poll survey, which this research relies on, does not supply sufficient information for a comprehensive analysis of the election outcome. Below, the limited information gathered from the poll is used to examine whether the China factor had a significant impact on the 2012 presidential election and also on political competition in general. The preliminary findings seem to suggest that the China factor did contribute significantly to the outcome of this particular election. In addition, the findings also suggest that this same factor is likely to frame political competition in the future, largely to the DPP's disadvantage, so long as the trend towards cross-Strait economic integration continues and China adheres uncompromisingly to its position on the 1992 Consensus. But as the data in this chapter also shows, there may be some leeway for the DPP to escape from its disadvantageous position. This, however, will require vision, imagination and most of all leadership on the part of its leaders.

Independent voters: the key to winning elections

Among the various factors that influence voting behaviours, party identification may be the most important, whether in the US (Campbell *et al.* 1976; Miller and Shanks 1996), Europe (Budge *et al.* 1976) or Taiwan. Party identification is mostly long-term and often stable. It may be formed during the years of adolescence and may persist throughout a voter's adult life. It thus becomes the deciding factor in both electoral support and the stability of a country's political environment. It is generally formed by the parties' positions during major historical events: for example, in the case of the United States of America, these could be the Civil War, the economic depression in the 1920s, and the civil rights movement in the 1960s. In Taiwan, the most important eras that have formed party identities were the Japanese colonization from 1895 to 1945 and the KMT authoritarianism from 1945 to 1987. Life experiences during these two eras has largely determined the party allegiance of Taiwanese voters. The generations who came of age in the era after democratic transition have inherited their party identity mainly from their parents through family socialization (Wu 1999).

We can see from Table 8.1 that, as for American voters, political identification is the most important factor in vote decisions. (In the current survey, the question that we have asked for the purpose of measuring party identification is: 'Which of the following political parties do you support: KMT, DPP, Taiwan Solidarity Union, or the New Party?') Among those who identified with both of

Table 8.1 Party identity and voting, 2013 (*N* (%))

[Question] *Which of the following political parties are you a supporter of?*

	Voting				
	Ma (KMT)	*Tsai (DPP)*	*Absentee*	*Others*	*Total*
KMT	352	5	42	31	430
	(81.9)	(1.2)	(9.8)	(7.2)	(100)
	(66.8)	(1.7)	(19.0)	(18.1)	(35.3)
People First Party	12	4	9	12	37
	(32.4)	(10.8)	(24.3)	(32.4)	(100)
	(2.3)	(1.3)	(4.1)	(7.0)	(3.0)
New Party	4	0	1	1	6
	(66.7)	(.0)	(16.7)	(16.7)	(100)
	(.8)	(.0)	(.5)	(.6)	(.5)
DPP	14	198	28	14	254
	(5.5)	(78.0)	(11.0)	(5.5)	(100)
	(2.7)	(66.4)	(12.7)	(8.2)	(20.9)
Taiwan Solidarity Union	1	10	1	3	15
	(6.7)	(66.7)	(6.7)	(20.0)	(100)
	(.3)	(3.4)	(.5)	(1.8)	(1.2)
Independents	144	81	140	110	475
	(30.3)	(17.1)	(29.5)	(23.2)	(100)
	(27.3)	(27.2)	(63.3)	(64.3)	(39.0)
Total	527	298	221	171	1217
	(43.3)	(24.5)	(18.2)	(14.1)	(100)
	(100)	(100)	(100)	(100)	(100)
(Actual turn-out) (%)	51.6	45.6	25.6		74.4

Notes
Chi-square=678.089.
df=10.
$p<0.001$.

the main political parties, around 80 per cent voted for the party with which they identify. Those who voted for the opposing party were few (1.2 per cent of KMT identifiers voted for Tsai Ying-Wen, the DPP candidate, while 5.5 per cent of DPP identifiers voted for Ma Ying-Jeou, the KMT candidate). The high overlap between party identification and electoral support shows that very few, if any, other factors affected the voting choice of party identifiers. A party identifier either votes for the party he/she identifies with or does not vote at all. To evaluate the effect of the China factor in Taiwanese elections, we may have to focus on those voters who do not identify with any particular political party, that is, the independent voters. In the absence of any allegiance to any political party, their voting decisions are more likely to be influenced by policy positions or a candidate's performance. In order to evaluate the impact of the China factor on the 2012 presidential election, we thus have to investigate how the independent voters' decisions were affected by their attitude to the 1992 Consensus.

A preliminary examination of independent voters' voting behaviours reveals, first, that they contributed the highest percentage of absentee voting (29.5 per cent) among all party-allegiance groups. Compared with voters with party identification, the independent voters have a more indifferent attitude to politics. Similar findings have been revealed in European and American voting studies. In the 2012 presidential election in Taiwan, independent voters were three times more likely to abstain from voting than those who identified with the two main political parties. But the more important question for the purpose of this chapter is how they voted. As the figures in Table 8.1 show, the independent voters were more significantly inclined to vote for the KMT than for the DPP, 30.3 per cent to 17.1 per cent. The same table also shows that, among the general electorate, the proportion of the KMT identifiers was already higher than that of the DPP identifiers (35.3 per cent and 20.9 per cent respectively). Together, these two sets of figures create a great disadvantage for the DPP. As party identity is largely formed by long-term trends and factors, these can hardly be turned around by any political party. The question that needs to be tackled, therefore, with regard to understanding the impact of China's rise on Taiwan's political competition is: what sort of role does the China factor play in the independent voters' support for the KMT? If the China factor played a significant role in the independent voters' voting decisions, it could lead to the conclusion that the China factor will also frame future political competition in the country.

When probing the issue of the independent voters' significantly higher support for the KMT, the first potential factor to consider is national identity. National identity is the most significant issue in the country's current politics. It also forms the only dividing line between the two political parties. Most voters who identify with the DPP tend to be Taiwanese nationalists, while those are inclined to identify with China are more likely to support the KMT. Although independent voters lack any specific party allegiance, they still retain their national identity to some extent. Could the disparities in the independent voters' support for the two parties be caused by their stance on national identity? Did the independent voters show more support for the KMT because they were more inclined towards Chinese nationalism, or at least less resistant to the latter ideology?

An analysis of the independent voters' voting decisions, however, does not reveal any significant relationship between national identity and voting behaviours. Table 8.2 seems to illustrate some relationship between voting and national identity. Among the independent voters, only Taiwanese nationalists were more likely to vote for the DPP. The DPP is at a disadvantage compared with all other nationalist groups. The proportion of Chinese nationalists who voted for the DPP was very low – less than 10 per cent. Those with 'dual identities' (do not oppose either Taiwan independence or Chinese unification) were three times more likely to vote for the KMT than for the DPP (50 per cent and 15 per cent respectively). Those who preferred the status quo (opposed to both independence and

Table 8.2 National identity and voting: independent voters, 2013 (*N* (%))

[Questions]
If Taiwan independence would not precipitate a war, do you agree that Taiwan should become an independent country?
If Taiwan and China were to become comparatively developed economically, socially and politically, do you agree that the two sides should be unified into one country?

[Questions]
Did you vote last year in the 2012 presidential election?
If so, whom did you vote for?

	Voting				
	Ma (KMT)	*Tsai (DPP)*	*Absentee*	*Others*	*Total*
Taiwanese nationalist	39 (23.2) (27.1)	44 (26.2) (54.3)	51 (30.4) (36.4)	34 (20.2) (35.8)	168 (100) (36.5)
Dual identity	20 (50.0) (13.9)	6 (15.0) (7.4)	11 (27.5) (7.9)	3 (7.5) (3.2)	40 (100) (8.7)
Chinese nationalist	27 (48.2) (18.8)	5 (8.9) (6.2)	15 (26.8) (10.7)	9 (16.1) (9.5)	56 (100) (12.2)
Status-quo	50 (33.3) (34.7)	22 (14.7) (27.2)	49 (32.7) (35.0)	29 (19.3) (30.5)	150 (100) (32.6)
Others	8 (17.4) (5.6)	4 (8.7) (4.9)	14 (30.4) (10.0)	20 (43.5) (21.1)	46 (100) (10.0)
Total	144 (31.3) (100)	81 (17.6) (100)	140 (30.4) (100)	95 (20.7) (100)	460 (100) (100)

Notes
Chi-square=44.794.
df=12.
p<0.001.

unification) were two times more likely to vote for the KMT than for the DPP (33.3 per cent and 14.7 per cent respectively). But although the DPP had an advantage due to the Taiwanese nationalists, this advantage was not substantial – 26.2 per cent of this group voted for the DPP, while as many as 23.2 per cent voted for the KMT. The difference is small. We can conclude from these figures that the DPP lost support in all the nationalist groups among the independents, even in its strongest constituency of Taiwanese nationalists. Thus national identity did not seem to be a factor in the independent voters' rejection of the DPP, but the question remains as to whether the China factor played a part in their rejection of the DPP.

The construction of the 1992 Consensus

It was through disagreement on the 1992 Consensus that the China factor manifested itself in the previous presidential election. The 1992 Consensus has been a much-debated topic in Taiwanese politics for the last 10 to 15 years, especially during the DPP's rule from 2000 to 2008. The Consensus originated in October 1992 when the governments of Taiwan and China first engaged in semi-official dialogue. Officials of the two governments met in Hong Kong to discuss the issue of the authentication of official documents – one side represented by China's Association for Relations Across the Taiwan Strait (ARATS) and the other by Taiwan's Straits Exchange Foundation (SEF). Before the meeting was held, China's ARATS promulgated adherence to the 'One China Principle' as a precondition for the signing of any document authentication agreement which would be on the table for the talks. To substantiate this precondition, China made a side proposal referring to five different modes, including the principle that 'the authentication of documents between the two sides of the Strait belongs to China's domestic affairs' and that 'both sides of the Strait strongly uphold the One China Principle' (Su and Cheng 2002).[2] This was rejected by Taiwan's SEF. Meanwhile, Taiwan's now-defunct National Unification Council adopted a resolution for the One China Principle: 'The two sides of the Strait have different opinions as to the meaning of "One China". To the Chinese Communist authority, "one China" means the "People's Republic of China (PRC)".... We, on the other hand, consider "one China" to mean the Republic of China (ROC), founded in 1911'.

When the formal negotiations started in Hong Kong, Taiwan responded to China's One China Principle by noting that 'while the two sides of the Taiwan Strait, in the process of their common effort to achieve national unification, both adhere to the principle of one China, they differ from each other on the acknowledgement of the meaning of One China'. As expected, China did not accept this formulation of the One China Principle. During the course of the negotiations, Taiwan's government authorized the SEF to propose a solution to the disagreement by suggesting that both sides 'orally' state their own formulation of the One China Principle. Immediately after rejecting Taiwan's proposal that the two sides state their positions in a verbal announcement, China's delegates left Hong Kong. Days later, however, China's ARATS sent a cable message to Taiwan's SEF, saying that it was willing to 'respect and accept' the SEF's proposal that each side announce its position in an oral statement. Two weeks later, the ARATS wrote to the SEF, stating: 'At these working-level negotiations in Hong Kong, SEF representatives proposed that each side use respective verbal announcements to state the One China Principle. We will respect and accept the proposal'. Many who took part in the negotiations on behalf of Taiwan considered this in terms of the 1992 Consensus between the two sides of the Strait: both agree on the One China Principle, but each side verbally states its respective interpretation of 'One China'. In 1993, the ARATS chairman Wang Daohan and the SEF chairman Koo Chen-Fu met in Singapore for high-level negotiations. Neither party disputed the One China Principle.

Then, in June 1995, when President Lee Teng-Hui visited Cornell University, China's ARATS claimed that the visit was an amplification of the 'One China, Different Interpretations' principle, and that it also constituted a violation of the One China Principle. China's ARATS, in the meantime, denied the existence of the 1992 Consensus. Less than one year later, during Taiwan's first direct presidential election in March 1996, China fired test missiles into the seawaters near Taiwan. Not only were cross-Strait dialogues disrupted, but Chinese government officials also publicly denied that the two governments had reached consensus on 'One China, Different Interpretations'. In July 1999, Lee Teng-Hui proclaimed his 'Two State Theory', which was a clear indication that the Taiwanese government would no longer honour the principle of 'One China'. The 1992 Consensus was thus dismissed by both China and Taiwan.

In 2000, when the pro-independence DPP won its first presidential election, the Chinese government changed its previous attitude to the 1992 Consensus. In response to Chen Shui-Bian's inaugural address, the Chinese government stated that for cross-Strait dialogues to resume, both sides 'must consent to the agreement reached in 1992 that both sides would uphold orally the One China principle'. Concurrently, the political forces in Taiwan that supported unification (or at least were opposed to Taiwan's achieving independence) had begun propagating the recognition of the 1992 Consensus as the basis for resuming dialogues with China. In the 2004 presidential election that followed, however, the KMT presidential candidate and party chairman Lien Chan surprisingly pledged at an international press conference that his party would abandon its long-held goal of unification: 'There's no dispute that there are two different states on each side of the Strait', he said (*China Times*, 17 December 2003). In the last days of the election campaign, Lien Chan even demonstrated that he identified with Taiwan by kneeling on the ground to kiss Taiwan's soil. However, these sentiments, which came in the midst of a political campaign, did not last beyond the election season. Shortly afterwards, the KMT camp accepted the 1992 Consensus; ever since the KMT regained power in 2008, it has continued semi-official talks with China on the basis of the 1992 Consensus. Meanwhile, the DPP has continued to reject the Consensus and has sometimes even denied its existence.

(Mis-)understanding the 1992 Consensus

In order to assess the influence of policies on voters' voting decisions, we first have to establish the voters' positions on the specific issues. We then have to see if the voters are aware of the position of each party/candidate on these issues. Lastly, we have to assess whether the position of the policy concerned is a significant factor in voters' decisions. Therefore, to evaluate the effect of the 1992 Consensus on the election result, we first need to look at the voters' stances, especially those of the independent voters, on the issues. Many academic researchers in the US have found that American voters generally have poor knowledge of public policy issues in the election campaigns.[3] How well, one may ask, do Taiwanese voters understand the issues that shape the two political parties' major policies and directions? Table 8.3 reveals some information that is both important and interesting. First, despite the fact that the 1992 Consensus was the most disputed topic in the run-up to the election and was also deemed to be the most decisive factor, it did not seem to have any overwhelming public support. On the whole, less than 40 per cent of those sampled supported the Consensus. Although the KMT identifiers showed more support for the Consensus than the DPP identifiers or the independent voters, only 60 per cent of the KMT supporters backed the policy.

Another interesting observation to be drawn from Table 8.3 is that voters generally thought they did not understand this policy – although it had generated such intense discussions and disputes between the opposing candidates in the election. As many as 62.9 per cent of the respondents reported that they did not understand the 1992 Consensus and only 20.4 per cent said that they fully

Table 8.3 Attitudes concerning the 1992 Consensus (*N* (%))

[Questions]
If your friend asks you to explain the 1992 Consensus, do you feel you understand the issue enough to do that?
Do you or do you not support the 1992 Consensus?

Total KMT identifiers DPP identifiers Independent voters	Understand	Don't understand	Never heard of it	Total
Support	172 (35.9)	307 (64.1)		479 (38.6)
	109 (38.9)	171 (61.1)		280 (59.2)
	9 (25.0)	27 (75.0)		36 (13.4)
	52 (33.8)	102 (66.2)		154 (32.4)
Don't support	72 (21.7)	260 (78.3)		332 (26.8)
	6 (10.3)	52 (89.7)		58 (12.3)
	38 (24.5)	117 (75.5)		155 (57.6)
	26 (22.6)	89 (77.4)		115 (24.2)
Others (did not care/others/ declined to respond)	7 (8.6)	74 (91.4)		81 (6.5)
	3 (12.0)	22 (88.0)		25 (5.3)
	2 (18.2)	9 (81.8)		11 (4.1)
	1 (2.3)	42 (97.7)		43 (9.1)
Don't know	2 (1.4)	140 (98.6)		142 (11.4)
	0 (.0)	43 (100)		43 (9.1)
	0 (.0)	31 (100)		31 (11.5)
	2 (3.0)	64 (97.0)		66 (14.1)
Never heard of it			207 (100)	207 (16.7)
			67 (100)	67 (14.2)
			36 (100)	36 (13.4)
			96 (100)	96 (20.2)
Total	253 (20.4)	781 (62.9)	207 (16.7)	1241 (100)
	118 (24.9)	288 (60.9)	67 (14.2)	473 (100)
	49 (18.2)	184 (68.4)	36 (13.4)	269 (100)
	81 (17.1)	297 (62.7)	96 (20.3)	474 (100)

understood the Consensus. This self-reported lack of understanding is found across all the lines of party support. More KMT identifiers (24.9 per cent) than DPP identifiers or independent voters (18.2 per cent and 17.1 per cent) said that they understood the Consensus. In other words, despite the fact that the KMT identifiers showed more support for the 1992 Consensus, they were hardly any more knowledgeable about the issue than other groups of voters.

The most important phenomenon emerging from Table 8.3, however, is that the supporters of the 1992 Consensus greatly outnumbered those who said they understood the Consensus. A mere 20 per cent of respondents said they understood it, but almost twice as many said they supported it (38.6 per cent). Among them, the KMT identifiers were in the majority, constituting almost 60 per cent of the group (59.2 per cent). The DPP identifiers who also supported the Consensus made up the smallest group, at around 10 per cent. The great difference between the numbers of those who claimed to understand the 1992 Consensus and those who supported it means that many people who supported the Consensus actually did not think they understood it. As many as 64.1 per cent of those supporting the Consensus said that they did not know what it was. If the majority of the public did not understand the Consensus, then what exactly were they supporting? And with regard to those on the other side, what exactly were they opposing?

Furthermore, as shown by Table 8.4, a sweeping majority of the general public (77.9 per cent) was opposed to employing the Consensus as a principle for discussing economic issues with China. Only 19.4 per cent of respondents agreed to employ the underlying principle of the Consensus, that 'there is only one China, and Taiwan is a part of China'. But, as previously demonstrated, close to 40 per cent of the total number of respondents said they supported the 1992 Consensus. That is, out of all those respondents who said they supported employing the Consensus as the basis for discussing economic issues with China, only half agreed with its content. The percentage of KMT identifiers who supported the notion of employing the Consensus and the underlying principle mentioned above as the basis for economic exchanges with China (28.9 per cent) was slightly higher than that of the DPP identifiers (16.7 per cent) and independent voters (25.3 per cent) who held the same view. The differences, however, are much less significant than commonly assumed. Close to 70 per cent of the KMT identifiers who supported the 1992 Consensus did not agree with its content (68.9 per cent). Similarly, in the case of the independent voters concerned, more than 70 per cent of those who supported the 1992 Consensus did not agree with the content.

To sum up, from the findings mentioned above, the following intriguing phenomena emerge:

1   Only 32.4 per cent of the Taiwanese general public supported the 1992 Consensus.
2   Among those who supported the 1992 Consensus, the majority (64.1 per cent) said that they did not understand its content.
3   Among these same supporters of the 1992 Consensus, an even larger majority (71.6 per cent) did not agree with its content.

Table 8.4 1992 Consensus, support and awareness, 2013 (*N* (%))

[Questions]
Do you support the 1992 Consensus?
Do you agree with applying the principle of 'there is only one China, and Taiwan is a part of China' to Taiwan's economic relationships with China?

Total KMT identifiers DPP identifiers Independent voters	Agree	Don't agree	Other	Total
1992 Consensus				
Support	128 (26.7)	343 (71.6)	8 (1.7)	479 (38.5)
	81 (28.9)	193 (68.9)	6 (2.1)	280 (59.2)
	6 (16.7)	30 (83.3)	0 (0.0)	36 (13.4)
	39 (25.3)	113 (73.4)	2 (1.3)	154 (32.4)
Not support	28 (8.4)	303 (91.3)	1 (0.3)	332 (26.7)
	9 (15.5)	49 (84.5)	0 (0.0)	58 (12.3)
	11 (7.1)	144 (92.9)	0 (0.0)	155 (57.6)
	8 (7.0)	106 (92.2)	1 (0.9)	115 (24.2)
Other	19 (23.2)	58 (70.7)	5 (6.1)	82 (6.6)
	7 (28.0)	17 (68.0)	1 (4.0)	25 (5.3)
	1 (9.1)	10 (90.9)	0 (0.0)	11 (4.1)
	11 (25.6)	28 (65.1)	4 (9.3)	43 (9.1)
Don't know	25 (17.5)	116 (81.1)	2 (1.4)	143 (11.5)
	10 (23.3)	33 (76.7)	0 (0.0)	43 (9.1)
	4 (12.9)	27 (87.1)	0 (0.0)	31 (11.5)
	11 (16.4)	54 (80.6)	2 (3.0)	67 (14.1)
Never heard of it	41 (19.8)	148 (71.5)	18 (8.7)	207 (16.7)
	17 (25.4)	46 (68.7)	4 (6.0)	67 (14.2)
	4 (11.1)	31 (86.1)	1 (2.8)	36 (13.4)
	19 (19.8)	65 (67.7)	12 (12.5)	96 (20.2)
Total	241 (19.4)	968 (77.9)	34 (2.7)	1243 (100)
	124 (26.2)	338 (71.5)	11 (2.3)	473 (100)
	26 (9.7)	242 (90.0)	1 (0.4)	269 (100)
	88 (18.5)	366 (77.1)	21 (4.4)	475 (100)

We see a similar pattern in the group of independent voters concerned here: only around 30 per cent supported the 1992 Consensus, 65 per cent said that they did not understand what it was, and 73 per cent did not agree with its content. It may be concluded from the above findings that the 1992 Consensus was not the main contributing factor in the DPP's defeat in the presidential election and, further, that it was not the main factor in the high levels of support shown by the independent voters for the KMT. These conclusions, however, should not be accepted without further examination; there may be some other explanation, as will be discussed below.

One possible explanation could be that although the general public did not fully understand the 1992 Consensus, they still saw it as a clue to understanding the respective parties' positions on economic relations with China. For example, the independent voters may not have fully understood the 1992 Consensus, but by observing whether the parties and candidates opposed or supported it they were able to gain a picture of the fundamental positions of the parties and candidates on Taiwan's economic relationship with China. On the other hand, some of the independent voters also held their own specific views on this issue and cast their votes accordingly.

Between economic gains and political loss: a dilemma

The 2011 survey revealed that Taiwan's general public was faced with two dilemmas at the same time regarding economic relations with China. The first dilemma concerned the co-existence of potential economic gain and potential political loss. On the one hand, the majority of the public (56.6 per cent) had a positive attitude towards cross-Strait economic relations. On the other, the majority (61.5 per cent) also believed that cross-Strait economic relations would make it more difficult for Taiwan to maintain the status quo and would also make unification easier (60.1 per cent). This dilemma had not disappeared even two years later. In the 2013 survey, 55.8 per cent of the respondents had a positive attitude towards cross-Strait economic relations, while 56.0 per cent also believed that cross-Strait economic relations would make it more difficult for Taiwan to maintain the status quo, and 61.4 per cent of them believed that this would make unification easier. These three percentages, which revealed the co-existence of a positive attitude towards economic relations with China (because of potential economic benefits) and a negative attitude towards economic relations with China (because of concern about political losses), did not change over the two-year period.

In addition to the dilemma posed by potential economic benefits and political losses, Taiwanese voters were faced with a second dilemma, deriving from their concerns about the two main political parties, albeit for different reasons. In the 2011 survey, 50.0 per cent of the respondents agreed that the DPP was 'overly opposed to relations with mainland China'. At the same time, 53.9 per cent believed that the KMT was 'overly accommodative to the position of Chinese government'. In the 2013 survey, these two figures had not changed. Out of all the respondents, 56.9 per cent agreed that the DPP was 'overly opposed to relations with mainland China', while 59.7 per cent thought that the KMT was 'overly accommodative to the Chinese government'. The Taiwanese voters' dissatisfaction with the two political parties remained – one party was considered overly opposed to China and the other overly inclined towards China.

Independent voters' attitudes were consistent with those of all the respondents as a whole. The former, too, were trapped in the dilemma posed by potential economic benefits and potential political losses and shared the same feelings of concern and dissatisfaction regarding the two political parties. Among the independent voters, 55.4 per cent thought that the DPP was 'overly opposed to relations with mainland China', while 61.9 per cent thought that the KMT was 'overly accommodative to the position of Chinese government'. When dissatisfied with both of the political parties, how did the independent voters cast their votes? It could be speculated that those who thought the DPP was overly opposed to China were more likely to vote for the KMT, and those who thought the KMT was overly inclined towards China were more likely to vote for the DPP. Tables 8.5 and 8.6 reveal that this speculation is only partially correct. Independent voters who thought that the DPP was overly opposed to China were twice as likely to vote for the KMT as for the DPP. It is not surprising that those who thought the DPP was overly opposed to China were more inclined to vote for the KMT. It should be noted, however, that the votes of the independent voters who thought that the KMT was overly inclined towards China were split almost equally between the DPP and the KMT. The DPP did not receive the overwhelming support of those who opposed the KMT's overly accommodative position towards China. In other words, independent voters who found the KMT overly inclined towards China did not show stronger support for the DPP.

Another observation is related to voters who were not happy with the positions of the parties. Close to 40 per cent of the independent voters (37.7 per cent) thought that while the DPP was overly opposed to China, the KMT was also overly inclined towards China. Among this group of voters who had doubts about both political parties, 60 per cent supported the KMT and 40 per cent supported the DPP. One cause of this imbalance may have been that the economic benefits outweighed the concern aroused by the KMT's inclination towards China. It is possible that although some thought that the KMT was overly

Table 8.5 The DPP's position on China: independent voters, 2013 (*N* (%))

[Question] *Some people say 'The DPP is overly opposed to relations with Mainland China'. Do you agree with them?*

Voting for					
DPP overly opposed to China	Ma (KMT)	Tsai (DPP)	Absentee	Other	Total
Agree	97	42	69	48	256
	(37.9)	(16.4)	(27.0)	(18.8)	(100)
	(67.4)	(51.9)	(49.3)	(49.5)	(55.4)
Don't agree	43	37	63	39	182
	(23.6)	(20.3)	(34.6)	(21.4)	(100)
	(29.9)	(45.7)	(45.0)	(40.2)	(39.4)
Don't know/declined to answer	4	2	8	10	24
	(16.7)	(8.3)	(33.3)	(41.7)	(100)
	(2.8)	(2.5)	(5.7)	(10.3)	(5.2)
Total	144	81	140	97	462
	(31.2)	(17.5)	(30.3)	(21.0)	(100)
	(100)	(100)	(100)	(100)	(100)

Notes
Chi-square = 18.461.
df = 6.
$p < 0.01$.

Table 8.6 The KMT's position on China: independent voters, 2013 (*N* (%))

[Question] *Some people say 'The KMT is overly inclined towards the Chinese government'. Do you agree with them?*

Voting for					
KMT overly inclined towards China	Ma (KMT)	Tsai (DPP)	Absentee	Others	Total
Agree	78	72	84	52	286
	(27.3)	(25.2)	(29.4)	(18.2)	(100)
	(54.2)	(88.9)	(60.0)	(53.6)	(61.9)
Don't agree	62	8	47	35	152
	(40.8)	(5.3)	(30.9)	(23.0)	(100)
	(43.1)	(9.9)	(33.6)	(36.1)	(32.9)
Don't know	4	1	9	10	24
	(16.7)	(4.2)	(37.5)	(41.7)	(100)
	(2.8)	(1.2)	(6.4)	(10.3)	(5.2)
Total	144	81	140	97	462
	(31.2)	(17.5)	(30.3)	(21.0)	(100)
	(100)	(100)	(100)	(100)	(100)

Notes
Chi-square$=39.323$.
df$=6$.
$p<0.001$.

inclined towards China, the fundamental directions of cross-Strait relations were in keeping with their expectations. Below, the information that was gathered in the survey is used to analyse the stance of the independent voters on cross-Strait relations and the relationship between this stance and their voting decisions.

First, we examine the independent voters' basic attitudes towards cross-Strait economic relations. Table 8.7 reveals that more than half (53.2 per cent) of the independent voters believed that an economic relationship with China is benefi-cial to Taiwan's economy. Close to 40 per cent (36.1 per cent) believe other-wise. These attitudes are not so different from the rest of the respondents: 55.8 per cent and 36.8 per cent respectively. Meanwhile, Table 8.7 also illustrates the high correlation between the independent voters' stance on cross-Strait relations and their voting decisions. The independent voters who believed that relations with China are beneficial to Taiwan's economy mainly voted for the KMT, if they chose to vote at all. Setting aside those who did not vote, 80.8 per cent of those favouring economic relations with China voted for the KMT. Only 19.2 per cent voted for the DPP. The difference is most significant. Since the inde-pendent voters mainly favoured economic relations with China, the dominant majority of this group, who tended to vote for the KMT, made a great difference in the election turnout.

The analysis of the statistical model also confirms the importance of the inde-pendent voters' attitudes to cross-Strait economic relations in their voting

Table 8.7 Evaluation of cross-Strait economic relations: independent voters, 2013 (N (%))

[Question] *Do you think the current development of cross-Strait relations is good or bad for Taiwan's economy in the long term?*

Voting for					
Effect on Taiwan's economy	Ma (KMT)	Tsai (DPP)	Absentee	Others	Total
Good	101	24	80	41	246
	(41.1)	(9.8)	(32.5)	(16.7)	(100)
	(70.1)	(29.6)	(57.1)	(42.3)	(53.2)
Bad	30	47	48	42	167
	(18.0)	(28.1)	(28.7)	(25.1)	(100)
	(20.8)	(58.0)	(34.3)	(43.3)	(36.1)
No difference	5	3	5	3	16
	(31.3)	(18.8)	(31.3)	(18.8)	(100)
	(3.5)	(3.7)	(3.6)	(3.1)	(3.5)
Don't know	8	7	7	11	33
	(24.2)	(21.2)	(21.2)	(33.3)	(100)
	(5.6)	(8.6)	(5.0)	(11.3)	(7.1)
Total	144	81	140	97	462
	(31.2)	(17.5)	(30.3)	(21.0)	(100)
	(100)	(100)	(100)	(100)	(100)

Notes
Chi-square = 44.483.
df = 9.
$p < 0.001$.

decisions. In predicting the support for Ma instead of for Tsai among the independent voters, only two variables emerge as significant contributors. One is 'disagreeing that the KMT is overly inclined towards China'; the other is the belief that 'economic relations with China are beneficial to Taiwan's economy'. The first opinion seems to be related to the independent voters' overall evaluation of the Taiwan–China situation. They tend to think either that economic relations between the two sides are a fair game or that it is natural and understandable that China, a rising and strong power with a large market, dictates to some extent the relations between the two sides. The other variable which allows us to predict voting support for the KMT is 'having a favourable attitude towards economic relations with China'. Each of the two variables seem to contain the same essential element: a positive attitude towards economic relations with China. On the other hand, the variable of 'supporting the 1992 Consensus' is not significant in predicting voting for the KMT (see Appendix 2). The 1992 Consensus per se does not seem to have been an important factor in the last presidential election. The heated debate on the 1992 Consensus during the election campaign only reflected each political party's position on economic relations with China. The independent voters cast their votes with reference to these positions, not with reference to the issue of the 1992 Consensus per se.

Conclusion

The goal of this chapter is to evaluate the effect of the China factor on Taiwan's electoral competition. The following results have been drawn from the data and information gathered from the survey findings:

1   There is a considerable overlap between party identification and voting behaviours. Independent voters are the key to the outcome of electoral competition.
2   Incongruent with conventional wisdom, the 1992 Consensus did not seem to be a decisive factor in the 2012 presidential election; the independent voters and the other voters in general did not show strong support for the 1992 Consensus.
3   Most of the independent voters and the other voters in general did not understand the content of the 1992 Consensus; they even opposed the tenets of the 1992 Consensus.
4   Political parties' positions on the 1992 Consensus, however, served as a clue for the independent voters with regard to understanding each party's position on Taiwan's economic relationship with China.
5   Independent voters' positive attitudes towards economic relations with China appeared to be the most significant factor contributing to their overwhelming support for the KMT, which favours economic integration with China. This factor took priority over their national identification and over their reluctance to vote for the KMT, which was believed to be overly inclined towards China.

As a result of Taiwan's close economic ties with China over the past decade, the DPP has apparently been placed at a disadvantage on the electoral front. If this trend continues and if Taiwan's voters, especially the independent voters, continue to support this trend, it is unlikely, although by no means impossible, that the DPP will regain the edge in the electoral competition for governing power. The electoral framework seems to be very much structured by the China factor. This framework, for the time being, has obviously placed the DPP at a disadvantage. According to the data presented in this chapter, however, it appears that this may not be an unchangeable situation, even if the DPP continues to uphold its official position of standing for an independent and sovereign Taiwanese state. First, a large majority of the electorate are concerned that economic relations with China, although beneficial to Taiwan's trade, come at a high price, i.e. loss of political autonomy. Second, a large majority of the electorate is concerned about the KMT's overly accommodating position towards the demands from and interests of the Beijing government. In other words, although the DPP suffers from a serious disadvantage in the national electoral competition framed by the China factor, it is by no means doomed. The party's comeback depends, of course, like every grand political move, on the political leaders, their leadership, and their visions on how to manoeuvre the circumstances to their advantage.

Appendix

Table A8.1 The national identity of Taiwan's general public, 1990–2013 (*N* (%))

[Questions]
If Taiwan independence would not precipitate a war, do you agree that Taiwan should become an independent country?
If Taiwan and China were to become comparatively developed economically, socially and politically, do you agree that the two sides should be unified into one country?

	Unification if there are no cross-Strait disparities			
1992 1996 2000 2004 2008 2011 2013	*Agree*	*Don't know*	*Don't agree*	*Total*
Independence no war				
Agree	II 311 (25.0)	29 (2.3)	I 116 (9.3)	456 (36.7)
	540 (38.8)	38 (2.7)	296 (21.3)	874 (62.8)
	485 (34.4)	35 (2.5)	338 (24.0)	858 (60.9)
	435 (23.9)	65 (3.6)	525 (28.8)	1025 (56.2)
	366 (19.2)	69 (3.6)	662 (34.8)	1097 (57.6)
	99 (8.1)	30 (2.5)	444 (36.5)	573 (47.1)
	102 (8.2)	11 (0.9)	495 (39.9)	608 (49.0)
Don't know	45 (3.6)	82 (6.6)	12 (1.0)	139 (11.2)
	46 (3.3)	173 (12.3)	9 (1.4)	238 (17.1)
	33 (2.3)	127 (9.0)	8 (0.6)	168 (11.9)
	36 (2.0)	190 (10.4)	31 (1.7)	257 (14.1)
	24 (1.3)	172 (9.0)	37 (1.9)	233 (12.2)
	15 (1.2)	92 (7.5)	50 (4.1)	157 (12.9)
	5 (0.4)	9 (0.7)	29 (2.3)	43 (3.5)
Don't agree	III 472 (38.0)	39 (3.1)	IV 137 (11.0)	648 (52.1)
	235 (16.9)	5 (0.4)	40 (2.9)	280 (20.1)
	272 (19.3)	18 (1.3)	93 (6.6)	383 (27.2)
	273 (15.0)	46 (2.5)	222 (12.2)	541 (29.7)
	241 (12.7)	36 (1.9)	297 (15.6)	574 (30.1)
	140 (11.5)	41 (3.4)	306 (25.2)	487 (40.0)
	160 (12.9)	13 (1.0)	416 (33.5)	589 (47.5)
Total	828 (66.6)	150 (12.1)	265 (21.3)	1243 (100.0)
	821 (59.0)	216 (15.6)	355 (25.5)	1382 (100.0)
	790 (56.1)	180 (12.8)	439 (31.2)	1409 (100.0)
	744 (40.8)	301 (16.5)	778 (42.7)	1823 (100.0)
	631 (33.1)	277 (14.5)	996 (52.3)	1904 (100.0)
	253 (20.8)	163 (13.4)	801 (65.8)	1217 (100.0)
	267 (21.5)	33 (2.7)	940 (75.8)	1240 (100.0)

Notes
I   Taiwanese nationalists.   III   Chinese nationalists.
II Duo-identity.   IV   Status-quo.

Table A8.2 Logistic models predicting voting for Ma Ying-Jeou, 2013

	(1)	(2)
	Ma Ying-Jeou (for Tsai Ing-Wen)	Ma Ying-Jeou (Absentee)
Gender (male)	−0.56	−0.44
	(0.37)	(0.28)
Age (above 50)	1.53	−1.18*
~29	(0.79)	(0.53)
39	1.26*	−0.23
	(0.58)	(0.40)
49	0.29	−0.67
	(0.46)	(0.37)
Ethnicity (native Taiwanese)	−0.73	−0.31
	(0.66)	(0.46)
Education (college)		
Primary and lower secondary school	0.76	−0.44
	(0.61)	(0.49)
High school	1.47**	0.10
	(0.47)	(0.33)
Support for 1992 Consensus	0.69	1.14***
	(0.39)	(0.30)
DPP overly opposing China	0.72*	0.83**
	(0.37)	(0.29)
Favouring cross-Strait economic relations	1.32***	0.35
	(0.36)	(0.29)
KMT overly inclined towards China	−2.30***	−0.08
	(0.51)	(0.29)
(constant)	0.72	−0.13
	(0.86)	(0.56)
N	218	267
pseudo R^2	0.302	0.119
Log likelihood	−99.634673	−162.90214

Notes
* $p < 0.05$.
** $p < 0.01$.
*** $p < 0.001$.

Notes

1 See www.youtube.com/watch?v=Kcgr53WML0A (accessed 3 July 2014).
2 For details of the negotiations between the two sides and the consensus that was finally achieved, see Su and Cheng (2002); the facts, quotations and material presented in this section also derive from this work.
3 For a recent study on this phenomenon which has long been troubling political scientists and democratic theorists, see Somin (2013).

References

Budge I., Crewe, I., and Farlie, D. (1976) *Party Identification and Beyond*, London: John Wiley and Sons.

Campbell, A., Converse, P. E., Miller, W. E., and Stokes, D. E. (1976) *The American Voter*, Chicago: University of Chicago Press.

Miller, W. E., and Shanks, J. M. (1996) *The New American Voters*, Cambridge: Harvard University Press.

Somin, I. (2013) *Democracy and Political Ignorance*, Stanford: Stanford University Press.

Su, C., and Cheng, G. A. (eds) (2002) *The History of 'One China, Different Interpretations' Consensus* (in Chinese), Taipei: Foundation for the Studies of National Policies.

Wu, Nai-Teh (1999) 'Family Socialization and Political Ideology: The Generational Difference of Taiwanese Voters' (in Chinese), *Taiwanese Sociological Studies*, 3: 53–85.

Wu, Nai-Teh (2012) 'Will Economic Integration Lead to Political Assimilation?' in Chow, Peter C. Y. (ed.) *National Identity and Economic Interest: Taiwan's Competing Options and Their Implications for Regional Stability*, New York: Palgrave Macmillan.

Part II

The China impact on Taiwanese society

9 The social basis of Taiwan's cross-Strait policies, 2008–2014

Chih-Jou Jay Chen

This study explores the social basis of Taiwan's cross-Strait policies since 2008, observing the various groups who support and/or reject particular cross-Strait policies. More specifically, it examines how various factors, such as gender, ethnicity, social status, party identification and national identity, influence the possibility of supporting or opposing particular cross-Strait policies. These divisions in opinions reflect the social impact of the rapidly changing cross-Strait relationship in Taiwan.

Since the second change in ruling parties in 2008, Taiwan's relationship with China has significantly warmed. Between 2008 and 2014, the two have held ten talks and signed 21 trade and investment pacts, have initiated direct cross-Strait flights and have made Taipei the first market outside Hong Kong that is able to clear Renminbi transactions. Thus, cross-Strait relations have become the centre of politics and the principal site of public disputes in Taiwan. Some Taiwanese would tend towards the view that boosting cross-Strait trade and investment will contribute positively towards driving Taiwan's economic growth, while others are perturbed that it will only exacerbate the hollowing out of Taiwan's manufacturing industries. In June 2010, the signing of the Economic Cooperation Framework Agreement (ECFA) opened up stronger cross-Strait ties in the fields of trade, finance and commerce. Cultural, educational and social exchanges have followed. In August 2010 Taiwan's legislature passed a bill recognizing 41 Chinese university degrees, and as of 2014 the number of recognized Chinese universities had increased to 129. Meanwhile, Taiwan has started to allow its universities and colleges to admit Chinese degree-seeking students. These events were a continuation of the June 2008 opening of Taiwan to Chinese tour groups, which has reached a daily quota of 5,000 Chinese citizens since April 2013. Earlier, the number of Chinese visitors to Taiwan increased from an average of 3,600 a day, after the daily quota was raised from 3,000 to 4,000 in early 2011, with the stipulation that Chinese visitors to Taiwan should travel as part of organized groups. Then, after June 2011, a maximum of 500 individual tourists per day from three Chinese cities (Beijing, Shanghai and Xiamen) were allowed to visit Taiwan. As of August 2014, 36 Chinese cities have been approved to grant individual tourist visits to Taiwan, reaching a daily quota of 4,000 tourists and further promoting tourism and social interaction between the two societies.

Taiwan's ruling party, the Kuomintang (KMT), claims that the above-mentioned trends have aided Taiwan's development over recent years, suggesting that they have helped the island achieve manufacturing goals and assisted in the realization of cross-Strait harmony. The opposition raised a hue and cry, arguing that this economic opening had substantially hollowed out Taiwan's manufacturing and high-tech industry and increased the disparity in wealth between rich and poor. Other critics were also wary of sacrificing Taiwan's political autonomy and cultural identity by helping Beijing realize its known intention of further binding Taiwan to the mainland. Given that Taiwan's media have indeed already taken up these talking-points on cross-Strait relations, the clamour in the legislature has belatedly mimicked the media. Although intensive debates and queries were conducted on the issue, the KMT still appeared to have control over the main direction of cross-Strait policies until the spring of 2014, when protesters linked with the Anti-Trade Pact Movement occupied the island's parliament to show their opposition to a trade pact with China.

In 2014, the Anti-Trade Pact Movement (also known as the Sunflower movement) protested against the Cross-Strait Service Trade Agreement proposed by the ruling party KMT in the legislature. The protesters felt that the trade pact with China would hurt Taiwan's economy and leave it vulnerable to political pressure from Beijing, while advocates of the treaty argued that increased economic relations would provide a necessary boost to Taiwan's economy. The movement has, to a great extent, weakened public support for accelerating the process of negotiating cross-Strait agreements. Meanwhile, the KMT failed to make headway on three related bills even after two extra legislative sessions in the summer of 2014.[1]

Cross-Strait issues are often presented in the media and in the legislature as a two-sided debate, with each side rigidly staking out its own position without the ability to compromise or to provide room for any suggested alternatives. Indeed, in cross-Strait debates, parties rarely deviate from their positions, so that party positions ultimately end up deciding party preferences for cross-Strait policies. The media and politicians rarely examine other factors that may be influencing their citizens' positions and views on cross-Strait relations.

In the midst of these debates, people's attitudes have been constantly overlooked. It is true that the media often draws on public opinion, but there is still a lack of understanding as to the factors that affect public opinion in cross-Strait policies in Taiwan. Given the fact that supporters of the main political parties will follow their party's preferences and positions, what are the views of those 'independent' or 'undecided' voters who are fence-sitters supporting neither party? Furthermore, are there other factors that affect cross-Strait attitudes apart from political rhetoric, such as socio-economic status, gender or locality? In addition to the main issues (ECFA, Chinese tourists and other related issues), what are citizens' attitudes towards other social issues in cross-Strait affairs? A clear picture of the specific factors influencing Taiwanese cross-Strait relations and preferences cannot be adduced without a full understanding of the complex issues that govern Taiwanese responses.

Social differentiation and social cleavages have led to differences in positions and attitudes on cross-Strait issues in Taiwan. Different social groups of gender, class and party identification could certainly have different opinions on cross-Strait policies. These attitudinal differences and their consequences reflect not only Taiwan's social differentiation and social cleavages but also the social impact of China's rapid rise in the global economy and its powerful influence over cross-Strait relations. In particular, since these cross-Strait policies are at a pioneering stage in Taiwan, they will have lock-in effects on cross-Strait institutional development. These policies are related to each other; their legitimacy and implementation will have long-term effects on Taiwanese society and future cross-Strait relations.

Data and measurement

This study draws on data obtained from two rounds of telephone surveys conducted in 2010 in Taiwan. These surveys were part of a long-term institutional research project, the Taiwan Social Image Survey, conducted by the Institute of Sociology at Academia Sinica. The interviewees were Taiwanese citizens over the age of eighteen. The first survey was conducted between 1 and 22 June and consisted of 1,242 respondents. The second survey was conducted between 16 and 26 December and consisted of 1,238 respondents.[2]

The attitudes of those surveyed towards five cross-Strait issues were examined:

1   support for or opposition to the signing of ECFA;
2   support for or opposition to the recognition of Chinese university degrees;
3   support for or opposition to allowing Chinese degree-seeking college students to study in Taiwan;
4   support for or opposition to opening Taiwan to individual Chinese tourists;
5   support for or opposition to increasing the cap on the daily number of Chinese group tourists.

These policy issues referred to different dimensions of the cross-Strait relationship. With regard to the ECFA question, it was the extent of mutual economic opening and trade ties with apparent economic implications. On the topic of Chinese tourists, it was a question of social interaction and people-to-people exchanges, embodying substantive social implications. On the topic of recognizing Chinese university degrees, it was 'institutional acknowledgement', in the context of acknowledging and accepting a different institution and system in mainland China. Of course, there could certainly be mixed considerations on the part of individual respondents. For example, with regard to relaxing restrictions for Chinese tourism, in addition to considerations of social interaction and human contact, there could also be economic considerations. However, at the fundamental level, this would still fall into the original category of social interaction, since social interaction engenders economic effects. As far as the general population is concerned, attitudes deriving from sentimental and instrumental motives are reasonable and common.

The descriptive statistics of people's attitudes towards five cross-Strait issues revealed the trends in their minds (Table 9.1). In the categories of economic opening and cultural exchange, those in favour outnumbered those who opposed the issue. On the ECFA, 45 per cent of the respondents supported the issue and 32 per cent were against (23 per cent did not know or abstained from answering). On allowing Chinese students to study in Taiwan, 50 per cent supported the proposal while 45 per cent were opposed to it (5 per cent did not know or abstained from answering). Conversely, on the issues related to institutional acknowledgement and social interaction, the opponents outnumbered supporters. On the topic of recognizing Chinese university degrees, 44 per cent supported and 50 per cent opposed the proposal. On opening Taiwan to individual Chinese tourists, 43 per cent supported and 48 per cent opposed the proposal. On increasing quotas for Chinese group tourists, 39 per cent supported and 44 per cent opposed the proposal.

From the frequency distributions of the variables, it appears that deep divisions exist among the Taiwanese people on policy issues related to cross-Strait

Table 9.1 Attitudes towards cross-Strait policies in Taiwan

	N	%
Economic opening		
(1) Support signing the ECFA?		
Support	558	45
Don't support	395	32
Don't know (abstained from answering)	289	23
Educational exchange		
(2) Support allowing Chinese students to study in Taiwan?		
Support	618	50
Don't support	559	45
Don't know (abstained from answering)	65	5
Institutional acknowledgement		
(3) Support recognition of Chinese degrees?		
Support	541	44
Don't support	623	50
Don't know (abstained from answering)	78	6
Social interaction		
(4) Support allowing individual Chinese tourists into Taiwan?		
Support	535	43
Don't support	597	48
Missing values	106	9
(5) Relax restrictions on number of Chinese group tourists to Taiwan?		
Support	477	39
Don't support	540	44
Don't know (abstained from answering)	221	18

Sources: (1)–(3): first survey, conducted 2 June 2010; (4)–(5): second survey, conducted 16 December 2010.

relations. A large proportion of the respondents supported economic openings and cultural exchanges, but a large proportion also opposed institutional acknowledgement and social interaction. On the issue of the ECFA, support outweighed opposition by 13 per cent, but a high percentage of people abstained from answering the question (23 per cent). Apart from this issue, the differences in opinion on other policy issues was less than 5 per cent, indicating that there was no common meeting ground on these issues in Taiwan. A comparison with other surveys conducted in 2010 by the media or other organizations also revealed a similar trend. On the question of the ECFA and Chinese students attending Taiwanese universities, support outweighed opposition. However, on the question of recognition for China's university degrees, there was no clear trend towards support or opposition.[3] On the topic of increasing the number of Chinese tourists, it seems most people supported a 'slow opening' to Chinese individual tourists.[4]

In order to explain the differences in the opinions on cross-Strait policies, we considered the effects of variables including the following: individual social positions, socio-economic status, residential locality, party identification, preference for independence or reunification, and other factors (outlined in Appendix I). These variables are explained below.

1 Individual social positions included gender, age, marital status and ethnicity. Age referred to the age of the respondent in the year of the survey. Marital status was categorized as 'not married' or married. Ethnicity was determined by the father's native place of birth and could be Taiwanese Minnan, Taiwanese Hakka or mainlander (there were too few Aboriginal respondents and they did not, therefore, present themselves as a category).

2 Socio-economic status was indicated by education and income. Education was divided into three categories: junior high and below, high school, vocational college and above. For income, there were fourteen income categories for both individual and household income, from no income to over NT$200,000 per month.

3 Residential locality was coded into two categories according to where respondents lived, namely, in southern Taiwan (Tainan, Kaohsiung and Pingdong) and elsewhere. This was for the purpose of obtaining a sense of the geographical differences between north and south Taiwan.

4 Party identification was measured from the questions the survey posed. The answers were divided into five categories: blue (KMT and PFP), green (DPP and TSU), those who chose candidates and not parties, those who supported both, and those who did not support any.

5 National identity for independence or reunification was measured from the questions the survey posed. The answers were grouped into four choices: reunification (including immediate reunification and maintaining status quo now but reunifying later), independence (including immediate independence and maintaining status quo now but independence later), maintaining status quo forever, and 'wait and see'.

6   Impact of the ECFA on Taiwan's wealth disparities. The original question was: 'Do you think the ECFA will increase, decrease, or have no impact upon Taiwan's wealth disparities?' Answers were grouped by either 'increase', 'decrease' or 'no impact'.

7   ECFA considerations. The original questions were: 'In cross-Strait relations, some people think that Taiwan's economic position is most important, while others think that Taiwan's sovereignty is most important. What do you think is most important?' Respondents were given three answers to choose from 'economy', 'sovereignty' or 'both'.

8   Impressions of Chinese tourists. Three questions were asked in order to assess the respondents' impressions of Chinese tourists:

   a   'After opening Taiwan to Chinese tourists what is your overall impression of China's society: Do you feel closer to China, further from China, or no different?'

   b   'Do you have a good impression of Chinese tourists in Taiwan?' Answers were coded into two categories:

      i   'have a good impression' (including behaviour and attitude);
      ii   'do not have a good impression' or 'no opinion'.

   c   'Do you have a bad impression of Chinese tourists in Taiwan?' Respondents were again given three answers to choose from: 'have a bad impression (including behaviour and attitude)', 'do not have a bad impression' or 'no opinion'.

Results

To examine the effects of various factors on different cross-Strait policies, binary logistic regression models were used and presented as follows. First, Table 9.2 shows the variables that may have influenced people's support for the ECFA, which will lead to further economic opening and trade relations. In model (1) through model (5), the effects of various independent variables were quite consistent. With regard to personal characteristics, the greater the age (although the influences were not that significant in model (4), it was still near the significance level of 0.05) and the higher the education level and individual income, the stronger was the support for the ECFA. Furthermore, mainlanders were more likely to support the ECFA than Taiwanese Minnan people. Also, unmarried respondents showed more support for the ECFA than married respondents. With regard to party identification, those who supported the blues were more likely to support the ECFA than those who supported the greens and those who were 'middle voters'. On national identity, those who supported independence were less likely to support the ECFA than those who supported reunification and maintaining the status quo. Similarly, on the issue of the ECFA creating greater wealth disparities, those who thought the ECFA would make the disparities greater were less likely to support the ECFA than those who thought it would

Table 9.2 Factors influencing support for signing the ECFA

Model	1	2	3	4	5
	β	β	β	β	β
Age	0.03***	0.03**	0.02*	0.02	0.03*
Education level (below lower secondary school)					
High school	0.79**	0.81**	0.76*	0.88***	0.82*
Associate college and above	1.03***	1.08***	1.11***	1.14***	1.04**
Female (male)	0.21	0.10	0.11	0.05	−0.2
Unmarried (married)	0.35	0.56*	0.60*	0.54	0.56
Southern Taiwan (other areas)	−0.2	0.25	0.27	0.31	0.31
Average monthly income	0.11***	0.11**	0.11**	0.13**	0.16***
Ethnicity (Minnan)					
Hakka	0.26	−0.1	−0.2	−0.1	−0.1
Mainlander	1.74***	1.17***	1.02**	1.15**	1.20**
Party affiliation (KMT)					
DPP		−4.2***	−3.6***	−3.3***	−3.0***
Choose candidate/policy		−1.9***	−1.8***	−1.4***	−1.3***
Support all		−1.7***	−1.6***	−1.3***	−1.1*
Support none		−2.1***	−2.0***	−1.7***	−1.6***
Tendency to support independence or reunification (maintain status quo)					
Reunification			0.37	0.35	0.23
Independence			−1.3***	−1.2***	−0.1***
Wait and see			−0.3	−0.4	−0.3
ECFA rich–poor influence (no influence)					
Greater wealth disparities				−2.1***	−2.1***
Smaller wealth disparities				0.02	−0.1
Emphasis on cross-Strait business negotiations (national sovereignty)					
Economic advantage					1.33***
Both economic advantage and national sovereignty					0.46
Intercept	−2.7***	−0.8	−0.5	0.88	−0.4
Chi-square	111***	366***	397***	477***	510***
Df	9	13	16	18	20
N	827	827	827	827	827

Notes

* $p<0.05$.

** $p<0.01$.

*** $p<0.001$.

Dependent variable: 1: 'Support ECFA'; 0: 'Don't support ECFA'.

A variable in brackets refers to the reference group.

have no impact at all. Finally, those who thought that, in cross-Strait trade, Taiwan's economic advantage should be put first were more likely to support the ECFA than those who thought sovereignty should be put first.

In conclusion, those who supported further opening up the cross-Strait economy and trade relations by means of the ECFA were older citizens with higher socio-economic status (education and income) who supported the blues and opposed Taiwan's independence. Furthermore, other variables being equal, those who thought that the ECFA would not influence wealth disparities and those who thought that, in trade relations, Taiwan's economic advantage should be given primacy were more likely to support the ECFA.

Second, on the issue of educational and cultural exchanges, Table 9.3 presents binary logistic regression models to show the effects of various variables on the

Table 9.3 Factors influencing support for allowing Chinese students into Taiwan

Model	1	2	3	4
	β	β	β	β
Age	0.01*	0.01	0.01	0.01
Education level (below junior high school)				
High school	0.49*	0.45*	0.41	0.37
Associate college and above	0.84***	0.80***	0.81***	0.79***
Female (male)	−0.22	−0.32*	−0.33*	−0.42**
Unmarried (married)	0.33	0.40	0.44*	0.41
Southern Taiwan (other areas)	−0.11	0.10	0.13	0.12
Average monthly income	0.09***	0.08**	0.08**	0.08*
Ethnicity (Minnan)				
Hakka	0.15	−0.07	−0.10	−0.10
Mainlander	1.05***	0.58*	0.45	0.42
Party affiliation (KMT)				
DPP		−2.44***	−2.09***	−1.94***
Choose candidate/policy		−0.90***	−0.74***	−0.66**
Support all		−0.50	−0.42	−0.30
Support none		−1.05***	−0.96***	−0.91***
Tendency to support independence or reunification (maintain status quo)				
Reunification			0.74*	0.68*
Independence			−0.74***	−0.63**
Wait and see			0.17	0.17
Emphasis on cross-Strait business negotiations (national sovereignty)				
Economic advantage				0.58***
Both economic advantage and national sovereignty				0.41
Intercept	−1.63***	−0.41	−0.43	−0.86
Chi-square	94.9***	225.3***	254.7***	266.3***
Df	9	13	16	18
N	1,029	1,029	1,029	1,029

Notes
* $p<0.05$.
** $p<0.01$.
*** $p<0.001$.
Dependent variable: 1: 'Support the government opening Taiwan to Chinese students to come to study'; 0: 'Don't support the government opening Taiwan to Chinese students to come to study'. A variable in brackets refers to the reference group.

attitude towards permitting Chinese degree-seeking students to study in Taiwan. For personal characteristics, model (1) shows that the greater the respondent's age and the higher the education level and individual income, the more likely it is that they would support allowing Chinese students to study in Taiwan. Similarly, mainlanders were more likely to support such an opening than Taiwanese Minnan people. Model (2) shows that, when combined with party identification, several factors such as education, individual income and ethnicity (mainlanders versus Minnan) were still significant, but age became insignificant. At this stage, gender became a significant factor in that more females than males tended to oppose allowing Chinese students to study in Taiwan. The insignificant effect of age implied that it was party identification rather than age that had an influence on the respondents' attitudes towards allowing Chinese students to study in Taiwan. Similarly, non-blue voters (greens and 'middle-voters') were more likely not to support allowing Chinese students than blues. In model (3), the inclusion of national identity variables (i.e. support for independence/unification) rendered the effect of ethnicity insignificant. Relative to those advocating the status quo, unification supporters were more likely to support allowing Chinese students to study in Taiwan, and independence supporters were more likely to oppose such a policy. Also, those who were unmarried were more likely to support allowing Chinese students than those who were married. In model (4), those who emphasized Taiwan's economic advantage over sovereignty were more likely to support allowing Chinese students to study in Taiwan.

In conclusion, supporters of educational and cultural exchanges in the form of allowing Chinese degree-seeking students to study in Taiwan exhibited these characteristics: male, higher socio-economic status (education and income), blue-camp supporters, and pro-unification and anti-independence. Furthermore, they were more likely to give primacy to Taiwan's economic position over the country's political sovereignty. Conversely, females, people with lower socio-economic status, green-camp supporters and middle voters, pro-independence supporters, and those who emphasized sovereignty over economic advantage tended not to support allowing Chinese degree-seeking students into Taiwan.

Third, on policies related to institutional acknowledgement, Table 9.4 provides models that show support for recognizing Chinese university degrees. From models (1) to (4), the effects of variables are highly consistent. Overall, model (4) reveals that older, more highly-educated male mainlanders who are blue-camp supporters, pro-unification and have higher incomes tended to support the recognition of Chinese university degrees. Also, those who gave primacy to economic advantage over national sovereignty were more likely to support the recognition of Chinese university degrees.

In summary, the characteristics of those who supported the recognition of Chinese university degrees were the following: older, high socio-economic status, male, mainlanders, blue-camp supporters and pro-unification supporters. Furthermore, they were more likely to give primacy to the economy over sovereignty. Conversely, those who were younger, female, with lower socio-economic status, non-blue supporters, pro-independence supporters, and with a preference

Table 9.4 Factors influencing support for recognition of Chinese degrees

Model	1	2	3	4
	β	β	β	β
Age	0.02**	0.02*	0.02*	0.02**
Education level (below lower secondary school)				
High school	0.81***	0.76***	0.74**	0.71**
Associate college and above	1.11***	1.06***	1.10***	1.07***
Female (male)	−0.25	−0.35*	−0.33*	−0.47**
Unmarried (married)	0.27	0.33	0.35	0.32
Southern Taiwan (other areas)	−0.28	−0.10	−0.11	−0.11
Average monthly income	0.09***	0.09**	0.08**	0.08*
Ethnicity (Minnan)				
Hakka	0.18	0.01	−0.01	0.00
Mainlander	1.33***	0.94***	0.81***	0.80***
Party affiliation (KMT)				
DPP		−2.36***	−2.01***	−1.79***
Choose candidate/policy		−0.93***	−0.74***	−0.63**
Support all		−0.46	−0.37	−0.19
Support none		−0.87***	−0.74***	−0.67***
Tendency to support independence or reunification (maintain status quo)				
Reunification			1.16***	1.09***
Independence			−0.73***	−0.55*
Wait and see			0.06	0.06
Emphasis on cross-Strait business negotiations (national sovereignty)				
Economic advantage				0.87***
Smaller wealth disparities				0.48
Intercept	−2.40***	−1.34**	−1.40**	−2.11***
Chi-square	132.5***	247.3***	283.5***	308.3***
Df	9	13	16	18
N	1,027	1,027	1,027	1,027

Notes
* $p<0.05$.
** $p<0.01$.
*** $p<0.001$.
Dependent variable: 1: 'Support government recognition of Chinese degrees'; 0: 'Oppose government recognition of Chinese degrees'. A variable in brackets refers to the reference group.

for sovereignty over economic opportunity were more likely to oppose the recognition of Chinese university degrees.

Fourth, on the issues of cross-society interaction, Table 9.5 presents models for opening Taiwan to individual Chinese travellers. It shows that ethnicity (mainlander versus Taiwanese Minnan) as a factor did not negatively impact on support for opening Taiwan to individual Chinese travellers, and that differences were associated with party identification. Non-blue voters were more likely to oppose opening up Taiwan than blue voters. Highly educated, unmarried people were more likely to support increasing cross-Strait economic interaction than

Table 9.5 Factors supporting opening up Taiwan to Chinese individual tourists

Model	1	2	3	4	5	6
	β	β	B	β	β	β
Age	0.0***	0.0**	0.0**	0.0**	0.0**	0.0*
Education (below lower secondary school)						
High school	0.5*	0.4	0.4	0.4	0.5	0.5
Associate college and above	0.9***	0.8**	0.8**	0.8**	0.9***	1.0***
Female (male)	−0.3	−0.4*	−0.3*	−0.4*	−0.4*	−0.3
Unmarried (married)	0.4	0.5*	0.5*	0.6*	0.5*	0.5*
Southern Taiwan (other areas)	−0.2	−0.1	0.0	−0.1	0.0	0.0
Household income	0.1	0.0	0.0	0.0	0.0	0.0
Ethnicity (Minnan)						
Hakka	0.3	0.3	0.2	0.3	0.2	0.2
Mainlander	0.8***	0.4	0.4	0.3	0.2	0.2
Party affiliation (blue)						
Green		−1.3***	−1.0***	−0.8**	−0.6*	−0.6*
Choose candidate/policy		−0.9***	−0.8**	−0.7**	−0.6*	−0.5
None		−0.6**	−0.5*	−0.3	−0.2	−0.2
Unification or independence (status quo)						
Unification			0.7	0.6	0.6	0.7
Independence			−0.8***	−0.6**	−0.6*	−0.4
Impressions of Chinese tourists						
Feel closer to China[a] (no)				0.9***	0.8***	0.8***
Good impressions[b] (no)					0.8***	0.8***
Bad impressions[c] (no)						−0.7***
Intercept	−2.3***	−1.5*	−1.5**	−1.9***	−2.1***	−1.9**
Chi-square	56	89	105	131	146	160
Df	9	12	14	15	16	17
N	671	671	671	671	671	671

Notes
* *p*<0.05.
** *p*<0.01.
*** *p*<0.001.
Dependent variable: 1: 'Support opening Taiwan to individual Chinese travellers'; 0: 'Oppose opening Taiwan to individual Chinese travellers'. A variable in brackets refers to the reference group.
a Since the opening of Taiwan to Chinese tourists, do you feel closer to China?
b Do you have a good impression of Chinese tourists in Taiwan?
c Do you have a bad impression of Chinese tourists in Taiwan?

people with a lower level of education. However, women were more likely to oppose these issues than males. People's feeling of relatedness to Chinese travellers and their impressions of Chinese tourists as good or bad significantly influenced their responses to opening up Taiwan. Those who felt closer and those who had a good impression of Chinese tourists were also more likely to support economic liberalization across the Taiwan Strait in the long term.

162   C.-J.J. Chen

Lastly, on social interaction, Table 9.6 presents models for increasing the Chinese tourist quota to Taiwan. Females were less likely to support such a policy, as were native Taiwanese Minnan people. Ethnicity was not a factor in this context; rather the case rested upon party identification. Non-blue voters were more likely than blue voters to oppose increasing the number of Chinese visitors; those who supported independence were more likely to oppose increases

Table 9.6 Factors influencing increasing the number of Chinese group tourist quotas

Model	1	2	3	4	5	6
	β	β	β	β	β	β
Age	0.0	0.0	0.0	0.0	0.0	0.0
Education (below lower secondary school)						
High school	−0.1	−0.2	−0.2	−0.3	−0.2	−0.2
Associate college and above	0.3	0.2	0.2	0.1	0.2	0.2
Female (male)	−0.5**	−0.6***	−0.6***	−0.7***	−0.7***	−0.7***
Unmarried (married)	−0.1	−0.1	0.0	−0.1	−0.1	−0.1
Southern Taiwan (other areas)	−0.1	0.0	0.0	0.0	0.0	0.0
Household income	0.0	0.0	0.0	0.0	0.0	0.0
Ethnicity (Minnan)						
Hakka	−0.1	−0.3	−0.3	−0.3	−0.3	−0.4
Mainlander	0.6*	0.2	0.1	0.1	−0.1	−0.1
Party affiliation (blue)						
Green		−1.6***	−1.2***	−1.0***	−0.9***	−0.9***
Choose candidate/policy		−0.5*	−0.5	−0.3	−0.3	−0.2
None		−0.8***	−0.7***	−0.5*	−0.5*	−0.5*
Unification or independence (status quo)						
Unification			0.5	0.3	0.4	0.4
Independence			−0.9***	−0.8**	−0.7*	−0.6*
Impressions of Chinese tourists						
Feel closer to China[a] (no)				1.0***	0.9***	0.9***
Good impressions[b] (no)					0.7***	0.8***
Bad impressions[c] (no)						−0.4*
Intercept	−0.6	0.5	0.6	0.3	0.2	0.4
Chi-square	29	72	88	118	130	135
Df	9	12	14	15	16	17
N	621	621	621	621	621	621

Notes
* $p<0.05$.
** $p<0.01$.
*** $p<0.001$.
Dependent variable: 1: 'support increasing quotas'; 0: 'quotas can decrease or remain the same'.
A variable in brackets refers to the reference group.
a Since the opening of Taiwan to Chinese tourists, do you feel closer to China?
b Do you have a good impression of Chinese tourists in Taiwan?
c Do you have a bad impression of Chinese tourists in Taiwan?

than those who supported the status quo. The feeling of closeness and the good or bad impressions of Chinese visitors also had an influence on respondents' support or non-support for increasing the quota of visitors. Those who had good impressions or felt closer to Chinese tourists were more likely to support an increase in the quota of visitors, whereas those who had a bad impression were less likely to opt for a quota increase.

Discussion

The results of the above analysis show that there are significant differences in the various factors that affect people's attitudes towards the government's cross-Strait policies, in which social differentiation and social cleavages have played a key role. Furthermore, these differences reflect the ways in which cross-Strait policies and the rise of China have affected different social groups in Taiwan. These policies relate to different aspects of cross-Strait interactions, including economic cooperation (the ECFA), educational exchange (allowing Chinese degree-seeking students), institutional acknowledgement (recognizing Chinese university degrees) and social interactions (allowing more group and individual Chinese tourists into Taiwan). With regard to personal background, the older the individual and the higher his/her socio-economic status, the more likely he/she was to support policies related to increasing exchanges with China. This is also to say, the younger the individual and the lower his/her socio-economic status, the more likely he/she was to oppose further interactions with China. In short, age and socio-economic status played a vital role in whether the respondents supported or opposed cross-Strait policies.

Table 9.7 provides a breakdown of the percentages of group support for the various cross-Strait policies. The issues of analysis are: (1) the ECFA; (2) allowing Chinese degree-seeking students to study in Taiwan; (3) recognizing Chinese university degrees; (4) opening to individual Chinese tourists; and (5) increasing the daily quota for Chinese group tourists. The percentage of older respondents (over 42 years of age) who supported these issues were: (1) 48 per cent; (2) 51 per cent; (3) 45 per cent; (4) 45 per cent; and (5) 40 per cent. In comparison, the percentages of support among younger respondents (under 42 years of age) were: (1) 42 per cent; (2) 50 per cent; (3) 43 per cent; (4) 44 per cent; and (5) 40 per cent. These figures show that, overall, older respondents showed higher levels of support for these policies than younger respondents. At the same time, those with higher levels of education were more likely to support these policies. The percentages in this category were: 58 per cent, 61 per cent, 55 per cent, 54 per cent, and 46 per cent for those who were educated above high school level, with 35 per cent, 42 per cent, 35 per cent, 37 per cent, and 35 per cent for those educated to below high school level.

Why do the younger groups with relatively low socio-economic status tend to oppose the strengthening of economic and social interaction with China? One explanation could be found in their perceived economic interests and collective identities. With regard to economic interests, the younger groups with low

Table 9.7 Cross tables of personal characteristics and cross-Strait policies (percentages of respondent sample)

	(1)	(2)	(3)	(4)	(5)
	ECFA (N = 1,185)	Allow Chinese students (N = 1,185)	Recognize Chinese degrees (N = 1,185)	Open to individual travellers (N = 1,143)	Increase group tourist quotas (N = 1,143)
Age					
Young	42	50	43	44	40
Old	48	51	45	45	40
Education					
Below high school	35	42	35	37	35
Associate college and above	58	61	55	54	46
Gender					
Male	48	55	49	50	47
Female	44	46	40	39	33
Party affiliation					
Blue	77	72	65	59	58
Middle	37	47	40	41	33
Green	8	19	15	26	22

Notes
1 The figures show the percentages for 'support'; other items include 'oppose' and 'don't know' (abstained from answering).
2 'Young' refers to those born in 1968 and after. 'Old' refers to those born in 1967 and before.
3 Blues include KMT and PFP. Greens include DPP and TSU.
4 Middle voters include those who voted for the candidate or policy and not the party, who support all parties, or who support no party.

socio-economic status have a more vulnerable position on the labour market. They are subjected to media influence on the disadvantages for their interests in cross-Strait relations, such as stories about tougher job market competition and rising prices for housing and commodities. For these reasons, they tend to oppose the further liberalization of cross-Strait economic relations. Young people describe themselves as a 'crash generation', with stagnating wages and limited upward mobility. For this reason, they may have doubts about further opening interactions with China. The Sunflower movement in March 2014 was mainly composed of young people who were opposed to the KMT government's proposed Cross-Strait Service Trade Agreement. This student movement was a clear expression of the anxiety of young people in Taiwan with regard to further cross-Strait economic exchanges. In addition to competitive economic interests, those who have grown up since the 1990s have been less subject to the social and educational influences of the KMT, which leans towards Chinese identity and pro-reunification platform. Young people identify more strongly with Taiwan and they also have fewer connections with China than the older generations. In fact, on the contrary, the increasing threats and impacts of China in recent years have touched a nerve in many people, which has led to their having reservations with regard to strengthening cross-Strait relations.

The reserved attitude towards cross-Strait policies seems to have developed in recent years in conjunction with growing Taiwanese identity and anti-China sentiment. For example, in a 2014 island-wide survey, the percentage of those respondents who lean towards Taiwanese independence or are hoping that independence will be achieved quickly reached 24 per cent, a record high since 1994. It is clear that this anti-China trend was strengthened by the student protests in March. The same survey showed that 60 per cent of the respondents identified themselves as Taiwanese, the highest level since such surveys began in 1992, while 33 per cent identified as Taiwanese and Chinese and only 4 per cent as Chinese, both these figures being the lowest since the surveys began (BBC Chinese 2014).

The so-called 'southern Taiwan factor' does not, in fact, have any significant effect on people's position on cross-Strait policies. The category of 'mainlander' is a significant variable when controlling other variables in light of people's attitudes towards economic opening up by the ECFA and towards institutional acknowledgement by the recognition of Chinese degrees. With regard to permitting Chinese students to study in Taiwan and increasing the quotas of group tourists, the mainlander effect disappeared when party identification and national identity were taken into consideration.

On the surface, the influence of identification with the party on the positions of respondents with regard to cross-Strait policies appears to correspond with our expectations. Green supporters showed a strong tendency towards opposing policies for greater interaction with China. But it is worth pointing out that green and blue support does not make up the entire spectrum of Taiwan political affiliation. Together, the greens and the blues only make up about 50 per cent of the population (blue 34 per cent, green 17 per cent). What is the position on cross-Strait policies of the other 50 per cent which does not have a strong party identification? Generally speaking, these citizens were located precisely between the blues and the greens. Given the similarity of their personal backgrounds with regard to age, gender, socio-economic status and ethnicity, middle voters who were neither blue nor green tended to show less support for cross-Strait policies than blue supporters.

Lastly, the surprising impact of gender on support for cross-Strait policies is noteworthy and demands an explanation. This study found that a higher percentage of Taiwanese women than men opposed the increases in social exchanges with China. There were few differences between women and men with regard to their positions on economic issues, such as the ECFA. However, when background factors such as marriage status and income were taken into account, men and women were found to be deeply divided in their opinions on social issues. These issues included cultural and educational exchanges, recognition of Chinese diplomas and social interaction.

Table 9.7 shows quite clearly that male support for cross-Strait policies is consistently higher than female support for the same policies. The issues and corresponding figures for male and female are:

1 ECFA (48 per cent vs 44 per cent);
2 allowing Chinese degree-seeking students to study in Taiwan (55 per cent vs 46 per cent);
3 recognizing Chinese university degrees (49 per cent vs 40 per cent);
4 open to individual tourists (50 per cent vs 39 per cent);
5 increasing group tourist quota (47 per cent vs 33 per cent).

When economic openings were placed alongside other factors, the differences in the percentages between the genders were not imbalanced. However, with regard to other issues such as educational exchanges, institutional acknowledgement and social interaction, taking into account personal background (education, marriage, income and ethnicity), females showed a stronger tendency towards opposing policies than males.

Tables 9.8 to 9.11 analyse the relationship between gender, party identification and each of the policies under consideration. Table 9.8 shows that, on the topic of the ECFA, gender was not a factor with regard to support for the policy

Table 9.8 Cross tables of gender, party and the ECFA (%)

Party affiliation		ECFA		
		Support (N = 280)	Oppose (N = 32)	Total (N = 312)
Blue	Male	51	56	52
	Female	49	44	48
		Support (N = 198)	Oppose (N = 317)	Total (N = 515)
Non-blue	Male	56	55	56
	Female	44	45	45

Table 9.9 Cross tables of gender, party and allowing Chinese students into Taiwan (%)

Party affiliation		Allowing Chinese students		
		Support (N = 277)	Oppose (N = 92)	Total (N = 369)
Blue	Male	55	36	50
	Female	45	64	50
		Support (N = 274)	Oppose (N = 386)	Total (N = 660)
Non-blue	Male	54	49	51
	Female	46	51	49

Table 9.10 Cross tables of gender, party and recognition of Chinese degrees (%)

Party affiliation		Recognition of Chinese degrees		
		Support (N = 250)	*Oppose (N = 113)*	*Total (N = 363)*
Blue	Male	55	38	50
	Female	45	62	50
		Support (N = 233)	*Oppose (N = 431)*	*Total (N = 664)*
Non-blue	Male	56	49	52
	Female	44	51	49

Table 9.11 Cross tables of gender, party and opening to individual tourists (%)

Party affiliation		Opening to individual travellers		
		Support (N = 160)	*Oppose (N = 88)*	*Total (N = 248)*
Blue	Male	58	35	50
	Female	43	65	50
		Support (N = 162)	*Oppose (N = 261)*	*Total (N = 423)*
Non-blue	Male	53	49	50
	Female	48	51	50

among blue and green voters. The difference between male and female blue voters expressed as a ratio was small (51 per cent; 49 per cent).

Table 9.9 shows that for educational exchanges, the gender difference among the non-blue voters was not significant. However, among the blue voters, females were relatively more strongly opposed to the policy of opening to Chinese students than males. Among the non-blue voters, opposition to the same policy was split between 49 per cent of the males and 51 per cent of the females. Conversely, among the blue voters, 36 per cent of the males and 64 per cent of the females were opposed to the educational exchange issue. The same gender discrepancy exists among the blue voters with regard to the issues of recognizing Chinese university degrees and increasing the quota of Chinese tourists. In Table 9.10, a gender difference was not obvious among the non-blue voters on the issue of recognizing Chinese degrees. However, among the blue voters, 38 per cent of the male respondents were opposed to recognizing Chinese degrees, against 62 per cent of the female respondents. As for opening Taiwan to individual Chinese travellers, the non-blue gender difference was negligible, but for the blue voters, 35 per cent of the male respondents and 65 per cent of the female respondents were opposed to this issue (Table 9.11). Similarly, 36 per cent of the male blue voters were opposed to increasing group tourist quotas, against 64 per cent of the female blue voters (Table 9.12).

Table 9.12 Cross tables of gender, party and increasing Chinese group tourist quotas (%)

Party affiliation		Increasing Chinese group tourist quotas		
		Support (N = 148)	*Oppose (N = 89)*	*Total (N = 237)*
Blue	Male	59	36	50
	Female	41	64	50
		Support (N = 141)	*Oppose (N = 243)*	*Total (N = 384)*
Non-blue	Male	56	45	49
	Female	44	55	51

This analysis shows that, in Taiwan, the female respondents adopted a position on cross-Strait policies that differed from that of their male counterparts. On economic opening and trade, the differences in the responses of the women and the men were not so marked. However, on non-economic policies, women were more likely to adopt an opposing position than men, for example on policies pertaining to institutional acknowledgement and social interaction. Why is this the case? A final explanation has not yet been found, but a few working hypotheses present themselves. First, the differences may derive from a personal need for stability, in particular for stable homes and committed relationships. The issues of permitting Chinese students to study in Taiwan, recognizing Chinese degrees and increasing group tourist quotas would have an immediate impact on people's living environment and social networks. For housewives and single women, such policies would have the potential to overturn or disrupt the predictability and stability of everyday life. The last 20 years have witnessed Taiwanese businessmen going away to China and sending money back home to their wives, who have tended to feel that this development threatens the stability of their marriages and the security of their valued home environment. Although only a few women live in separated families because their husbands work in China, the impact of the feelings of insecurity that this has engendered has been widely acknowledged within Taiwanese society. In fact, women would be more likely to take a conservative position on increasing cross-Strait interaction in order to ensure that it remains in the realm of predictability and stability.

Second, these differences may reflect the gender differences in moral values that affect political attitudes. For example, recent scholarship suggests that, in the US, men and women responded differently when asked about cultural issues such as anti-war matters, civil rights, abortion rights, women's rights and homosexual rights (Kaufmann 2002, 2006); women tend to be more concerned about social welfare issues, while men tend to be more concerned about economic issues (Thorson and Stambough 1994). In Taiwan, women are more concerned about social issues than men, and this may produce a gender difference in party support and electoral behaviour (Yang 2006, Yang and Liu 2009). This can lead to their having different attitudes towards cross-Strait social policies.

Third, Taiwanese women may feel that they face a potential threat from Chinese mistresses. Even if Taiwan's economy benefits from the ECFA, those who are making money and enjoying life are mainly men, while women have to bear the brunt of the social consequences resulting from the increasing cross-Strait interaction. For example, the Taiwanese media has recently reported many stories about the 'Chinese mistress' which has engendered further distrust among women on policies of cross-Strait interactions and led them to feel victimized in cross-Strait social interactions (Shen 2005, 2008). Many women do not see benefits accruing from further cross-Strait social exchanges. In fact, they feel disadvantaged by these social exchanges and feel that they do not stand to benefit from them (Shen 2014). Finally, the differences may be related to concerns about the impact on the marriage market. Increasing social interaction with China would have the effect of stimulating the marriage market, leaving unmarried Taiwanese women with the feeling that they are now in competition with Chinese women. This could place the fear in the minds of Taiwanese housewives that their young children may find potential marriage partners among the Chinese men and women on the college campus. It could be argued that, as a result of these factors, the effects of party identification, socio-economic status, age and gender on social policies remain independent and significant variables in today's Taiwanese society.

Conclusion

In Taiwan, for some social groups – females, the younger generation, and people with lower socio-economic status – the reservations expressed with regard to cross-Strait policies specifically reflect the collective concerns and anxieties caused by the surging China impact, particularly after the acceleration in cross-Strait exchanges after 2008, which eventually led to the Anti-Trade Pact Movement in 2014. These social groups are economically vulnerable and relatively disadvantaged in Taiwanese society. They seem uncomfortable and insecure in the face of increasing social interactions with Chinese people coming to Taiwan. This kind of collective anxiety did not exist in previous years, i.e. before 2008. For example, studies on Taiwanese attitudes towards immigration policies for bride immigrants from China and Southeast Asia have shown that, in the early 2000s, gender, age and socio-economic status had little effect on people's attitudes regarding immigration policies. During that period, when cross-Strait contacts were not so intensive and interactions not so frequent, people's attitudes regarding cross-Strait policies were shaped mainly by partisan competition and political rhetoric, instead of socio-economic status and self-interest (Chen and Yu 2005; Tsai 2011). However, when cross-Strait exchanges intensified and everyday life was affected, people's attitudes altered, reflecting their emotional feelings and interpretations of China's rising impact on civil society in Taiwan.

This chapter shows that the reservations with regard to cross-Strait policies in Taiwan that have accumulated since 2008 are not only drawn along partisan lines, and that they have long transcended the pattern of Taiwanese party politics. It is noteworthy that middle voters who are neither pro-KMT nor pro-DPP tend to show significantly less support for cross-Strait policies than pro-KMT people. In fact, it was the middle voters who decided the 2008 and 2012 elections by casting their votes overwhelmingly for Ma. Their support for cross-Strait liberalization policies has apparently been declining since then. In addition to party lines, those opposed to the further liberalization of cross-Strait relations come from different social groups and are not limited to traditional DPP supporters. They are found among the younger generation and have low or moderate incomes. Furthermore, women are less likely than men to support liberalization. The dispute on the Cross-Strait Trade in Services Agreement in early 2014 has shed light on an interesting fact: if the proposed agreement had been perceived simply as an economic issue, it might have garnered the support of the majority of the public. However, the Sunflower student movement encouraged each professional and social group to scrutinize and unravel the agreement, revealing the economic losses and negative social consequences that could result, and this sharply reduced the social support basis for strengthening cross-Strait exchanges.

President Ma's success in the 2008 presidential election has apparently not translated into sustainable support for his cross-Strait policies. In fact, public support for cross-Strait liberalization and the hopes placed in increased exchanges and interaction gradually evaporated after 2008. Subsequent surveys have revealed that two main factors created support for increased cross-Strait liberalization: first, the belief that China would democratize, and second, the belief that cross-Strait trade would ameliorate their own economic conditions. In addition to age, gender, education, income and political position, these two factors still have a significant effect (Chen 2013). All other conditions being equal, those who believe in China's democratization and who believe that they stand to benefit from cross-Strait interaction tend to support cross-Strait liberalization and trade policies. But the problem is that these two conditions cannot be taken for granted. If people start to think that China's political system will not change or that their personal economic situation will not improve as a result of cross-Strait trade liberalization and social integration, then their support for both will decrease. Since the Sunflower movement in the spring of 2014, it seems clear that public sentiment has begun to change. Those groups that reject the agreement are mainly students and young white-collar workers, and they have led the public and media circles to seriously assess the economic losses, political risks and consequences of growing inequality in wealth and power. These groups are not necessarily anti-Chinese, but they are certainly opposed to undemocratic one-party rule in China, and they are even more concerned that Taiwan will become simply an extension of Chinese Communist Party politics.

Appendix I

Table A9.1 Descriptive statistics

Variable	First round 2010/06 (N = 1,242)				Second round 2010/12 (N = 1,238)			
	N	%	Mean	S.D.	N	%	Mean	S.D.
Age	1219	98	47	15	1188	96	48	15
Education								
Below junior high school	299	24			344	28		
High school	364	29			359	29		
Higher degree	575	46			530	43		
Gender								
Male	604	49			601	49		
Female	638	51			637	52		
Marriage status								
Married	964	78			994	80		
Unmarried	276	22			236	19		
Area								
Southern Taiwan	321	26			302	24		
Other areas	915	74			936	76		
Ethnicity								
Hakka	152	12			145	12		
Minnan	894	72			891	72		
Mainlander	170	14			170	14		
Missing values	26	2			32	3		
Individual/household monthly	1200	97	5.0	2.8	973	79	7.5	3.5
Income	(3~4,000 NT dollars)				(5~6,000 NT dollars)			
Missing values	42	3			265	21		
Party affiliation								
Blue	416	34			416	34		
Green	207	17			206	17		
Choose candidate (or policy)	202	16			204	17		
Support all	49	4						
Support none	333	27			365	30		
Missing values	35	3			47	4		
Unification or independence sentiment[1]								
Unification	111	9			206	17		
Independence	253	20			77	6		
Depends on situation	463	37						
Maintain status quo	348	28			858	69		
Missing values	67	5			97	8		

continued

Table A9.1 Continued

Variable	First round 2010/06 (N = 1,242)				Second round 2010/12 (N = 1,238)			
	N	%	Mean	S.D.	N	%	Mean	S.D.

Do you think the signing of the ECFA will increase wealth disparities in Taiwan, decrease them, or not have any impact?

Increase	632	51						
Decrease	78	6						
No influence	246	20						
Missing values	193	16						

In cross-Strait economic interaction what do you think is most important: Taiwan's economic advantage, Taiwan's sovereignty, or are both equally important?

Economic advantage	665	54						
National sovereignty	391	32						
Both are important	137	11						
Missing values	49	4						

After the opening of Taiwan to Chinese tourists, do you feel closer to China?

Yes (closer)					457	37		
No (more distant or no different)					667	54		
Missing values					114	9		

Do you have a good impression of Chinese tourists?

Yes					301	24		
No					721	58		
Missing values					216	17		

Do you have a bad impression of Chinese tourists?

Yes					482	39		
No					614	50		
Missing values					142	12		

Notes
'Missing values' include those who did not know how to respond, abstained from answering, evaded the question, had no opinion, or gave some other answer that could not be categorized.
1 There was a discrepancy in the questions in the two different rounds of interviews. See text for discussion.

Notes

1 The three bills delayed in the legislature until the summer of 2014 include the setting up of free economic pilot zones, a monitoring mechanism for cross-Strait pacts, and the endorsement of the Cross-Strait Service Trade Agreement with China signed the previous year. These three issues were listed as the KMT' top priorities in the upcoming session of the legislature slated for September 2014.
2 For details of these two telephone surveys, see Institute of Sociology, Academia Sinica (2013).
3 For example, a telephone poll conducted on 22 April 2010 by the *China Times* showed that 47 per cent of the Taiwanese supported Chinese students coming to Taiwan, but only 40 per cent supported the recognition of Chinese degrees. And on 21–22 April 2010, a TVBS telephone survey found that 51 per cent of the Taiwanese supported

accepting Chinese degree-seeking students in Taiwan, but only 35 per cent supported the recognition of Chinese degrees. See www.tvbs.com.tw/FILE_DB/DL_DB/yijung/201005/yijung-20100504120818.pdf (accessed 15 October 2012).

4 A survey conducted by the Mainland Affairs Council from 1 to 5 September 2010 reported that 60 per cent of the population supported a 'slow opening' to Chinese individual tourists. See www.mac.gov.tw/public/Attachment/09211884354.pdf (accessed 15 October 2012).

References

BBC Chinese (2014) 'Taiwan mindiao: taidu zhichilü pan xingao' [Taiwan Poll: Taiwan Independence Reached Record High], 14 July, available at www.bbc.co.uk/zhongwen/trad/china/2014/07/140714_polls_tw_independence.shtl (accessed 31 July 2014).

Chen, Chih-Jou Jay (2013) 'Converging or Diverging? The Dynamics of Cross-Strait Social Relations', paper presented at IOS-IASA Joint Conference for Young Sociologists, University of Tokyo.

Chen, Chih-Jou Jay, and Yu, Te-Lin (2005) 'Taiwan minzhong dui wailai pei'ou yimin zhengce de taidu' [Public Attitudes towards Taiwan's Foreign Spouses Immigration Policies], *Taiwanese Sociology*, 10: 95–148.

Institute of Sociology, Academia Sinica (2013) *Shehui yixiang diaocha zhixing baogao* [Reports on Social Image Survey], Taipei: Academia Sinica.

Kaufmann, Karen M. (2002) 'Culture Wars, Secular Realignment and the Gender Gap in Party Identification', *Political Behaviour*, 24: 283–307.

Kaufmann, Karen M. (2006) 'The Gender Gap', *Political Science and Politics*, 39: 447–453.

Shen, Hsiu-Hua (2005) ' "The First Taiwanese Wives" and "the Chinese Mistresses": The International Division of Labour in Familial and Intimate Relations across the Taiwan Strait', *Global Networks*, 5, 4: 419–437.

Shen, Hsiu-Hua (2008) 'Becoming "the First Wives": Gender, Intimacy, and Regional Economy between Taiwan and China', in Liu, Jieyu, and Jackson, Stevi (eds) *East Asian Sexualities: Modernity, Gender and New Sexual Cultures*, London: Zed Books, 216–235.

Shen, Hsiu-Hua (2014) 'Stay in Marriage across the Taiwan Strait: Gender, Migration, and Transnational Family', in Davis, Deborah, and Friedman, Sara (eds) *Marriage and Family in Cosmopolitan China*, Stanford, CA: Stanford University Press, 262–284.

Thorson, Gregory R., and Stambough, Stephen J. (1994) 'Understanding the Gender Gap through the Paradigm of the Michigan Model', paper presented at the Annual Meeting of the American Political Science Association, New York.

Tsai, Ming-Chang (2011) 'Cong jiechu dao jieshou? Hunyin yimin zhichi taidu de zaijianshi' [From Contact to Acceptance: Reexamining Attitudes Towards Marriage Immigrants], *Journal of Taiwan Studies*, 7: 1–23.

Yang, Wan-Ying (2006) 'Xingbie chongzu huo jiezu? Bijiao Oumei toupiao xingbie chaju de jieshi moshi' [Gender Realignment or Dealignment? Comparing the Explanatory Models of the Gap between European and American Gender Voting], *Issues and Studies*, 45: 103–131.

Yang, Wan-Ying, and Liu, Jie-Wei (2009) 'Tantao tongdu taidu de xingbie chaju: heping zhanzheng yu fazhan liyi de guandian' [Exploring Gender Differences on Attitudes towards Independence/Unification: Perspectives on Peace and War and Development-Interest], *Journal of Electoral Studies*, 1: 37–66.

10 Cross-Strait trade and class cleavages in Taiwan

Thung-Hong Lin

Cross-Strait trade has become a controversial political issue in Taiwan. During the last two decades, Taiwan's degree of dependency on cross-Strait trade continuously increased from 4 per cent in 1990 to more than 23 per cent in 2010 (Taiwan Mainland Affairs Council 2011). In the same period, Taiwanese capital constantly flowed into China. The investment dependency ratio, calculated by dividing Taiwan's investment amount in China by Taiwan's total overseas direct investment amount, augmented from less than 20 per cent to more than 80 per cent (Lin and Hu 2011). The expansion of cross-Strait trade and capital flow has instigated political debates on developmental strategy and national identity in Taiwan. In 2010, the signing and ratification of a free trade agreement titled the Economic Cooperation Framework Agreement (ECFA), a major economic and cross-Strait policy of the Ma Ying-Jeou administration, triggered large-scale protests. The DPP Chairperson, Tsai Ing-Wen, the leader of the opposition, criticized the ECFA, claiming that it would lead to increasing income inequality, particularly among peasants and workers (*Taipei Times*, 27 April 2010). In 2014, the Cross-Strait Agreement on Trade in Services, another open trade policy, led to the occupation of the Legislative Yuan by the student-led 'Sunflower' movement in protest against the pact.

The expanding economic integration with China has also given rise to some unintended social consequences. For example, the unemployment rate rose from about 1.5 per cent in the early 1990s to more than 4 per cent in the last decade; the Gini coefficient, a popular index of income inequality, also amplified from 0.31 to higher than 0.34. In addition, the number of families under the official poverty line doubled in Taiwan during the same period. As Figure 10.1 illustrates, Taiwan's rising poverty rate is robustly associated with the trade and investment dependency ratios on China in the last two decades. Most families in poverty suffer from unemployment and lower income as a result of factory closures and the importation of low cost manufactured goods and agricultural products from China. Cross-Strait economic integration has produced winners and losers and has reshaped the distribution of wealth in Taiwan.

On the other hand, some scholars have found that class voting has influenced Taiwan's electoral turnouts during the last decade. Hu *et al.* (2009) examined the Taiwan Social Change Survey (TSCS) datasets between 1992 and 2004, and

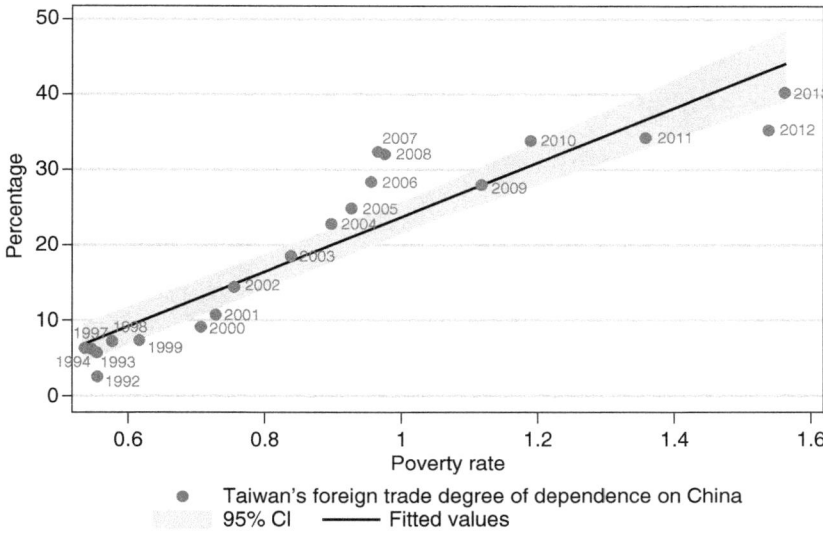

Figure 10.1 Cross-Strait trade and poverty rate in Taiwan, 1992–2013 (source: poverty rate – household income < 60% basic household consumption – was obtained from the Directorate General of Budget, Accounting and Statistics 2012 'Macro Database', website of National Statistics, http://61.60.106.82/pxweb/Dialog/statfile9L.asp; the trade dependence rate was obtained from the Bureau of Foreign Trade, the Ministry of Economic Affairs 2012 'Trade Database', website of Bureau of Foreign Trade, http://cus93.trade.gov.tw/fsci/, accessed 13 May 2012).

discovered that before 2000, pan-green voters mainly came from the self-employed and upper-middle classes, while pan-blue voters were mainly administrators, peasants and workers. This finding is consistent with the observation that Taiwan's middle classes were the main supporters of the political opposition in the process of democratization (Hsiao 1989; Huntington 1991). However, after 2000, workers and peasants switched their political affiliation to the pan-green camp, while the upper-middle class, mainly capitalists and managers, shifted their support to the pan-blue camp (Lin and Hu 2011). The changes in class politics have also been reflected in the turnouts for local elections during the last decade.

Figure 10.2 illustrates the voting turnouts for the 1998 local election and for the 2004 and 2012 presidential elections at county level. Electoral districts that were won by the (blue) Chinese Nationalist Party (KMT) are marked in white, and electoral districts that were won by the (green) Democratic Progressive Party (DPP) are marked in dark grey. As Figure 10.2 shows, deepening class cleavages have reshaped the geographical distribution of pan-green and pan-blue voters. Paralleling the other developing countries under democratization (Huntington 1991), in the late 1990s, the DPP candidates won the majority of the middle-class votes in large cities. In contrast, at least starting with the presidential

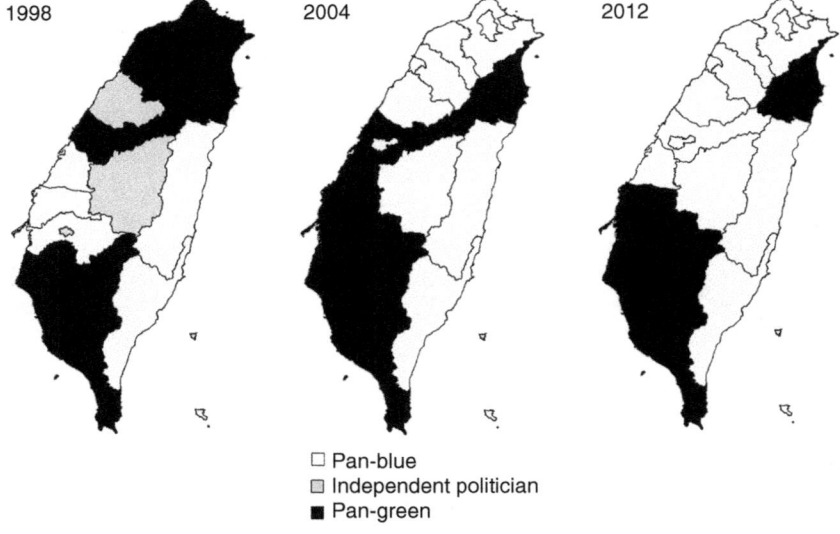

Figure 10.2 Changing geography of pan-blue- and pan-green-dominated cities/counties in Taiwan: 1998 = turnout for local election; 2004 = turnout for presidential election; 2012 = turnout for presidential election (source: Central Election Commission 2013 'Election Statistics', http://engweb.cec.gov.tw/files/103429.php, accessed 17 April 2013).

election in 2004, the DPP government has mainly been sustained by voters in southern Taiwan who, to a great extent, are blue-collar workers and peasants, while employers and the middle classes overwhelmingly shifted their support to the KMT. The new political landscape, which partially reflects the geographical distribution of social classes, has been taken for granted and dubbed 'blue sky (north), green earth (south)' by the mass media in Taiwan.

It seems that there was a 'class realignment' of Taiwan politics around 2000–2004. Since this realignment occurred, the social foundation of the green and blue parties has gradually approached the left-wing–right-wing cleavage in Western democracies. Although the 'class voting' phenomenon was confirmed by a recent survey in 2010 (Lin and Hu 2011), without a commitment to socialist ideology and organizational supports from trade unions, it is difficult to explain why the DPP became more attractive for workers and peasants during the last decade (Chang and Chang 2010). Although some of the recent social surveys have provided evidence of the rising working-class identity and the relative deprivation of the workers (Lin 2013), it is difficult to sustain the argument that a working class is forming as a result of increasing class consciousness in Taiwan.

As some authors have argued, one possible origin of Taiwan's new 'class politics' is the China impact through economic integration (Wong 2010; Lin and

Hu 2011). This chapter investigates the relationship between cross-Strait trade and class inequality in Taiwan. According to the literature on open economy politics (OEP), for a relatively advanced economy, the adoption of an open trade policy by a developing economy increases the income gap between employers and employees as well as the wage gap between skilled workers and unskilled workers. The deterioration of income distribution creates coalitions of social classes for and against expanding trade relations. The relationship between the cross-Strait open trade policy and the deepening class cleavages in Taiwan is a typical case of OEP theories.

In this study, I use a pooled dataset from two national surveys conducted during 2010–2013 to demonstrate the relationships between cross-Strait trade, income inequality and class voting. The statistical results support the contention that cross-Strait trade has changed life chances and material returns for different social classes. With regard to income distribution, the employers and the middle classes have benefited from cross-Strait trade, but the self-employed, the peasants and the workers have not. The deepening of income inequality has also influenced people's opinions on open-trade policies: i.e. in the case of the ECFA, the employers and the middle classes have welcomed the policy but the peasants and the workers are sceptical of it. Finally, mediated by the different cross-Strait trade policy preferences, class backgrounds have influenced people's voting behaviour in Taiwan's recent elections.

Classes and trade

The politics of trade is a conventional issue in the international relations literature (Gourevitch 1978; Putnam 1988; Milner 1997), but only a few empirical studies have linked the issue with social stratification models (Evens *et al.* 1993). Taking cross-Strait trade as a typical case of economic globalization, this chapter examines the association between open trade and class cleavage. The OEP literature lays out an appropriate theoretical framework for discussing the relationship between cross-Strait trade and class politics in Taiwan.

In economics literature, the Heckscher-Ohlin (H-O) model, which builds on the Ricardian theory of comparative advantage and is sometimes extended by the Stolper-Samuelson (S-S) theorem (in this combined form, referred to as the HO-SS theorem), explains the association between the endowment of production factors (namely, assets in class analysis) and the income distribution effects under free trade conditions. This model implies that, with regard to the cross-national differences in production factors' endowment, open trade policies impact on the profits made by the owners of production factors (namely assets). The owners of a relatively abundant production factor who are faced with high domestic market competition and low profits can benefit from exporting their products for a better price to another economy where the same production factor is relatively scarce. In contrast, the owners of a relatively scarce asset may enjoy a domestic market shortage or a monopoly and higher prices, and would suffer disadvantage as a result of cheaper products being imported. Therefore, although

open trade benefits the owners of relatively abundant assets, it impacts negatively on the owners of relatively scarce assets in an economy (Lake 2009).

In a simplified two-country and two-factor (labour/capital) HO-SS model, for
example in the case of more developed countries with abundant capital and
scarce labour (i.e. economies enjoying lower interest rates and higher wage
levels), open trade policies benefit capital owners (i.e. the employer), especially
the exporters of capital-intensive products, through increasing prices and profit
rates, while open trade policies disadvantage labour (i.e. the employee), especially by reducing employment and wage levels through the import of cheaper
labour-intensive products. In contrast, in less developed countries with abundant
labour and scarce capital (i.e. economies with higher interest rates and lower
wage levels), open trade policies benefit labour because of the increasing export
of labour-intensive products and, therefore, gradually rising employment and
wage levels. The policies may suppress the capital-intensive industries (so-called
infant industries) in the less developed countries because of the negative impact
of imports on their sales and profit rates.

Rogowski (1989) developed a class-politics model, based on the HO-SS
theorem, which he used to analyse historical cases of trade policy. He constructed this model with three types of asset owners: the owner of capital, the
owner of land (peasant), and the owner of labour power (working class). In political struggles over trade policy, the classes that hold relatively scarce assets who
expect to suffer economically as a result of open trade tend to form a protectionist coalition, while the classes who hold relatively abundant assets and expect to
benefit as a result of open trade tend to support free trade policies. Depending on
the relative scarcity or abundance of asset endowments, a range of different class
coalitions that are for or against open trade policies may be formed and realigned
in different countries and eras in international trade negotiations.

Rogowski's three-class model – coalitions and struggles among the bour-
geoisie, the working class and the farmers – fitted well with the historical experiences of European trade politics in the nineeenth century and the early twentieth
(Rogowski 1989). In the twenty-first century, the attention of scholars has been
drawn to the role played by skilled workers in the process of globalization
(Wood 1994). As Atkinson (2008) discovered, the extended HO-SS model can
be applied to examine the increasing wage gap between the skilled workers and
unskilled workers in OECD countries. Wage inequality has become the major
source of deteriorating income distribution in the advanced economies.

Revising Rogowski's model, Hiscox (2002) argued that skilled workers and
managers, (i.e. 'the new middle classes' in the neo-Marxist class schema, see
Wright [1985]), also play important roles in OEP. In more advanced economies,
open trade benefits the relatively technology-intensive industries and more
highly skilled workers, who may thus be persuaded to support open trade policies. In contrast, open trade damages the more labour-intensive industries and
unskilled workers, who may tend to support protectionist policies.

Second, this new theory focuses on the capacity of factor mobility in international trade. In the original HO-SS theory, production factors are assumed

immobile, but this assumption is not realistic. Reconsider the two-country and two-factor model. If one factor is allowed to move across two countries, which means opening the market to the asset owners, the effect is indeed similar to that obtained under open trade conditions. The owners, whose asset is relatively abundant in their country, can move to another country to obtain a higher factor price; in contrast, the owners whose asset is relatively scarce may suffer disadvantage from the factor market competition. For example, migrant workers from developing countries may benefit by moving to a developed economy, where the labour supply is limited and wages are comparatively high because of unionization. However, with regard to wage levels and employment opportunities, unionized workers may not favour a liberal migrant policy (Wood 1994). In advanced economies, in contrast, capitalists and professionals can take advantage of international trade, not only because of factor abundance but also because of their own capacity to move their capital to developing countries, where the wage levels of unskilled workers are low, which increases the capitalists' profit margin (Hiscox 2002). In addition, some scholars have argued that the assets' higher transnational mobile capacity increases the level of market information, the bargaining power and the rent-seeking opportunities of the asset owners, while lower transnational mobile capacity impacts negatively on the life chances and bargaining power of the other classes (i.e. Acemoglu and Robinson 2005).

Recently, some studies have identified links between trade policies and partisanship. Milner and Judkins (2004), for instance, examined the changes in trade policies in 25 advanced economies from 1945 to 1998 by conducting an analysis of cross-national panel data at the aggregate level. The results of this analysis showed that left-wing governments tend to sustain protectionism, and right-wing administrations tend to improve free trade. They concluded that the traditional class cleavage and political ideologies – socialism or neo-liberalism – shaped the ruling party's trade policy in the democratic countries of the developed world (Milner and Judkins 2004).

Another important issue is the role played by voters in the formulation of trade policy. Since the OEP researchers mainly relied on historical comparative methods and aggregate data, their studies largely neglected the empirical evidences of voting behaviour. Without an individual foundation, such as surveys on trade policy preferences among voters in different social classes, the OEP studies cannot provide a satisfactory explanation for the incentives that encourage partisanship among voters. In addition, the OEP scholars have never linked their theory to major stratification models, neo-Marxist class analysis (Wright 1997), the neo-Weberian class schema (Erikson and Goldthorpe 1992), etc. On the other hand, social class theorists did not show interest in OEP theory until the debate on economic globalization started to emerge in the last two decades (Babb 2005). Moreover, very few empirical studies on trade policies can be found in the social stratification literature (see e.g. Grusky 2008).

The HO-SS model and the 'Rogowski-Hiscox' theory can be applied to test the class voting hypothesis in the case of the cross-Strait trade policy between

China and Taiwan. Although testing the class voting hypotheses on trade in the context of China's authoritarian government may seem questionable, it is feasible to investigate the theory of income inequality and the class politics of cross-Strait trade in Taiwan's democracy. By applying an appropriate social stratification model, we can test the OEP hypotheses by analysing the social surveys mentioned above.

Applying the simplified schema of neo-Marxist class analysis (Wright 1985, 1997), I divided Taiwan's workforce into four class locations: the capitalists (the owners of capital), the new middle classes (the owners of skills and authority), the self-employed (including peasants, the owners of farmland) and the working class (the owners of labour power). As the OEP studies imply, the expansion of trade between Taiwan and China would change the respective income distribution and voting behaviour of all four groups.

According to the HO-SS model, expanding cross-Strait trade would benefit the owners of capital and skills, which are relatively abundant in Taiwan but scarce in China, and would disadvantage the owners of farmland and labour power, which are relatively scarce in Taiwan but abundant in China. In addition, in comparison with peasants and workers, the owners of capital and skills are more likely to move across the Taiwan Strait and, hence, benefit from their capabilities and mobility. The distribution effects of open trade on earning could increase the average income of the capitalists and new middle classes (Hypothesis 1a) but could also, in relative terms, reduce the average income of the unskilled workers and self-employed/peasants (Hypothesis 1b).

Following the Rogowski-Hiscox theory, the potential winner and loser of trade would become the foundation for the political coalitions supporting or opposing free trade policy. In the case of Taiwan, it is assumed that the capitalists and the new middle classes support open trade policies (Hypothesis 2a), while the working class and peasants favour protectionism (Hypothesis 2b).

Similarly to the situation in European countries, the social cleavage between those supporting and those opposing free trade is reflected in party politics in Taiwan. Since the pan-blue politicians are committed to cross-Strait trade liberalization, as embodied in the ECFA, capitalists, managers and skilled workers will vote for the pan-blue parties (Hypothesis 3a). Although it is difficult to argue that the pan-green parties consistently promoted policies that oppose economic globalization, they generally show support for Taiwan's independence and have recently started to criticize cross-Strait trade policies. Therefore, since the pan-green parties claim that they will prevent Taiwan's political integration with China, the working class and farmers will tend to support the pan-green camp (Hypothesis 3b).

Table 10.1 displays the three falsifiable hypotheses derived from the OEP theories. In the next section, I use a pooled dataset from two recent representative national surveys conducted in 2010–2013 to test the OEP hypotheses of income distribution, trade policy preference and class voting on an individual base.

It should be noted that, in this chapter, the concept of 'class politics' is applied in a more flexible way. The class voting may not imply that trade policy

Table 10.1 Hypotheses from the literature of open economy politics

Hypothesis	Cross-Strait trade's impacts on Taiwanese society
HO theory (H1)	H1a: Benefit the owners of capital and skills (middle classes) H1b: Damage the self-employed (peasant) and working class
Rogowski-Hiscox theory (H2)	H2a: Employers and middle classes support free-trade policy H2b: Workers and self-employed are in favor of protectionism
Class voting (H3)	H3a: Employers and middle classes vote for pan-blue camp H3b: Workers and self-employed vote for pan-green camp

has triggered the formation of a strong working class in Taiwan. Some trade unions and labour NGOs mobilized against the ECFA, but their political influence was relatively weak. At the same time, although the DPP, in the name of lower-class people, organized protests against the ECFA (*Taipei Times*, 27 April 2010), the debate did not lead to an obvious left turn in the party's ideology. In the context of Taiwan, new class politics mean that voters link their class interests and trade policy preference, and some voters change their party preference. Therefore, it can be said that the impact of cross-Strait trade politics on social class reshaped the political landscapes in the recent elections.

Measurement and data

The dataset for this chapter is drawn from two national representative telephone surveys conducted by Academia Sinica's Institute of Sociology in Taiwan during 2010–2013. The first survey, the Taiwan Social Image Survey (TSIS) 2010, can be viewed as the pre-test for the second, with a sample consisting of 1,242 adults – including 638 females and 604 males aged over 20 – interviewed in June 2010 when the ECFA was signed and ratified. Valid national samples were collected in 2011, 2012 and 2013 for the second survey, which was entitled the China Impact [in Taiwan] Survey project. The two surveys asked not only about the interviewees' opinions and expectations regarding cross-Strait trade but also about their monthly income, the number of trips that they had made to China in the last year, and their voting behaviour. After the information obtained from the two surveys had been pooled, the dataset consisted of 4,876 adults.

As the social stratification literature shows, the theoretical definition and empirical categorization of social classes are a contested terrain in sociology (Erikson and Goldthorpe 1992; Wright 1997; Hout 2008). Here, I will not comment directly on the debates on competing class theories; for practical reasons, I will employ neo-Marxist class analysis and introduce the simplified four-class typology – the capitalist, the self-employed, the new middle classes and the working class (Wright 1985). Empirically, the term 'employer (capitalist)' refers to business owners with employees, the term 'self-employed' refers to peasants and business owners without employees; the term 'new middle classes' refers to skilled workers and managers; and the others belong to the category of unskilled workers (e.g. the proletariat or working class).[1] As we will see, the four-class model matches the OEP assumptions very well.

Class cleavage is not the only factor that determines the political preferences of Taiwanese voters. As most studies on Taiwan elections have repeatedly emphasized, ethnicity and national identity are also major issues that shape the island's political landscape (Wang 2005). Some scholars have argued that ethnicity, class and their interaction influence Taiwanese voters' choice (Wu 1996). In addition, using the surveys of the 1996, 2000 and 2004 presidential elections without trying to link class analysis with the OEP literature, Wong (2010) claimed that cross-Strait economic integration has led to the emergence of class cleavages in Taiwan. Following the insights gained from earlier electoral studies, Lin and Hu (2011) displayed a voting behaviour model based on class and ethnicity. Some scholars have argued that there are interactions between ethnic background and class location (Yang 2007), while other studies show that the effect of class–ethnicity interactions on voting behaviour is not statistically significant (Hu *et al.* 2009). In my pooled dataset, the interactions are complex and mostly insignificant. To single out the effects of classes, I adopted the parsimonious principle, taking class and ethnicity as independent variables in most statistical models.

Figure 10.3 illustrates the link between class and ethnic cleavages and Taiwanese voters' political preference. The figure displays three cause-effect chains. First, the class location determines people's mobility capacity and material returns associated with cross-Strait trade policy (H1). Therefore, the first set of statistical models focuses on the factor mobility and income inequality of members of different social classes. The number of trips made to China in one year is used to measure the mobility capacity of the members of different classes, while the monthly income is used to measure the material returns from trade. Because the income data is skewed to the left rather than normal distribution, I used a natural logarithmic transformation to normalize it. The results are used to test the HO-SS hypotheses (H1a and H1b).

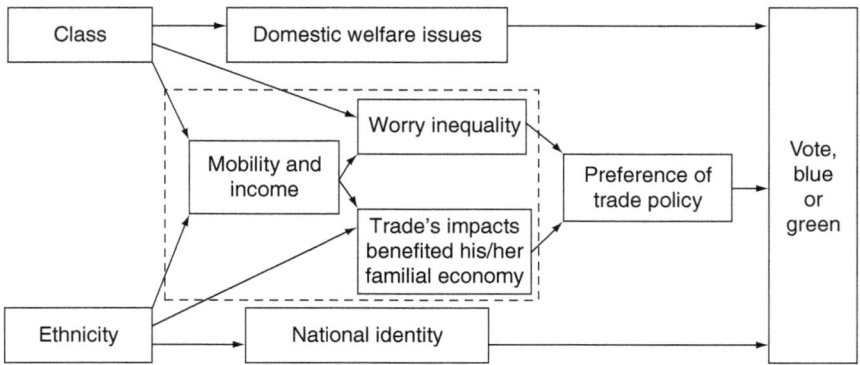

Figure 10.3 Causality among classes, trade and voting behavior in Taiwan (source: revised from Lin and Hu 2011).

Second, class interests or damage to trade influence people's subjective attitudes toward the trade policy. (H2). Two questions are asked to measure people's subjective attitudes on trade with China. The first is 'Do you think that the expansion of cross-Strait trade benefits or damages your family economy?' The second is 'Do you think that the expansion of cross-Strait trade increases or decreases Taiwan's income gap between the rich and the poor?' For an easier understanding of the responses to the two questions, the answer is transferred to the three-point Likert scale; positive means benefit or increase, and negative means disadvantage or decrease. The results are used to test the Rogowski-Hiscox model (H2a and H2b).

Third, after controlling the main effects of ethnicity, national identity and class background, we look at how people's attitudes on trade policy have shaped voters' electoral preferences (H3). It has been mentioned that there is neither strong working-class identification nor socialist ideology within the DPP. This being the case, it is reasonable to argue that the 'class voting' phenomenon in Taiwan is largely related to the voters' subjective attitude to cross-Strait trade. In the 2010 TSIS, respondents were asked 'which party is better at representing the interests of your social class?' In the 2011 wave of CIS, the question was framed as 'which party do you support?' In the 2012 and 2013 waves of the CIS, the question was 'which presidential candidate did you vote for in the 2012 election?' I used the different questions because the surveys revised the questionnaires from time to time. Not surprisingly, the responses to the different questions are highly correlated. I categorized the DPP and the Taiwan Solidarity Union (TSU) as the pan-green camp, and the KMT, the New Party (NP) and the People First Party (PFP) as the pan-blue camp. Although policy differences, competition and conflicts among the parties in the same camp certainly exist, with regard to the parties' general policy line towards China and cross-Strait trade liberalization, the blue/green dichotomy largely holds in election studies on Taiwan (Wu 1996).

In all three-level models, the main control variables are national identity and ethnicity. National identity is measured by the dichotomous variable, pro-independence or anti-independence. The ethnic variable, divided into four groups – Holo, Hakka, mainlander and Aboriginal/others – is determined by the ethnic background of the respondent's father. The other control variables include age, gender, education, marriage status and year of survey dummies. In the subsequent models, the dummies for the class and ethnicity variables are based on the non-workforce and Taiwanese (Holo) group. The descriptive statistics and simple correlations of the selective variables are shown in Tables 10.2 and 10.3.

Method and results

As mentioned earlier, the models are divided into three levels. The two regression models on the first level are displayed in Table 10.4. In model (1) the dependent variable is the number of visits to China in one year, which is the measurement of class mobility. According to the regression results, the significantly positive

Table 10.2 Descriptive statistics of selective variables in the 2010–2013 surveys

Variables	N	Mean	S.D.	Min.	Max.
Log (income)	4,405	10.542	0.904	8.517	12.231
(Number of) visits to China	4,876	0.357	0.898	0	4
Pro-independence	4,873	0.421	0.494	0	1
Benefited/damaged from trade	4,876	0.267	0.880	−1	1
Worry inequality	4,876	0.533	0.714	−1	1
Support pan-blue	4,367	0.409	0.492	0	1
Class location					
Unskilled worker	4,876	0.345	0.476	0	1
New middle classes	4,876	0.281	0.450	0	1
Self-employed (+ peasant)	4,876	0.223	0.416	0	1
Employer	4,876	0.094	0.291	0	1
Non-workforce	4,876	0.057	0.232	0	1
Father's ethnicity					
Holo	4,876	0.736	0.441	0	1
Hakka	4,876	0.108	0.311	0	1
Mainlander	4,876	0.128	0.334	0	1
Aboriginal/others	4,876	0.027	0.163	0	1
Control variable					
Year of schooling	4,872	12.802	3.78	0	18
Female	4,876	0.507	0.500	0	1
Age	4,869	46.917	13.924	19	93
Married	4,876	0.525	0.499	0	1

coefficients imply that employers, the new middle classes and the more highly educated travel much more frequently to China than the self-employed/unskilled workers and non-workforce reference group (Figure 10.4). It can thus be assumed that that the capitalists and the new middle classes have the strongest cross-Strait mobility capacity and social networks in China among all four classes. With regard to the control variables, as Wong (2010) has found, the mainlanders and the aged population (including the first generation of mainlanders) also have better opportunities to move across the Taiwan Strait, possibly because of their stronger Chinese national identity and their familial networks in China.

In model (2) the dependent variable is the logarithmic monthly income. The significant coefficients show that employers and the new middle classes dispose of a much higher income than the self-employed and the working class. Although the main effect of class location has been controlled, the number of trips to China in one year also significantly increases the income standard. Without the real panel data, the cross-sectional data would not be sufficient to track the net changes in income. Furthermore, the brief telephone surveys lasting only a few minutes would not allow enough time to gather the full details of each interviewee's income sources, which would make it difficult to derive the figures for the net increase in income from cross-Strait trade for each class.

Table 10.3 Correlation matrix of selective variables in the 2010–2013 China impact surveys

	Visits to China	Log (income)	Pro-independence	Benefited/damaged	Worry inequality	Pan-blue
Log (income)	0.16*					
Pro-independence	-0.10*	-0.01				
Benefited/damaged	0.09*	0.16*	-0.25*			
Worry inequality	-0.04*	0.04*	0.19*	-0.26*		
Support pan-blue	0.05*	0.16*	-0.18*	0.41*	-0.22*	
Non-workforce	-0.01	-0.26*	-0.01	-0.01	-0.08*	0.04*
Unskilled worker	-0.09*	-0.05*	0.03	-0.03*	0.04*	-0.06*
New middle classes	0.08*	0.29*	-0.04*	0.07*	0.04*	0.04*
Self-employed (+ peasant)	-0.02	-0.06*	0.04*	-0.04*	0.01	-0.05*
Employer	0.09*	0.15*	0.00	0.00	0.02	0.00
Holo	-0.05*	-0.04*	0.134*	-0.14*	0.11*	-0.18*
Hakka	-0.01	0.01	-0.03	0.02	-0.01	0.03
Mainlander	0.08*	0.06*	-0.15*	0.16*	-0.11*	0.20*
Aboriginal/others	-0.01	-0.04*	0.01	0.01	-0.05*	0.02
Year of schooling	0.10*	0.53*	-0.02	0.15*	0.07*	0.09*
Female	-0.07*	-0.11*	0.01622	0.00671	-0.03*	0.07*
Age	0.10*	-0.18*	-0.06*	-0.04*	-0.11*	0.05*
Married	0.07*	-0.10*	-0.05*	-0.04*	-0.00	-0.04*

Note
Two-tails t-test.
* $p < 0.05$.

Table 10.4 Class inequality related to cross-Strait mobility and income in Taiwan, 2010–2013

	(1) OLS	(2) OLS
	N of visits to China	Log (income)
Class (non-workforce)		
Unskilled worker	−0.0508	0.2929***
	(−1.5249)	(11.6881)
New middle classes	0.0909*	0.4880***
	(2.4565)	(17.6186)
Self-employed	0.0009	0.2060***
	(0.0188)	(6.0443)
Employer	0.3382***	0.8722***
	(5.9108)	(20.4700)
Ethnicity (Holo)		
Hakka	−0.0237	0.0313
	(−0.5873)	(1.0593)
Mainlander	0.1107**	0.0095
	(2.9150)	(0.3424)
Aboriginal/others	0.1311+	−0.0647
	(1.7012)	(−1.1314)
Year of schooling	0.0441***	0.1266***
	(10.9029)	(40.0488)
Female	−0.0698**	−0.0775***
	(−2.7274)	(−4.1320)
Age	0.0114***	0.0048***
	(10.1120)	(5.6867)
Married	0.0305	0.3452***
	(0.9694)	(14.7904)
Year 2011	−0.2655***	1.0929***
	(−6.5620)	(37.1787)
Year 2012	−0.2861***	0.0165
	(−8.0917)	(0.6074)
Year 2013	−0.3805***	−0.0317
	(−10.8776)	(−1.2281)
Visits to China		0.0964***
		(9.1801)
Constant	−0.5299***	7.9316***
	(−5.5253)	(108.9336)
N	4866	4398
R-sq	0.0802	0.5547
Adj *R*-sq	0.0776	0.5532

Note

Two-tails t-test.

+ $p<0.1$.

* $p<0.05$.

** $p<0.01$.

*** $p<0.001$.

The higher income of 2011 comes from the special survey month: the February is the Lunar New Year.

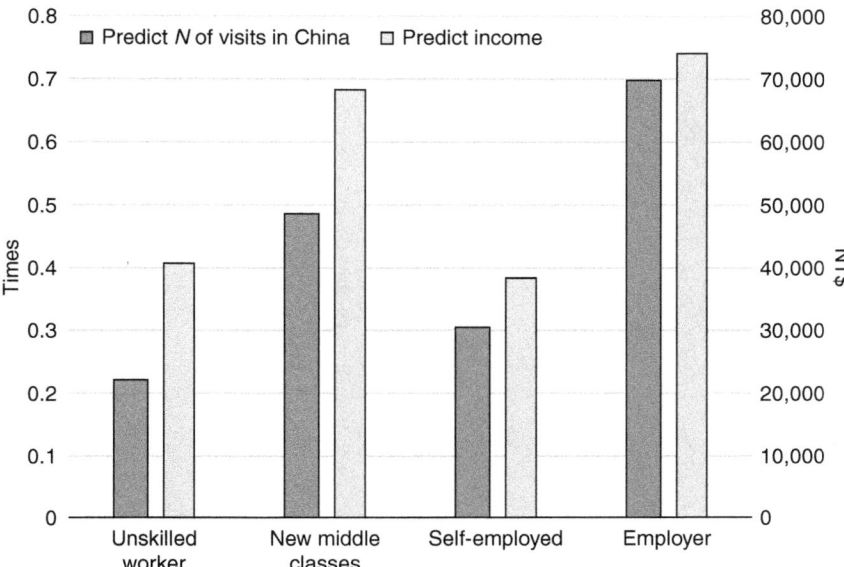

Figure 10.4 Cross-Strait mobility and income inequality of social classes in Taiwan (source: predicted value from model (1) and model (2)).

One method of calculating the trade advantage is to estimate the monthly income from cross-Strait mobility. From the results of model (1), we learn that the capitalists and the new middle classes are more capable of moving across the Taiwan Strait (at least 0.48 and 0.17 times more than the unskilled worker each year). Calculated from the results of model (2), the predicted value of each visit to China is more than NT$2,500 added to the average monthly income.[2] Based on the estimates of model (1) and (2), on average, from male respondents, the employer's benefit from cross-Strait mobility is a net gain of NT$7,944, the new middle classes' benefit is NT$1,439, and the unskilled workers' net loss is NT$657 per year. Although, without additional information, these figures are obviously underestimated, the outcomes of both models reflect the earning advantage of the capitalists and new middle classes, not only from their assets per se but also from their cross-Strait mobility capacity.

The models on the second level are displayed in Table 10.5. In model (3) the dependent variable is the respondent's answer as to whether the respondent and his/her family are positively or negatively affected by cross-Strait trade. I applied the ordered logit regression to fit the three-order Likert scale responses (1 = benefited, 0 = no impact, −1 = lost). A positive coefficient implies that the family benefits from cross-Strait trade, while a negative coefficient implies that they suffer economic loss. The results show that mainlanders, the more highly educated, and especially higher-income and higher-mobility groups feel that their

188   *T.-H. Lin*

Table 10.5 Subjective feelings of inequality connected to cross-Strait trade, 2010–2013

	(3) Ordered Logit	*(4) Ordered Logit*
	Benefited/damaged	*Worry inequality*
Class (non-workforce)		
Unskilled worker	−0.1480⁺	0.1581⁺
	(−1.7480)	(1.7441)
New middle classes	−0.0656	0.2122*
	(−0.6573)	(2.0604)
Self-employed	−0.1702	0.0830
	(−1.5033)	(0.6856)
Employer	−0.2639⁺	0.3264*
	(−1.7235)	(1.9854)
Ethnicity (Holo)		
Hakka	0.2340*	−0.1515
	(2.3527)	(−1.4463)
Mainlander	0.8015***	−0.5264***
	(7.4025)	(−5.6395)
Aboriginal/others	0.4635*	−0.7464***
	(2.3818)	(−4.0642)
Year of schooling	0.0367**	0.0190
	(3.0571)	(1.5095)
Female	0.0639	−0.1043
	(1.0068)	(−1.5540)
Age	−0.0021	−0.0156***
	(−0.7441)	(−5.2397)
Married	−0.1339⁺	0.2778***
	(−1.6744)	(3.3316)
Year 2011	0.6231***	0.5848***
	(5.5429)	(5.0277)
Year 2012	0.8993***	0.1588⁺
	(9.4756)	(1.6791)
Year 2013	0.5996***	0.5550***
	(6.7775)	(5.8651)
Visits to China	0.1376***	−0.0189
	(3.5315)	(−0.5244)
Log (income)	0.2181***	−0.0339
	(4.3241)	(−0.6367)
Pro-independence	−1.1058***	0.8209***
	(−16.5459)	(11.1000)
N	4,397	4,397
Pseudo *R*-sq	0.0725	0.0526
Log likelihood	−3,936.0766	−3,558.9545

Note
Two-tails t-test.
+ $p<0.1$.
* $p<0.05$.
** $p<0.01$.
*** $p<0.001$.

family economy benefits from increasing cross-Strait trade. In contrast, unskilled workers and some employers, who may be the owners of local small-scale enterprises, feel that their family economy is damaged by cross-Strait trade. The opposing feelings concerning the pros and cons of free trade with China clearly reflect the political struggle between the pan-blue and pan-green parties over the ECFA in 2010 (Lin and Hu 2011).

The dependent variable of model (4) is the respondent's three-ordered reply to the question of whether they think that the expansion of cross-Strait trade increases or decreases Taiwan's income inequality. A positive coefficient means that the respondents tend to think that the income inequality increases and a negative coefficient means that they think it decreases. The results of the ordered logit regression show that not only the working class but also the employers and the new middle classes tend to think that expansion of cross-Strait trade increases income inequality. Ethnicity and national identity also matter – mainlanders tend to think that trade reduces income inequality. These results can be explained as showing that not only the economically disadvantaged but also the wealthy have noticed the effects of cross-Strait trade on income distribution.

The models on partisan preference are displayed in Table 10.6. In both logit regression models, the dependent variable is a binomial choice: pan-blue (=1) or pan-green (=0). As usual, national identity and ethnicity remain the most important factors in influencing voting behaviour, but in model (5), referring to the non-workforce, the marginally significant coefficients show the different voting preferences of the four classes. The unskilled workers and the self-employed prefer the pan-green camp, while the employers and the new middle classes prefer the pan-blue camp. These outcomes match the findings that I obtained in earlier studies (Hu *et al.* 2009; Lin and Hu 2011).

The result of model (6) clarifies the effects of the intermediated variables on cross-Strait trade. The differences between model (5) and model (6) are four additional variables – the number of visits to China, pro-independence or anti-independence, the expanding trade benefits/damages family economy and agreement/disagreement on the increasing inequality statement – employed in model (6). Because of these additional variables, the coefficients of the dummies for class turn to be insignificant. This implies that, in Taiwan's elections, the 'class voting' phenomenon is largely mediated by people's attitudes towards cross-Strait trade and income distribution.

To sum up, the first level models confirm that, in relative terms, the capitalist class and the new middle classes benefit from their assets and mobility capacity (H1a), but that the working class and the self-employed either remain in a status quo or are negatively affected by cross-Strait trade (H1b). The second level models show that the capitalist class, skilled workers and managers welcome an open trade policy approach to China (H2a), but that unskilled workers are concerned about the growth in income inequality (H2b). The wealthy, however, also identify negative effects on income distribution. The last two models verify that class position influences Taiwan's voters' partisan preferences: the capitalists and the new middle classes tend to support the pan-blue camp, while the

Table 10.6 Trade policy and class voting in Taiwan, 2010–2013

	(5) Logit	*(6) Logit*
	Support pan-blue	*Support pan-blue*
Class (non-workforce)		
Unskilled worker	−0.1478[+]	−0.0902
	(−1.6583)	(−0.9233)
New middle classes	0.0361	0.0482
	(0.3709)	(0.4513)
Self-employed	−0.3466**	−0.2279
	(−2.7101)	(−1.6120)
Employer	0.0173	0.0254
	(0.1191)	(0.1592)
Ethnicity (Holo)		
Hakka	0.4626***	0.3949***
	(4.3916)	(3.4068)
Mainlander	1.2074***	0.8349***
	(12.0793)	(7.6680)
Aboriginal/others	0.6028**	0.2824
	(2.9528)	(1.2429)
Year of schooling	0.0647***	0.0389**
	(5.9060)	(3.1939)
Female	0.3850***	0.4565***
	(5.6535)	(6.0887)
Age	0.0157***	0.0139***
	(5.2444)	(4.1933)
Married	0.1051	0.1251
	(1.2968)	(1.4106)
Year 2011	1.6227***	1.9268***
	(13.7561)	(14.2641)
Year 2012	0.8138***	1.0050***
	(8.8552)	(9.5607)
Year 2013	0.8119***	1.1824***
	(8.8981)	(11.1834)
Visits to China		0.0541
		(1.3212)
Pro-independence		−0.6055***
		(−7.5541)
Benefited/damaged		0.8865***
		(18.8018)
Worry inequality		−0.3832***
		(−7.4166)
Constant	−3.1125***	−2.8227***
	(−11.9020)	(−9.7975)
N	4,359	4,356
Pseudo *R*-sq	0.0905	0.2172
Log likelihood	−2,682.1241	−2,307.1948

Note
Two-tails t-test.
+ *p*<0.1. * *p*<0.05. ** *p*<0.01. *** *p*<0.001.

self-employed and the workers tend to support the pan-green camp (H3a and H3b). Therefore, the 'class voting' phenomenon in contemporary Taiwan is, to a great extent, connected to voters' interests and attitudes towards cross-Strait trade and increasing economic interaction.

Discussion and conclusion

Class voting is an evergreen issue in social science. From the late 1980s onwards, scholars have continuously claimed that class voting is fading away in post-industrial societies. They have argued that de-industrialization, the declining organization rate of trade unions and the collapse of communist regimes have together undermined the political power of the social classes (Clark *et al.* 1993; Evans 1999). In contrast, as (most) empirical evidence shows, dissenting voices hold that class is still useful as a means of explaining voting behaviours in the developed countries (Hout *et al.* 1995; de Graaf *et al.* 1995).

In contrast to the early dispute in the late 1980s, the class voting debate has returned in recent studies on 'globalization'.[3] Globalization theorists argue that due to the invention of informational technology, the essential features of the neo-liberal era are the deregulation of the labour market and the flexibility of production organizations (Babb 2005; Castells 2000). The transformation into a freer market and a more flexible mode of production will affect lifetime employment, undermine the political power of trade unions and lead to the retrenchment of welfare states (Giddens 1999; Huber and Stephens 2001; Gray 1998).

As critics have pointed out, only a few globalization theorists have seriously examined the evidence of class inequality (Hirst and Thompson 1999; Goldthorpe 2002). In developed countries, nevertheless, the empirical findings on the link between globalization and class politics are contradictory. Some studies display the continuity of class politics in Western Europe and the rise of class voting in Eastern Europe (Andersen and Heath 2002; Chan and Goldthorpe 2007; Domañski 2008), and some point to the constant retrenchment of European welfare states (Korpi and Palme 2003), while others rarely find any association between economic openness and the political power of trade unions (Scruggs and Lange 2002). As a result, social class theorists are usually sceptical about globalization theories.

For those who argue that class politics will fade away under globalization, the OEP theories pose a real challenge. As the HO-SS theory predicted, economic openness, in the name of 'globalization', will deepen class inequality in most advanced economies; the impact will lead to the forming of class coalitions that support or oppose globalization and facilitate the return of class voting in democratic countries. The association between class inequality and class voting depends to some extent on the mobilization and formation of class coalitions in the struggles over trade politics.

After considering Taiwan in the context of the class politics of trade, I confirm that increasing cross-Strait trade has led to changes in income distribution as well as in voters' attitudes towards cross-Strait trade and their voting behaviours. The beneficiaries of cross-Strait trade, mainly capitalists and the new middle classes, who are most probably living in the north, tend to form a pro-trade coalition supporting the blue camp, while the victims of cross-Strait trade, mainly workers, self-employed and peasants, who are most probably living in the south, try to protect their livelihoods by supporting the green camp.

This chapter's analysis of the surveys in 2010–2013 reveals the emerging class politics of cross-Strait trade in Taiwan. It claims neither that a strong Taiwanese working class is coming to the fore nor that the DPP is turning to the left. The author agrees that national identity and ethnic politics are still the most important issues in party politics in Taiwan. However, the statistical findings show that intermediated by the policy debate on cross-Strait trade, class is also significant.

As already mentioned, cross-Strait trade policies have given rise to political struggles among those supporting or opposing them. In 2013, the Sunflower movement, in protest against the passing of the Cross-Strait Service Trade Agreement, occupied the Legislative Yuan between 18 March and 10 April 2014. The protesters, from a coalition of students and civic associations, raised at least three concerns: (1) the improper procedure of endorsement; (2) the potential economic losses of specific industries and the lower classes; (3) the increasing political pressures from China. In this chapter, the OEP theory explains the social foundations, class cleavages and industrial interest conflicts of open trade that culminated in the protests of the Sunflower movement.

In contrast to earlier globalization theories, which claimed that class voting would decline, the OEP theory on class interests explains the rising class inequality and enduring class politics in democracies. It also helps us to understand the class origins of the rising anti-globalization movements, such as the Battle of Seattle during the World Trade Organization Ministerial Conference in 1999 and the Occupy Wall Street movements in various places in the United States in 2011. The class voting and social protests in Taiwan that stem from cross-Strait trade can well be added to the debate on contemporary class politics in the era of economic globalization. The China impact on class cleavage, furthermore, may persistently reshape the political landscape and the future of the island.

Notes

1 The interviewees are divided into four class categories according to their responses to the following survey questions: (1) 'Do you work for yourself, or do you work for others?' Those who answered 'work for myself' are labelled as 'owner'; the others are labelled as 'employee'. (2) 'Do you hire/manage others in your workplace?' The owners who answered 'yes' are labelled as 'employer' and the employees who answered 'yes' as 'manager'. In addition, the owners who answered 'no' are labelled as 'self-employed'. The responses to these questions, however, are of little help in measuring the skill level of employees. Therefore, the International Standard Classification of Occupations 1988 (ISCO-88) is adopted to adjust the class schema. According to the digital version of ISCO-88, an occupation is a skilled job if it is categorized by ISCO-88 as coded less than 400.

2 The average monthly log (income) is 10.542, and for each visit to China adds 0.0964 to it. Through the operation of exponentiation (exp), the difference between exp (10.606) and exp (10.542) is 2503. Because the *R*-square of the model (2) is 0.555, it can explain only around half of the income difference. By calculating from the explained log (income) from model (2), the log (income) of employer (male) is 9.903 (+0.033 as the benefit from their visits to China), the log (income) of the new middle classes is 9.519 (+0.009), and the log (income) of the unskilled worker is 9.324 (–0.005, a net negative time of visits to China). This is the yearly net income difference of the classes.

3 From the economic aspect, globalization simply refers to the levels of integration of markets for capital, labour, goods and services among economies around the world (Babb 2005).

References

Acemoglu, Daron, and Robinson, James A. (2005) *Economic Origins of Dictatorship and Democracy*, Cambridge: Cambridge University Press.

Andersen, Robert, and Heath, Anthony (2002) 'Class Matters: The Persisting Effects of Contextual Social Class on Individual Voting in Britain, 1964–97', *European Sociological Review*, 18: 125–38.

Atkinson, A. B. (2008) *The Changing Distribution of Earnings in OECD Countries*, New York: Oxford University Press.

Babb, Sarah (2005) 'The Social Consequences of Structural Adjustment: Recent Evidence and Current Debates', *Annual Review of Sociology*, 31: 199–222.

Castells, Manuel (2000) *The Rise of the Network Society*, New York: Basil Blackwell.

Chan, Tak Wing, and Goldthorpe, John H. (2007) 'Class and Status: The Conceptual Distinction and its Empirical Relevance', *American Sociological Review*, 72, 4: 512–532.

Chang, Chin-Fen, and Chang, Heng-Hao (2010) 'Who Cares for Unions? Public Attitudes toward Union Power in Taiwan, 1990–2005', *China Perspectives*, 3: 64–78.

Clark, Terry, Seymour, Nicholas, Lipset, Martin, and Rempel, Mike (1993) 'The Declining Political Significance of Social Class', *International Sociology*, 8: 293–316.

De Graaf, Nan Dirk, Nieuwbeerta, Paul, and Heath, Anthony (1995) 'Class Mobility and Political Preferences: Individual and Contextual Effects', *The American Journal of Sociology*, 100: 997–1027.

Domański, Henryk (2008) 'A New Dimension of Social Stratification in Poland? Class Membership and Electoral Voting in 1991–2001', *European Sociological Review*, 24, 2: 169–182.

Erikson, Robert, and Goldthorpe, John H. (1992) *The Constant Flux: A Study of Class Mobility in Industrial Societies*, Oxford: Clarendon Press.

Evans, Geoffrey (ed.) (1999) *The End of Class Politics? Class Voting in Comparative Context*, Oxford: Oxford University Press.

Evens, Peter B., Jacobson, Harold K., and Putnam, Robert D. (eds) (1993) *Double-Edged Diplomacy: International Bargaining and Domestic Politics*, Berkeley: University of California Press.

Giddens, Anthony (1999) *The Third Way: The Renewal of Social Democracy*, Cambridge: Polity Press.

Goldthorpe, John H. (2002) 'Globalisation and Social Class', *West European Politics*, 25, 3: 1–28.

Gourevitch, Peter (1978) 'The Second Image Reversed: The International Sources of Domestic Politics', *International Organization*, 32, 4: 881–912.

Gray, John (1998) *False Dawn: the Delusions of Global Capitalism*, New York: New Press.

Grusky, David B. (ed.) (2008) *Social Stratification: Class, Race, and Gender in Sociological Perspective*, Boulder CO: Westview Press.

Hirst, Paul, and Thompson, Grahame (1999) *Globalization in Question: The International Economy and the Possibilities of Governance*, Malden: Polity Press.

Hiscox, Michael J. (2002) *International Trade and Political Conflict: Commerce, Coalitions, and Mobility*, Princeton: Princeton University Press.

Hout, M., Brooks, C., and Manza, J. (1995) 'The Democratic Class Struggle in the United States, 1948–1992', *American Sociological Review*, 60: 805–828.

Hout, Michael (2008) 'How Class Works in Popular Conception: Most Americans Identify with the Class Their Income, Occupation, and Education Implies for Them', in Lareau, Annette, and Conley, Dalton (eds) *Social Class: How Does It Work?* New York: Russell Sage Foundation.

Hsiao, Hsin-Huang Michael (1989) 'The Middle Classes in Taiwan: Origins, Formation and Significance', in Hsiao, Hsin-Huang Michael (ed.) *Taiwan: A Newly Industrialized State*, Taipei: Department of Sociology, National Taiwan University, 151–166.

Hu, Alfred, Lin, Thung-Hong, and Wong, Raymond (2009) 'Class and Ethnic Cleavages in Electoral Politics: Stability and Changes in Taiwan Since 1984', paper presented at the Spring Meeting of RC28, International Sociological Association, Beijing, May 2009.

Huber, Evelyne, and Stephens, John D. (2001) *Development and Crisis of the Welfare State: Parties and Policies in Global Markets*, Chicago: University of Chicago Press.

Huntington, Samuel P. (1991) *The Third Wave: Democratization in the Late Twentieth Century*, Norman: University of Oklahoma Press.

Korpi, Walter, and Palme, Joakim (2003) 'New Politics and Class Politics in the Context of Austerity and Globalization: Welfare State Regress in 18 Countries, 1975–95', *American Political Science Review*, 97, 3: 425–446.

Lake, David A. (2009) 'Open Economy Politics: A Critical Review', *Review of International Organizations*, 4, 3: 219–244.

Lin, Thung-Hong (2013) 'The Lost Decade: Changing Class Identity and Ideology in Taiwan', *Journal of Social Sciences and Philosophy*, 25, 4: 689–734 (in Chinese).

Lin, Thung-Hong, and Hu, Alfred (2011) 'Cross-Strait Trade and Class Politics in Taiwan', *Thought and Words*, 10: 95–134 (in Chinese).

Milner, Helen V. (1997) *Interests, Institutions, and Information: Domestic Politics and International Relations*, Princeton NJ: Princeton University Press.

Milner, Helen V., and Judkins, Benjamin (2004) 'Partisanship, Trade Policy, and Globalization: Is There a Left–Right Divide on Trade Policy?' *International Studies Quarterly*, 48, 1: 95–119.

Putnam, Robert D. (1988) 'Diplomacy and Domestic Politics: The Logic of Two-Level Games', *International Organization*, 42, 2: 427–460.

Rogowski, Ronald (1989) *Commerce and Coalition: How Trade Affects Domestic Political Alignments*, Princeton NJ: Princeton University Press.

Scruggs, Lyle, and Lange, Peter (2002) 'Where Have All the Members Gone? Globalization, Institutions, and Union Density', *Journal of Politics*, 64, 1: 126–153.

Taipei Times (2010) 'Tsai questions Ma on job losses from signing ECFA', 27 April, available at www.taipeitimes.com/News/taiwan/archives/2010/04/27/2003471594 (accessed 16 June 2013).

Taiwan Central Election Commission (2013) Election Statistics, available at http://engweb.cec.gov.tw/files/11-1030-4429.php (accessed 17 April 2013).

Taiwan Directorate General of Budget, Accounting and Statistics (2012) Macro Database, available at http://61.60.106.82/pxweb/Dialog/statfile9L.asp (accessed 17 April 2013).

Taiwan Mainland Affairs Council (2011) 'The Share of Cross-Straits Trade in Taiwan Total Foreign Trade', available at www.mac.gov.tw/public/Attachment/12149433186. pdf (accessed 26 February 2011).

Taiwan Ministry of Economic Affairs (2012) 'Trade Database', available at http://cus93. trade.gov.tw/fsci (accessed 13 May 2012).

Wang, Fu-Chang (2005) 'Why Did the DPP Win Taiwan's 2004 Presidential Election? An Ethnic Politics Interpretation', *Pacific Affairs*, 77, 4: 691–696.

Wong, Tze Wai Kevin (2010) 'The Emergence of Class Cleavage in Taiwan in the Twenty-First Century: The Impact of Cross-Strait Economic Integration', *Issues and Studies*, 46, 2: 127–172.

Wood, Adrian (1994) *North-South Trade, Employment and Inequality: Changing Fortunes in a Skill-Driven World*, Oxford: Oxford University Press.

Wright, Erik Olin (1985) *Classes*, London: Verso.

Wright, Erik Olin (1997) *Class Counts*, London: Verso.

Wu, Nai-Teh (1996) 'Class Identity without Class Consciousness? Working Class Consciousness in Taiwan', in Perry, Elizabeth (ed.) *Putting Class in Its Place: Worker Identity in East Asia*, Berkeley CA: Institute of East Asian Studies.

Yang, David D. (2007) 'Classing Ethnicity: Class, Ethnicity, and the Mass Politics of Taiwan's Democratic Transition', *World Politics*, 59, 4: 503–538.

11 Escalator or merry-go-round?

Taiwanese skilled migration to China

Yen-Fen Tseng

> It is hard not to think about landing a job in China; it is like being on board a small ship sailing along with a giant aircraft carrier.
>
> (*Commonwealth Magazine* 2009, September, 430)

China, as a job-generating machine, has caused large numbers of Taiwanese to migrate, searching for better jobs or greater job diversity. Regulations have gradually loosened for Taiwanese people to work in China. According to a newly revised act passed in 2005, the Taiwanese can work in any sector as long as they are proven to be healthy, to be between 18 and 60 years old and to have entered China legally (Ministry of Commerce of People's Republic of China 2005). As a result, the Taiwanese enjoy favourable residency and employment rights that are unavailable to other foreigners. According to the 2010 Chinese census data, there were already over 700,000 Taiwanese migrants or settlers in the greater Shanghai region alone at that time (Lan and Wu 2011). Moreover, surveys have found that the majority of Taiwanese migrants in China have a tertiary education background (Lee and Peng 2009). This profile makes the Taiwanese one of the largest migrant communities of skilled labour in the world.

There have been two distinctive waves of migration from Taiwan to China. The first wave that occurred in the late 1980s was associated with the relocation of manufacturers seeking to reduce labour costs in the shoe-making, garment and houseware sectors. Migrants of this type included key personnel sent by their parent companies as well as small business owners who closed down their operations in Taiwan and moved to China to manage their new factories. The majority of them were male, and they tended to move alone, without the other members of their families (Shen 2005). The second wave of migration began around 1998, when some of the powerhouses of Taiwan's high-tech industries expanded their manufacturing sites to the greater Shanghai area. At about the same time, the business service and retail sectors targeting the China market began to invest in China. This wave of investment was mainly Shanghai-bound, to take advantage of the booming economy of Shanghai and its position as a regional hub in the Yangtze River delta (Ken 2002).

The migration patterns of the second wave of Taiwanese migrants differed from those of the first wave. First of all, the second wave often involved the relocation of the nuclear family. Second, these migrants were motivated more by their own independent career planning than simply following company personnel deployment policies. Even those who moved to China on overseas assignments were likely to move on, very quickly, to other jobs in the local market. The reason why I refer to these second wave migrants as *independent movers* is because their decisions to move or to stay on in China resulted from their own career planning. While most of these independent movers were in mid-career, some of them started their working lives in China. Third, compared with the first wave of migration, which was heavily involved in manufacturing, the second wave of Taiwanese migrants worked in a much more diverse array of jobs in the industrial and service sectors, such as retailing, wholesaling, trading, business services and design. Lastly, female migrants were prominent among these independent movers. The female-to-male ratio was even greater than in the traditional manufacturing sector, because female skilled workers were already prominent in these employment sectors in Taiwan.

Previous research on Taiwanese migration to China concentrated on capital-linked migrants such as business owners and expatriates working for them. Little understanding has been developed concerning the salaried workers whose decisions to move or to settle have been made independently of organizational assignments. The numbers of these new salaried migrants, whom I term 'independent movers', can be expected to grow in the future. There is a lack of systematic research on the reasons for which they came to China in such large numbers and then decided to stay. This chapter aims to fill this gap. The empirical data is based on in-depth interviews with Taiwanese people who currently live or used to live and work in Shanghai or Beijing. The profile of these interviewees reflects a sample that is skewed toward those who have been pulled by attractive career paths, rather than pushed by job insecurity or professional disadvantages back home. In other words, the sample draws heavily on those who have been able to choose whether to move or not to move. By investigating the employees who are freer to choose than others, information can be obtained about their choices of life and work options and also whether these choices eventually work out. Since such migration choices might be experienced very differently by different gender groups, I intentionally included a significant number of women among my respondents.

The aim of this chapter is to analyse the China impact on Taiwanese skilled workers and the future waves of migration. The chapter is structured as follows. First, I turn to the causes of migration; I argue that in assessing skilled migration, we should go beyond the traditional push-and-pull typology, focusing more on the regionalization of skilled labour markets in terms of both the demand and the supply of jobs. Second, by looking at two groups of new migrants – women and young workers – we can learn more about these new migrants' decisions and their settlement prospects. The last section discusses the policy responses of the home state to its hyper-mobile citizens. The chapter concludes with a discussion on the possible long-term trends in middle-class migration from Taiwan to China.

Data

This chapter draws on 45 in-depth interviews conducted during 2007 and 2008 with Taiwanese skilled workers who were working or had worked in Shanghai. Following the international migration literature, skilled workers are defined as professionals, managers, and technical specialists. I relied on snowball sampling via informants in various occupations. The sample was created to document diverse migration channels and occupations. It covered four major types of work: manufacturing, cultural products industry (design, media etc.), business services (banking, consulting) and international trading. A few interviews were conducted with housewives who had moved to China after their spouses had relocated there. I also interviewed five migrants who have moved into and out of Shanghai more than once. Interviewees were asked to talk about their job history, professional life, migration and housing choices, and to reflect on the decisions that they had made with regard to migration and whether they were thinking of moving on to other Chinese cities or back to Taiwan. The interviews used in this chapter are denoted by a reference number and the year in which they took place.

Background: moving to China

Taiwan's economy has been dwarfed by the giant growth machine across the Taiwan Strait – a booming China. For businesses that benefit from this growth, this means that a win-win situation has been developing between the two sides. For example, according to Forbes' 'Taiwan's 50 Richest' (*Forbes Magazine*, 23 May 2012), the new rich in Taiwan are those who have established their businesses in China. The owners of the Want Want Snack Food and Dinshin Instant Noodle Groups are ranked first and third respectively on this list. They have topped their Taiwanese 'old' rich counterparts, the property giants and finance tycoons who are mainly or solely based in Taiwan. Another source lists the top 50 foreign-born richest in China, with the Taiwanese placed in the first and second positions, and Taiwan-born billionaires accounting for half of the individuals included on the list.

In contrast to entrepreneurs taking the initiative to generate wealth from new businesses in China, for salaried workers, cross-border employment is often the consequence of jobs being shifted to China. This first occurred in the export-oriented manufacturing sector, with companies moving to southern China to tap cheap labour; middle management jobs followed. More job shifts came as a result of the regional headquarters of transnational firms moving to Shanghai or Beijing to gain proximity to the market. Taiwan lost many jobs as a result, and many people had to move, especially in service sectors such as advertising and investment banking. More recently, the Taiwanese have been drawn to China beyond the above-mentioned waves of job transplantation. When the world's most populated country grew into a huge consumption market, new jobs were created by both local and foreign-owned enterprises (including Taiwanese) in retail, hotel services, catering, marketing etc.

According to the 2011 survey conducted by the 104 Human Bank, which is the largest Taiwanese website for job offers in China, the demand for Taiwanese personnel in China's manufacturing sector has been declining significantly, while on the other hand, job listings in the electrical appliances business as well as the retail and wholesale sectors have grown steadily (104 Human Bank 2011). The highest demand for Taiwanese labour is in the sales sector. Such a demand profile fits well with the sources of economic growth in China. Although most attention has been paid to the foreign investment manufacturing sectors that produce for global markets, the true driving force behind economic growth has been local investment, which has accounted for the greatest part of GDP growth. Cox (2012) points to the fact that investment in plants, machinery, buildings and infrastructure amounted to about 48 per cent of China's GDP in 2011. Rapid urbanization creates new business sectors to serve the consumption needs of urban residents, such as convenience stores, restaurants, department stores and warehouses. These are areas where Taiwanese employees are well represented today.

However, in addition to demand, there is a supply side story that has been much neglected. According to various survey results, the majority of the Taiwanese migrated to China to actively pursue their careers; they were not driven to leave Taiwan for economic reasons. Many Taiwanese went to China before they had even secured a job offer in the first place. And as a survey based on a sample over-represented by highly skilled workers indicates, a high percentage (44 per cent) of respondents would go to China if they were offered a job there (*Wealth Magazine* 2007). The same survey showed that the higher the ranking of respondents' job positions, the stronger the propensity to migrate. Those who have already had jobs in China are more likely to move than those who are still looking for jobs. To sum up, the migration of skilled labour is mainly self-motivated and constitutes a steady supply of Taiwanese personnel for Chinese companies.

What is especially noticeable is that when the barriers of residence and employment in China are lifted, many Taiwanese people feel encouraged to take a chance, to travel around in China or to live there for a short period, after which they decide to stay on for employment reasons. The Taiwan Social Change Survey found that about one fourth of all respondents in 2006 were willing to move to and work in China if employment opportunities were available (Academia Sinica Institute of Sociology 2007). Those who expressed their willingness to move given appropriate opportunities were motivated by both push and pull factors. The main reasons for which they opted for migration were: more opportunities for professional achievement and promotion; a higher income; a booming domestic market in China; the possibility of accumulating more human capital than in Taiwan; and pessimism about the economic prospects of the Taiwanese economy. From this list, it becomes clear that the supply of Taiwanese highly-skilled migrants mainly stemmed from both positive assessments of China and negative expectations of individual opportunities in Taiwan.

According to the above-mentioned 2011 survey by the 104 Human Bank, the Taiwanese migrants who are now working in China explain their reasons for moving as follows: a growing China market, better salaries, and the prospect of gaining experience and enhancing professional credentials. The lack of opportunities in Taiwan, a push-side factor, is strikingly absent from this list. To go or not to go to China has become a major issue, particularly among middle-class Taiwanese with professional experience and managerial backgrounds. According to a 2007 *Wealth Magazine* survey, the higher the status of the respondents' job positions, the stronger the propensity to migrate. And those who already have jobs are more likely to move than those still looking for them. An open-border job market across the Taiwan Strait is a magnetic attraction for the Taiwanese, even if they do not have any precise plans regarding where to go and how to begin.

Escalator or merry-go-round?

Although most interviewees expected to find better career prospects in China, their career patterns have changed from climbing job ladders in a hierarchical company organization to career advancement by 'job-hopping' from company to company in different regions. Globalization increases the feelings of fear and insecurity in Taiwanese labour migrants and hence reduces their loyalty to one particular company. Those with higher human capital, i.e. better education, more work experience and more extensive social networks, are constantly looking for better jobs via internet job search services. Head-hunters play a crucial role here as well. Moving across the border to find jobs beyond corporate ladders is therefore often understood as a way to enhance employment opportunities and labour mobility.

An investigative report by the leading Taiwanese business magazine *Commonwealth*, entitled 'My Boss is Posting in China', drew a familiar picture for middle-management workers in today's China (*Commonwealth Magazine* 2009). The most frequently mentioned rationale of Taiwanese migrants for leaving their homeland, according to the report, is the regionalization of business firms. The companies they worked for moved their regional headquarters to Shanghai or Beijing to cover the Taiwan market, and they consequently downsized their Taiwan offices and/or downgraded their decision-making powers. Some closed down their Taiwan offices altogether.

Taiwanese migration to China can be compared with migration communities sharing similar cultural links between the sending and the host society. For example, New Zealanders have long regarded London as a place to pursue ambitions that cannot be fulfilled in New Zealand because their country's economy is small and rather undifferentiated (Conradson and Latham 2005).

What is interesting about the current pattern of labour migration, in this case, is not simply the volume of people involved, however, but the fact that 'so many of these individuals clearly treat migration to London as a temporally bounded activity': 'Despite their ability to obtain well remunerated jobs and the opportunities for obtaining residence status, these individuals continue to organize their lives around an opportunity horizon that remains focused on "home"' (Conradson and Latham 2005: 165).

Fielding (1992) also argued that the focal points provided by capital cities for attracting people from other regions might be transitional in nature. For example, many migrants moving to London actually see their stay in the city as an escalator – 'stepping on the escalator, being taken up to a higher level by the escalator, and stepping off the escalator' (Fielding 1995:176). The final step refers to their homebound trip with the sort of credits to be transferred back that will enable them to continue working at that level. By contrast, many of my interviewees considered Shanghai to be equipped with enough capital, ideas and people to facilitate their career advancement in China. As a result, most of them would prefer to stay on, rather than to use Shanghai as an escalator to move somewhere else, including a homebound journey. An expatriate working in the banking sector said:

> I am on an overseas assignment and have never changed my job here. But if I leave my current job, I will still look for another job opportunity in Shanghai. I have learned a lot from my customers since they do business both locally and globally. Through them, I can learn about new developments on a wider geographical scale than in Taiwan. I also benefit a lot from Shanghai's international resources, such as the broadcasting network that covers world news in much more scope and depth than Taiwan. In Taiwan, your vision is narrowed by the more and more marginalized business environment.
>
> (17–2007)

An interviewee working as a retail manager expressed a similar view:

> If I go back to Taiwan, I think I will be equipped with very valuable experience accumulated here in Shanghai and would therefore easily find a job back home. I think 'international' experience is what we can take back from Shanghai to Taiwan. But I would prefer to stay here, because in Shanghai, it feels as if you are in a world champion game, but in Taiwan, it only feels like a domestic game. It is more challenging in Shanghai and I like that.
>
> (18–2007)

For this reason, although most interviewees perceived their current employment to be of a temporary nature, most of them stated that they would choose to move on to another job in China, or even to different cities, rather than to move back to Taiwan. This is more like a 'merry-go-round', moving on the same level in an organizational hierarchy but in different firms and/or locations. In other words, these Taiwanese respondents do not expect to move up by moving back to their homeland, unlike the New Zealanders.

While success stories still inspire Taiwanese people to cross the Taiwan Strait, this tendency has gradually given away to fears of losing out on career opportunities by staying in Taiwan. In fact, migration to China must be seen as being driven both by aspirations (pull) and preoccupations (push). One additional preoccupation refers to the possibility that the salaries to be earned in China will gradually be trimmed down to local Chinese levels – or that Taiwanese employees will be completely replaced by local employees. Indeed, the job prospects for younger mid-level professionals are increasingly being threatened by this trend. Even in the retail sector, to which the Taiwanese have been heavily drawn in the past, local competition is fierce. According to an industry report (Sheng 2012), one of the largest department stores in China, owned by Taiwanese who used to place their compatriots as top managers, has retained fewer than half of them, while the remainder of the positions have been filled by Chinese. This is a development generally considered as a good indicator of business localization. However, for the time being, the Taiwanese still enjoy an advantage at management level because of their loyalty and work ethic.

Moving to China is not always perceived as positive. From the 2007 Taiwan Social Change Survey, we learn that the number of respondents who consider that migrating to China was harmful to their job prospects *once they return to Taiwan* exceeds those who think otherwise. Many interviewees expressed such fears in greater detail, explaining that it might be difficult for them to find a proper position and salary, or that their China experiences might not be appreciated by local businesses once they enter the Taiwanese job market.

'I am not a migrant'

Many of my interviewees responded to my first question – 'Please tell me your migration history' – by saying 'I am not a migrant'. This objection to being classified as a migrant is a curious feature that requires explanation. Such thinking reflects, in most cases, their uncertainty about being able to live and work in China beyond a period of five years. Although they can easily apply for a one-, two- or five-year resident permit with the Public Security Bureau, many do not bother to do so. They continue to hold tourist visas, and travel back to Taiwan at least once a year to make sure that they qualify for re-entry and another period of temporary residency. Their legal status is 'resident of the Taiwan region' as well as 'Chinese national' without registered household status (*huji*, 戶籍). The Chinese government defines the status and rights of Taiwanese migrants in terms of household registration. The 'residents of the Taiwan region' in China are a special status group, considered neither as ordinary 'Chinese citizens' nor as 'foreigners'. According to current regulations, the main requirement for becoming a regular resident of the People' Republic of China is marriage to a Chinese citizen. In other words, the Taiwanese are segregated by a distinct legal category, and this makes them a collective group which can be targeted by Chinese law. A fine line keeps people within these legal boundaries, and even if policy-makers can move this line close to the legal status of a full citizen, they do not cross it.

The great majority of interviewees had a very ambivalent attitude towards their long-term plans, with most being unable to say for certain that they would stay in China for more than five years. Many times, when I first introduced myself to interviewees explaining that I was conducting research on Taiwanese immigrants in China, the notion of 'immigrants' was deemed to not apply to them, because the word 'immigrant' (*yimin*, 移民) invokes the implication of long-term settlement. A manager in electronic construction engineering put it this way:

> I don't know for how long I will continue to be appreciated as a valuable worker. In general, if you come here to work for others (*dagong*, 打工), you tend to keep alert to the possibility that, one day, the local Chinese might learn the trade and take over your job.
>
> (2–2008)

It is interesting how this manager has adopted the term *dagong* to refer to her employment situation. The term *dagong* is used mainly to refer to those who take temporary jobs in low-end sectors, such as student part-timers, and in Taiwan a manager will never use *dagong* to refer to his or her employment status. It shows that migrating to work in China, in the case of this interviewee and of many others, has eroded their long-term job security, at least in subjective perspectives.

Women warriors

According to the above-quoted 2007 *Wealth Magazine* survey, men showed a stronger propensity than women to move to China, with a 10 per cent difference between the sexes. However, the percentage of women who would like to move was as high as 30 per cent. Indeed, the recent wave of migration has been constituted more and more by women. Kofman (1999) once observed that even if female labour migration is gradually gaining recognition as a significant phenomenon, it is given scant scholarly attention because of the notion that it only mirrors the migration of men. In fact, in earlier literature on Taiwanese migrant workers in China, woman were not studied in their own right; they were seen either as spouses following men or as employees behaving like men. I intend to show, however, that not only do women make up a significant part of migration flows to China, but that the majority of them should be conceptualized as 'independent movers'. They have been making migration decisions and facing subsequent settlement patterns very different from those of men. The considerations of Taiwanese women concerning migrant destinations and the life–work balance, their professional experiences and their acculturation in Chinese society follow quite distinct trajectories. Although my interviews with women migrants include spouses, I focus on discussing those who moved as white-collar workers.

Shanghai is a favourite destination among those women who move alone, for it is perceived as modern, international and above all safe. South China, on the contrary, is often depicted as backward, parochial and prone to crime. Female migrants are indeed most visible in Shanghai. In 2002, an association catering to Taiwanese career-women, the Taiwanese Professional Women's Society (TPWS, or 1881台灣職業婦女俱樂部), was established in Shanghai. The association has since grown to a membership of some 100 regular and another 300 associate members. It was founded to facilitate the lives of migrant career women by offering regular forums and social activities to serve as platforms for networking, as well as for exchanging information and ideas (Li Po 2007). In contrast to the male-dominated Taiwanese business associations in China's major cities, TPWS has so far remained the only organization exclusively serving Taiwanese career women in China.[1]

This is a strong indication that Shanghai is the concentration hub for Taiwanese career women. These women tend to build migration decisions not only around career considerations but also on the assumed effects on their personal life. The barriers they have to face when trying to gain the approval of their parents to move, especially if they move alone, are higher than those for men. A journalist who pioneered as a single Taiwanese female migrant to China in 2004 provides the following testimony: 'Although I am a second-generation mainlander, I never set foot in China before 2004 when I arrived in Beijing for work. At that time, my family was worried about my safety' (Gong 2012: 5).

The 'supply shortage' of potential future spouses is a worrying issue for these women as well as their families. Following the social norm for women to marry 'up' on the socio-economic ladder, the Chinese are considered a less attractive choice as spouses because they tend to be devalued by the Taiwanese, including migrant women. Therefore, the first barrier for a single woman migrating to China involves the perception of how such a move would affect her chance of getting married. However, many of my respondents emphasized the pursuit of independence as an essential part of their choices for migration. The following interviewee, a landscape designer and single parent (being legally separated from her husband), reflected on another advantage of moving to China, especially to Shanghai: 'For myself, I can go anywhere. But as a mother supporting a child alone, I have to come to work in Shanghai, for I can earn more money here by working on more projects going on at the same time' (11–2008).

Most of the women migrants that I talked to emphasized the fact that they had experienced more respect for their work performance after moving to China. Their male counterparts agreed that Shanghai was unique in its gender equality culture, which privileges women in both the domestic and public spheres. This gender equality culture was frequently cited by my respondents as facilitating their career development and settlement. Also, business dinners and socializing in Shanghai were regarded as less male-oriented than in Taiwan. An architect highlighted her experience of being excluded from office building design in Taiwan:

I did not have any chance of being put in charge of designing office build-ings. I resented this very much because I was trained to do that. I blame such a lack of opportunity on my being a woman within a male-dominated business. Men simply do not value women's capabilities. In addition to that, the way in which male architects do business with their clients heavily involves wining and dining, and that often means excluding woman col-leagues. As an architect, I am more highly qualified, but as a woman, I am considered an inconvenience on such occasions where business is to be done. You don't have such informal norms here in Shanghai. They ask for my input of professional skill, and that is all they are looking for.

(23–2007)

Other interviewees stressed that women were well respected in their workplaces in Shanghai, and no one mentioned any experience of being discriminated against for simply being a woman. Some said that, as women, they even gained greater respect. One respondent working in real estate spoke of her deep satis-faction when Chinese colleagues recognized her efforts and expressed their appreciation of 'my courage with regard to traveling extensively and doing busi-ness with people in various parts of China'.

The China impact on young workers

In the autumn of 2000, from the moment when I stepped into the gate of Peking University as a graduate student, I felt I had chosen a road that Robert Frost described as 'the one less travelled by', and indeed 'that has made all the difference'.

(Lee 2009: 10)

The interviewees who migrated to China at a young age often emphasized the difficulties they encountered as pioneers, as the first independent movers, and as a minority within a large expatriate population. Their perception of themselves and their situation was similar to that of the author of the above quotation (who is now a university lecturer and a writer). At that time, very few young people were moving to China or studying there; today, however, seeking out job oppor-tunities in China has become an attractive option for graduates from institutions such as National Taiwan University, especially business school students. Spe-cific lecture courses and internships bring students to China and into contact with Chinese companies. Connections built up during courses or internships enable these graduates to find jobs in China once they have graduated. Among such internship opportunities, the Jade Mountain Programme (玉山計畫), organized and sponsored by the Chinese Scientists' Association, is the largest and most prestigious. This programme recruits 200 students from major universities in Taiwan each year and matches them with a list of prominent Chinese companies in Beijing. For instance, a student from NTU's sociology department, with the help of the Jade Mountain Programme, gained an internship with a major Beijing media group. Even before she graduated, she was recruited by the same media group to write reports on Taiwan. After she graduated, she was formally offered a job as a correspondent based in Taiwan (Hu 2011).

In an advanced industrial country such as Taiwan, the normal route taken by those who wish to lead a middle-class life is first to enter a college of good reputation, to earn a salary that is on or above the average, then to have a family and be able to count on the welfare state to ease the burdens of life or assist if things go exceptionally wrong. How does labour migration to China impact on this scenario? To begin with, the job prospects for young Taiwanese people have become gloomy. For more than a decade now, average salaries in Taiwan have not risen and starting salaries for university graduates have even plummeted. Young workers are also exposed to increasing levels of casual employment. In 2008, 20 per cent of all young workers between 15 and 24 years of age were dependent on casual employment, in contrast with only 9 per cent of the general population (Lin 2011: 128).

However, working on the other side of the Taiwan Strait does not guarantee better conditions or a more promising future. The salaries of the Taiwanese, in comparison with those of the local Chinese employees, shrink along the way down the age line. According to the 104 Human Bank survey, Taiwanese employees earn 50 per cent more on average than their Chinese colleagues. The most surprising finding of this survey, however, was that a large majority (70 per cent) of Taiwanese employees currently working in China consider their Chinese local colleagues to be equally competent. Only 15 per cent felt superior in job ability and work performance compared with their Chinese counterparts. And many respondents were concerned that their jobs would soon be taken by local employees.

Despite these pessimistic claims that the Taiwanese are 'falling out of favour', there are still sufficient promising challenges and opportunities to make a move worthwhile. The story of Mr Young, a 29-year-old interviewee, illustrates many facets of the opportunities that can arise after migration. Mr Young was transferred to a post in China by his employer, a firm of architects, only one year after he had graduated. As a junior designer, back in Taiwan, he would not have stood any chance of being put in charge of the wide variety of projects that he was entrusted with in China – a shopping centre, a kindergarten, a tourist centre, etc. He later moved on to a prominent Chinese firm of architects, doubling his salary in the process; after two years, he was recruited by an American firm of architects in Shanghai. He eventually left the job because of the lack of promotion opportunities and returned to Taiwan. He provided the following advice to upcoming young architects and designers:

> I know that the Chinese government has tight control over foreign young workers in the architectural sector, for they do not wish to see their own workers unemployed. For example, the American firm of architects I worked with in Shanghai tried to apply for a work permit for a young American designer to stay and work for them. But her application was turned down.

It is only the Taiwanese who have unrestricted access to the Chinese job market. I think it is worth taking the opportunity, especially in architecture, even if you do not plan to stay on. You will be given much more exciting projects to carry out. Within a short period of time, juniors are allowed to try out their skills on various projects from scratch to full design, enjoying professional autonomy. The pay by working for Taiwanese employers in China is too low; we earned a salary package the same as junior designers in Taiwan. But my Taiwanese colleagues perform far fewer tasks than we do here. I was working non-stop, all hours of the day and night and I felt constantly chased by all kinds of deadlines. However, this is a real golden opportunity for a young architect to develop and learn. Since it is usually much harder to work in China than in Taiwan, many older peoples do not wish to move. Therefore, there are plenty of opportunities for the young.

(1–2011)

Mr Young returned to Taiwan, where he founded an environmentally-friendly design line for home appliances and products and gave up architectural design. He attributed his ability to make such a career change to his stay in Shanghai, where many new ideas spring up and international exhibitions take place. He learned about environmentally-friendly design from his American boss in Shanghai, whose projects were mostly related to renovating old houses. Now Mr Young still returns to Shanghai at least once a year to display his work at an environmental design exhibition.

In recent years, more and more students, the so-called Taisheng (台生; Taiwanese college graduates from Chinese universities), have been studying at Chinese universities and graduate institutes (Lan and Wu 2011). They are potential migrants to find jobs in China. Some local governments have initiated policies to attract migrants to settle in their regions. For example, Fujian provincial government has attempted to attract well-educated Taiwanese to Pingtan Island on the south coast by means of the 'one thousand talents' programme, with the intention of recruiting 1,000 Taisheng. The programme covers subsidized housing and offers other incentives to lure potential medical doctors, engineers and business creators to Pingtan (China Benpost 2012).

The swing: between homeland identity and global nation[2]

In discussions on the citizenship rights of migrants, much more attention has been paid to the host state's policies than to those of the homeland state. This is understandable, since the host state's policies are of practical concern for the survival and success of migrants living there (Freeman and Ogelman 1998). Yet the homeland state's policies of maintaining or cutting ties with nationals in the diaspora also have both symbolic and practical consequences for migrants. In my analysis of the actions of Taiwan as a home state with regard to Taiwanese migrants in China, I rely on Smith's (2003) differentiation between two types of home state policies governing nationals abroad: homeland policies and global nations' policies. Homeland policies aim at maintaining links with the migrants overseas to encourage their eventual return to their homelands and, at the same time, to discourage them from settling abroad. Global nations' policies encourage the nationals living abroad to assimilate while maintaining ties, especially economic ones, with their homelands.

The Taiwanese state governs its migrants in two important domains, i.e. registered resident status and universal health coverage. While Taiwanese migrants, like their counterparts in other countries, are entitled to enjoy universal health coverage, arguably under even better conditions than non-migrants, they have to choose between registered residence in either China or Taiwan. Once they give up their resident status in Taiwan, their social entitlements, such as universal health coverage, are taken away from them. As a matter of fact, Taiwanese migrants consider universal health coverage as the most important social benefit, in the sense that it motivates them to keep their Taiwanese citizenship. Taiwan's universal health care policy therefore discourages migrants from obtaining Chinese citizenship.

Single choice

When Taiwanese migrants began to move to China in large numbers in the mid-1990s, the question of whether they should be considered residents of China rather than of Taiwan rapidly arose. Previous regulation (prior to 2001) governing the citizenship status of such migrants in China mandated that after four years of continuous stay in China without any return visit to Taiwan, the migrants' registered resident status would be designated 'ineffective' and they would automatically lose their citizenship status. In 2000, after public concerns emerged over a number of disputes involving Taiwanese who had been banned from entering Taiwan with their Taiwanese passports after they had resided in China for more than four years, new legislation was set on track to recognize dual citizenship. In other words, Taiwanese migrants were able to keep their Taiwanese citizenship and also to acquire citizenship in China (Legislative Yuan Meeting Records 2002).

However, this was a short-lived reform. Since 2002, according to new regulations, Taiwanese migrants in China have had to renounce their registered resident status in Taiwan upon acquiring citizenship in China. While Taiwanese migrants in other countries are allowed to have dual citizenship, those migrating to China are not. However, Taiwanese citizens are able to reclaim their resident status upon renunciation of their Chinese citizenship. During the legislative debates over the new policy, the head of the Council of Mainland Affairs who drafted this 'single choice' policy offered the following justification for the policy change: While migration and settlement choices remain basic rights of our people, one has to take into account the potential conflicts between such individual choices and national interests' (Legislative Meetings Records 2002). The shift from dual citizenship to single citizenship is now the backbone of Taiwan's homeland policy towards Taiwanese migrants in China. By adopting a single citizenship stance, the Taiwan state discourages its citizens from enjoying rights and accepting obligations as citizens in China. The rationale behind this policy, according to the government, is that citizenship is inseparable from national loyalty. However, the same logic does not apply to Taiwanese citizens residing elsewhere, because they are allowed to keep their Taiwanese citizenship after becoming naturalized in other countries. The state–diaspora relations in the case of Taiwanese migrants in China are therefore are different from those in countries such as the US.[3]

Universal health coverage

In Taiwan, the requirements for nationals to join the universal health coverage system are tied to the household registration system: only those resident in Taiwan qualify for coverage. I found that my respondents unanimously viewed universal health coverage as a most precious entitlement which they wished to keep under all circumstances. When discussing their retirement plans, many interviewees talked of going back to Taiwan precisely because of their concerns about medical insurance and medical care quality:

> I would like to retire in Taiwan because of medical insurance coverage. This will become more significant as I grow older.
>
> (1–2008)

> If I were planning to stay in China, medical care and costs would be the main barriers. Although medical care in China has improved, quality care is very expensive. Most of the time I do not use the insurance back home, but I continue to pay the monthly premium just in case an emergency arises.
>
> (6–2008)

> If there is no solution to medical care in sight, I would consider retiring in Taiwan because medical care is the most important thing during retirement.
>
> (1–2007)

To retain their membership in the universal health coverage system, migrants need to go back to Taiwan at least once every two years and must also continue to pay the monthly premiums. The current policy of universal coverage allows migrants to apply for a temporary suspension of payments when they are abroad for at least six months and to resume the payments when they come back. This measure, of course, cuts the costs of long-term migrant citizens since they do not have to pay the premiums to maintain their health coverage. Many migrants take advantage of this generous offer and resume coverage only when they need to come back for medical care. There has been much criticism of this policy, to the effect that it allows citizens living abroad to evade responsibility for sharing the costs of health insurance but then allows them enjoy the full benefits when they return. Some critics have drawn attention to the burden imposed on the

Taiwanese health care system by Taiwanese migrants living in China, because of their sheer numbers among all overseas Taiwanese. From statistics available from 2005 to 2007, around 60–70 per cent of reimbursements for medical expenditures from the National Health Care System were made for the medical needs of Taiwanese migrants in China (Lin 2008).

However, many migrants living abroad who continue to be covered by health insurance in Taiwan have their own complaints. The reimbursement of medical costs incurred overseas takes a long time and involves tedious procedures. Taiwanese migrants in China often feel that they are victims of the system since they have to pay the premiums nonetheless. They are demanding simpler and speedier reimbursement procedures for their medical expenditures. Taiwanese business associations in China have lobbied intensively for these procedures to be simplified by permitting Taiwanese migrants to use their insurance cards in Taiwanese-owned hospitals in China (Central News Agency 2008).

At the same time, there has been public concern that although these reimbursements require notarization on medical and expenditure records in China, there have been instances of fraud, which raises doubts about the credibility of the medical expenditures in China claimed by Taiwanese insurers.

The rationale behind this costly policy is both political and economic. First, it allows the Taiwan state to show that it does not wish to alienate Taiwanese citizens, even if they migrate to the territory of its rival state, China. Universal health coverage is an important 'diaspora integration' mechanism, as Gamlen (2008: 851) put it, by which the Taiwan state extends its sovereignty by reaching out to its extra-territorial citizens. Second, ensuring that the Taiwanese diaspora continues to identify with the homeland entails potential economic gains, since Taiwanese migrants are considered by the political elites in Taiwan to be a symbol of national wealth and pride (Wang 2000).

Conclusion

'I am a Scotsman', Sir Walter Scott once famously wrote, 'therefore I had to fight my way into the world'. This 'Scottish mentality', according to historian Arthur Herman (2002), is a mixture of humbleness and pride that can also be found among the Taiwanese, who perceive themselves as fighters struggling against unfavourable conditions, historically as well as geographically. Like Scotland, Taiwan is also known as one of the main emigrant-producing countries, from which the brightest individuals, in particular, go abroad (Findlay and Garrick 1990; Tseng 1995). Taiwanese people have 'had to fight their way into the world' by connecting themselves with the world; as keen learners they import ideas and technology from abroad, as producers they export commodities, and as migrants they export themselves.

This mentality has sustained continuous waves of emigration over several decades, mostly to industrially advanced countries and especially to the United States (Tseng 1995). In the last two decades, however, migrants from Taiwan have moved in large numbers to major cities in China.[4] Understanding how

China's economic growth has changed the landscape of job prospects for highly skilled Taiwanese migrants is important, not only at the individual level but also at the societal level. For individuals, a growing job market brings opportunities but also risks, since educated local people seem to be preparing to take over the jobs of the Taiwanese migrants. On the other hand, at the societal level, faced with one million Taiwanese citizens living and working in China, Taiwan has to calculate the costs and benefits involved in maintaining citizens' entitlements for the sizable Taiwanese diaspora.

The Chinese government, for its part, provides legal privileges for Taiwanese migrants as incentives for long-term political integration. And they gain extra brain-power in many economic sectors which are in urgent need of talent. From the economic perspective, Taiwanese workers have access to a larger job market in China while, on the other hand, China gains skilled workers 'free of cost' in terms of education and training. The Chinese legal framework incorporates the Taiwanese as subjects who move between two nation-states but within a seam-less job market. This poses challenges for the Taiwan government with regard to its efforts to maintain a distinctive political community. Since the opening up of the Chinese job market for Taiwanese citizens is motivated by the PRC's drive for unification, the separation of job market issues from political integration is not as easy as one might think.

Although working in China is such a strong option for Taiwanese white-collar workers, the rapid outmigration is still very much neglected. However, radical positions have been taken by commentaries; an example is a widely read and discussed article published in the *Wall Street Journal* by a Taipei observer, who noted that 'it's no secret that if you're young, talented and motivated, you're better off launching your career in Shanghai or Beijing' (Chen 2013). The commentary was listed as one of the 'most read' pieces in *Business Magazine*, which posted the web link to the article, with more than 300,000 visits. Another author from *Business Magazine* made a similar comment (Huang 2013).

But what lies ahead for those who have the potential to move to China? My research suggests that, first, salaries are shrinking for Taiwanese migrants and the likelihood of being replaced by local workers is rising. Second, Taiwanese are valued more when it comes to transnational team work, for they are deemed to be more capable of communicating bi-culturally than other foreign nationals. Third, latecomers have to be prepared to move to inland cities in China, since the labour markets in coastal cities are becoming too competitive. Fourth, the most important benefit of Taiwanese citizenship is that of being covered by universal health insurance in Taiwan. However, if they are not qualified to join pension insurance schemes back home, migrants (especially young ones) might rather opt to seek higher salaries in China in order to save enough money for their retirement.

With regard to assessing potential future developments, however, further research is needed to find answers to questions such as which segments of the population tend to migrate to China, which tend to stay in Taiwan, and what are the reasons underlying these tendencies. Most importantly, what are the differences between middle-class life in Taiwan and the life of a middle-class migrant employee in China? For many, the 'China rush' began with the excitement of being 'invited' to be part of China's economic growth machine, but many years have elapsed since those days, and the lives of Taiwanese migrants have become increasingly contingent and transient: they are without any expectation of long-term settlement on the one hand, but at the same time without any return plan in sight. Whereas initially the mobility options offered to Taiwanese middle-class migrants have privileged them to access job markets across the Taiwan Strait, the greatest challenge for them and future generations of migrants will be how to integrate in the host society.

Notes

1 In other areas where the Taiwanese have settled in China, there are migrant women's organizations for wives of expatriates, such as 'New Universes of Taiwanese Spouses': see www.taimaclub.com (accessed 25 July 2014).
2 This section is based on a previously published article from 2011 (co-authored with Wu Jieh-Min): 'Reconfiguring Citizenship and Nationality', *Citizenship Studies*, 15, 2: 265–282.
3 Since 2005, nationality law has changed to officially recognize dual nationality: see http://rosseauism.kscg.gov.tw/asw5/law2.asp (accessed 25 July 2014).
4 Between 1996 and 2000, the number of Taiwanese moving to countries other than China reached over 100,000 in total, but the figure shrank to just half this number between 2001 and 2005 (Lee and Peng 2009).

References

Academia Sinica Institute of Sociology (2007) *Taiwan Social Change Survey: Basic Findings*, Taipei: Academia Sinica.
Central News Agency (2008) 'Barriers Ahead for Taiwanese to Use Insurance Card in Chinese Hospitals', available at www.epochtimes.com/b5/9/6/24/n2568773.htm (accessed 24 July 2014).
Chen, Jennifer (2013) 'In Taipei, Life on the Slow Lane', *Wall Street Journal*, 14 March, available at http://blogs.wsj.com/scene/2013/03/14/in-taipei-life-in-the-slow-lane/(accessed 28 July 2014).
China Benpost (2012) 'Pingtan Industrial District Offers Incentive Packages for Taishen', 28 March, available at http://chaiwanbenpost.blogspot.tw/2012/03/37_28.html (accessed 28 July 2014).
Commonwealth Magazine (2009) 'My Boss is Posting in China and Taiwan is Part of "Great China"', September.
Conradson, D., and Latham, A. (2005) 'Transnational Urbanism: Attending to Everyday Practices and Mobilities', *Journal of Ethnic and Migration Studies*, 31, 2: 227–233.
Cox, S. (2012) 'Pedalling Prosperity: China's Economy is Not as Precarious as it Looks', *The Economist*, 26 May, 3.
Fielding, A. (1992) 'Migration and Social Mobility: South East England as an Escalator region', *Regional Studies*, 26, 1: 1–15.
Fielding, A. (1995) 'Migration and Middle-class Formation in England and Wales, 1981–1991', in Butler, T. and Savage, M. (eds) *Social Change and the Middle Classes*, London: UCL Press.

Findlay, Allan, and Garrick, Lesley (1990) 'Scottish Emigration in the 1980s: A Migration Channels Approach to the Study of Skilled International Migration', *Transactions of the Institute of British Geographers*, 15, 2: 177–192.

Forbes Magazine (2012) 'China Success Lifts Snack Food Billionaire to No. 1', 23 May, available at www.forbes.com/taiwan-billionaires/ (accessed 23 July 2014).

Freeman, G., and Ogelman, N. (1998) 'Homeland Citizenship Policies and the Status of Third Country Nationals in the European Union', *Journal of Ethnic and Migration Studies*, 24, 4: 769–788.

Gamlen, A. (2008) 'The Emigration State and the Modern Geopolitical Imagination', *Political Geography*, 27: 840–856.

Gong, L. (2012) *China Incredible!* [Dalu bu siyi!], Taipei: Shangxun Culture.

Herman, A. (2002) *How the Scots Invent the Modern World: The True Story of How Western Europe's Poorest Nation Created Our World and Everything In It*, New York: Three Rivers Press.

Hu, Jiajie (2011) 'My Days of Being a Journalist in Beijing', available at www.lihpao.com/?action-viewnews-itemid-116832 (accessed 24 July 2014).

Huang, Chi-Yuan (2013) 'Talented Young People should Not Stay in Taipei', *Business Magazine*, 19 March.

Human Bank (2011) 'Survey on West-Bound Workers', available at www.104.com.tw/cfdocs/2000/pressroom/message900224.htm (accessed 24 July 2014).

Kofman, E. (1999) 'Female 'Birds of Passage' a Decade Later: Gender and Immigration in the European Union', *International Migration Review*, 33, 2: 269–299.

Ken, S. (2002) 'National Identity among Taiwanese High-Tech Entrepreneurs in Shanghai', unpublished paper, Institute of International Relations, Taipei: Chengchi University.

Lan, P. C., and Wu, Y. F. (2011) 'Between 'Homeland' and 'Foreign Country': Liminal Identity and Boundary Work of Taiwanese Students in China', *Taiwanese Sociology*, 22: 1–57.

Legislative Yuan Meeting Records (2002) *Legislation Debate, First Committee Meeting of Interior Affairs and Ethnic Minorities Committee on Revising Laws Governing Relations between Taiwan Residents and China Residents*, Taipei: Legislative Yuan.

Lee, Y., and Peng, S. L. (2009) 'The Impact of International Migration on Taiwan Economy and Policy Responses', paper presented at International Migration and Taiwan Economy Conference, Taipei.

Lee, Z. L. (2009) *Into Urban China: A Taiwanese Cultural Memoir after a Decade in China*, Taipei: Xiari.

Li, Po (2007) 'Taiwanese Career Women Active in Shanghai', available at www.lihpao.com/?action-viewnews-itemid-95115 (accessed 28 July 2014).

Lin, T. H. (2011) 'Working Poor', in Lin, T. H. *et al.* (eds) *Generational Decline*, Taipei: Taiwan Labour Union Front.

Lin, W. D. (2008) *Evaluations of Overseas Reimbursements of National Health Insurance*, Pingtung: Chang-Rong University.

Ministry of Commerce of People's Republic of China (2005) 'Taiwan, Hong Kong, Macau Residents Employment Act', Beijing: Ministry of Commerce of People's Republic of China.

Shen, H. H. (2005) '"The First Taiwanese Wives" and "the Chinese Mistresses": The International Division of Labour in Familial and Intimate Relations across the Taiwan Strait', *Global Networks*, 5, 4: 419–437.

Sheng, P. (2012) 'Along with Increasing Consumption Demand, Department Stores Stock Soar', available at http://tw.money.yahoo.com/news_article/adbf/d_a_120501_3_34pkk (accessed 28 July 2014).

Smith, R. C. (2003) 'Diasporic Memberships in Historical Perspective: Comparative Insights from the Mexican, Italian and Polish', *International Migration Review*, 37: 724–759.

Tseng, Y. F. (1995) 'Beyond Little Taipei: Taiwanese Immigrant Businesses in Los Angeles', *International Migration Review*, 29: 33–58.

Wang, H. L. (2000) 'Rethinking the Global and the National: Reflections on National Imaginations in Taiwan', *Theory, Culture and Society*, 17: 93–117.

Wealth Magazine (2007) 'Mid-Career Crisis in Taiwan', July.

12 Taiwan's immigration policy and the China impact

The case of cross-Strait families

Jian-Bang Deng[1]

The movement of peoples is often related to the development of human civilization. In the contemporary world, global capital flows and better transport technologies have greatly facilitated cross-border movement. Unlike the early flows of migration, which were largely directed towards the north and well-developed countries, modern migration flows follow a more diversified route towards the south and newly-developed countries (Massey 2002 [1998]). This indicates that contemporary international migration does not only impact on a few developed or less-developed countries but is becoming a global phenomenon involving more and more countries.

Among the vast number of works on international migration, labour migration has attracted a great deal of attention (Butcher 2006; Hannerz 1998), particularly in the context of Asian societies, where the export of semi-skilled or unskilled labour is widespread. As Massey (2002 [1998]) points out, many countries have switched from simply exporting labour to both exporting and importing it. In fact, the cross-border movement of skilled migrants, as a result of the trend towards globalization and new forms of the international division of labour, has increased in significance during the past two decades (Favell *et al.* 2006). As shown in Manning and Bhatnagar (2006: 60), even in Southeast Asia, the traditional labour-exporting areas of Singapore, Malaysia and Thailand were already hosting 60,000–70,000 professionals and managerial personnel in 2002, while Indonesia and the Philippines had permitted the entry of 10,000–20,000 skilled workers.[2] Manning and Bhatnagar's research also revealed that manpower from Taiwan accounted for 4.6 per cent, 6.3 per cent and 4.7 per cent of skilled migrants in Malaysia, Thailand and the Philippines respectively, and Taiwan is accordingly listed as one of the top five import areas for skilled labour in the above-mentioned countries (2006: 61).

Nevertheless, there is another country which has attracted more Taiwanese skilled workers during the past two decades: the People's Republic of China. According to an estimate by an expert at the Taiwan Research Institute at the Chinese Academy of Social Sciences, the number of Taiwanese business people and expatriates residing in China had reached more than one million people in 2008 (Overseas Chinese News 2008).[3] Ming-Chang Tsai and Chin-Fen Chang (2010) showed that 10.3 per cent of the respondents in the Taiwan Social Change

Survey 2005 claimed to have worked in China at some time or other. If responses to the survey questions such as, 'having family (6.3 per cent), relatives (20.1 per cent), neighbours and/or friends (29.3 per cent), or co-workers (9.3 per cent) who have worked in China' are included, it becomes clear that moving to China to work has become a striking feature of the career plans and daily lives of Taiwanese people in the various strata of society.

Taiwanese business people and expatriates have also been the focus of many recent studies that have employed a broader approach, incorporating perspectives from sociology, social anthropology and political science (Hsing 1997; Tseng 2000, 2008; Chen 2006). There have even been calls for 'Taishang [Taiwanese entrepreneurs] Studies' as an interdisciplinary approach to this emerging research field (Keng *et al.* 2012). This reflects not only the increase in economic and social interaction between Taiwan and China in the recent past, but also the growing importance of China in the East Asian region and globally. Studies on Taiwanese entrepreneurs to date have tended to focus on their economic influence on cross-Strait relations and on the political impact of the huge capital flows to China, by adopting, for example, analytical perspectives at the macro level. Because capital flows are always linked with the mobility of people, however (Tseng 2000), there is also a need to provide analytical perspectives at the micro level. Indeed, Taiwanese business people and expatriates as individual migrants have been drawing increased attention from scholars during the last few years. These studies explore, for example, the social dynamics of expatriates during the migration processes, their identities and feelings of belonging after migrating to China, and the issue of keeping mistresses that is so common among Taiwanese businessmen (Jones and Shen 2008; Shen 2008; Keng and Schubert 2010).

Little attention, however, has been given to the increasing number of cross-border marriages between expatriates and local Chinese people. This does not mean that this issue has been absent from recent studies on migrants or lacks importance in Taiwan. On the contrary, many scholars from different disciplines have contributed to this research agenda in the last decade, highlighting the huge impact of new immigrants to Taiwan both socially and politically (Wang and Hsiao 2009; Wang and Chang 2002; Lu 2008). They have addressed issues such as the large-scale commercialization of the marriage market in Taiwan, including cross-border marriages and the social adaptation processes of foreign and Chinese spouses in Taiwan as well as the kind of education problems that are faced by the children of new immigrants. This research goes beyond the dominant explanation, which is based on the economic disparities between the sending and receiving countries, and shows how other factors, such as the uneven development of the international political economy, the role played by matchmakers and individual desires for cross-border marriage, have all played a part in the rapid increase in marriage migrants to Taiwan. These studies have also served to draw public attention to the interaction between personal migration experiences and the social constraints faced by cross-border marriage migrants by unveiling the discrimination and other unfair treatment based on the racial, class and gender prejudices experienced by new immigrants. Nevertheless, up to now, this work on migration has focused on marriage migrants in Taiwan proper and has paid much less attention to those who live outside Taiwan. This chapter will show that a great number of Chinese spouses have not registered for permanent residence in Taiwan, and also that this is not a marginal phenomenon but one that is well worth serious examination, especially with respect to the Chinese spouses of Taiwanese expatriates.

The objective of this chapter is to provide a more comprehensive explanation of the reasons why the majority of Chinese spouses married to Taiwanese expatriates tend to choose to reside in China rather than in Taiwan, and how their citizenship is arranged. One line of argumentation followed here is that these marriages should be termed transnational, rather than cross-border marriages, in order to emphasize the role played by marriage migrants as active agents in the migration process. This chapter also argues that citizenship for Taiwanese expatriates with Chinese spouses, under the given restrictions in immigration policy in Taiwan, is first and foremost a 'family-based dual citizenship' arrangement. Many Chinese marriage migrants do not give up their PRC citizenship and decide not to reside in the host society; this is a pattern of migration behaviour that differs greatly from older patterns. Lastly, this chapter calls for the reconsideration of Taiwan's current immigration policy.

Demographic characteristics of Chinese spouses in Taiwan

Table 12.1 presents the number of registered marriages according to the nationalities of the spouses from 1998 to 2013 in Taiwan. It shows that the number of cross-border marriages with foreign and PRC nationals has increased steadily since the late 1990s. In 2003, the number of cross-border marriages reached a high point, constituting 31.86 per cent of all marriages in Taiwan. Although cross-border marriages had dropped to 13.01 per cent by 2011, there were 157,630 foreign and 329,073 Chinese spouses, with a total number of 486,703 marriage migrants registered in the official statistics of marriage migration, making them a significant group within Taiwanese society (Table 12.2).

Immigration regulation, citizenship and Chinese spouses

In order to respond to this rapid increase in new immigrants, the government in Taiwan has launched a series of new policies in the past few years. These have included, in 2005, the setting up of a 'Foreign Spouses Care and Counselling Fund' of three billion NT dollars (equivalent to some US$100 million) for a period of ten years, and the founding of the National Immigration Agency (NIA) in 2007. It seems obvious that these policies were configured, on the one hand, for the purpose of establishing stricter immigration regulations, for example the implementation of a limited annual quota for marriage migration applications as well as interviews conducted by immigration officials with marriage migrants at the airport. On the other hand, the government has also provided extra care

Table 12.1 Registered number of marriages according to nationality of spouses, 1998–2013

Year	All marriages	With foreign spouses*	With Chinese spouses**	With foreign or Chinese spouses/all spouses (%)
1998	145,976	10,454	12,451	15.69
1999	173,209	14,674	17,589	18.63
2000	181,642	21,338	23,628	24.76
2001	170,515	19,405	26,797	27.10
2002	172,655	20,107	28,906	28.39
2003	171,483	19,643	34,991	31.86
2004	131,453	20,338	10,972	23.82
2005	141,140	13,808	14,619	20.14
2006	142,669	9,524	14,406	16.77
2007	135,041	9,554	15,146	18.29
2008	154,866	8,957	12,772	14.03
2009	117,099	8,620	13,294	18.71
2010	138,819	8,169	13,332	15.49
2011	165,327	8,053	13,463	13.01
2012	143,384	7,887	12,713	14.37
2013	147,636	7,950	11,542	13.20

Source: National Immigration Agency, Ministry of Interior, ROC, www.immigration.gov.tw/ct.asp?xItem=1268370&ctNode=29699&mp=1 (accessed 8 July 2014).

Notes
* Spouses from countries other than China.
** Spouses including those from Mainland China, Hong Kong and Macao.

Table 12.2 Registered number of foreign spouses and Chinese spouses, 1987–2013

Chinese spouses (%)			Foreign spouses (%)			Total (%)
Female	Male		Female	Male		
308,232	20,841	329,073 (67.61)	142,752	14,878	157,630 (32.39)	486,703 (100)

Source: National Immigration Agency, Ministry of the Interior, ROC, www.immigration.gov.tw/ct.asp?xItem=1247109&ctNode=29699&mp=1 (accessed 8 July 2014).

benefits for these new immigrants in Taiwan because they were making a new start in the host society under less favourable social circumstances compared with the rest of the population. According to a government report, the 'Care and Counselling Fund' was set up with the aim of helping to 'solve life adjustment problems due to cultural differences which foreign and Chinese spouses may experience, and helping them to integrate as soon as possible into Taiwanese society' (MOI 2013a). In other words, foreign and Chinese spouses, from the government's point of view, were all to be treated as 'immigrants'. The official 'Care and Counselling Fund' was supposed to encourage new immigrants to learn the official language and absorb the social and cultural practices of the receiving community. The immigration policies in Taiwan, therefore, were advocated from the perspective of assimilation.

These immigration policies were formulated on the assumption that many people from the PRC and from other foreign countries, in particular Southeast Asian countries, seek to reside in Taiwan permanently and are willing to adopt Taiwanese citizenship after their marriages with Taiwanese citizens. However, among the registered 329,073 Chinese spouses (Table 12.3), probably only those who hold a 'resident visa with long-term residency' or a 'resident permit' have been resident for a long period of time in Taiwan. According to Taiwan's immigration laws, Chinese spouses can visit Taiwan with a tourist visa or claim the status of dependent relative and apply for a resident visa, but they are only allowed to apply for a resident visa with long-term residency after they have stayed in Taiwan for more than 183 days in four consecutive years. After they have held a resident visa with long-term residency for two years and have stayed in Taiwan for more than 183 days in two consecutive years, they can apply to change the resident visa to a resident permit. That is to say, the visa status of the spouses who hold a tourist visa (108,932 individuals; see Table 12.3) or 'dependent relative' visa (70,279 individuals) does not show whether they are actually seeking to reside permanently in Taiwan.

If the numbers of tourist visa holders and resident visa holders are included with those claiming the status of 'dependent relatives', it appears that more than half of all registered Chinese spouses (54.46 per cent) still remain at the first stage of their marriage migration to Taiwan. It is not clear whether these marriage migrants have made the decision to reside in Taiwan and to apply for long-term or permanent residency. Although many Chinese spouses who hold a resident visa and have the status of 'dependent relative' may actually stay in Taiwan and wait for a visa with long-term residency to be granted, the high proportion of Chinese spouses holding a tourist visa highlights the fact that nearly one third of all Chinese marriage migrants hold a temporary resident visa only.

Another statistic in the 'White Paper with Interviews Conducted with Chinese Spouses Coming to Taiwan to Join Family Members' (大陸地區人民來台團聚面談工作白皮書) (IONPA 2005) shows that 199,419 Chinese residents applied to travel to Taiwan for the purpose of marriage migration in 2005, but only 109,726 Chinese spouses were actually still resident in Taiwan at the end of that year. 89,793 marriage migrants, or 45 per cent of all applicants, decided to leave again after they had entered Taiwan. Table 12.4 shows the ratio of Chinese

Table 12.3 Registered number of Chinese spouses according to visa status, 1987–2013

Tourist visa (visiting relative or family reunification)	Resident visa		Resident permit	Total
	Resident visa for dependent relative	Long-term residency		
108,932 (33.10%)	70,279 (21.36%)	36,668 (11.14%)	113,194 (34.40%)	329,073 (100%)

Source: National Immigration Agency, Ministry of the Interior, ROC, www.immigration.gov.tw/ct.asp?xItem=1247109&ctNode=29699&mp=1 (accessed 8 July 2014).

Table 12.4 Number of Chinese spouses remaining in Taiwan according to visa status in
IONPA's White Paper (2005)*

	Tourist visa (visiting relative or family reunification)	*Resident visa (resident visa for dependent relative/ long-term residency)*	*Resident permit*	*ID card*
Number of Chinese spouses staying in Taiwan(A)	43,027	31,935	24,701	NA
Number of Chinese spouses(B)	107,808	88,265	27,137	10,063
Ratio(A/B) (%)	39.9	36.2	91.0	NA

Source: IONPA (2005).

Note
* The White Paper with interviews conducted with Chinese spouses was provided by the Immigration Office of the National Police Agency. This was only published once, in 2005, and the figures have not yet been updated.

spouses staying in Taiwan in 2005 according to their visa status. While 91 per cent of all those holding resident permits stayed in Taiwan in 2005, only 36.2 per cent holding resident visas and 39.9 per cent holding tourist visas chose to stay in Taiwan during the same period. This illustrates the fact that, in 2005, 63.8 per cent of the Chinese spouses holding resident visas and 60.1 per cent of those holding tourist visas, i.e. more than 60 per cent holding both tourist and resident visas, did not stay continuously in Taiwan.

Table 12.5 shows that the proportion of Chinese spouses without a resident permit or ID card, i.e. without proper household registration in Taiwan, but still continuously resident in Taiwan was only 47.4 per cent, 45.2 per cent and 42.3 per cent for the period from 2005 to 2007. That is to say, more than half of all the Chinese spouses without such registration in the period mentioned were not continuously resident on the island. Paradoxically, as it may seem, the statistics concurrently show that there was a steady increase in marriage migrants from 2005 to 2007, but that the number of those continuously resident in Taiwan actually decreased.

Although strict government immigration regulations may have increased the difficulties in obtaining a resident permit and this may have led to many Chinese spouses having to wait longer, usually more than six years, to be naturalized, there is still no clear explanation as to why so many Chinese spouses remain at the first stage of their visa status after their marriage to Taiwanese citizens. Chinese spouses, even after their cross-border marriages, did not seem to have any intention of being continuously resident in Taiwan. For this reason, it appears that a different perspective is required to explain the migratory behaviours of Chinese spouses married to Taiwanese citizens.

Table 12.5 Percentage of Chinese spouses without household registration who stayed continuously in Taiwan*

Year	Number of Chinese spouses without household registration in Taiwan**	Number of Chinese spouses without household registration continuously staying in Taiwan***	Percentage
2005	196,073	93,012	47.4
2006	201,811	91,158	45.2
2007	205,906	87,018	42.3

Sources: Ministry of the Interior, ROC; MOI (2007) and www.immigration.gov.tw/ct.asp?xItem=10 84047&ctNode=29699&mp=1 (accessed 8 July 2014).

Notes
* The Ministry of the Interior (ROC) published only once, in 2007, a detailed report containing three years of data regarding the continuous and non-continuous residence of citizens and non-citizens in Taiwan. Table 12.5 therefore provides statistics only for the period from 2005 to 2007.
** Chinese spouses without household registration in Taiwan: all registered Chinese spouses, minus those who obtained a resident permit and ID card.
*** A continuous stay: resident in Taiwan for more than 183 days in the year.

Theoretical framework: cross-border marriages vs. transnational marriages

Why did marriage migration become popular in the era of globalization? The push-and-pull theory in international migration has frequently been used to explain the decision-making processes underlying migrant marriages (Lee 1966; Thomas 1973; Espenshade 1989; Golini *et al.* 1991). However, recent findings have shown that factors such as economic disparities between sending and receiving countries or the poverty of individual people alone cannot fully explain the motivations underlying marriage migration. The 'mail-order brides' in Western industrial countries and the emergence of a commercial marriage market in Asian societies during recent years have revealed the importance of another factor: marriage matchmakers (Constable 2003; Lu 2008). Without marriage matchmakers, it would not be possible for a large number of cross-border marriages to take place in the space of only a few weeks or even a few days. In recent cross-border marriages in Taiwan, in particular those involving women from Southeast Asian counties, the help of matchmakers in mate choice has proved crucial. Despite this common trend, marriages between Taiwanese expatriates and Chinese spouses, according to a survey (MOI 2004),[4] are love matches and do not rely on matchmakers.

Mueller-Schneider's (2000: 219) study of recent marriage migration to Western industrial countries showed that marriage migration is not only a phenomenon related to gender, but also an indication of the high correlation between marriage on the one hand and migration on the other. According to his research, women from a developing-world country who marry into a Western country are not just seeking to participate in the lifestyle of Western societies but are also, through 'global hypergamy',[5] seeking to acquire citizenship in the host country in order to obtain better life-style opportunities. However, this factor fails to explain why a high percentage of Chinese spouses, as mentioned earlier, do not act actively seek to obtain ROC citizenship and do not decide to reside permanently in Taiwan. Charsley and Shaw (2006: 335) show, in their study, that not all cross-border marriages necessarily entail cross-border migration. In a more globalized world, the emergence of more divergent migration behaviours and patterns of cross-border marriages could actually be expected.

Lu (2007: 3) proposed that a sharper difference be made between the two terms, i.e. 'cross-border marriage' and 'transnational marriage', which are both commonly used to refer to the same thing in the international migration literature. From Lu's point of view, both of these terms can refer to cross-cultural or same-culture marriages. However, the term 'cross-border marriage' emphasizes the 'geographical, national, racial, class and gender and cultural borders constructed in the hosting societies'. Marriage migrants, particularly females from less developed areas, decide to marry mainly for economic reasons, citizenship and welfare or a better lifestyle in the receiving society. In contrast, transnational marriage is defined by Lu (2007:3) as 'a transnational network and space created by the actors themselves; as well as the transactions of economic resources, symbols and political and cultural practices between the sending and receiving communities'. This kind of interpretation of marriage migration is obviously strongly influenced by the perspective on transnationalism found in recent migration studies conducted by scholars such as Glick-Shiller *et al.* (1997, 2004). Transnationalism studies emphasize the ongoing importance of the nation-state in the modern globalized world and also tend to focus more on 'the human agency or adaptive strategies of transnational migrants' (Jackson *et al.* 2004: 8). In other words, analyses of transnational marriage focus on how marriage migrants, under the restrictions imposed by the nation-state, act as active agents in the migration process.

As Aihwa Ong's (1999) research on Hong Kong's middle- and upper-class migration to the United States shows, many migrants develop a flexible notion of citizenship as a strategy for accumulating capital and power. For the above-mentioned reasons, these business migrants do not seek 'merely to engage in profit making' but also tend to acquire US citizenship or passports from other countries that help them to 'acquire a range of symbolic capitals' to 'facilitate their positioning, economic negotiation, and cultural acceptance in different geographical sites' (Ong 1999: 18). An instrumental attitude toward citizenship helps these migrants to accumulate individual capital and power in their hosting societies. Ong describes this kind of cultural logic of capital accumulation among many overseas Chinese who migrate to the US as 'flexible citizenship'. This chapter takes the perspectives of both Lu and Ong in order to gain a more appropriate description of a different type of marriage migration. I examine the way in which citizenship is arranged in the families of Taiwanese expatriates and their Chinese spouses by focusing on the viewpoint of actors' opportunities and choices under the given cross-Strait immigration regulations.

Methodology

Apart from the demographic data provided by the statistics of government departments published online and the collection of government reports related to immigration policy, the primary data for this study were gathered during field research between 2005 and 2010, and in particular during two years of fieldwork on the marriage processes involving Taiwanese expatriates and Chinese spouses from August 2007 to September 2008 in China's Pearl River Delta and Yangtze River Delta. I chose these two areas for my fieldwork mainly because of the high spatial concentration of Taiwanese manufacturing industries in these regions, and thus the greater likelihood of obtaining more interviews with Taiwanese expatriates and their Chinese spouses.

For this research, I have mainly employed a methodological approach based on narrative in-depth interviews and participant observation. I adopted a snow-ball strategy in the first phase of the research to identify interviewees, and this was combined with a sampling strategy of 'maximum variation' (Flick 2005) at subsequent stages of the interview process by taking into account variables such as age, gender, occupation, position in the companies of Taiwanese expatriates and the occupations of the Chinese spouses and the existence of children in the family. In total, 37 in-depth interviews were conducted, each lasting one to two hours, with 25 male Taiwanese expatriates, 1 female Taiwanese expatriate and 11 female Chinese spouses. Nine couples among the interviewees had a spousal relationship. In order to obtain more detailed information, four participans were interviewed twice. I had several opportunities to take part in family gatherings with my respondents, which proved to be very useful with regard to completing my data pool.

The majority of interviews conducted with cross-Strait married couples were with male Taiwanese expatriates who had married local Chinese females. Only one respondent was a female Taiwanese expatriate married to a Chinese male. However, the under-representation of such cases, such as that found in my sample, is not unusual and is well-documented in official statistics on cross-Strait marriages. According to data provided by Taiwan's NIA in January 2014, only 20,841 Chinese males compared with 308,232 Chinese female spouses had made cross-Strait marriages, which gives a male/female Chinese spouse ratio of 5:74 (Table 12.2).

During the interview process, I used a questionnaire with several research sub-questions including the interviewees' motivations for making a cross-Strait marriage, their stereotypes concerning the other side of the Taiwan Strait, the process of their marriage migration, their choices of main residence for the family, and their preferences concerning citizenship for their spouses and children. All the interviews were recorded and transcribed in word text for later analysis. Various types of field notes were taken after each interview.

The interviews were then analysed and classified according to the arrangement of citizenship for each respondent and his/her family during the migratory process. Tables 12.6.1 and 12.6.2 show that none of the interviewed Taiwanese

Table 12.6.1 List of interviews with Taiwanese expatriates

No.	Position level	Sex	Age	Assignment location	Citizenship after cross-Strait marriage	Types of spouses' residence status*	Note
I28	Manager	M	38	Shenzhen	–	Taiwan Resident Permit	
T02	Manager	M	57	Shanghai	ROC(Taiwan)	III	
T05	Manager	M	49	Suzhou	ROC(Taiwan)	III	
T42	Deputy General Manager	M	50	Shenzhen	ROC(Taiwan)	II	
S01	Assistant Manager	M	40	Shenzhen	ROC(Taiwan)	I	Spouse of S02
S04	Manager	M	48	Dongguan	ROC(Taiwan)	III	Spouse of S03
S05	Manager	M	39	Shenzhen	ROC(Taiwan)	III	Spouse of A01
S06	Assistant Manager	M	34	Dongguan	ROC(Taiwan)	III	
S08	Manager	M	44	Shanghai	ROC(Taiwan)	III	
S09	Manager	M	40	Shanghai	ROC(Taiwan)	III	
S10	Manager	M	41	Suzhou	ROC(Taiwan)	I	Spouse of S11
S12	Manager	M	35	Shanghai	ROC(Taiwan)	II	
S13	General Manager	F	35	Shanghai	ROC(Taiwan)	I	
S14	Executive Assistant to CEO	M	34	Ningbo	ROC(Taiwan)	I	Spouse of S15
S16	Head of Department	M	34	Ningbo	ROC(Taiwan)	II	Spouse of S17
S18	Manager	M	59	Dongguan	ROC(Taiwan)	I	
S19	Manager	M	38	Shenzhen	ROC(Taiwan)	I	Spouse of S20
A17	Engineer	M	32	Guangzhou	ROC(Taiwan)	III	Spouse of A18
A24	Manager	M	34	Shenzhen	ROC(Taiwan)	III	
A25	Manager	M	36	Shenzhen	ROC(Taiwan)	III	
A33	Manager	M	36	Shanghai	ROC(Taiwan)	II	Spouse of A34
A35	Manager	M	30	Kunshan	ROC(Taiwan)	III	
A37	Executive Director	M	36	Shanghai	ROC(Taiwan)	III	
A38	Manager	M	44	Shanghai	ROC(Taiwan)	II	
A39	Manager	M	38	Suzhou	ROC(Taiwan)	II	
A41	Manager	M	37	Suzhou	ROC(Taiwan)	II	

Note
* See Table 12.7.

Table 12.6.2 List of interviews with Chinese spouses

No.	With/without occupation	Sex	Age	Number of children	Place of birth	Citizenship after cross-Strait marriage	Types of residence status*
S02	W/O	F	28	1	Hubei	PRC	I
S03	W	F	31	0	Guangxi	PRC	III
S07	W	F	36	3	Hubei	ROC (Taiwan)	Taiwan Resident Permit
S11	W/O	F	30	2	Jiangsu	PRC	I
S15	W/O	F	28	2	Zhejiang	PRC	I
S17	W	F	26	1	Zhejiang	PRC	II
S20	W/O	F	31	2	Heilongjiang	PRC	I
A01	W	F	32	1	Jiangxi	PRC	III
A08	W	F	29	0	Hunan	PRC	III
A18	W	F	26	0	Hainan	PRC	III
A34	W	F	31	0	Zhejiang	PRC	II

Note
* See Table 12.7.

expatriates sought to change their citizenship status after marriage, i.e. they all continued to hold their original Taiwanese (ROC) citizenship. Most of the interviewed Chinese spouses, with the exception of cases S07 and T02, retained their PRC citizenship unchanged. The most significant difference concerning citizenship arrangements was related to whether Chinese spouses changed from rural to urban *hukou* (household registration) after having married Taiwanese expatriates.

Table 12.7 presents the different types of residence status of the interviewed Chinese residents before and after their marriage to Taiwanese expatriates. All cases of Chinese spouses related to only three out of four cell types with reference to their residence status. Not covered is the case of Chinese spouses holding an inherited urban *hukou* who exchanged this for a rural *hukou* after marriage, as this is only a theoretical option which is rarely chosen in contemporary China. The following three cases illustrate the complexity of cross-Strait marriages.

Narratives of cross-Strait marriages

He-Chen and Suyun's story (Type I)

He-Chen (born in 1966) is an expatriate who has been working in China for 14 years. He met his wife, Suyun (born in 1977), after he started to work in Suzhou, where for the first year he lived in a local hotel in which Suyun worked as a hotel receptionist. When his two-year contract was about to end, He-Chen decided not to return to Taiwan immediately but to continue with his expatriate career in China. In 1997, he married Suyun. After they were married, He-Chen and Suyun decided not to follow the usual route observed in marriage migration, which would have entailed Suyun joining He-Chen's family in Taiwan by obtaining resident status as a dependent relative, then converting this to a long-term residency visa, and finally applying to the Taiwanese authorities for a permanent resident permit. Instead, He-Chen went to great lengths to help Suyun change her inherited rural *hukou* into a Suzhou citizen's resident permit.

According to the 'Interim Measures for Access to Suzhou Household Registration' (蘇州市戶籍準入登記暫行辦法) (Suzhou City Government 2003), a

Table 12.7 Types of residence status of Chinese spouses of Taiwanese expatriates

| | | Current residence status of Chinese spouse | |
		Rural hukou	Urban hukou
Inherited residence status of Chinese spouse	Rural *hukou**	III	I
	Urban *hukou*	IX**	II

Notes
* *hukou*: household registration.
** IX shows that, in theory, the existence of such a case is possible, but no such case was found during the fieldwork.

rural *hukou* holder is entitled to apply for an urban *hukou* if he/she (1) has acquired a BA or higher degree abroad, (2) is classified as a professional, managerial or technical specialist who meets the current needs of Suzhou city, (3) has employment in Suzhou that requires a bachelor's degree or higher, (4) has invested more than RMB500,000 in Suzhou or pays taxes to the local government of RMB50,000 or more, and (5) has found employment in Suzhou and purchased commercial real estate (measuring more than 50 m² in the case of a single person and more than 75 m² in the case of a couple). Although she had been working in Suzhou for more than a decade, Suyun would not have been able to obtain a local *hukou* in Suzhou because she comes from a middle-income family and holds only a high school degree. However, with the support of He-Chen in buying a house in Suzhou, Suyun was finally able to obtain an urban *hukou*.

The first time Suyun visited Taiwan was in 1997, soon after her marriage to He-Chen had taken place, when she was three months pregnant. However, Suyun decided to return to Suzhou for the birth, since He-Chen's mother, due to ill health, would not at that time have been able to take care of the coming baby. Their first daughter was born in 1998 and the second in 2001. He-Chen applied for Suzhou household registration for their first daughter after birth, but he cancelled it three months later and applied for Taiwanese citizenship for her. Although the second daughter held PRC citizenship at the time of the interview, according to He-Chen, the authorities will allow her to change her citizenship from Chinese to Taiwanese before she is enrolled in school. Additionally, He-Chen will keep his Taiwanese citizenship unchanged because for him, holding the *Taibao* passport (Mainland Travel Permit for Taiwan Residents, 台灣居民來往大陸通行證) is more convenient than holding the alternative – that is, the Taiwan Travel Permit for Mainland Residents (大陸居民來往台灣通行證) – for those holding PRC citizenship.

The case of He-Chen and Suyun is a typical example of the way many Chinese spouses are married to Taiwanese expatriates. Why did Suyun not give up her PRC citizenship upon marriage? Obviously, for Suyun, obtaining Taiwanese citizenship and having to live permanently in Taiwan for this would have meant that she would have had to live away from her husband for six years or even longer. In addition, many of Suyun's relatives, including her parents and only brother, have moved to Suzhou. When Suyun was asked where home is for her, she answered that it was neither Taipei nor her parents' home in North Jiangsu, but Suzhou.

Jia-Qing and Xiaowei's story (Type II)

The interview with Jia-Qing (born in 1973) and Xiawei (born in 1981) was conducted in a brand new residential apartment located in the central city of Ningbo (寧波). Jia-Qing had been motivated by the good prospects offered by China's economy to accept an assignment to move to work in Shanghai in 2001. At the beginning of his expatriation he worked in the securities industry, but due to barriers for foreign investment in the finance sector in China, he changed jobs one year later and went to work in the electronic production industry in Ningpo. Xiawei was hired by this company during the same year. Although they had known and loved each other for a long time, they did not get married until 2006. Xiawei's parents are local residents of Ningpo. They did not want their only child to marry far away from home because she was the 'the apple of their eyes'.

At the time of the interview (August 2008), Xiawei was pregnant. When asked whether she would give birth in Taiwan and apply for Taiwanese citizenship, Xiawei answered without hesitation:

> I told him [Jia-Qing] I wanted to stay here even after marriage, otherwise I wouldn't fall in love with him and marry him. If I migrated to Taiwan, my degree in China would not be recognized, and I would have no choice but becoming a housewife there. To be honest, I feel that kind of life is quite boring.

Nevertheless, when it came to the household registration of their coming baby, although Xiawei wanted to give birth in Ningpo, they would still apply for Taiwanese citizenship for their child. The reason was quite simple, as Xiawei pointed out: 'Because after the child grows up, it can choose to work either in China or in Taiwan like his/her father'. For Xiawei and Jian-Qing, the ideal arrangement regarding the issue of citizenship in their family was for Jia-Qing and the child to hold the same Taiwanese citizenship, while Xiawei retained her Ningpo *hukou*.

Zhi-Heng and Linlin's story (Type III)

Zhi-Heng (born in 1968) was hired as an expatriate management trainee by a software company in Taiwan at the end of 2000. The following year, in June, he migrated to Shenzhen in China. Linlin (born in 1976) came from Jiangxi with a rural *hukou*. She migrated to work in Shenzhen after she graduated from college in 1998. A journey back home from the current location in Shenzhen usually takes her more than two days, but this is quite common for rural migrants who work in Chinese coastal cities. According to one report, there are more than 120 million rural migrants in China and most of them are female (CECC 2006; Gransow 2003; see also Ngai 1999). Linlin's first job was in a manufacturing company in a suburb of Shenzhen; two years later she started to work for a software company for which Zhi-Heng was working at the time. They became acquainted with each other during a Chinese Moon Festival party organized by the company and were married in 2004. They held wedding banquets not only in Jiangxi at Linlin parents' home with all her relatives, but also in Shenzhen with all their colleagues from the company, and in Taiwan with Zhi-Heng's family. It was thus a wedding ceremony held in three places across the Taiwan Strait. When asked about his wife's Taiwan resident permit visa status, Zhi-Heng was hesitant for a while and then answered that Linlin would not consider applying for such a permit, even though she was on the annual quota list for immigration to Taiwan. Many of his friends who were married to Chinese people, Zhi-Heng said, were in the same situation. When the spouse was informed that he/she was on the list for immigration and would need to reside in Taiwan for 'long-term residency', she/he would give up.

Linlin is a trained professional with a good background in international trade. She could easily find good career opportunities in the migration city of Shenzhen, but probably not in Taipei or elsewhere in Taiwan. Back in China, Linlin might even have the opportunity to earn a salary higher than that of his many colleagues in the parent company in Taipei, Zhi-Heng said. She retains a rural *hukou* registration inherited from her parents. Zhi-Heng did try to help his wife to obtain a local *hukou* in Shenzhen, but the policy of 'obtaining the household registration by house buying' (買房入戶) in Shenzhen was, for various reasons, abolished in 2003.[6] Nevertheless, they do not intend to give up hope of eventually obtaining a local *hukou*. For instance, a foreign company, according to the Shenzhen city government, with a continuous tax-paying contribution can be rewarded with an annual quota for their employees to change to a local *hukou*. If the company is granted such a quota in the coming years, Zhi-Heng said, they will apply for it.

Zhi-Heng and Linlin's child was born in 2006. They applied to the local government authorities for the 'confirmation of non-acquisition of PRC citizenship' (未入籍證明)[7] for their child immediately after the birth. Zhi-Heng said this will help their child obtain Taiwanese citizenship when he returns to visit Taiwan. However, they do not have plans for the further relocation of any of their family members to Taiwan. For both Zhi-Heng and Linlin, Shenzhen is the city that provides them with the most opportunities for career development and a better quality of family life.

Negotiating citizenship arrangements between the families of Taiwanese expatriates with Chinese spouses

Each of these stories represents one of the main types of citizenship arrangements between Taiwanese expatriates and their Chinese spouses: Type I, inheriting a rural Chinese *hukou* but changing to an urban hukou (He-Chen and Suyun); Type II, staying with an inherited urban *hukou* (Jia-Qing and Xiaowei); Type III, remaining with an inherited rural *hukou* (Zhi-Heng and Linlin). These three types represent different choices for the rural/urban household registration of Chinese spouses before and after marriage. Clearly, Taiwanese expatriates and their Chinese spouses tend not to abrogate their original Taiwanese or PRC citizenship. Citizenship for Taiwanese expatriates with Chinese spouses therefore becomes a 'family-based dual citizenship' arrangement.

Why do Taiwanese expatriates and their Chinese spouses tend to adopt the strategy of holding two different citizenships in one family? Two reasons can be given for this: on the one hand, under the current immigration regulations in Taiwan and China, it is impossible for a Taiwanese or Chinese citizen to acquire dual citizenship. The nation-state and its immigration policy still play a key role in controlling the mobility of people and access to citizenship (Zollberg 1999; Ellermann 2009; Kaur 2006; Morris-Suzuki 2006; Thränhardt and Hunger 2003). Tseng and Wu (2010) point out that the Taiwanese government adopts 'homeland policies' for the citizenship processes of Taiwanese migrants in China. If these migrants acquire a PRC passport, they have to relinquish their Taiwanese citizenship; Chinese spouses have to relinquish their PRC citizenship upon being granted a Taiwanese passport.

On the other hand, however, as Ong (1999: 18) noted, many overseas Chinese have adopted a more flexible strategy toward obtaining or holding citizenship in order to accumulate their cultural capital and find greater social acceptance in the hosting society. This flexibility can also be found in cross-Strait marriage migration processes. First, in the case of Taiwanese expatriates, most of them migrated to China as professionals, benefiting from the favourable conditions for residency which the Chinese government provided and which were so much better than the policies the Taiwanese government applied to Chinese citizens migrating to Taiwan. In addition, Taiwanese expatriates also enjoyed continuous Taiwanese citizenship so that they remained covered by national health insurance back in Taiwan. Second, most of the Chinese spouses who were interviewed had married Taiwanese expatriates but chose not to reside in Taiwan and did not have any strong inclination to acquire Taiwanese citizenship. Instead, great efforts were made to enable the Chinese spouses to change their *hukou* status from rural to urban.

Why does an urban *hukou* mean so much to a Chinese citizen? The *hukou* (household registration) system was implemented in China in the mid-1950s. The Chinese population was divided into urban and rural according to their birthplaces (Lin 2011: 254). The *hukou* system was initially a tool for obtaining demographic data and for the management of social stability. However, the system became more rigid during the economic crisis following the 'Great Leap Forward' at the end of the 1950s, when limits were imposed on the rights of ordinary citizens to choose their permanent place of residence. Since the introduction of economic reforms in the late 1970s and early 1980s, migrants who lack a local *hukou* have been confronted with discrimination at their workplaces and have been denied access to education and social welfare systems in the localities in which they work and live (CECC 2006). For example, migrants who obtain a Beijing 'Green Card' have access to healthcare, old-age insurance and low-interest housing loans provided by the city, as well as access to schooling for their children and the right to purchase 'affordable housing' (經濟適用房), buy a car, travel abroad easily, etc. (Deng 2009). Wu (2009) used the term 'differential citizenship' to describe the existing situation of serious inequalities in the urban and rural treatment of rural migrants in China. They are seen as temporary residents in the cities and face a very high threshold when seeking to convert a rural *hukou* into an urban *hukou* (Chan and Li 1999). It is for these reasons that Taiwanese expatriates help their mainland spouses to acquire an urban *hukou* before they think of moving to Taiwan, if they think of it at all.

Why do Chinese spouses not want to relinquish their PRC citizenship and acquire Taiwanese citizenship, which would allow them to enjoy more freedom of movement across the Taiwan Strait? A look at the three types of cross-Strait marriages reported in this chapter reveals several factors that might contribute to this decision. The first factor, as Suyun's story shows, is the link between obtaining Taiwanese citizenship and the separation from family members and family life across the Taiwan Strait for many years. The second factor is that many Chinese spouses with good jobs in China are often not able to find employment in these sectors after moving to Taiwan. This, among other reasons, is related to the current education policy of the Taiwanese government, according to which degrees awarded in China are not recognized. However, the third and probably most important factor is the opportunity for Chinese spouses who marry a Taiwanese person to convert a rural *hukou* to an urban *hukou* by house-buying, tax-paying or applying for a *hukou* by means of the annual quota programme granted to foreign companies with significant investment in China. Cross-Strait marriages thus facilitate upward mobility as a result of the urban–rural social divide in China.

Finally, current attitudes toward citizenship are also shaped by planning the futures of the children from a cross-Strait marriage. Here it is not national loyalty that matters, but flexibility, mobility and competence. A cross-Strait family with children holding Taiwanese citizenship does not necessarily have a strong Taiwanese identity, but rather both Taiwanese expatriates and their Chinese spouses believe that holding Taiwanese citizenship offers more options in terms of career opportunities and healthcare benefits for their children. These children, when they are older, can choose to work in either Taiwan or China. When working in China, they will even be treated as expatriates and enjoy more benefits than local citizens. In addition, with Taiwanese citizenship, children of cross-Strait marriages can join Taiwan's national health insurance systems as dependent relatives of their Taiwanese parent. Moreover, they can travel move easily across the Taiwan Strait to visit relatives or to attend school. Even taking university entrance exams in China is easier for people with Taiwanese citizenship, since they can enjoy the benefit of gaining extra points for the entrance exams to qualify for Chinese universities.

In other words, the Taiwanese people who hold a *Taibaozheng* (台胞證), which is available to Taiwanese citizens for travelling to and residing in China, obviously enjoy many advantages compared with Chinese citizens in Taiwan: easier enrolment in Chinese universities, quick access to China's employment market (also more opportunities to join several professional licensing exams), local healthcare insurance, etc.[8] Moreover, a Taiwanese citizen can reside for longer periods of time or can even gain permanent de facto residence in China through the unlimited extension of their residence visa (Tseng and Wu 2010). Finally, the continuous relaxation of residency and work permit regulations for Taiwanese citizens by the Chinese government explains why a *Taibaozheng* is still a strategic choice for Taiwanese expatriates and for their children when it comes to the issue of citizenship.

Conclusion: Chinese spouses' strategic decisions and the China impact

This chapter draws attention to the link between citizenship and cross-Strait marriages. I argue that it is not appropriate to classify all Chinese marriage migrants as Taiwanese immigrants. It is sometimes taken for granted that Chinese women aspire to and often achieve upward mobility through cross-border marriages, since marriage mobility commonly involves the movement of female spouses from less-developed locations to more developed ones (Constable 2005). However, this study shows that most of the Chinese spouses of Taiwanese expatriates achieve upward mobility not by migrating to Taiwan or by applying for Taiwanese citizenship, but rather by remaining in China and seeking opportunities to change from a rural to an urban *hukou*.

These strategic decisions made by Chinese spouses not only affect themselves and their families but also have a huge impact on the migration landscape in Taiwanese society. First, from the analysis of official statistics, we find that a high percentage of Chinese spouses do not continuously stay in Taiwan. The stories presented in this chapter explain very clearly why a great number of them do not choose to reside in Taiwan or to exchange their PRC citizenship for a Taiwanese passport. It is obvious that although these Chinese spouses have engaged in a marriage that is classified as cross-border, it does not follow the expected cross-border migratory behaviour. Cross-border marriages between Chinese citizens and Taiwanese expatriates have thus created new challenges to the notion and perception of marriage migration across the Taiwan Strait.

Second, the rapid increase in cross-border marriages in the last two decades seems, at first sight, to have made Taiwan an immigrant country. But reality is somewhat different. According to statistics published by the Ministry of the Interior, Taiwan continued to have more emigrants than immigrants in the period from 1999 to 2013, and the only exception to this pattern was in the year 2006 (MOI 2014). The decision of many Chinese spouses and their Taiwanese husbands or wives, i.e. Taiwanese expatriates, to remain in China has contributed significantly to making Taiwan an emigrant country over the last decade.

Finally, the current KMT government has made a great effort to develop a friendlier immigration policy towards Chinese spouses since 2008, which includes allowing them to work soon after their arrival, lifting the ID application quota of 6,000 per year, removing the restrictions that fixed the maximum amount of inheritance at NT$2 million, and shortening the required duration of residency to acquire Taiwanese citizenship from eight to six years (and probably to only four years in the near future) (*China Post* 2008a, 2008b). However, it seems that these reforms to Taiwan's immigration policy still cannot generate sufficient incentives to encourage Chinese spouses who have chosen to reside in China to change their minds and become permanent residents in Taiwan. For instance, more than 100,000 Chinese spouses to date, as mentioned earlier (about one-third of all registered Chinese spouses), still hold tourist visas and remain at the first stage of their marriage migration to Taiwan although the latest relaxing of the immigration regulations means that they would easily be able to obtain a resident visa.

The China impact thus has many faces. For national security reasons, the previous DPP government implemented more restrictive rules for the naturalization of Chinese spouses than for those who emigrated from other countries. The present KMT government, on the contrary, has relaxed immigration regulations in order to encourage more Chinese spouses to move to Taiwan. However, the strategic decision made by many Chinese spouses reveals that the present immigration policy is only attractive to those who are already inclined to reside in Taiwan – but not to all Chinese marriage migrants per se.

China has had and will always have a strong impact on Taiwan, particularly in the context of cross-Strait migration. Cross-border marriages in Taiwan during the past 15 years reached a high point in 2003 and remained fairly constant over the next eight years, ranging from 14,619 in 2005 to 11,542 in 2013, while marriages with citizens from Southeast Asia, which once constituted the most important source of foreign spouses in Taiwan, reached a peak in 2004 with 18,103 cases but dropped dramatically to 4,823 in 2013 (see Table 12.1; MOI 2013b). This is an indication that cross-Strait marriages might start to play an even more important role in Taiwan in the near and long-term future. Chinese spouses are expected to continue to constitute the largest group of cross-border marriage migrants in Taiwan. With the rise of China, marriages between Taiwanese women and Chinese men might also become more visible in the future, although they were under-represented in this study. In fact, official statistics from the Ministry of the Interior show that marriages between Chinese bridegrooms and Taiwanese brides steadily increased from 3.69 per cent in 2004 to 8.67 per cent in 2012 as a proportion of all cross-Strait marriages (NIA 2012).[9] Following this trend, it is also to be expected, in the next decades, that a large number of Chinese spouses will not register for permanent residence in Taiwan and will consider alternative citizenship arrangements such as those reported in my case studies. All the new migration patterns mentioned above should help to shift the immigrant policies in Taiwan into a new framework by simultaneously emphasizing Taiwan's position as an immigrant and emigrant country.

Notes

1 This research was financially supported by the Ministry of Science and Technology in Taiwan (project numbers: NSC 94–2412-H-032–003 and NSC 98–2410-H-032–060-MY2). I would like to thank Gunter Schubert, Yen-Fen Tseng, Yun Fan, Hsin-Huang Michael Hsiao, Mau-Kui Chang, Jih-Wen Lin and Thung-Hong Lin for their constructive comments, and Anna Mackay for her excellent proof-reading.

2 These statistics are taken from Manning and Bhatnagar (2006); more recent figures were not available at the time of writing.

3 There are no exact figures on the number of Taiwanese business people and expatriates currently residing in China. According to the Sixth National Population Census of the People's Republic of China in 2010, the registered number of Taiwanese residents in China showed only 170,283 (National Bureau of Statistics of the People's Republic of

China 2011). Taiwanese business associations in China as well as researchers on Tais-hang (Taiwanese business people) studies, however, agreed that this figure had been greatly underestimated. A more reliable estimate provided by the Mainland Affairs Council in Taiwan showed that around 850,000 Taiwanese business people, Taiwanese expatriates and their relocated family members are currently residing in China (Hong 2014).

4 The 2003 survey of foreign and Chinese spouses' cultural adaption in Taiwan by the Ministry of the Interior pointed out that cross-Strait couples first meet each other mainly of their own volition (28.3 per cent) or through their relatives and friends (60.8 per cent), and only 9.6 per cent through matchmakers (MOI 2004).

5 The term 'hypergamy' is used specifically to denote women marrying up into a higher socio-economic group. Global hypergamy, therefore, indicates the behaviour of marriage mobility from the poor and less-developed global south to the wealthy and developed north (Constable 2005:10).

6 The Shenzhen city government launched the 'Measures for Promoting the City's Real Estate Market Development' [Guanyu cujin woshi fangdichan shichang fazhan de ruogan guiding] in the Baoan and Longgan district of Shenzhen in 1995. This policy was intended to reduce the large development disparities between Shenzhen's inner city (Special Economic Zones) and outskirts (Baoan and Longgan district). However, after eight years of implementation, although the benefits stemming from this policy in terms of economic growth could be observed, the real-estate market had overheated. In addition, according to official statistics, 84.7 per cent of homebuyers who benefited from the guidelines were graduates of junior or senior high school, and only 15.3 of these held a college diploma or higher. The Shenzhen city government considered that this would entail 'negative effects' for the population composition in the long term, and therefore decided to abolish the above-mentioned policy. See www.southcn.com/estate/news/zsjls/200305070 106.htm (accessed 17 July 2013).

7 In order to obtain Taiwanese citizenship for their children, Taiwanese residents in China have to apply, after the birth of their children, for a 'confirmation of the non-acquisition of PRC citizenship' from the responsible local authorities.

8 Taiwanese citizens working in China can enjoy both Chinese and Taiwanese health insurance. In recent years, particularly in some coastal cities such as Beijing or Shanghai, local governments have asked residents from Taiwan, Hong Kong and Macao to subscribe to the local insurance system (*Sina News* 2012).

9 At the time of writing, the National Immigration Agency (NIA) statistics on the 'registered number of foreign spouses and Chinese spouses by bridegrooms and brides' had not been updated since September 2012.

References

Butcher, M. (2006) 'White Collar Filipinos: Australian Professionals in Singapore', in Kaur, Amarjit, and Metcalfe, Ian (eds) *Mobility, Labour Migration and Border Controls in Asia*, New York: Palgrave Macmillan, 172–192.

Chan, K. W., and Li, Z. (1999) 'The Hukou System and Rural-Urban Migration in China. Processes and Changes', *China Quarterly*, 160: 818–855.

Charsley, K., and Shaw, A. (2006) 'South Asian Transnational Marriages in Comparative Perspective', *Global Networks*, 6, 4: 331–344.

Chen, C. J. (2006) 'Forging Social Capital in the Alien Motherland: Taiwanese Business Associations in China', paper presented at the Annual Meeting of the Association for Asian Studies, San Francisco, 6–9 April.

China Post (2008a) 'Work Rules for Chinese Spouses Nixed', 12 December.

China Post (2008b) 'Quota for Chinese Spouse IDs Cancelled', 30 December.

Congressional-Executive Commission on China (CECC) (2006) *Annual Report: Monitoring Compliance with Human Rights*, available at www.cecc.gov/publications/annual-reports (accessed 9 July 2014).

Constable, N. (2003) *Romance on a Global Stage: Pen Pals, Virtual Ethnography, and 'Mail-order' Marriages*, Berkeley and Los Angeles: University of California Press.

Constable, N. (2005) 'Introduction: Cross-border Marriages, Gendered Mobility, and Global Hypergamy', in Constable, N. (ed.) *Cross-border Marriages: Gender and Mobility in Transnational Asia*, Philadelphia: University of Pennsylvania, 1–16.

Deng, Jian-Bang (2009) 'Skilled Workers Recruitment Measures and their Impacts in Major Cities of China: Beijing, Shanghai and Shenzhen', *Mainland China Studies Newsletter*, 92: 30–33.

Ellermann, A. (2009) *States against Migrants. Deportation in Germany and United States*, Cambridge: Cambridge University Press.

Espenshade, T. J. (1989) 'Growing Imbalances between Labor Supply and Labor Demand in the Caribbean Basin', in Bean, F. D., Schmandt, J., and Weintraub, S. (eds) *Mexican and Central American Population and US Immigration Policy*, Austin: University of Texas Center for Mexican American Studies, 113–160.

Favell, A., Feldblum, M., and Smith, M. P. (2006) 'The Human Face of Global Mobility: A Research Agenda', in Smith, M. P., and Favell, A. (eds) *The Human Face of Global Mobility: International Highly Skilled Migration in Europe, North America and the Asia-Pacific*, New Brunswick NJ: Transaction, 1–25.

Flick, U. (2005) *Qualitative Sozialforschung* [Qualitative Social Research], Hamburg: Rowohlt.

Glick Schiller, N., Basch, L., and Blanc, C. S. (1997) 'From Immigrant to Transmigrant: Theorizing Transnational Migration', in Pries, L. (ed.) *Transnationale Migration* [Transnational Migration], Baden-Baden: Nomos, 121–140.

Glick Schiller, N., Basch, L., and Blanc, C. S. (2004) 'Transnationalism: A New Analytical Framework for Understanding Migration', in Mobasher, M. M., and Sadri, M. (eds) *Migration, Globalization, and Ethnic Relations. An Interdisciplinary Approach*, Upper Saddle River NJ: Pearson Prentice Hall, 213–227.

Golini, A., Gerano, G., and Heins, F. (1991) 'South–North Migration with Special Reference to Europe', *International Migration*, 29, 2: 253–279.

Gransow, Bettina (2003) 'Gender and Migration in China: Feminization Trends', in Morokvašić, M., Erel, U., and Shinozaki, K. (eds) *Crossing Borders and Shifting Boundaries*, Opladen: Leske und Budrich, 137–154.

Hannerz, U. (1998) 'Transnational Research', in Bernard, H. R. (ed.) *Handbook of Methods in Cultural Anthropology*, Lanham MD: AltaMira Press, 235–255.

Hong, Sin-Chi (2014) 'How Many People Working Abroad? Minister Being Criticised for Failing to Provide the Exact Number', *China Times*, 21 April, available at www.chinatimes.com/realtimenews/20140421003 029–260405 (accessed 16 December 2014).

Hsing, Y. T. (1997) *Making Capitalism in China. The Taiwan Connection*, New York and Oxford: Oxford University Press.

IONPA (Immigration Office of the National Police Agency, Ministry of the Interior) (2005) *White Paper with Interviews Conducted with Chinese Spouses Coming to Taiwan to Join Family Members* (in Chinese), Taipei: Ministry of the Interior.

Jackson, P., Crang, P., and Dwyer, C. (2004) 'Introduction: The Spaces of Transnationality', in Jackson, P., Crang, P., and Dwyer, C. (eds) *Transnational Spaces*, London: Routledge, 1–23.

Jones, G., and Shen, H. H. (2008) 'International Marriage in East and Southeast Asia: Trends and Research Emphases', *Citizenship Studies*, 12, 1: 9–25.

Kaur, A. (2006) 'Order (and Disorder) at the Border: Mobility, International Labour Migration and Border Controls in Southeast Asia', in Kaur, A., and Metcalfe, I. (eds) *Mobility, Labor Migration and Border Controls in Asia*, New York: Palgrave Macmillan, 23–51.

Keng, S., and Schubert, G. (2010) 'Agents of Unification? The Political Role of Taiwanese Businessmen in the Process of Cross-Strait Integration', *Asian Survey*, 50, 2: 287–310.

Keng, S., Schubert, G., and Lin, E. R. (eds) (2012) *Taishang Studies*, Taipei: Wunan.

Lee, E. (1966) 'A Theory of Migration', *Demography*, 47: 49–56.

Lee, H. K. (2009) 'Cross-Border Marriage Partners and their Food: A Case Study in Fuli Village, Taiwan', in Wang, H. Z., and Hsiao, H. H. M. (eds) *Cross-Border Marriages with Asian Characteristics*, Taipei: Centre for Asia-Pacific Area Studies, Academia Sinica, 61–88.

Lin, Thung-Hong (2011) 'Market Transformation and Social Inequalities', in Wang, J. H., Tang, C. P., and Song, G. C. (eds) *Studies on Mainland China and Cross-Strait Relations* (in Chinese), Taipei: Chuliu Publishers, 249–281.

Lu, M. (2007) 'Transnational Marriage in Asia', *IIAS Newsletter*, 45: 3.

Lu, M. (2008) 'Commercially Arranged Marriage Migration: Case Studies of Cross-border Marriages in Taiwan', in Palriwala, Rajni, and Uberoi, Patricia (eds) *Marriage, Migration and Gender*, London: Sage, 125–151.

Manning, C., and Bhatnagar, P. (2006) 'Coping with Cross-border Labour Flows within Southeast Asia', in Kaur, A., and Metcalfe, I. (eds) *Mobility, Labor Migration and Border Controls in Asia*, New York: Palgrave Macmillan, 52–72.

Massey, D. S. (2002 [1998]) 'New Migrations, New Theories', in Massey, D. S., Arango, J., Hugo, G., Kouaouci, A., Pellegrino, A., and Taylor, J. E. (eds) *Worlds in Motion. Understanding International Migration at the End of the Millennium*, Oxford: Clarendon Press, 1–16.

Ministry of the Interior (MOI) (2004) *The 2003 Survey of Foreign and Chinese Spouses' Cultural Adaption in Taiwan*, Taipei: Ministry of the Interior.

MOI (2007) *Analysis of Continuous and Non-continuous Residence of Citizens and Non-citizens in Taiwan*, available at www.moi.gov.tw/stat/week.aspx (accessed 8 July 2014).

MOI (2013a) *Care and Counselling Measure for Foreign and Chinese Spouses*, available at https://www.immigration.gov.tw/public/Data/42279154571.doc (accessed 8 July 2014).

MOI (2013b) *Registered Number of Foreign Spouses and Chinese Spouses, 1988–2013*, available at www.immigration.gov.tw/ct.asp?x Item=1183521&ctNode=29699&mp=1 (accessed 8 July 2014).

MOI (2014) *Migration Registration of Resident Population*, available at http://sowf.moi.gov.tw/stat/month/list.htm (accessed 8 July 2014).

Morris-Suzuki, T. (2006) 'Changing Border Control Regimes and their Impact on Migration in Asia', in Kaur, A., and Metcalfe, I. (eds) *Mobility, Labor Migration and Border Controls in Asia*, New York: Palgrave Macmillan, 8–22.

Mueller-Schneider, T. (2000) *Zuwanderung in Westlichen Gesellschaften. Analyse und Steuerungspositionen* [Migration in Western Societies. Analysis and Positions of Regulation], Opladen: Leske und Budrich.

National Bureau of Statistics of the People's Republic of China (2011) *The Sixth National Population Census Statistics of the People's Republic of China on the Residents from Macao, Hong Kong and Taiwan and other Foreign Countries*, available at www.stats. gov.cn/tjsj/tjgb/rkpcgb/qgrkpcgb/201104/t20110429 _30329.html (accessed 16 December 2014).

National Immigration Agency (NIA) (2012) *Registered Number of Foreign Spouses and Chinese Spouses by Bridegrooms and Brides, 1988–2012*, available at www. immigration.gov.tw/ct.asp?xItem=1185022&ctNode=29699&mp=1 (accessed 8 July 2014).

Ong, A. (1999) *Flexible Citizenship: The Cultural Logics of Transnationality*, Durham NC: Duke University Press.

Overseas Chinese News (2008) 'Taiwanese Business People in Mainland China: Interview with the Director of Economic Studies, Taiwan Research Institute, Chinese Academy of Social Sciences (CASS)', available at www.chinaqw.com/zgqj/qkjc_ hnyhw/200804/24/114635.shtml (accessed 10 July 2014).

Pun, N. (1999) 'Becoming *Dagongmei* (Working Girls): The Politics of Identity and Difference in Reform China', *China Journal*, 42: 1–18.

Shen, H. H. (2008) 'Becoming the First Wives: Gender, Intimacy and Regional Economy between Taiwan and China', in Jackson, S., Liu, J. Y., and Woo, J. Y. (eds) *East Asian Sexualities: Modernity, Gender and New Sexual Cultures*, London: Zed Books, 216–235.

Sina News (2012) 'New Regulation of Social Insurance in Beijing: Obligation to Join the Insurance System for Residents from Taiwan, Hong Kong and Macao', available at http://finance.sina.com.cn/money/insurance/bxdt/20120917/090113155122.shtml (accessed 10 July 2014).

Suzhou City Government (2003) 'Interim Measures for Access to Suzhou Household Registration' (in Chinese), available at www.southcn.com/law/fzzt/fgsjk/200503070877.htm (accessed 10 July 2014).

Thai, H. C. (2008) *For Better or For Worse: Vietnamese International Marriages in the New Global Economy*, New Brunswick NJ: Rutgers University Press.

Thomas, B. (1973) *Migration and Economic Growth: A Study of Great Britain and the Atlantic Economy*, Cambridge: Cambridge University Press.

Thränhardt, D., and Hunger, U. (eds) (2003) *Migration im Spannungsfeld von Globalisierung und Nationalstaat* [Migration between Globalization and the Nation-State], Wiesbaden: Westdeutscher Verlag.

Tsai, M. C., and Chang, C. F. (2010) 'China-Bound for Jobs? The Influences of Social Connections and Ethnic Politics in Taiwan', *China Quarterly*, 203: 639–655.

Tseng, Y. F. (2000) 'The Mobility of Entrepreneurs and Capital: Taiwanese Capital-linked Migration', *International Migration*, 2: 143–168.

Tseng, Y. F. (2008) 'Taiwanese Middle Classes in Shanghai: Migration Patterns of Skilled Taiwanese to China', paper presented at the International Symposium on Comparing Middle Classes in Ethnic Chinese Societies in Modern Asia-Pacific, Taipei.

Tseng Y. F., and Wu, J. M. (2010) 'Bring Politics Backs In: Regulating Dual Citizenship of Taiwanese Migrants in China' (in Chinese), *SOCIETAS*, 32: 93–143.

Wang, H. Z., and Chang, S. M. (2002) 'The Commodification of International Marriages: Cross-border Marriage Business in Taiwan and Vietnam', *International Migration*, 40, 6: 93–116.

Wang, H. Z., and Hsiao, H. H. M. (eds) (2009) *Cross-border Marriages with Asian Characteristics*, Taipei: Centre for Asia-Pacific Area Studies, Academia Sinica.

Wu, J. M. (2009) 'Rural Migrant Workers and China's Differential Citizenship: A Comparative-Institutional Analysis', in Whyte, M. K. (ed.) *One Country, Two Societies: Rural–Urban Inequality in Contemporary China*, Cambridge MA: Harvard University Press.

Zollberg, A. R. (1999) 'Matters of State: Theorizing Immigration Policy', in Hirschmann, C., Kasinitz, P., and DeWind, J. (eds) *Handbook of International Migration*, New York: Russell Sage Foundation, 71–93.

13 Taiwanese youth in mainland China

Fragile identity in the shadow of China

Ping Lin[1]

The rise of China in the past two decades and its impact on the rest of the world have caught the attention of scholars from various disciplines. One of the most important issues is the extent to which China, with its investment and development aid, can affect the politics and economy of other countries (Alden 2007; Brautigam 2011; Monson 2009; Roett and Paz 2008). Some scholars have argued that China's investments and aid help the receiving countries (Powles 2010; Tarte 2010; Zhang 2010); others are concerned that the rise of China will generate more conflict in these countries (Izumi 2010; Porter and Wesley-Smith 2010). However, most of these studies examine the situation from the perspective of political economy, and few pay attention to the viewpoints of the people in these countries: how they perceive China and whether their perceptions have changed in the past two decades are issues that have rarely been subject to analysis. Taiwan, a country with strong historical connections to China and facing serious disputes with China over its political status, feels the China impact more strongly than other countries in the region. Given that more than a million Taiwanese people have moved to China, it is crucially important to understand how these people, especially their children's generation who have been raised on the mainland, perceive China in order to predict how Taiwan might be affected by China in the future.

Since the lifting of martial law and the removal of the restrictions on travel in 1987, more than a million Taiwanese people have moved to China for business reasons, to start new careers, to be with family, etc. Many studies have focused on the question of whether increased cross-Strait economic interaction will entail political integration, as suggested by the theory of neo-functionalism (Chao 2003; Wei 1997). Some of these studies have also considered whether China will be able to influence the politics and economy of Taiwan via Taiwanese entrepreneurs in China (Keng and Schubert 2010). The ways in which Taiwanese people with 'experience of China' perceive China can therefore help to measure the potential influence of a rising China on Taiwan and other countries nearby.

While most studies on Taiwanese people who have resided in China, temporarily or permanently, focus on Taiwanese adults (Deng 2002; Deng and Wei 2010; Tseng 2011; Lin 2009, 2013), this chapter concentrates on the experiences of young Taiwanese people growing up in China. Previous studies have shown that most Taiwanese adults with experience of China, excluding a few tycoons, do not support political integration across the Strait (Lin 2011, 2013; Lee 2014), but little research has been carried out on how Taiwanese youth perceive China (Deng and Wei 2010; Lan and Wu 2011; Lin 2012). All the individuals discussed in this chapter were born in Taiwan but moved to China during their childhood. After moving to China, all of them studied at one of the Taishang Schools (see below) for at least three years. How they identify themselves (especially with respect to the common 'Taiwanese or Chinese' dichotomy) is one of the questions that I will address in this chapter. By exploring their identity, we may also be able to better predict their perception of the cross-Strait relationship in the future. After associating with these young Taiwanese people for several years, I realized that they had gone through a special process of identity transformation: from being Taiwanese and wishing to return to Taiwan, to being Taiwanese and regarding China as the place to build their homes. This transformation shows how China has partially affected the lives and thinking of this specific category of Taiwanese people.

Literature review: teenagers on the move

If we look at the literature published before the early 2000s that focused on why Taiwanese people move to China, the answer becomes clear immediately: to make money and get rich. The study of Taiwanese migrants in China is often referred to as Taishang studies (台商研究), which means, literally, 'studies on Taiwanese business people' (Keng and Schubert 2010; Keng *et al.* 2012). It seems that 'making money to get rich' is the main reason that more than a million Taiwanese people have so far moved to China. Although this making-money discourse partially explains why Taiwanese people think of themselves as 'sojourners' instead of 'settlers' in China (Tseng 2005; Deng 2009), it excludes the experiences of those without a professional career in China, such as the elderly and young Taiwanese people. It also tells us little about how (and how much) these 'permanent sojourners' are affected by their Chinese experiences.

Most studies on teenage migrants concentrate on the second generation of people belonging to an ethnic minority and, in particular, on how they interact with the majority local population. As a result of being educated and living in the host country, these children find it easier to assimilate into the local society than the first generation. However, this assimilation can be limited. Some studies published in the US have argued that although teenage migrants may integrate in the local society in some respects, they maintain a distance from it in others; this partially-mixed feature is often described as 'segmented assimilation' (Portes and Zhou 1993; Portes and Rumbaut 2001). This segmented assimilation also means that minorities with different backgrounds may encounter different barriers on their routes to integration (Zhou 1997; Levitt and Waters 2002; Kasinitz *et al.* 2003).

Apart from the interaction with the majority local population, one of the most important issues to address is how teenage migrants interact with the country of their birth or parental origin. Although many scholars employ the concept of 'transnationalism' to analyse and illustrate the interaction between the migrants and their home country, others argue that it is unconvincing to speak of a 'transnational relationship' (Rumbaut 2002; Kasinitz *et al.* 2002). If the relationship between the sending and host countries is friendly and stable, some affluent teenage migrants may indeed have some level of interaction with people in their country of origin. However, their relationships with the people in that country are often too limited to be conceptualized as 'transnationalism' (Levitt 2002; Smith 2002; Fouron and Glick-Schiller 2002). Although teenage migrants may hold various forms of a hybrid identity, it is often mainly composed of elements of the host country and not based on their experiences of life in their country of origin (Kasinitz *et al.* 2003; Butterfield 2004; Portes and Rumbaut 2001).

In these studies on the second generation, one specific type of young migrant is often disregarded: that is, the so-called '1.5 generation', which refers to people who are born in one country but move to another during their childhood. These people usually have more understanding of the country of residence than the first generation of migrants (their parents) and still feel more closely related to their country of origin than the second generation of migrants who were born in the host country. Therefore, the formation of their identity is usually more complex than that of the second-generation migrants discussed above (Ryu 1991; Park 1999; Rumbaut 2002; Bartley and Spoonley 2008; Bartley 2010; Danico 2004; Suarez-Orozco *et al.* 2008).

These studies generally assume a certain level of interaction between the teenage migrants and the local society because they have been educated together. However, this assumption overlooks the fact that some teenage migrants do not enrol in the same schools as the majority of the local population. Affluent migrant communities may have a better lifestyle than the local population (O'Reilly 2000; Fechter 2007; Croucher 2009) and may have their children educated separately from the children of the local population (Moore 2008; O'Reilly 2009). However, as already mentioned, little research has focused on teenage migrants, especially those who follow different education trajectories from those of young local people. How this 'educational divide' may affect teenage migrants will be the main issue addressed in this chapter.

Taiwanese overseas schools and the case of China

To begin with, it is not clear how many Taiwanese young people are living in China today. However, three schools for Taiwanese immigrants have been established in Guangdong province and Shanghai metropolis. All the students in these schools were born in Taiwan but moved to China during their childhood. Therefore, students and graduates of these schools will be treated as a 'proxy' for that of Taiwanese young people in China.

Apart from these three schools in China, five Taiwanese Schools have been established in Southeast Asia. All eight of these institutions are officially recognized as 'schools' by the Taiwanese government and the respective governments of the receiving countries. These eight schools are usually referred to as Taishang Schools (schools established by Taiwanese business people), because most of their funding comes from overseas Taiwanese entrepreneurs for the education of the children of Taiwanese business people or expatriates.

Since all the Taishang Schools are officially treated as formal institutions of education by the Taiwanese government, most of the teachers, staff and teaching materials come from Taiwan. The curricula of Taishang Schools also follow the national curricula adopted by schools in Taiwan. Graduates of Taishang Schools can either stay overseas or return to Taiwan to continue their education. By supporting Taishang Schools, the Taiwanese government hopes to maintain the connections between its nationals overseas and their 'home country' (Mou 2001; Lin 2002; Hsia 2004; Wu and Chen 2006).

Since one of the underlying aims of these schools is to sustain the Taiwanese identity of overseas students, how these schools actually contribute to the identity formation of the students is an important issue. Although some studies have emphasized the success of Taishang Schools in reducing the impact of China on the identity of Taiwanese students (Chen and Wu 2006; Tao 2009; Tseng *et al.* 2012), these are all observational studies conducted during specified time periods. Up to now, no study has been undertaken on the graduates of Taishang Schools. By comparing how students respond to questions concerning their identity while they are still studying and working towards graduating from Taishang Schools, we can gain a better understanding of the identity formation processes and changes in these young migrants.

Methodology

Because of the political disputes across the Strait, the issue of 'identity' is usually viewed as a sensitive topic of discussion. Some studies have argued that researchers without a good deal of field experience are likely to be 'cheated' by the 'politically correct' answers provided by their respondents, especially if fieldwork is conducted during only a limited period of time (Wu 2004; Lin 2009). These factors were taken into account in the research that I am presenting here, which is therefore based on participant observation and extensive informal interviewing conducted during two fairly lengthy periods of time, 2004–2005 and 2008–2010. All the individuals discussed in this chapter were still teenagers in 2004–2005.

The approach that I employed during the first period of fieldwork (2004–2005) is similar to that used for other studies based on fieldwork in schools (Holmes 1998; Kasinitz *et al.* 2003; Fong 2004): I worked as a school teacher in two Taishang Schools in 2004 and 2005.[2] During this period, I taught several courses (English, Discovering Society in Taiwan, Civil Education, and Geography) to students from year 7 to year 12. More than half of my courses were related to political developments in Taiwan and the cross-Strait relationship. The ways in which students talked about Taiwan and China on my courses provided me with numerous access points to explore their views on China. Apart from teaching in the school, I also joined in with some students' off-campus activities. Comparing students' viewpoints and behaviours both on and off the school campus enabled me to examine the extent to which their identity was formed in the school and modified by their day-to-day lives in China.

During the second period of fieldwork (2008–2012), I returned to Taiwan. All my students had graduated from the Taishang Schools of Dongguan and Huadong. Some were continuing their education in China, some had returned to Taiwan, and a few of them had moved to a third country, such as Australia, Japan, the US or the UK, for higher education. Between 2008 and 2012, I had numerous casual talks with 14 people from the two Taishang Schools. The basic information related to these 14 people is listed here. Eight were graduates from the two Taishang Schools (four from each). All eight of the graduates are now (2014) aged between 22 and 30. Apart from these eight graduates, six respondents were faculty members (teachers and staff) of Taishang Schools. Although these six respondents were not graduates of Taishang Schools, they had worked in Taishang Schools for certain periods of time. The information obtained from these six faculty members therefore complements the information provided by the eight graduates. In addition to telephone conversations, exchanges of emails, and social gatherings (meals, for example) with my respondents, I maintained contact with other individuals at Taishang Schools via Facebook and blogs.[3] I also read a number of Master's dissertations that focused on the issues of Taishang Schools. These various sources of information helped to further my understanding of the lives and perceptions of the young Taiwanese migrants.

Of course, there are limitations to my approach. First, although I knew that some of my former students, after graduating, were continuing their studies in a third country, I did not have the opportunity to talk to them. Second, since the third Taishang School in China had been established in Shanghai after my fieldwork periods had ended, I was not able to include data from that school. Nevertheless, this study offers a good starting point for exploring the self-perception and identity formation of young Taiwanese migrants over time and provides a preliminary set of empirically-based assumptions that may be validated by more systematic research in the future.

Findings: from being in the Taiwanese diaspora to being Taiwanese overseas

One of the aims of establishing Taishang Schools in China is to reduce the impact of China on Taiwanese students' identity (Mou 2001; Lin 2002). Some scholars have confirmed the success of the Taishang Schools in this respect. Most Taiwanese students in China still retain a certain level of Taiwanese identity even after they have been living in China for several years (Chen and Wu 2006; Tseng *et al.* 2012). When I started my fieldwork, I was under a similar impression. However, a longer period of observation revealed that the influence of China was greater than I had expected. Students' identity also changed during the course of time. Although initially students did not really identify with China, they gradually came to think of the coastal cities of China, not Taiwan, as their homes.

Taishang Schools as a replacement for Taiwan

When I started teaching at the Taishang Schools, I found that almost all students clearly identified themselves as people of Taiwan, not people of China. Since most of the teaching material and staff were from Taiwan, this did not seem surprising. However, since all the teaching material which had any connotations of Taiwan independence was censored, it was still difficult to understand why the students emphasized their differences from the Chinese people. There had to be something other than the teaching contributing to the formation of the students' Taiwanese identity. I found that the strength of this 'we are not people of China' picture was largely attributable to the Taishang Schools functioning as a surrogate Taiwan in China.

Most schools in Taiwan have their own PTA (Parent–Teacher Association). The PTA is often expected to act as a support organization for non-academic activities, such as preparing for the schools' anniversary celebrations and summer trips. For many parents, participating in PTA activities and PTA committee work is a time-consuming task. Most parents are happy to know that their children are well looked after, but only a few have enough energy and money to actively participate in a PTA (Huang 2006). This 'free-rider' image has led to most PTAs in Taiwan being seen as weak and irrelevant organizations; the PTAs in Taishang Schools, however, are quite different. These schools generally have their own permanent offices for PTA meetings and the members often organize weekly activities (such as gardening and singing) in which all parents are invited to participate.[4] I often met parents at the PTA offices in the Taishang Schools; some were PTA members, but others were just 'ordinary' parents who were spending some of their spare time there.

These parents were often the mothers of students and they were usually referred to, by students and staff, as 'Love Mothers', because of the help (love) that they offered to the school. Some 'Love Mothers' would stay on the campus for entire days; if the school authorities needed any help, the 'Love Mothers' would simply volunteer. Otherwise, they would spend their time chatting in the PTA office, waiting to meet their children after class. Some of the 'Love Mothers' established such close relationships with each other that they even lived together in rented houses near the school. Apart from gathering at the campus on weekdays, they would also go to the city centre together, on shopping trips and for meals during the weekend. For these 'Love Mothers', the Taishang School was not only a place to educate their children but also a place to socialize with other Taiwanese people. This close relationship between parents has rarely been heard of in most schools in Taiwan.

The 'Love Mothers' were not alone in devoting close attention to the Taishang Schools; the Taiwanese government, the Chinese government and local

Taiwanese business people also treated the school as an informal community centre where they could distribute and collect information. It was common to see the Taishang Schools hosting visits from a variety of different organizations in Taiwan, China or a third country.[5] On various occasions, teachers of Taishang Schools participated in events in China and in Taiwan, acting as representatives of the 'voice' of the Taiwanese community in China.[6] All these factors contributed to creating the image of the Taishang Schools as the core of the Taiwanese community. The Taishang School served not only as a place for education but also as a hub for the Taiwanese community to get together and exchange information. This social function made the Taishang School seem like a substitute for Taiwan in China. Most students therefore treated their Taishang Schools as a replicated social field of Taiwan, just the way their parents did. The social function of the Taishang Schools explained why most students strongly identified themselves as Taiwanese even when they had lived in China for years. However, the students' Taiwanese identity was actually fragile because it mainly derived from their lives in the Taishang Schools and not from real experiences in Taiwan proper.

Life in the Taishang Schools (2004–2005)

If my research had been based on teaching and interviews carried out during a very limited time period, the fragility of the students' Taiwanese identity could easily have been overlooked. As a result of teaching in Taishang Schools for one year, however, I gradually realized that the students' Taiwanese identity was not supported by any real knowledge of Taiwan but was based mainly on life at the Taishang Schools. For these students, 'being Taiwanese' was behaving either in the same way as people in the Taishang Schools or differently from the people outside the Taishang Schools; 'being Taiwanese' had little to do with Taiwan itself. The content and fragility of their Taiwanese identity became obvious when students exchanged their experiences of visiting Taiwan.

The Taishang Schools organize a two-week study tour for Year 8 students to Taiwan every year, which is partly sponsored by the Taiwanese government.[7] Apart from these study tours, most students visit Taiwan during their summer or winter vacations. I sometimes posed the question 'Where are you from?' at the beginning of a casual conversation while I was teaching. What surprised me was not which Taiwanese city the students named, but the way in which they discussed it. Their conversation was reminiscent of the way that some people talk about their experience of travelling somewhere, rather than their experience of returning home. It was most telling that the students misnamed the cities they had visited even when they were referring to these places as 'my hometown'.[8] I discovered that almost no solid link was made between their hometown in Taiwan and their real life in China. When students said that they were originally from somewhere in Taiwan, it usually meant nothing more than a reference to a place they would visit once or twice a year, or where their relatives (uncles, aunts or grandparents) lived. Because they had so little knowledge about life in

Taiwan, their conversations about Taiwan usually ended up in a statement comparing something good in Taiwan and something bad in China (such as the clean metro in Taipei and the crowded underground in Shanghai). Although the students knew that the information they exchanged might be inaccurate or even wrong, they did not really care. It seemed that the purpose of their conversation was not to exchange information about Taiwan, but to construct a 'we Taiwanese' sense of belonging in order to highlight the boundary between people in and outside Taishang Schools.

From the students' limited knowledge of Taiwan and the way in which they discussed Taiwan, I could see just how unstable their Taiwanese identity was. A deeper understanding of this 'Taiwanese identity by name' was gained by analysing the students' off-campus behaviour. Apart from teaching courses in school, I also participated in students' activities in their spare time. On some of these occasions, I noticed that some students spoke to local Chinese people in a fluent local dialect (Cantonese or Shanghainese), or behaved like Chinese people (such as 'making a toast' by hitting the drinking glass on the table rather than touching the glass of another person). When I showed surprise at the students' proficiency in the dialect and the Chinese-styled 'toasts', students sitting next to me simply commented matter-of-factly that 'He learned [Cantonese] from the nanny at home' or 'He has lived here since he was five'.

It was not my intention to criticize the students for their poor knowledge of Taiwan. It was also reasonable that they had learnt the local dialects and body language from the Chinese people. What surprised me, however, was that the Chinese dialects and Chinese-styled body language were all used quite naturally off the school campus but were rarely used on the campus. It seemed these students had internalized two types of behaviour: one for their lives inside the schools, and the other for their lives outside the schools. By the way that students highlighted the similarities between the Taiwanese people in the Taishang Schools (by sharing the origin of Taiwan) and downplayed the similarities between people inside and outside the Taishang Schools (by sending out 'no surprise' signals to my curiosity), it was clear that the students' Taiwanese identity was mainly based on the subjective selection and interpretation of life in China. This 'Taiwanese identity by name' not only confirms my argument on the social function of the Taishang School in the previous section but also supports Barth's argument that the formation of identity is primarily based on day-to-day personal interactions and is less determined by similarities in physical (ontological) features (Barth 1969).

To sum up, the Taishang School is not only a place for education but also a 'replacement' for Taiwan. Because of this function, students developed two types of language and body behaviours: one type for addressing people from Taiwan (actually mainly people at the Taishang Schools) and the other type for addressing Chinese people. Although students paid regular visits to Taiwan, these short-term visits did not help them to discover and understand the differences between the Taishang School-based Taiwanese community and real life in Taiwan. By comparing the students' behaviours on and off the campus of Taishang School, we can judge the extent to which their claimed Taiwanese identity was based on subjective selection as well as its fragility. Although this fragility was not easily perceived, it was gradually even noted by the students themselves. The longer they lived in China, the more they sensed their distance from Taiwan. This sense of distance eventually turned into a sense of anxiety over the following years.

Life after Taishang School (2008–2012)

No systematic study has yet been carried out to track the graduates of Taishang Schools. Although one study on the Taishang School in Dongguan showed that the number of students returning to Taiwan for higher education rose from 38 per cent in 2005 to 78 per cent in 2008,[9] a study on the Taishang School in Shanghai in 2012 found that the number of students returning to Taiwan might fall as a result of the favourable policies launched by the Chinese government.[10] All we know for sure is that only a small proportion of these students continue their studies in a third country, for example in the US or Europe. The following part of this chapter, therefore, focuses on those who choose to continue their studies in either China or Taiwan.

Students still living in China: anxiety about the future

In 2010, those who had attended my class as Year 8 students in 2005 were now in Year 12, the final year of study at the Taishang School. During these five years, I had also moved on, from being employed as a part-time teacher at the Taishang Schools to a position as a junior lecturer (assistant professor) at a university in Taiwan. Partly due to my new job, one of my former colleagues asked me to give a lecture on higher education in Taiwan and to provide students with some advice on how to apply. When I told students, 'For those intending to study in Humanities and Social Sciences, you should highlight your experience of studying in Shanghai. Many scholars in Taiwan will be interested in your Chinese experiences', one of my former students, Flora, suddenly responded 'I think I am different from those studying in Taiwan'. The entire conversation suddenly took a turn and students started to discuss 'the strange feeling [I got] when [I was] returning to Taiwan'. I was surprised that the students who had quite clearly told me 'I am from Taiwan' in 2005 were now expressing a feeling of distance from Taiwan. It seemed that many of my previous students were encountering similar emotional problems.

Meanwhile, all my students who had been in Years 10–12 in 2005 had graduated from the Taishang School in 2010. Some of them were continuing their education in China. Initially, I thought that those who were continuing their education in China would successfully integrate into Chinese society and get along well with the Chinese students. However, I found that most of them still kept their social circle limited to people who had graduated from Taishang Schools or to Taiwanese people who had grown up in China; most of them had only a nodding acquaintance with Chinese students. Although a few of my former students had dated Chinese people, they described their relationships with Chinese partners as less serious than those with Taiwanese compatriots. This sense of social alienation from the host society caused one student, when I asked about future career plans, to suddenly burst into tears and exclaim 'I just want to return to Taiwan, to catch up on what I have lost over the years'. I felt sad for her, so I asked her to think about what she would do in Taiwan before returning: 'You cannot just come back without any preparation', I said. What made me even sadder was her response: 'I don't know. Anything is better [than working in China]'. Although many of my former students had talked for years about returning to Taiwan, few of them actually had any clear idea about how to put their plans into practice.

The students who had told me 'I think I am different from those studying in Taiwan' had something in common with the one who said 'I just want to return to Taiwan, to catch up on what I have lost over the years'. After living in China for years, they had gradually discovered their distance from Taiwan. After identifying themselves for years as Taiwanese people, they felt anxious when talking about this distance or discussing any serious plans related to returning to Taiwan. This anxiety further confirms my previous contention regarding the fragility of their Taiwanese identity, which now seemed more fragile and even weaker than before. This sense of anxiety would continue until the time of their actual return or until the time when they made the decision not to return.

Students returning to Taiwan: lost in reintegration

While the students who continued their education in China were 'lost in anxiety', I imagined that those who had returned to Taiwan might be happy because they had finally returned to their homeland as they had long hoped. And certainly, those returning to Taiwan were actually happy at first. One student told me he had felt happy because 'the air is clean and everything is more organized'. However, after a couple of honeymoon weeks, they gradually encountered the other side of Taiwan, most importantly the anti-China climate in daily life. What surprised these young Taiwanese 'returned migrants' was not the gap in economic development or lifestyle discussed, for instance, in studies on the Taiwanese who had returned from Australia (Chiang and Liao 2008; Chiang 2011), but the fact that their Taiwanese identity was challenged by Taiwanese society. This challenge was felt on many occasions, for example, as a result of the political issues raised during election campaigns, heated debates on the internet, or even any event related to China that was mentioned in everyday conversations. Although my former students roughly understood how this anti-China climate had developed, they still felt uncomfortable or humiliated when asked questions such as 'Are you Chinky Chinese?'[11] They had no idea why their Taiwanese identity was being denigrated by some people in Taiwan just because they had studied in China for years.

One incident which led to the students feeling uncomfortable involved the school anthem in 2012. This anthem was condemned by some politicians in

Taiwan, who described it as 'unacceptable' and 'pro-China' because of some of the lyrics, for example, 'working together to establish a Great China（共創我大中華' and 'Although I was born in the Island Taiwan, I have settled down with my parents in Shanghai, a city of my motherland (我出生於臺灣島，跟隨爸媽奔向祖國落腳上海)'.[12] Although many students were also unhappy with the lyrics, they doubted whether any positive outcome could be expected after the comments that had been made by these high-profile politicians.[13] Actually, these comments gave my students the feeling that their national loyalty was being called into question by Taiwanese society. All these unhappy experiences made them feel even more alienated from the people in Taiwan. Some respondents eventually described their relationship with the local students as being 'a gap' or 'something I do not fit into'.

This sense of 'something I do not fit into' also occurred when respondents talked about the day-to-day interaction with their schoolmates in Taiwan. Although my respondents complained about their lives in China, they felt more independent and capable than their schoolmates in Taiwan because of their Chinese experiences. One girl described the difference between herself and other Taiwanese students as follows: 'They are so childish. The activities they organize [in university] are even simpler than what we have experienced in Taishang School', and 'Just a tiny car accident [in Kaohsiung], and [he] rang his parents [in Chiayi] at midnight for help. He should have rung the police instead'. One boy commented on the naivety of the schoolmates he encountered in Taiwan: 'There is nothing serious I can talk about with them. All my talk with them is nothing but gossip'. This comment, 'they are so naive', also occurred after my respondents had been talking about China with their schoolmates. Initially, respondents were happy that some of their schoolmates were showing any interest at all in their Chinese experiences, but they soon realized that the latter did not have any sound understanding of developments in China: 'They [schoolmates] regard China either as the only hope for the future or as the source of all evils'. Therefore, 'there is nothing serious I can talk about with students in Taiwan'.

I am not pronouncing judgement on my previous students and their schoolmates. What I am presenting here is a picture of the feeling of social exclusion experienced by the young Taiwanese students who have graduated from a Taishang School. This feeling of social exclusion leads them to remain in close contact, as good friends, with others who have attended Taishang Schools when they return to Taiwan. Few of my respondents became involved in romantic relationships with people in Taiwan. Although they have returned to Taiwan, their social lives are quite different to those of the local students in Taiwan, but rather similar to the lives of ethnic Chinese students from Southeast Asia.

Retrospection and future planning (2012–2013)

In 2012 and 2013, all the students who had attended my courses in 2004–2005 had graduated from the Taishang Schools. Some had also graduated from university and were starting their careers. After moving back and forth for around ten years, those working in China had gradually given up thinking of Taiwan as a place to return to and now considered it just as a place to visit. What surprised me again was that those who were working in Taiwan also looked at China in terms of a place to make a career. No matter where they were studying or working, most of them selected China, rather than Taiwan, as their destination, as the place where they would spend their lives in the future.[14] In the case of those studying and working in China after graduating from Taishang Schools, all of them opted for China as their future destination, including the one respondent who had once told me that 'I just want to return to Taiwan to catch up on what I have lost'. In the case of those who had studied at universities in Taiwan after graduating from Taishang Schools, most of them had moved back to China again, just as one respondent reported: 'He is back in Kunshan. Now he has his own bakery shop'. Even those who were studying or working in Taiwan at the time right now expressed their strong intention of moving to China eventually because 'the market in Taiwan is too small. It is easier to start one's career in China'.

It would be too easy, however, to say that the students' motives for moving to China derived solely from the job market in China or from the desire to be reunited with their parents. I would argue that there is something beyond these reasons. Their plans for building a career in China also result from their reflections on and personal adjustments to their 'Taiwanese identity'. With the experience of moving back and forth across the Taiwan Strait over several years, they have gradually discovered that the reality in Taiwan is far removed from what they had originally expected. While one respondent sadly expressed her nostalgia – 'Although the local train in Taipei is clean and safe, it is not what I experienced and remembered from years ago' – another emphasized her confidence in the future development of China: 'Although the development of China is still behind Taiwan, it has really improved a lot. I am also getting used to [some drawbacks of] it'. These two remarks help to explain why so few of them are considering Taiwan as the place to make their future lives.

I also asked my respondents to re-evaluate their experience of living in China by asking them questions, such as, 'If you had children and you could choose, would you have them study in China, or in Taiwan?' Although my respondents had divergent viewpoints regarding the education they had received at the Taishang Schools, they all agreed that they would want their children to study in China, not in Taiwan. Some of them even specified that their first choice would be that their children attend 'a Chinese school in China' rather than a Taishang School in China. This response shows that they see China not only as a place to work but also as a place to have a family. This kind of response, 'making a home in China', should not be seen as an indication that my respondents are emotionally attached to China. What they are really emotionally attached to is the experience of living in a Taiwanese community in the coastal cities of China. This type of 'identity of Taiwanese overseas' helps bring graduates from different Taishang Schools who live in the same city close to one another. It also leads graduates from the same Taishang School but living in different cities to contact each other regularly as a group. At these gatherings, they usually reflect on their previous experiences of living in China and their future plans.

The way that these young migrants re-evaluated their lives at Taishang Schools, discussed their futures and organized their get-togethers leads me to suggest that their Taiwanese identity is in transition from being part of the 'Taiwanese diaspora' to being 'Taiwanese overseas'. While the former implies that they expect to return to Taiwan as their home country one day, the latter implies that they gradually come to think of China as home. This new type of Taiwanese identity does not derive from the dichotomy between Taiwanese and Chinese identities, but from a combination of both. It is not based on the imagined homeland of Taiwan, but on their real experiences in the community of young Taiwanese people in China. Their Taiwanese identity can be seen in terms of three layers: the Taiwanese community in China as the core, the reference to the people in Taiwan as the second, and the reference to the people of China as the third. This transformation of identity will arguably encourage them to become more involved in cross-Strait issues than their parents, to act as a 'bridge' across the Taiwan Strait and to support some level of political integration between the two sides in the future.

Conclusion

Most studies concentrating on the impact of China adopt a political-economy perspective and few have paid attention to the viewpoints of people with profound experience of China. How such people perceive China and how their perceptions change over time has seldom been explored in the literature up to now. Taiwan, a country with strong historical connections to China and facing serious disputes with China over its political status, feels the China impact more strongly than other countries in the region. Given that more than a million Taiwanese people have moved to China, it is crucially important to understand how these people, especially their children's generation who have been raised on the mainland, perceive China in order to predict how Taiwan might be affected by China in the future.

All the young Taiwanese people discussed in this chapter are people who were born in Taiwan and moved to China in their childhood. When they studied at the Taishang Schools in Dongguan or Shanghai, they clearly identified themselves as not belonging to China. This 'non-Chinese' identity was actually formed as a result of the Taishang School functioning as a 'filter' to limit the impact of China. However, China still affected these respondents, as my observations of their body language on and off the school campus revealed. Chinese-style gestures were not displayed within the school campus but were naturally employed outside, at gatherings where local Chinese people were present. These two facets of their behaviour, 'being different from the Chinese when at the Taishang School' and 'being similar to the Chinese when outside the Taishang School', show how the Taishang Schools and China together have constituted the fragile Taiwanese identity of these young migrants.

The impact of school life and China on the identity of these Taiwanese became clearer after graduation. The respondents who returned to Taiwan quickly discovered their differences and distance from the people in Taiwan. The respondents who stayed in China gradually grew to appreciate their environment and the development of Chinese society. Most of them named the cities of coastal China, rather than Taiwan, as the place in which they would establish their future homes. This transformation of their identity (from being part of Taiwan to being part of China) shows how these young Taiwanese migrants are affected by China. It also shows how the anti-China climate in Taiwan reinforces the China impact if we look at the difficulties encountered by my respondents when they were trying to (re-)integrate in Taiwan. Since their knowledge about China is seldom appreciated and often denigrated, it should not come as a surprise that most of them would like to move back to China – and eventually do so.

What else can and should we expect from these young Taiwanese people? When protests against a proposed trade deal with China erupted in Taipei in March 2014, the grave concerns of many people in Taiwan about the rise of China and its potential impact on Taiwan came to the fore. They called for more caution to be exercised with regard to issues concerning China and cross-Strait interaction. As a matter of fact, it is not surprising that many people in Taiwan will not support economic integration taking place across the Strait before the political disputes between Beijing and Taipei have been sorted out. However, this chapter provides us with another perspective from which to consider the rise of China and related developments in Taiwan. As one of my respondents said, 'people in Taiwan are naive about the development of China. They treat China either as the only hope for Taiwan, or the source of all evils in Taiwan'. However, China is neither the only hope nor the only source of all evil. It is something in between. Any relationship with China can be beneficial or detrimental to Taiwan, and although people in Taiwan are generally well aware of this fact, they seldom explore China in a way that would allow them to gain a realistic picture of the dangers and opportunities on the other side of the Taiwan Strait. Most people in Taiwan are quick to pronounce judgement on China, whether this is positive or negative; more considered judgements are seldom heard.

Most Taiwanese people do not know much about developments in China and keep a distance from the mainland, but this is certainly not a good way of dealing with the potential (and unavoidable) impact of China. Taiwanese people with extensive Chinese experience (such as the respondents featured in this chapter) should be appreciated, because their knowledge about China can help people in Taiwan to understand what China actually is or means for Taiwan. However, such a dialogue has not yet developed because of strong fears of a rising China. What people should worry about is not the rise of China but the fear of a rising China. This fear is troublesome, because it will hinder Taiwan's efforts to deal effectively with China in the future.

Notes

1 This chapter is based on research partially supported by the National Science Council of Taiwan (The Local Response to Taiwanese Investment in China, 100–2420-H-194–005-MY3). Some sections were published in the *Journal of Population Studies* in June 2013. However, these sections have been thoroughly revised and more recent information has been added for the purpose of this chapter.

2 These two schools are Dongguan Taishang School and Huadong Taishang School. The third school, the Shanghai Taishang School, was established in September 2005 after I had already left Shanghai. I therefore did not have the opportunity to collect data from the third Taishang School by working there.

3 Students who have studied in the two Taishang Schools have their own groups on Facebook. See www.facebook.com/?sk=welcome#!/groups/4681397242/ for people from Dongguan Taishang School and www.facebook.com/?sk=welcome#!/groups/175010725846155/ for people from Huadong Taishang School (accessed 13 April 2013).

4 Most of the information about the PTA's regular activities is also available online. See http://blog.sina.com.cn/htcsparent; www.td-school.org.cn/3WS0570/jzh/new.asp (accessed 13 April 2013).

5 For example, the Taishang School in Dongguan hosted more than 400 visitors during the first ten months of 2004. These visitors included officials from both sides of the Taiwan Strait, schools from Taiwan, China and other countries. See HTTP: www.td-school.org.cn/3ws 0608/schoolhistory.htm (accessed 13 April 2013).

6 See e.g. *Xinhua News* (2002).

7 This study tour is usually hosted by one university in Taiwan to accommodate students from the three Taishang Schools in China at the same time. Some information about these study tours is available online. See e.g. 'Happy Study Tour for Taishang School students in Taiwan', www.cna.com.tw/postwrite/cvpread.aspx?ID=86582 (accessed 30 March 2012).

8 For example, students could easily tell where Taibei, Taichung, and Tainan were located geographically because '-bei', '-chung' and '-nan' mean 'north', 'middle' and 'south' in Mandarin. However, they were confused about the locations of other cities (such as Chiayi and Hsinchu) even if these cities were referred to as 'hometown' (*jiaxiang*).

9 For further details, see: 'Study on the Graduates from Dongguan Taishang School', www.npf.org.tw/post/3/4924 (accessed 10 April 2013). This study provides information drawn from the school's records that show how many graduates had actually returned to Taiwan in past years.

10 For further details, see: 'A Study on Enhancing Government Guidance Policy for Taiwanese Children's School', http://nccuir.lib.nccu.edu.tw/retrieve/82169/102301.pdf (accessed 10 April 2013). This study was focused on students currently attending the Huadong Taishang School with the aim of predicting where they might continue their education after graduation. There are no records or figures in this report to show where they eventually went.

11 People in Taiwan employ various terms to refer to people in China, such as 'zhongguoren' (people from the PRC), 'daluren' (people from the Chinese mainland) and 'ala'ar' (Chinky Chinese). The first two terms are neutral; the third is offensive.

12 For further details, see *Taipei Times* (2012).

13 As I have observed for years, there are many unofficial arrangements and informal understandings between the Taishang School and the Chinese government which allow the Taishang Schools some political space in China. For example, despite the 'textbook censorship' at Taishang Schools, many sensitive political issues can still be discussed because teachers can provide students with additional related materials. However, the comments made by Taiwanese politicians pose a threat to this political

space, which could easily result in the unofficial arrangements being changed into explicit requirements.

14 Only one respondent selected Taiwan as her first choice for her future professional career: a girl who had obtained her BA in Taiwan. By participating in domestic politics, she had developed a sense of belonging in Taiwan.

References

Alden, C. (2007) *China in Africa: Partner, Competitor or Hegemon?* London: Zed Books.

Barth, F. (1969) *Ethnic Groups and Boundaries: The Social Organization of Culture Difference*, Boston: Little Brown.

Bartley, A. (2010) '1.5 Generation Asian Migrants and Intergenerational Transnationalism: Thoughts and Challenges from New Zealand', *National Identities*, 12, 4: 381–395.

Bartley, A., and Spoonley, P. (2008) 'Intergenerational Transnationalism: 1.5 Generation Asian Migrants in New Zealand', *International Migration*, 46, 4: 63–84.

Brautigam, D. (2011) *The Dragon's Gift: The Real Story of China in Africa*, Oxford: Oxford University Press.

Butterfield, A. (2004) 'We Are Just Black: The Racial and Ethnic Identities of Second-Generation West Indians in New York', in Kasinitz, P., Mollenkopf, J., and Waters, M. (eds) *Becoming New Yorkers: Ethnographies of the New Second Generation*, New York: Russell Sage Foundation.

Chao, C. (2003) 'Will Economic Integration between Mainland China and Taiwan Lead to a Congenial Political Culture?' *Asian Survey*, 43, 2: 280–304.

Chen, K., and Wu, C. (2006) 'Homeland or Strange Land? The Identity-Images of Taiwanese Businessmen's Children as Formed through their Learning Experiences' [Shi guxiang, haishi yixiang? Cong dong wan tai xiaoxuesheng de xuexi jingyan kann taishang zinu de shenfen renting yixiang], *Journal of Taiwan Normal University*, 51, 2: 173–193.

Chiang, L. (2011) 'Return Migration: The Case of the 1.5 Generation of Taiwanese in Canada and New Zealand',*China Review*, 11, 2: 91–124.

Chiang, L., and Liao, P. (2008) 'Back to Taiwan: Adaptation and Self-Identity of Young Taiwanese Trans-nationals', *Journal of Population Studies*, 36: 99–135.

Croucher, S. (2009) *The Other Side of the Fence: American Migrants in Mexico*, Austin: University of Texas Press.

Danico, M. (2004) *The 1.5 Generation: Becoming Korean American in Hawaii*, Honolulu: University of Hawaii Press.

Deng, J. (2002) 'The Distance of Interaction between Taiwanese Managers and Chinese Employees at Taiwanese Firms' [Jiejin de juli: Zhongguo dalu taizichang de hexin dalu yuangong yu taishang], *Taiwanese Sociology*, 3: 211–251.

Deng, J. (2009) 'Making A Living on the Move: Transnational Lives of Taiwanese Managers in the Shanghai Area' [Chixu di huijia: da shanghai taiji jingliren de yiju shenghuo], *Taiwanese Sociology*, 18: 139–179.

Deng, J.-B., and Wei, M.-G. (2010) 'Family Firms and Generational Change: Taiwanese Manufacturing Business in the Pearl River Delta' [Jiating qiye yu shidai bianqian: Yi zhusanjiao diqu zhi zaoye taishang wei li], *Mainland China Affairs*, 53: 25–51.

Fechter, A. (2007) *Transnational Lives, Expatriates in Indonesia*, Aldershot: Ashgate.

Fong, V. (2004) *Only Hope: Coming of Age under China's One-child Policy*, Stanford: Stanford University Press.

Fouron, G., and Glick-Schiller, N. (2002) 'The Generation of Identity: Redefining the Second Generation within a Transnational Social Field', in Levitt, P., and Waters, M. (eds) *The Changing Face of Home: The Transnational Lives of the Second Generation*, New York: Russell Sage Foundation.

Holmes, R. (1998) *Fieldwork with Children*, New York: Sagel.

Hsia, C. (2004) 'The Current Situation and Prospect of Overseas Taipei School' [Haiwai taibei xuexiao de zhanwang yu xiankuang], *Hsuan Chuang Humanities*, 3: 1–56.

Huang, Y.-C. (2006) 'The Policy and Thesis Research of Parents' Participation in Education in Taiwan from 1995 to 2004' [Yijiujiuwu zhi erlinglingsi nian Taiwan jiazhang canyu xuexiao jiaoyu de zhengce yu xuewei lunwen yanjiu fenxi], *Educational Policy Forum*, 9: 27–46.

Izumi, K. (2010) 'China's Advances in Oceania and Japan's Response', in Wesley-Smith, T., and Porter, E. (eds) *China in Oceania: Reshaping the Pacific?* New York: Berghahn Books.

Kasinitz, P., Mollenkopf, J., and Waters, M. (2003) 'Becoming Americans/Becoming New Yorkers: Immigrant Incorporation in a Majority Minority City', in Reitz, J. (ed.) *Host Societies and Reception of Immigrants*, San Diego: Center for Comparative Immigration Studies, University of California.

Kasinitz, P., Waters, M., Mollenkopf, J., and Anil, M. (2002) 'Transnationalism and the Children of Immigrants in Contemporary New York', in Levitt, P., and Waters, M. (eds) *The Changing Face of Home: The Transnational Lives of the Second Generation*, New York: Russell Sage Foundation.

Keng, S., and Schubert, G. (2010) 'Agents of Unification? The Political Role of Taiwanese Businessmen in the Process of Cross-Strait Integration', *Asian Survey*, 50, 2: 287–310.

Keng, S., Lin, R., and Schubert, G. (2012) 'Studies on Taishang: The Originality, Development, and Core Issues' [Taishang yanjiu: qiyuan, fazhan yu hexin yiti], in Keng, S., Schubert, G., and Lin, R. (eds) *Taishang Studies* [Taishang yanjiu], Taipei: Wunan Publishing.

Lan, P., and Wu, Y. (2011) 'Between "Homeland" and "Foreign Country": Liminal Identity and Boundary Work of Taiwanese Students in China' [Zai 'zuguo' yu 'waiguo' zhijian: lu zhong taisheng de rentong yu huajie], *Taiwanese Sociology*, 22: 1–57.

Lee, C. (2014) 'From Being Privileged to Being Localized? Taiwanese Businessmen in China', in Chiu, K., Fell, D., and Lin, P. (eds) *Migration To and From Taiwan*, London: Routledge.

Levitt, P., and Waters, M. (eds) (2002) *The Changing Face of Home: The Transnational Lives of the Second Generation*, New York: Russell Sage Foundation.

Lin, C. (2002) 'The Establishment of Taipei School Overseas: A Case Study on Dongguan Taiwanese Children School in China' [Wailai dongle de zhidu chuangxin: dongwan taishang xiehui chengli taishang xuexiao zhi yanjiu], unpublished MA thesis, Taipei: National Cheng Chi University.

Lin, P. (2009) 'Do They Mix? The Residential Segregation of Taiwanese People in China' [Cong juzhu kongjian kan taiwanren dui zhongguo dalu dangdi de rentong], *Taiwan Political Science Review*, 13, 2: 57–111.

Lin, P. (2011) 'Chinese Diaspora "at Home": Mainlander Taiwanese in Dongguan and Shanghai', *China Review*, 11, 2: 43–64.

Lin, P. (2012) 'Imagined Mobility: Taiwanese College Students in China' [Xiangxiang de jieceng liudong: Zhongguo dalu taiwan xuesheng de jiuxue jiuye fenxi], *Mainland China Affairs*, 55, 3: 57–84.

Lin, P. (2013) 'Taiwanese Women in China: Integration and Mobility in Gendered Enclaves', *China Information*, 27, 1: 107–123.

Monson, J. (2009) *Africa's Freedom Railway: How a Chinese Development Project Changed Lives and Livelihoods in Tanzania*, Bloomington: Indiana University Press.

Moore, F. (2008) 'The German School in London, UK: Fostering the Next Generation of National Cosmopolitans', in Coles, A., and Fechter, A. (eds) *Gender and Family among Transnational Professionals*, London: Routledge.

Mou, S. (2001) *A Research on the Schooling Model of Children of Taiwan Merchants in Mainland China – Based on a Middle and Primary School as an Example* [Dalu taishang zinü jiuxue moshi zhi yanjiu: yi zhongxiaoxue wei li], unpublished MA thesis, Taipei: Tamkang University.

O'Reilly, K. (2000) *The British on the Costa Del Sol: Transnational Identities and Local Communities*, London: Routledge.

O'Reilly, K. (2009) 'The Children of the Hunters: Self-realization Projects and Class Reproduction', in Benson, M., and O'Reilly, K. (eds) *Lifestyle Migration: Expectation, Aspirations, and Experiences*, Aldershot: Ashgate.

Park, K. (1999) 'I Really Do Feel I'm 1.5! The Construction of Self and Community by Young Korean Americans', *Amerasia Journal*, 25, 1: 139–164.

Porter, E., and Wesley-Smith, T. (2010) 'Introduction: Oceania Matters', in Wesley-Smith, T., and Porter, E. (eds) *China in Oceania: Reshaping the Pacific?* New York: Berghahn Books.

Portes, A., and Rumbaut, R. (2001) *Legacies: The Story of the Immigrant Second Generation*, New York: Russell Sage Foundation.

Portes, A., and Zhou, M. (1993) 'The New Second Generation: Segmented Assimilation and its Variants', *Annals of the American Academy of Political and Social Sciences*, 530: 74–98.

Powles, M. (2010) 'Challenges, Opportunities, and the Case for Engagement', in Wesley-Smith, T., and Porter, E. (eds) *China in Oceania: Reshaping the Pacific?* New York: Berghahn Books.

Roett, R., and Paz, G. (2008) 'Introduction: Assessing the Implications of China's Growing Presence in the Western Hemisphere', in Roett, R. and Paz, G. (eds) *China's Expansion into the Western Hemisphere: Implications for Latin America and the United States*, Washington DC: Brookings Institution Press.

Rumbaut, R. (2002) 'Served or Sustained Attachments? Language, Identity, and Imagined Communities in the Post-immigrant Generation', in Levitt, P., and Waters, M. (eds) *The Changing Face of Home: The Transnational Lives of the Second Generation*, New York: Russell Sage Foundation.

Ryu, C. (1991) '1.5 Generation', in Lee, J. (ed.) *Asian American Experiences in the United States*, Jefferson NC: McFarland.

Smith, R. (2002) 'Life Course, Generation, and Social Location as Factors Shaping Second-generation Transnational Life', in Levitt, P., and Waters, M. (eds) *The Changing Face of Home: The Transnational Lives of the Second Generation*, New York: Russell Sage Foundation.

Suarez-Orozco, C., Suarez-Orozco, M., and Todorova, I. (2008) *Learning a New Land: Immigrant Students in American Society*, Cambridge MA: Harvard University Press.

Taipei Times (2012) 'Taishang School Songs Have Pro-China Lyrics', 2 February, available at www.taipeitimes.com/News/taiwan/archives/2012/02/17/2003525695 (accessed 8 April 2013).

Tao, M.-C. (2005) *How do Taiwanese Immigrants in China Choose Schools for Their Children? Research on the Schooling Model of Children of Taiwan Merchants in Mainland China – Based on Middle and Primary School as an Example* [Taiwan yimin zai zhongguode zinü jiaoyang he xuexiao xuanze], unpublished master's thesis, Institute of Sociology, National Tsing Hua University, Hsinchu, Taiwan.

Tarte, S. (2010) 'Fiji's Look North Strategy and the Role of China', in Wesley-Smith, T., and Porter, E. (eds) *China in Oceania: Reshaping the Pacific?* New York: Berghahn Books.

Tseng, Y. (2005) 'Permanently Temporary: Taiwanese Business Nomads as Reluctant Migrants', in Lorente, B., Piper, N., and Shen, H. (eds) *Asian Migrations: Sojourning, Displacement, Homecoming and Other Travels*, Singapore: ARI, National University of Singapore.

Tseng, Y. (2011) 'Shanghai Rush: Skilled Migrants in a Fantasy City', *Journal of Ethnic and Migration Studies*, 37, 5: 765–784.

Tseng, Y., Tsao, M., and Keng, S. (2012) 'The Political Socialisation of Taishang School in Dongguan' [Zuowei zhengzhi shehuihua jizhi de dongwan taixiao], in Keng, S., Schubert, G., and Lin, R. (eds) *Taishang Studies* [Taishang yanjiu], Taipei: Wunan Publishing.

Wei, Y. (1997) 'From Multi-system Nations to Linkage Communities: A New Conceptual Scheme for the Integration of Divided Nations', *Issues and Studies*, 33, 10: 1–19.

Wu, J. (2004) 'The "Guanxi-Sensitive Zone" and "Symbolic Clustering" of Taiwanese Business Communities in China' [Taishang shequn de 'guanxi min'gandai' yu 'xiangzheng xingdong qunju'], *Contemporary China Newsletter*, 3: 37–40.

Wu, J., and Chen, C. (2006) 'The Current Situations of Taiwanese Schools Overseas and Taiwanese Business Schools in China' [Haiwai Taiwan xuexiao yu dalu taishang xuexiao zhi xiankuang yu zhanwang], paper presented at Conference on Education in the Chinese Societies, University of Macau, 29–30 April.

Xinhua News (2002) 'A Visit to Huadong Taishang School', 20 February, available at http://news.xinhuanet.com/newscenter/2002–02/20/content_282654.htm (accessed 15 January 2014).

Zhang, Y. (2010) 'A Regional Power by Default', in Wesley-Smith, T., and Porter, E. (eds) *China in Oceania: Reshaping the Pacific?* New York: Berghahn Books.

Zhou, M. (1997) 'Segmented Assimilation: Issues, Controversies, and Recent Research on the New Second Generation', *International Migration Review*, 34, 4: 975–1008.

Part III

The China impact on Taiwan's security

14 The rise of China and its implications for US–Taiwan relations

Cheng-Yi Lin

The dramatic growth of the Chinese nominal gross domestic product (GDP) has been far beyond the expectations of Chinese leaders and international observers. The rise of China and the rise of Brazil, Russia, India, China and South Africa (BRICS) have led to wide-spread discussion of the relative decline of the US and the coming of a post-US world (Zakaria 2008: 3; Kagan 2012: 24–25; Kupchan 2012: 63–64). Under the shadow of China's rise and the rapid development of warmer cross-Strait relations since May 2008, Taiwan's security environment has fundamentally changed. President Barack Obama has welcomed 'China's peaceful rise', believing that 'a strong and prosperous China is one that can help to bring stability and prosperity to the region and to the world'.[1] On the other hand, China is facing not just the US but a larger Western bloc of democratic states, and it is believed that China 'cannot fight a hegemonic war and it probably cannot remake the existing international order' (Ikenberry 2008: 114). Nevertheless, the rise of China has posed a challenge to 'the United States' long-term ability to continue playing what it regards a unique security role in the Asia-Pacific region' (Swaine 2011: 6; Sutter 2005: 289–305).

With the ending of the wars in Iraq and Afghanistan, the Obama administration initiated the pivot to the Asia strategy, which was later rephrased as rebalancing toward the Asia-Pacific, with the emphasis on four key areas – 'enhancing security, expanding prosperity, fostering democratic values, and advancing human dignity'.[2] Although this strategy is not aimed at containing a rising China, Beijing is keeping a wary eye on increasing US involvement in the East and South China Seas. The Obama administration welcomes the warming of cross-Strait relations, moving from a coexistence in conflict towards a relatively peaceful coexistence, but is not certain how long this will last. In addition to examining the meaning of China's rise, the second and third sections of this chapter argue that Taiwan will face more challenges when it comes to acquiring US arms and persuading the US to play a proactive role in the cross-Strait peace process. Taiwan will find itself in a situation where the ability of the US to maintain peace and stability in the Taiwan Strait is weaker than it has ever been since 1949. The chapter's fourth section concludes that China has not only been increasing its influence over Taiwan's relations with the US but also complicating Taiwan's standing with its closest neighbours with regard to the disputes in the East and South China Seas.

The rise of China and its implications

The most salient geopolitical factor in the Asia-Pacific region related to regional security is the rise of China. China's GDP overtook that of Japan in 2010, placing it second after the US. China has become the centre of media attention since the global financial crisis that started in 2008. Even with China's widening gap in income distribution, serious corruption and lower GDP per capita, if China maintains a 7–8 per cent annual economic growth rate in comparison to the US's 2.5 per cent, China's GDP will become the world's largest by 2025–2030 (see Table 14.1) (Subramanian 2011: 69; Babones 2011: 79–80).

China has long been the largest holder of US debt, with a total of US$1,144 billion in March 2011, US$1,169 billion in March 2012 and US$1,272 billion in March 2014.[3] Bilateral merchandise trade between the US and the People's Republic of China reached US$590.6 billion in 2014, with the US exporting US$124.0 billion to China while absorbing US$466.6 billion in Chinese goods (see Table 14.2). Noting the Chinese challenge, the US Secretary of State, Hillary Clinton, once asked 'How do you deal toughly with your banker?'[4] The same logic might be also applied to Taiwan. Taiwan is heavily dependent on

Table 14.1 GDP and projection of China, Japan and the US ($trillion)

	China	*Japan*	*US*
2010	5.87	5.45	14.65
2011	7.29	5.86	15.09
2015	10.06	6.37	17.99
2020	16.13	7.38	22.20
2025	24.16	8.00	24.91
2030	34.65	8.40	28.41

Source: International Monetary Fund and Tokyo Foundation, 2011.

Table 14.2 US trade in goods with China ($million)

	Total	*Exports*	*Imports*	*Balance*
2004	231,109.8	34,427.8	196,682.0	−162,254.3
2005	284,662.1	41,192.0	243,470.1	−202,278.1
2006	341,347.4	53,673.0	287,774.4	−234,101.3
2007	384,379.8	62,936.9	321,442.9	−258,506.0
2008	407,505.4	69,732.8	337,772.6	−268,039.8
2009	365,870.6	69,496.7	296,373.9	−226,877.2
2010	456,863.7	91,911.1	364,952.6	−273,041.6
2011	503,492.7	104,121.5	399,371.2	−295,249.7
2012	536,141.8	110,515.6	425,626.2	−315,110.6
2013	562,184.1	121,736.4	440,447.7	−318,711.3
2014	590,680.5	124,024.0	466,656.5	−342,632.5

Sources: US Census Bureau, www.census.gov/foreign-trade/balance/c5700.html, accessed 20 April 2015.

China's market, with the two-way trade volume hitting US$198.3 billion in 2014, and Taiwan enjoying a surplus of US$105.5 billion (see Table 14.3). Despite being a much smaller economy, Taiwan's exports to China have been larger than those to the US, resulting in a high degree of vulnerability for the island's economic security (Pan 2014: 1).

Beijing's quota and voting shares in the International Monetary Fund have expanded, and it was set to become the member country with the third largest quota share after the US and Japan in 2013–2014.[5] In October 2014, Beijing, which has pledged to contribute an initial US$50 billion in capital, announced the establishment of Asian Infrastructure Investment Bank (AIIB) to offer financing for infrastructure projects in developing countries across Asia, which has given officials in Japan and the US an entrenched suspicion of Chinese attempts. Speculation on a Group of Two (G-2) has been widespread in the Asia-Pacific region since March 2007 (Ferguson 2007). In China, senior state leaders have been cautious not to accept the invitation of co-management with the US over global issues, while younger experts and commentators are inclined to accept the G-2 arrangement. In the fourth round of the US–China Strategic and Economic Dialogue in May 2012, Beijing subtly declined the G-2 proposal and replaced it with a new name, urging more cooperation and coordination (C2) between the two countries.[6]

The rise of China has given the Chinese a sense of superiority, since they are enjoying the best-ever economic prosperity in Chinese communist history. Instead of being number two after the US, China is thought by some Chinese observers to actually be the number one among the developing countries not dominated by the US. For some observers, the 'Beijing Consensus' and Chinese methods of national development could serve as a model for other countries, in contrast to the 'Washington Consensus' (Wang 2011: 76). The PRC is wielding its economic power by promoting an amicable, tranquil and prosperous neighbourhood policy. The former President, Hu Jintao, has established strategic

Table 14.3 Taiwan's trade in goods with China ($million)

	Total	Exports	Imports	Balance
2004	78,323.8	64,778.6	13,545.2	+51,233.4
2005	91,234.0	74,684.4	16,549.6	+58,134.8
2006	107,884.2	87,109.0	20,735.2	+66,373.8
2007	124,480.0	101,021.7	23,458.3	+77,563.4
2008	129,217.5	103,339.6	25,877.9	+77,461.7
2009	106,228.2	85,722.9	20,505.3	+65,217.6
2010	145,370.5	115,693.9	29,676.6	+86,017.3
2011	160,031.8	124,919.9	35,111.9	+89,808.0
2012	168,963.0	132,183.9	36,779.1	+95,404.8
2013	197,280.5	156,636.9	40,643.6	+115,993.3
2014	198,314.3	152,029.5	46,284.8	+105,744.7

Sources: 'Mainland China Customs Statistics', Mainland Affairs Council, Executive Yuan, Republic of China, www.mac.gov.tw/public/MMO/MAC/263_1.pdf, accessed 20 April 2015.

partnerships with other major countries with the exception of Japan and the US. China's strategy may not feature a revisionist international agenda, but the critical question is whether China and the US 'are able to rise to the challenge of managing their inevitable disagreements in a world where China plays a more prominent and active role' (Goldstein 2005: 216).

For the first time in Sino-Japanese history, China's rise has placed the two countries on a more equal footing, and they have entered into a bumpy relationship in almost every dimension. After the Yasukuni Shrine visits under the Koizumi government, Japan and China released a joint statement with regard to building a strategic and reciprocal relationship, but Beijing and Tokyo have increasingly been protesting against each other's intentions and activities in the disputed islands in the East China Sea. In addition to an unstable governmental relationship, the animosity between the peoples of China and Japan has increased into the twenty-first century. A series of surveys released by Japan's cabinet office indicated that Japanese affinity toward China dropped dramatically from 32.4 per cent (2009) to 20 per cent (2010), 26.3 per cent (2011), 18.0 per cent (2012), and 18.1 per cent (2013), a record low since the first survey in 1978.[7] The survey might have been affected by an incident when a Chinese fishing boat collided with a Japanese Coast Guard ship within twelve nautical miles of the Diaoyutai (Senkaku) Islands in September 2010. A series of protests erupted in both China and Japan. Beijing sometimes links the disputed Dokdo (Takeshima) Island that lies between Japan and South Korea with the Diaoyutai issue, portraying Japan as a nation with territorial ambitions. For Japan, Chinese naval activities in waters surrounding Japan's remote islands to the southwest are most alarming (Kachi 2012).

To make matters worse, since Japan's nationalization of the Senkaku/Diaoyutai Islands in September 2012 and China's announcement with regard to establishing an Air Defence Identification Zone (ADIZ) in the East China Sea, these two countries have been on the brink of armed conflict in the overlapping ADIZ or Exclusive Economic Zones (EEZs). The People's Liberation Army (PLA) Navy fleet has been increasing its training drills by passing through waters between Japan's Okinawan islands and the Miyako Strait. In April 2010, a total of ten Chinese warships and submarines travelled from the East China Sea through the above-mentioned Strait to waters off the disputed Okinotori Islands – the southernmost point in Japan – in the Western Pacific Ocean. In July 2010, a destroyer and a frigate belonging to the Chinese Navy passed through these waters again. In addition, eight Chinese warships were detected in June 2011, six were spotted in November 2011, and three were detected in the same water areas in May 2012. These increasing Chinese naval activities have confirmed the US Pentagon's prediction in 2010 that by 2015–2020, 'it is likely that China will be able to project and sustain a modest sized force – perhaps several battalions of ground forces or a naval flotilla of up to a dozen ships – in low-intensity operations far from China' (Office of the Secretary of Defence 2010: 29). It seems that the Chinese moves are taking place more quickly than expected and that China will be able to project and sustain large forces in high-intensity combat operations far away from China, particularly in the waters between the first and the second island chains.[8]

China's thirst for oil to fuel its economic powerhouse has driven Beijing's leaders to tackle the Malacca Strait dilemma. Beijing has developed a string-of-pearls strategy to avoid its oil supply routes being blockaded by the US. The PLA Navy has increasingly projected power beyond Chinese EEZs. The PLA has conducted a series of opaque military exercises including satellite interception (January 2007), missile interception (January 2010) and a J20 flying test (January 2011), all of which gave rise to a great deal of international concern and debate. Five Chinese vessels blocked and surrounded a US surveillance ship, the *Impeccable*, in the South China Sea in March 2009. This indicates that China and the US have different interpretations regarding the military use of the EEZs (Zha 2011; Godement 2010: 21).

In April 2009, Hu Jintao and Barack Obama decided to build a positive, constructive and comprehensive relationship between the two countries. Nevertheless, Beijing has argued that this relationship has been undermined by US arms sales to Taiwan and constant US military intervention in Chinese EEZs. In 2010, Beijing reportedly included the South China Sea as part of its 'core interests' related to China's sovereignty and territorial integrity. In the summer of 2011, a ship belonging to China's State Oceanic Administration cut the cables of a Vietnamese oil exploration ship in the South China Sea, which led to a series of anti-Chinese protests in Vietnam, followed by an exchange of diplomatic fire between China and the US at the ASEAN Regional Forum annual meeting in Hanoi. In April 2012, the most serious maritime and diplomatic conflict between China and the Philippines erupted in waters around the Scarborough Shoal in the South China Sea. China was again portrayed as bullying its much weaker neighbour. In May 2014, China's placement of its first oil rig in disputed waters south of the Xisha (Paracel) Islands led to anti-China riots and the looting of foreign factories in several Vietnamese cities, where Taiwanese business people and Chinese migrant workers suffered the most direct consequences.

The rise of China is not always perceived in negative terms, and Beijing might have played an active role on the Korean Peninsula. China has been perceived by international observers as the key aid donor and economic partner of North Korea; for example, more than 80 per cent of North Korean consumer goods and crude oil come from China (Kim 2011: 136). Beijing has also acted as mediator and initiator of the Six-Party Talks in defusing crises on the Korean Peninsula. China and other parties, such as the US, Russia, Japan and South Korea, viewed the Six-Party Talks statements in September 2005, February 2007 and October 2007 as key documents which have laid the foundations for making the Korean Peninsula nuclear-free. After the sudden death of the North Korean leader, Kim Jong-il, in December 2011, Beijing dissuaded other concerned parties from taking provocative measures, while serving as the protector of Kim Jong-il's youngest son, Kim Jong-un (Glaser and Glosserman 2010; Bilefsky 2011). The North Korean nuclear dispute and the political succession have increased the opportunities for China to play an active role in Northeast Asia and for South Korea to seek security through cooperation with China (Ross 2010: 531). For the US, Sino-American co-management of any future crisis concerning North Korea could be a viable option or a test case for the two countries in maintaining stability in Northeast Asia, particularly with reference to the Taiwan Strait.

Beijing has sometimes tried to convince the US that China does not have any intention of challenging US leadership, since the overall Chinese weapons capability is lagging 20 years behind that of the US (Hodge 2011). However, China is developing the capability to attack at long range as well as military forces that could deploy or operate within the Western Pacific, which the US Department of Defence characterizes as 'anti-access' and 'area denial' (A2AD) capabilities. In order to respond to China's rapidly growing military capabilities, the US is pursuing an air-sea battle concept (ASBC) in its Defence Strategic Guidance released in January 2012 (Manyin 2012: 16). The application of ASBC comprises a variety of air, sea, undersea, space, counter-space and information warfare systems and operational concepts to counterbalance China's A2AD. In 2010, the former US Pacific Commander Robert Willard stated that 'China's rapid and comprehensive transformation of its armed forces is affecting regional military balances and holds implications beyond the Asia-Pacific region' (Gertz 2010). Additionally, the US and Japan set a common strategic objective to 'encourage China's responsible and constructive role in regional stability and prosperity, its cooperation on global issues, and its adherence to international norms of behaviour', and to 'improve openness and transparency with respect to China's military modernization and activities, and strengthen confidence building measures'.[9]

With the inauguration of the China-friendly President Ma Ying-Jeou and an anti-independence KMT government in place, Beijing and Washington have been temporarily relieved to see improved cross-Strait relations taking shape. China has taken advantage of the US preoccupation with wars in Iraq and Afghanistan and the détente across the Taiwan Strait by undertaking efforts to weaken US influence in Taiwan. Beijing regards Ma's presidency as a golden opportunity to further develop cross-Strait relations. The Chinese government has warned Taiwan and the US that the improvements in cross-Strait relations could be reversed if the Democratic Progressive Party (DPP) is returned to power on the island. Therefore, Beijing has not given a green light for the expansion of Taiwan's international space. The threat of Chinese pressure and the domino effect of diplomatic allies falling away will cast a shadow over Taiwan's international space.

With the 'back to Asia' policy espoused by the Obama administration, Beijing has encountered a hostile security environment along its southern borders, both in the East China Sea and the South China Sea. For Beijing, relations with the US are too comprehensive and pivotal to be handicapped by US arms sales to Taiwan, human rights issues or naval standoffs in China's EEZs. Since 2009, China and the US have been conducting an annual Strategic and Economic Dialogue that is aimed at building a cooperative partnership in fighting the global financial crisis and reducing regional instabilities from the Korean Peninsula to the Gulf of Aden. The Taiwan independence problem has been temporarily marginalized in the dialogue, but it is far from being resolved, and the arms sales issue continues to be a source of friction between Beijing and Washington.

Declining influence of the US in cross-Strait relations

The PRC's imminent military threat declined significantly when the KMT regained power and announced Taipei's acceptance of the 1992 Consensus, but Beijing continues to decry US arms sales to Taiwan. Beijing has tried to create the notion that the justifications offered for Taiwan's purchases of US arms are anachronistic. Since tensions across the Taiwan Strait have been greatly reduced, and direct air links had brought at least 3.9 million Chinese tourists to Taiwan in 2014, Beijing has some evidence-backed arguments that the US should cease arms sales to Taiwan on the basis of the 17 August 1982 communiqué.

The US provided Taiwan with a supply of carefully selected defence articles and services totaling about US$19 billion in three arms sales during the first Ma government.[10] However, the US has repeatedly put off the sale of F-16C/D fighters and has only agreed to upgrade 145 F16A/B fighters for Taiwan. Meanwhile, some US academics and experts have begun suggesting that the US should drop its security commitments to Taiwan or strike a grand bargain with China over arms sales to Taiwan (Glaser 2011: 80–91; Shambaugh 2010: 225). Michael Swaine, a senior security specialist at the Carnegie Endowment for International Peace, has suggested that

> It is time for Washington to consider negotiating directly with Beijing, in consultation with Taipei, a set of mutual assurances regarding Chinese force levels and deployments, on the one hand, and major U.S. arms sales and defence assistance to Taiwan, on the other hand – linked to the eventual opening of a cross-Strait political dialogue on the status of Taiwan.[11]

Even an offensive realist in the study of international relations, John Mearsheimer, a professor at the University of Chicago, doubts that the US will be able to succeed in defending Taiwan in the distant future: he explained quite bluntly that a powerful China is a nightmare for Taiwan and 'it is difficult to imagine American policy-makers purposely choosing to fight a war in which the U.S. military is not only going to lose, but is also going to pay a huge price in the process' (Mearsheimer 2014: 38).

China is developing an A2AD capability which is aimed at deterring the US from future military intervention in the Taiwan Strait, the East China Sea and the South China Sea. The PRC has deployed surface-to-air missiles and land-based cruise missiles that will place US fighters and ships in great jeopardy in areas close to Chinese coastal areas. Beijing has stressed that as long as Taiwan does not declare independence, China will not attack. Beijing has also said that if Taipei embraces the 'one China' principle, there will be no war, and Taiwan will no longer need to purchase US arms. For the KMT, the DPP and the US, a PRC that does not renounce the use of force but only reduces the number of missiles targeting Taiwan would pose further problems. Taipei would be under pressure to make solid concessions in terms of its military deployments on the offshore islands, such as Matsu or Kinmen, and the US would probably welcome Beijing's move, commending a reduction in missiles as a positive step. This would further weaken the foundations for continuing US arms sales to Taiwan.

Taiwan can no longer match China's armed forces, either in quantity or in quality of arms. China's rise has highlighted the fact that it is almost impossible for Taiwan to compete with the PRC in military modernization and that the island cannot stand on its own without US intervention. It also presents the US with a greater challenge with regard to selling new major weapons to Taiwan, owing to the political unpredictability of cross-Strait relations and the insurmountable task of maintaining a military balance across the Taiwan Strait. Whether the US will be able to succeed in a military intervention to defend Taiwan from Chinese attack is also under serious scrutiny.

In recent years, Beijing has watched with interest the debate within the US on whether to abandon Taiwan. Charles Glaser, a professor at George Washington University, believes that the rise of China might lead China and the US into a conventional and nuclear arms race if the US continues to sell arms to Taiwan (Glaser 2011: 88–91). The former National Security Advisor under the Carter administration, Zbigniew Brzezinski, suggested that Taiwan consider a formula of 'one country, several systems' in preserving its security and avoiding US–China contention because 'a separate Taiwan, protected indefinitely by US arms sales, will provoke intensifying Chinese hostility' (Brzezinski 2012: 103). In the same vein, John Mearsheimer argued that 'Once China becomes a superpower, it probably makes the most sense for Taiwan to give up hope of maintaining its de facto independence and instead pursue the "Hong Kong strategy"' (Mearsheimer 2014: 39).

For some US China policy experts, Taiwan's absorption by China is only a matter of time. After the Economic Cooperation Framework Agreement (ECFA) between Taiwan and China had been signed, David Shambaugh, a professor at George Washington University, declared 'game over' for Taiwan, claiming that the island had no option but to accept the One China formula (Shambaugh 2010: 224). Taiwan's government might consider a possible 'Finlandization' arrangement under China's rise, which would have the potential to relieve the US of the long-time security commitment burden for the island (Gilley 2010: 44–60). These remarks contrast sharply with that of a former National Security Council director of the Obama administration, Jeffrey Bader, who argued against abandoning Taiwan and who believes that 'there is a pretty strong consensus' in Washington 'about the importance of Taiwan – democracy, stability and the peaceful resolution [of cross-Strait differences]' (Shih 2012: 3). And Bader's viewpoints are not exceptional by any means.[12] In June 2011, the US House of

Representatives' Committee on Foreign Affairs held a hearing during which the Chairperson, Ileana Ros-Lehtinen, denounced some of the calls coming from Washington to stop selling weapons to Taiwan (US Congress 2011a: 3–4, 13–53). In October 2011, at the House Foreign Affairs Committee hearing on 'Why Taiwan Matters, Part II', Kurt Campbell, the Assistant Secretary of State for East Asian and Pacific Affairs, rejected an assertion that the US–China relationship 'would come at the expense of our relations with Taiwan' (US Congress 2011b: 15).

Immediately after Taiwan's 2008 election, the US President at that time, George W. Bush, responded by saying that 'the election provides a fresh opportunity for both sides [of the Taiwan Strait] to reach out and engage one another in peacefully resolving their differences'.[13] President Obama made a similar observation when he visited Beijing in November 2009, stating at a news conference that Americans 'applauded the steps that the People's Republic of China and Taiwan have already taken to relax tensions and build ties across the Taiwan Strait'.[14] The Obama Administration welcomed the signing of the cross-Strait ECFA in June 2010.

Regardless of the nature of cross-Strait relations, the US government has a policy of encouraging Taipei and Beijing to explore 'confidence-building steps that will lead to closer ties and greater stability across the Taiwan Strait'.[15] Two American scholars contributed an article on the formation and implications of a cross-Strait peace agreement as soon as the Ma government came to power (Saunders and Kastner 2009: 87–114). To weaken the rationale for Taiwan's maintenance of a competitive security strategy, Beijing has encouraged meetings between both sides of the Taiwan Strait to deal with topics related to military confidence-building measures (CBMs). It is believed that China has sent hundreds of spies or intelligence agents into Taiwan as Trojan horses to sabotage the security of Taiwan. Therefore, the DPP has been critical of KMT-loyal retired generals who frequently visit China to serve as mouthpieces for Beijing's Taiwan policy.

China is likely to freeze or reduce the number of missiles targeting Taiwan if the US reconsiders its position on arms sales to Taiwan. The implications of a possible cross-Strait CBM mechanism for the validity of the TRA could pose a challenge to US policy. Another concern is that if Taiwan reduces its military capabilities and the two sides continue to grow ever closer, then weapons systems provided by the US could fall into the hands of the PLA. In addition to attempting to stop US arms sales to Taiwan, Beijing will also seek to eliminate any possibility of the US playing a role in establishing a cross-Strait peace agreement. Since May 2008, Beijing has remained silent about the proposal that the US and China co-manage the Taiwan issue. Clearly, the implications of a possible cross-Strait peace agreement for the TRA could also include a policy challenge for the US. Given China's increasing strength and Beijing's increasing ability to direct cross-Strait relations, US influence has been diminished in the Taiwan Strait. China's growing strength is also making it increasingly complicated for the US and Taiwan to maintain a shared strategic view and can also be expected to call into question 'Washington's ability to credibly serve as guarantor of Taiwan's security in the future' (Shlapak *et al.* 2009: xix). Therefore, experts such as Robert Sutter and Shelley Rigger have proposed that the US government craft a new policy, or at least conduct a policy review and develop a response plan (Sutter 2009).

Leaders in China and the US were taken by surprise when they saw Taipei's Sunflower student movement in March–April 2014 sabotaging the Ma government's plan to get the Cross-Strait Service Trade Agreement passed in the Legislative Yuan. The US has seen fewer possible roles for itself to play in cross-Strait peace negotiations than in a Taiwan Strait crisis. A détente in the Taiwan Strait relieves the US from being forced into intervening in a Taiwan–China military confrontation. Washington, and even Beijing, can also focus attention on dealing with other regional flashpoints on the Korean Peninsula or in the South China Sea. Whether any increase in Chinese influence on Taiwan could challenge the vested interests of the US and other countries has been closely monitored by keen observers. The DPP has persistently argued that the actions of the KMT and the CCP are changing the status quo in the Taiwan Strait. Critically, Taiwan has been left out in the rebalancing-to-Asia strategy employed by the US in response to China's rise. And ironically enough, some members of the Obama Administration and US academics are concerned about a possible comeback by the DPP and the resumption of a provocative approach toward China (Bush 2011: 282–286). Just before the 2012 presidential elections, the Obama administration dispatched USAID Director, Rajiv Shah, and Deputy Secretary of Energy, Daniel Poneman, to Taiwan and warned that a victory by Tsai Ing-Wen could raise tensions with China, thus indicating tacit support for the reelection of President Ma Ying-Jeou. Whether the US is more accommodative to China's rise and weakening its impartiality in Taiwan's 2016 presidential elections remains to be seen.

Complicating disputes in East Asian waters

A situation in which Taiwan sided with the PRC in asserting Chinese historical claims either in the East or South China Seas could change the balance of power in the region, and Taiwan's dependence on the US for security protection could also be endangered. China has adjusted its policy on the Diaoyutai Islands since the Japanese government finalized its decision to nationalize the contested islands in September 2012. Beijing has shifted from a passive, indirect approach to one which is much more active and direct, by regularly dispatching its maritime reconnaissance ships to patrol within 12 nautical miles of the Diaoyutais. In the process, Taiwan has been downgraded from playing a part as a leading actor to that of playing a supporting role in the unfolding drama. In the South China Sea, China has also become more assertive in maritime law enforcement since the Scarborough Shoal incident in April 2012. The lingering territorial disputes in the context of China's rise and new assertiveness have rendered the security issue in the waters surrounding Taiwan precarious.

While Chen Shui-Bian was in office, Japan, ASEAN and the US were not concerned about any cross-Strait collaboration on strengthening Chinese legal claims on disputed islands in the South China Sea or the East China Sea. They knew that tensions in the Taiwan Strait could preclude such an option. The KMT government has modified the previous DPP government stance and has adopted a neutral position in conflicts in the South China Sea between China and the US. With the aim of defusing the suspicions of the US, President Ma Ying-Jeou has frequently stated that there are no plans to ally with the PRC to safeguard sovereignty claims in the waters surrounding Taiwan. While consolidating peaceful cross-Strait relations through agreements and regulations, President Ma is facing less friendly and diverse opinions among US China experts with regard to US–Taiwan policy under the shadow of China's rise.

President Ma Ying-Jeou has sought to maintain friendly relations with Japan, but this approach has backfired as a result of the constant clashes involving Taiwanese and Chinese fishing ships and Japan's law enforcement vessels in waters near the Diaoyutais/Senkakus. The first episode occurred soon after Ma's inauguration in June 2008. The Ma government was again caught in the middle, as Japan and the PRC confronted each other in the Diaoyutais in September 2010. Since Japan was urging the US to make a public commitment with regard to the defence of the Senkakus, Taiwan, by leaning toward China, could have been construed as a potential adversary of the US–Japan security alliance. Therefore, on the Diaoyutai issue, President Ma has constantly tried to assure the Japanese that Taiwan will not seek to cooperate with the PRC to settle the dispute. Fishing rights are a top priority for Taiwan, and there is a crucial need for separate and bilateral negotiations between Taiwan and Japan.[16] Beijing, however, has urged Taipei to take a stronger stand, as Beijing did in denouncing the Japanese claim of jurisdiction over the Diaoyutais, rather than a neutral position in the Sino-Japanese rift over Chinese territorial sovereignty.

In response to the nationalization of the Senkaku Islands by the DPJ (Democratic Party of Japan) government, President Ma travelled on 7 September 2012 to the offshore Pengjia Islet north of Taiwan and announced the Implementation Guidelines for his East China Sea Peace Initiative. Ma reiterated his proposal that the Peace Initiative should progress in two stages, starting with peaceful dialogue and mutually reciprocal negotiations, and followed by the sharing of resources and cooperative development among Taiwan, Japan and China. President Ma made a subtle and modest adjustment to the proposal by calling for an arrangement of three sets of bilateral negotiations. In addition to Japan/China and Taiwan/Japan, Ma, for the first time, revealed that Taiwan and China should also conduct negotiations over the settlement of the Diaoyutai dispute.[17]

On 25 September 2012, China's first aircraft carrier *Liaoning* was handed over to the navy of the People's Liberation Army amid rising tensions over disputed waters in the East China Sea. On the same day, dozens of Taiwan's fishing boats, with financial support from the *China Times* and an escort provided by Coast Guard Administration patrol vessels, entered waters surrounding the Diaoyutai Islands. Although the Taiwanese fishermen were conducting separate protest actions, Japan and the US had the impression that Taiwan and China were working in tandem. This led to the absence of senior US defence and diplomatic officials from the US–Taiwan Defence Industry Conference on 1 October 2012 (Mo 2012: 3).

In April 2013, Taipei and Tokyo surprisingly reached a fishing agreement over the Diaoyutai waters at the seventeenth round of fishery talks that had begun in 1996. The agreement gave Taiwan an additional fishing zone of 1,400 square nautical miles outside Taiwan's self-drawn temporary enforcement line dating from 2003. Waters within 12 nautical miles surrounding the Diaoyutai Islands were exempted from the agreement. Beijing was extremely concerned and reacted angrily, expressing the hope that 'Japan earnestly abides by its promises on the Taiwan issue and acts cautiously and appropriately'.(Shih 2013:1) Given the improvements in cross-Strait relations under the influence of China's rise, the Prime Minister Shinzo Abe (Liberal Democratic Party) apparently wanted to use the fishing agreement to 'prevent Taiwan and China from forming a joint front against Japan in the Senkaku dispute'.[18]

President Ma publicly supported the strengthening of the US–Japan security alliance through the settlement of the Futenma marine base relocation between the Obama administration and the Democratic Party of Japan.[19] Partly because of fluid and uncertain cross-Strait relations, and partly because of the Chinese navy's excursion into waters to the east of Taiwan, the Japanese government decided to extend the ADIZ of Yonakuni Island, which is located 100 km to the east of Taiwan, into the air space closer to Taiwan. Tokyo is also planning to station self-defence forces on Yonakuni Island. Such a move demonstrates that Japan is very concerned about Chinese naval activities near Taiwan and is not completely comfortable with the recent improvement of cross-Strait relations.[20] The Ma government has not accepted either Japan's expansion of its ADIZ or China's creation of the new ADIZ in the East China Sea. In February 2014, President Ma Ying-Jeou again called for multilateral negotiations to establish an East China Sea code of conduct covering both sea and air in order to reduce tensions in the region (Mo and Chung 2014: 3). The constraints and dilemmas that the KMT government faces exist not only in the East China Sea but also in the South China Sea.

Although the strategic value of the Spratly Islands is debatable, the US government has adamantly maintained that its interest lies in freedom of navigation and has indicated that it holds a neutral position on the claims of disputants on specific islands or reefs in the Spratlys (Dumbaugh *et al.* 2001: 9; Till 2009: 36–37). A series of standoffs in the South China Sea between China and the US erupted in 2009. For example, the USNS *Impeccable* was harassed by five Chinese ships in the South China Sea and accused of conducting illegal activities in the Chinese EEZs (Rahman and Tsamenyi 2010: 326). The US protested against Chinese attempts 'to place limits on the exercise of high seas freedoms with an exclusive economic zone' and established a high-level defence policy dialogue with Vietnam and Malaysia in 2009 to safeguard international maritime interest in the South China Sea (US Congress 2009: 11).[21] The Pentagon issued a warning in 2010 that 'a stronger regional military presence would position China for force projection, blockade, and surveillance operations to influence the critical sea lanes in the region' (Office of the Secretary of Defense 2010: 51).

In July 2010, the US Secretary of State Hillary Clinton raised the South China Sea issue at the ASEAN Regional Forum (ARF) by offering to facilitate moves to create a code of conduct in the region. Clinton also said to other members that 'legitimate claims to maritime space in the South China Sea should be derived solely from legitimate claims to land features' (Pomfret 2010). On 25 July 2010, the Chinese Foreign Minister Yang Jiechi sharply criticized the US for internationalizing the South China Sea issue, which he claimed would only make matters worse and complicate the situation. For Beijing, the best way to solve the disputes is through bilateral negotiations between China and individual claimants, without interference from non-claimants including the US and Japan.[22] Chinese harassment of US, Vietnamese and Philippine ships in the South China Sea led Jim Webb (Democratic senator from Virginia) to introduce Senate Resolution 217 (June 2011), which condemned the repeated use of force by naval and maritime security vessels from China and supported 'the continuation of operations by the United States Armed Forces to assert and defend freedom of navigation rights in international waters and air space in the South China Sea'.[23] The Chinese navy's dangerous manoeuvres in its EEZs in the South China Sea have not stopped: for example, the USS *Cowpens* was forced to take evasive action to avoid a collision with a Chinese military ship escorting the *Liaoning* aircraft carrier in December 2013.

Although the US has long claimed to maintain a neutral position on the competing territorial claims, the Obama administration has gradually adopted a less friendly position on assertive Chinese policies in the South China Sea. The US Department has criticized China's upgrading of the administrative level of Sansha City and urged China to stop its land reclamation projects in the South China Sea. The Obama administration has also supported the Philippine approach to take the nine-dash line dispute to international arbitration and calls for a freeze on construction in areas under dispute.

Cross-Strait cooperation projects on oil exploration in the northern part of the South China Sea were revived in December 2008, when oil corporations from both sides of the Taiwan Strait signed a Memorandum of Understanding (MOU) to extend exploration surveying every two years. Taipei and Beijing reacted separately but strongly in March 2009 over Filipino legislation that defined the archipelagic baselines of the Philippines as including the disputed islands and reefs of the Kalayaan (Spratly) archipelago and the nearby Scarborough Shoal (Adriano 2009). In May 2009, Taiwan and the PRC each issued a protest against a joint submission of claims by Malaysia and Vietnam related to jurisdiction over their continental shelf that extends beyond 200 nautical miles from the baselines to the United Nations Commission on the Limits of the Continental Shelf (CLCS).[24]

After Clinton's remarks at the ARF meeting in Hanoi, China and ASEAN decided to conduct intensive discussions to reach an agreement on the Guidelines for the Implementation of the Declaration on the Conduct of Parties in the South China Sea immediately before the ARF meeting in Bali in July 2011 (Yan 2011: 10–13). While the US welcomed the implementation guidelines agreement, Taiwan was once more left out of the negotiation process and therefore refuses to recognize any agreements related to the South China Sea.[25] Facing pressure from the US and ASEAN, Beijing has been more eager to enlist Taiwan's support to jointly assert Chinese sovereignty in the South China Sea. Beijing is appreciative of Taiwan's contribution to safeguarding Taiping Island when China was absent in the region before 1988. As cross-Strait relations become more cordial, military analysts in China have been anxious to propose joint studies, development, patrols, and defence of the sovereignty in the South China Sea.[26]

Some analysts in the US are worried that collaboration between China and Taiwan in the South China Sea will complicate the US's own relations with Southeast Asian countries (Pearson 2011: 8). In 2012, Kurt Campbell (at that time, an Assistant Secretary of State) raised the same concern with Taiwan, saying that 'Taiwan assured [the US] that it would be careful' (Kan 2014: 51). Improved cross-Strait relations might translate into the disappearance of Taiwan as a buffer between ASEAN and China over the Spratly disputes. Observations such as these are by no means groundless. Proposals of cross-Strait CBMs in the South China Sea initiated by Taiwan have been under examination, including the 'exchange of monitoring information on activities taken by other claimants' and 'setting up hotlines or notification mechanisms to assist stationed military and coast guard personnel' (Song 2005: 279). In the Indonesia-sponsored South China Sea Workshop in 2009, participants from Taiwan and China agreed that Taipei and Beijing could take turns to sponsor a marine scientific research training seminar in 2010 and 2011. Taiwan's retired generals and think tanks closely affiliated with the KMT in Taipei publicly recommended cooperation with Beijing in the South China Sea.[27]

A situation in which Taiwan joins hands with China to support Chinese legal claims against those of other ASEAN countries, while the US continues to sell arms to Taiwan, must seem completely unacceptable to US policy-makers. The Ma government appreciates the sensitivity of the South China Sea issue. Accordingly, Taipei has repeatedly claimed that it will not seek cooperation from Beijing in handling the Spratly Islands disputes.[28]

Taipei has, for the most part, remained quiet with regard to the rifts between China and Vietnam over oil exploration and the conflict between China and the Philippines over the sovereignty of the Scarborough Shoal and Second Thomas Shoal. The Ma government has not criticized any of these three claimants and simply issued a statement asserting that the ROC 'enjoys all rights over the islands and their surrounding waters, and that it does not accept any claim to sovereignty over, or occupation of, these areas by other countries' in the South China Sea. Beijing has urged Taipei to conduct joint maritime patrols in the South China Sea, but Taipei, ironically enough, has declined in order not to alienate the US defence community.[29] Responding to PRC military action against

Taiwan-controlled islands in the South China Sea is beyond the scope of the Taiwan Relations Act.

The growing US attention on the South China Sea has created constraints for Taiwan regarding cooperation with China both in joint oil exploration and in policy coordination vis-à-vis other ASEAN claimants. The concern over a potential conflict between the US and the PRC in the South China Sea region could place Taiwan in an awkward position. If Taiwan allies itself closely with the PRC in the South China Sea territorial disputes, the US may face more domestic calls to reconsider its role in defending Taiwan against the PRC's use of force. If Taiwan openly supports an increased US presence in the South China Sea, this could rekindle Beijing's suspicions about Taiwan's intentions and could possibly lead to a setback in the development of cross-Strait economic and functional cooperation.

Conclusion

The US is not totally free of challenges concerning the Taiwan issue, particularly those related to US arms sales to the island. It would hardly be possible for any cross-Strait CBMs or peace agreement drafts to deviate from Beijing's 'one China' principle. A public referendum before signing a peace agreement can attest that President Ma Ying-Jeou's pledge that Taiwan's future is in the hands of the 23 million Taiwanese and theirs alone. Under the shadow of China's rise, some doubts remain as to whether Taipei's leaders would be willing to fight to preserve the freedom of choice and also whether the US government would be willing to act in line with the principle it has cherished for centuries.

China's rise has increased Beijing's capacity to force Taiwan to accept its terms, using either the carrot or the stick. If the military, economic, social and diplomatic aspects are taken into consideration, cross-Strait relations still seem to be quite dynamic, and maintaining the status quo across the Taiwan Strait therefore appears impossible. When the DPP government was in office, Beijing urged the US to constrain President Chen, but now it is asking the US to keep its hands off the Taiwan issue. President Ma's policy toward China has given Beijing new hopes concerning unification, and Beijing has proposed that the two sides enter into political negotiations with no necessity of involving the US. The question now facing the US is whether, given that creeping independence is seen as destabilizing the status quo, Taiwan's creeping unification also poses a threat to the future stability of the region. The TRA was successful in its first 35 years, but this does not mean that it will be free from challenge, or effective, in future decades. The rise of China and the improvements in cross-Strait relations have created a different security environment and new challenges for policy-makers in Taipei and Washington.

Tensions in the Taiwan Strait have abated since President Ma took office, and Beijing might, as a consequence, believe that a window of opportunity has been created for cross-Strait cooperation in the South China Sea. For President Ma and the KMT, all the islands and reefs inside the U-shaped line drawn in 1947 by the ROC government in the South China Sea belong to the Chinese people. Nevertheless, President Ma is trying to walk a tightrope without tilting toward China in any joint military actions against other claimants. On the other hand, the Ma government is aware of the sensitive implications of tilting toward the US in a Sino-American conflict in waters in East Asia. Cross-Strait CBMs in the South China Sea cannot be dealt with separately from the situation in the Taiwan Strait, but it will be more difficult to establish them in the East China Sea due to Taipei's dependence on Japan's political support and the Japan–US security arrangements for Taiwan's security. Having encouraged CBMs in the Taiwan Strait for some time, the US does not seem to have any justification for blocking similar arrangements in the East China Sea or in the South China Sea. However, the US has remained vigilant because cooperation between China and Taiwan, whether in the Taiwan Strait, in the waters of the East China Sea or in the South China Sea, often has security ramifications for Japan, ASEAN and the United States.

Notes

1 *Xinhuanet* (2012).
2 Rice (2013).
3 'Major Foreign Holders of Treasury Securities' (n.d.).
4 BBC News (2010).
5 'IMF Quotas' (2012).
6 Wang (2012).
7 Japan Cabinet Office (n.d.).
8 The first island chain is referred to as a line through the Kurile Islands, the Ryukyu Islands, Taiwan and the Philippines. The second island chain runs from the Kurile Islands, the Bonins and the Marianas to the Carolines.
9 Security Consultative Committee (2011).
10 President Obama has provided Taiwan with the following military items: a retrofit package for Taiwan's 145 F-16A/B aircraft, including the advanced Active Electronically Scanned Array (AESA) radar, and other advanced technologies and weapons systems; an extension of the F-16 Pilot Training Programme; spare parts for F-5, C-130, and F-16A/B aircraft; 60 UH-60M Blackhawk Utility Helicopters; Patriot Advanced Capability-3 (PAC-III) Fire Units, Training Unit, and Missiles; Multifunctional Information Distribution Systems technical support for Taiwan's command and control system; 2 *Osprey*-class mine-hunter ships; Harpoon Telemetry Training Missiles; Hughes Air Defence Radar (Direct Commercial Sale); Indigenous Defence Fighter (IDF) Radar (Direct Commercial Sale); IDF Colour Display (Direct Commercial Sale); Small Arms (Direct Commercial Sale). See US Congress (2011a: 14–15).
11 Swaine (2011b).
12 Rigger (2011).
13 White House (2008).
14 White House (2009).
15 Steinberg (2009).
16 Office of the President, Republic of China (Taiwan) (2010a).
17 Office of the President, Republic of China (Taiwan) (2010b).
18 *Japan Times* (2013).
19 Office of the President, Republic of China (Taiwan) (2010a).

20 Matsuda (2009).
21 Scher (2009).
22 *China Daily* (2010).
23 'Inhofe, Webb Introduce Resolution' (2011).
24 See ROC Ministry of Foreign Affairs (2009). Under the United Nations Convention on the Law of the Sea, the coastal state shall establish the outer limits of its continental shelf where it extends beyond 200 nautical miles on the basis of the recommendation of the CLCS.
25 ROC Ministry of Foreign Affairs (2011).
26 *China Review* (2010).
27 Fu (2011); Kao (2010).
28 Le (2011).
29 Tzeng (2011).

References

Adriano, Joel D. (2009) 'China, Philippines Stoke Island Tensions', *Asia Times*, 27 March.

Babones, Salvatore (2011) 'The Middle Kingdom: The Hype and the Reality of China's Rise', *Foreign Affairs*, 90, 5: 79–80.

BBC News (2010) 'Australian PM Kevin Rudd "Sought Tough China Policy"', 6 December, available at www.bbc.co.uk/news/world-asia-pacific-11925438 (accessed 29 June 2014).

Bilefsky, Dan (2011) 'China Delays Report Suggesting North Korea Violated Sanctions', *New York Times*, 14 May.

Brzezinski, Zbigniew (2012) 'Balancing the East, Upgrading the West: U.S. Grand Strategy in an Age of Upheaval', *Foreign Affairs*, 91, 1: 103.

Bush, Richard (2011) 'Taiwan and East Asian Security', *Orbis*, 55, 2: 275–286.

China Daily (2010) 'Chinese FM Refutes Fallacies on the South China Sea Issue', 25 July, available at www.chinadaily.com.cn/china/2010–07/25/content110460 54.htm (accessed 29 June 2014).

China Review (2010), Major General Luo Yuan's remarks, 15 March, available at www.chinareviewnews.com/doc/1012/6/0/0/101260078.html?coluid=7&kindid=0&docid=101260078. (accessed 29 June 2014).

Dumbaugh, Kerry, Ackerman, David, Cronin, Richard, Kan, Shirley, and Niksch, Larry (2001) *China's Maritime Territorial Claims*, Washington DC: Congressional Research Service.

Ferguson, Niall (2007) 'Not Two Countries, But One: Chimerica', *Telegraph*, 4 March.

Fu, Ying-Chuan (2011) article, *Want Daily* (Taipei), 14 July.

Gertz, Bill (2010) 'Admiral: China's Buildup Aimed at Power Past Asia', *Washington Times*, 26 March.

Gilley, Bruce (2010) 'Not so Dire Strait: How the Finlandization of Taiwan Benefits US Security', *Foreign Affairs*, 89, 1: 44–60.

Glaser, Bonnie, and Glosserman, Brad (2010) 'China's Cheonan Problem', *PacNet*, 18 June.

Glaser, Charles (2011) 'Will China's Rise Lead to War?' *Foreign Affairs*, 90, 2: 80–91.

Godement, Francois (2010) 'The United States and Asia in 2009: Public Diplomacy and Strategic Continuity', *Asian Survey*, 50, 1: 21.

Goldstein, Avery (2005) *Rising to the Challenge: China's Grand Strategy and International Security*, Stanford CA: Stanford University Press.

Hodge, Nathan (2011) 'Beijing's Top General says U.S. Overstates China Threat', *Wall Street Journal*, 19 May.

Ikenberry, G. John (2008) 'The Rise of China: Power, Institutions, and the Western Order', in Ross, Robert, and Feng, Zhu (eds) *China's Ascent: Power, Security, and the Future of International Politics*, Ithaca NY: Cornell University Press.

'IMF Quotas' (2012), 30 March, available at www.imf.org/external/np/exr/facts/pdf/quotas.pdf (accessed 29 June 2014).

'Inhofe, Webb Introduce Resolution Condemning China's Use of Force in South China Sea' (2011), 13 June, available at www.inhofe.senate.gov/newsroom/press-releases/inhofe-webb-introduce-resolution-condemning-chinas-use-of-force-in-south-china-sea (accessed 29 June 2014).

Japan Cabinet Office (n.d.) 'Public Opinion on Foreign Relations', available at http://www8.cao.go.njp/survey/index-gai.html (accessed 26 June 2014).

Japan Times (2013) 'A Positive Step in Senkaku Dispute', editorial, 14 April, available at www.japantimes.co.jp/opinion/2013/04/14/editorials/a-positive-step-in-senkaku-dispute/#.UfCj6BUVFdg (accessed 29 June 2014).

Kachi, Hiroyuki (2012) 'Japanese Leader Warns on China's Military Buildup', *Wall Street Journal*, 19 March.

Kagan, Robert (2012) 'Not Fade Away: The Myth of American Decline', *New Republic*, 2 February, 24–25.

Kan, Shirley A. (2014) *Taiwan: Major U.S. Arms Sales since 1990*, Washington DC: Congressional Research Service.

Kao, Yung-Kuang (2010) 'An Analysis of Cross-Strait Cooperation in the South China Sea', National Policy Forum Commentary, 7 January, available at www.npf. org.tw/post/1/6923 (accessed 29 June 2014).

Kim, Yongho (2011) *North Korean Foreign Policy: Security Dilemma and Succession*, Lanham MD: Lexington Books.

Kupchan, Charles A. (2012) 'The Democratic Malaise: Globalization and the Threat to the West', *Foreign Affairs*, 91, 1: 63–64.

Le, Bryan (2011) 'Negotiations with a Giant: Taiwan's 'Win-Win' Strategy', *Asia Society*, 12 July, available at http://asiasociety.org/policy/strategic-challenges/intra-asia/negotiations-giant-taiwans-win-win-strategy (accessed 29 June 2014).

'Major Foreign Holders of Treasury Securities' (n.d.), available at www.treasury.gov/ticdata/Publish/mfh.txt (accessed 29 June 2014).

Manyin, Mark E. (2012) *Pivot to the Pacific? The Obama Administration's 'Rebalancing' Toward Asia*, Washington, DC: Congressional Research Service.

Matsuda, Yasuhiro (2009) 'Improve Cross-Strait Relations Confusing to the Japanese', Association of Japanese Institute of Strategic Studies Commentary, 80, 28 December, available at www2.jiia.or.jp/en_commentary/200912/28–1.html (accessed 29 June 2014).

Mearsheimer, John J. (2014) 'Taiwan's Dire Straits', *National Interest*, 130: 29–39.

Mo, Yan-Chih (2012) 'Diaoyutais Spat Hasn't Hurt US Ties: Ma'. *Taipei Times*, 3 October, 3.

Mo, Yan-Chih, and Chung, Jake (2014) 'Ma Urges Sea Code of Conduct to Counter China's ADIZ', *Taipei Times*, 27 February, 3.

Office of the President, Republic of China (Taiwan) (2010a), 'President Ma Interviewed by Japan's *Nihon Keizai Shimbun*', 13 May, available at http://english.president.gov.tw/Default.aspx?tabid=491&itemid=21473&rmid=2355&size=100 (accessed 29 June 2014).

Office of the President, Republic of China (Taiwan) (2010b) 'President Ma Interviewed by Japan's *Sankei Shimbun* Newspaper', 19 August, available at http://english.president.gov.tw/Default.aspx?tabid=491&itemid=22205&rmid=2355&size=100 (accessed 29 June 2014).

Office of the President, Republic of China (Taiwan) (2012) 'President Ma Visits Pengjia Islet', 7 September, available at http://english.president.gov.tw/default.aspx?tabid=491&itemid=28074&rmid=2355 (accessed 29 June 2014).

Office of the Secretary of Defense (2010) *Military and Security Developments Involving the People's Republic of China*, August.

Pan, Jason (2014) 'Reliance on China Makes Taiwan Vulnerable: Clinton', *Taipei Times*, 25 June, 1.

Pearson, Richard (2011) 'Taiwan and the South China Sea', *Taipei Times*, 1 July, 8.

Pomfret, John (2010) 'U.S. Takes a Tougher Tone with China', *Washington Post*, 30 July.

Rahman, Chris, and Tsamenyi, Martin (2010) 'A Strategic Perspective on Security and Naval Issues in the South China Sea', *Ocean Development and International Law*, 41, 4: 315–333.

Rice, Susan E. (2013) 'America's Future in Asia', remarks delivered at Georgetown University, Washington DC, 20 November, available at www.whitehouse. gov/the-press-office/2013/11/21/remarks-prepared-delive-ry-national-security-advisor-susan-e-rice (accessed 29 June 2014).

Rigger, Shelley (2011) 'Why Giving up Taiwan Will Not Help Us with China', speech at American Enterprise Institute, 29 November, available at www.aei.org/article/foreign-and-defense-policy/regional/asia/why-giving-up-taiwan-will-not-help-us-with-china (accessed 29 June 2014).

ROC Ministry of Foreign Affairs (2009) 'Statement on the Outer Limits of the ROC Continental Shelf', 11 May, available at www.mofa.gov.tw/News_ Content_M_2.aspx?n=5028B03CED127255&sms=5ED24855AD8E6C58&s=E250B02D16CDA92E (accessed 29 June 2014).

ROC Ministry of Foreign Affairs (2011), 20 July, available at http://web.pts.org.tw/hakka/news/detail.php?id=73739 (accessed 29 June 2014).

Ross, Robert S. (2010) 'The Rise of Chinese Power and the Implications for the Regional Security Order', *Orbis*, 54, 4: 531.

Saunders, Phillip C., and Kastner, Scott L. (2009) 'Bridge over Troubled Water? Envisioning a China–Taiwan Peace Agreement', *International Security*, 33, 4: 87–114.

Scher, Robert (2009) Testimony of the Deputy Assistant Secretary of Defense, Robert Scher, Asian and Pacific Security Affairs, Office of the Secretary of Defense, before the Subcommittee on East Asia and Pacific Affairs, Committee on Foreign Relations, United States Senate, 15 July, available at http://foreign.senate.gov/imo/media/doc/ScherTestimony 090715p1.pdf. (accessed 29 June 2014).

Security Consultative Committee (2011) 'Toward a Deeper and Broader US–Japan Alliance: Building on 50 Years of Partnership', Joint Statement, 21 June, available at www.mofa.go.jp/region/namerica/us/security/pdfs/joint1106_01.pdf (accessed 26 June 2014).

Shambaugh, David (2010) 'A New China Requires a New US Strategy', *Current History*, 109, 728: 224–225.

Shih, Hsiu-Chuan (2012) 'Abandoning Taiwan is 'Unthinkable', Ex-Obama Administration Official Says', *Taipei Times*, 28 March, 3.

Shih, Hsiu-Chuan (2013) 'Taiwan, Japan Ink Fisheries Agreement', *Taipei Times*, 11 April, 1.

Shlapak, David A., Orletsky, David T., Reid, Toy I., Tanner, Murray Scot, and Barry Wilson (2009) *A Question of Balance: Political Context and Military Aspects of the China–Taiwan Dispute*, Santa Monica CA: Rand.

Song, Yann-Huei (2005) 'Cross-Strait Interactions on the South China Sea Issues: A Need for CBMs', *Marine Policy*, 29, 3: 279.

Steinberg, James B. (2009) 'Administration's Vision of the U.S.–China Relationship', remarks delivered at Center for a New American Security, Washington DC, 24 September, available at www.state.gov/s/d/former/steinberg/remarks/2009/169332.htm (accessed 29 June 2014).

Subramanian, Arvind (2011) 'Inevitable Superpower: Why China's Dominance is a Sure Thing', *Foreign Affairs*, 90, 5: 69.

Sutter, Robert (2005) 'China's Regional Strategy and Why it May Not be Good for America', in Shambaugh, David (ed.) *Power Shift: China and Asia's New Dynamics*, Berkeley: University of California Press.

Sutter, Robert (2009) 'Cross-Strait Moderations and the United States – Policy Adjustment Needed', *PacNet*, 5 March.

Swaine, Michael (2011a) *America's Challenge: Engaging a Rising China in the Twenty-First Century*, Washington DC: Carnegie Endowment for International Peace.

Swaine, Michael (2011b) 'China, Taiwan, U.S.: Status Quo Challenged', *National Interest*, 11 October, available at http://nationalinterest.org/commentary/us-provoking-china-over-taiwan-5996 (accessed 29 June 2014).

Till, Geoffrey (2009) 'The South China Sea Dispute: An International History', in Bateman, Sam, and Emmers, Ralf (eds) *Security and International Politics in the South China Sea*, London: Routledge.

Tzeng, Emmanuelle, and Kuo, Deborah (2011) 'Taiwan Will not Consult China on Spratly Issue: MND', 5 August, available at http://focustaiwan.tw/ShowNews/WebNews_Detail.aspx?ID=201108050042&Type=aIPL (accessed 29 June 2014).

US Congress (2009) *Maritime Disputes and Sovereignty Issues in East Asia*, Hearing before the Subcommittee on East Asia and Pacific Affairs, Committee on Foreign Relations, United States Senate, 112th Congress, 1st Session (15 July), Washington DC: US Government Printing Office.

US Congress (2011a) *Why Taiwan Matters*, Hearing before the Committee on Foreign Affairs, House of Representatives, 112th Congress, 1st Session (16 June), Washington DC: US Government Printing Office.

US Congress (2011b) *Why Taiwan Matters, Part II*, Hearing before the Committee on Foreign Affairs, House of Representatives, 112th Congress, 1st Session (4 October), Washington DC: US Government Printing Office.

Wang, Jisi (2011) 'China's Search for a Grand Strategy', *Foreign Affairs*, 90, 2: 76.

Wang, Qi (2012) 'China and U.S. Not G2, But C2', 4 May, available at http://english.sina.com/china/2012/0503/464519.html (accessed 29 June 2014).

White House (2008) 'Statement by the President on Taiwan Election', 22 March, available at http://georgewbush-whitehouse.archives.gov/news/releases/2008/03/2008 0322–4.html (accessed 29 June 2014).

White House (2009) 'Joint Press Statement by President Obama and President Hu of China', 17 November, available at www.whitehouse.gov/the-press-office/joint-press-statement-president-obama-and-president-hu-china (accessed 29 June 2014).

Xinhuanet (2012) 'Obama Says U.S. Welcomes Peaceful Rise of China', 15 February, available at http://news.xinhuanet.com/english/world/2012–02/15/c1227016 85.htm (accessed 29 June 2014).

Yan, Yu (2011) 'Bridge over Troubled Water', *Beijing Review*, 54, 31: 10–13.

Zakaria, Fareed (2008) *The Post-American World*, New York: W. W. Norton.

Zha, Daojiong (2011) 'South China Sea Diplomacy: More Needs to be Done', *PacNet*, 19 July.

15 Cross-Strait integration and Taiwan's new security challenges

Jean-Pierre Cabestan

Many analysts argue that cross-Strait integration has directly contributed towards stabilizing the relationship between China and Taiwan (Kastner 211:9). This stabilizing factor was already perceptible under the Chen Shui-Bian presidency (2000–2008) and even at the end of the Lee Teng-Hui era, but has become more visible and obvious since Ma Ying-Jeou's election. Indeed, since 2008, on the surface, Taiwan's security has dramatically improved: not only has a genuine détente emerged, but also what Ma himself described as a 'rapprochement' has taken place across the Taiwan Strait. However, on the ground, Taiwan's military and non-military security challenges have intensified.

On the one hand, the capability of Taiwan (Republic of China, ROC) to defend itself and protect the island from outside aggression has deteriorated; in addition, since no military confidence-building measures (CBMs) have been initiated with mainland China (People's Republic of China, PRC) military incidents cannot be excluded or managed properly. More importantly, however, the growing capability of the People's Liberation Army (PLA) to project power and exert pressure on the island as well as the Ma administration's lack of investment in defence have made Taiwan more and more dependent on the de facto US security guarantee – the Taiwan Relations Act (TRA). At a time when the United States' relative decline has become more perceptible, Beijing has been intensifying its pressure on Washington to stop providing weapons to the island, and a debate is looming in the US on its own long-term capability and interest in the context of guaranteeing Taiwan's security.

On the other hand, Taiwan's accelerated economic and social integration with mainland China has deepened the former's dependence upon the latter, enhanced China's political influence and eased its united front work on the island, not only with the business community but also with the political and cultural elites as well as society as a whole.

To be sure, many of Taiwan's security challenges are not really new. Some have their origins in the end of the Chinese civil war in 1949 and the asymmetry between the territory, the population and the (potential) resources that both Chinese governments have respectively controlled since then. Others stem from the PRC's economic and military rise after Deng Xiaoping decided to reform and open up his country in 1979 and to speed up this process in 1992. Still others are directly related to Chiang Ching-Kuo's and his successors' acceptance of indirect and direct trade, people-to-people and non-official relations with mainland China. And the Taiwanese people's deep political divisions over the island's identity and status as well as the nature and the future of its relations with the PRC have also, especially since the beginning of the democratization process in 1986–1987, constituted a well-rooted security challenge.

Nevertheless, Ma's election and the Kuomintang (KMT)'s return to power in 2008 initiated an unprecedented mainland policy that has contributed towards increasing these challenges and creating new ones that are far from being all of a military nature. The growing interactions across the Strait have already multiplied the number of constituencies on the island that have a vested interest in maintaining a close and stable relationship with the mainland, creating tensions within Taiwanese society (see below); they also have the potential to modify the Taiwanese people's perception of the mainland, loosen Taiwan's security relationship with the US and eventually their perception of the PRC, their identity and their attachment to the status quo in the Strait – or what I would call the island's de facto independence – precisely at a time when the impression of a US strategic decline is gaining momentum.

In this chapter, I do not aim to address all these issues in detail but rather to provide some very tentative and provisional answers. My conclusion is that, while Taiwan, with US support, will be able to remain a distinct democratic political entity under the ROC constitutional framework, the island's room for manoeuvre and, possibly, its political autonomy will continue to shrink.

Taiwan's military challenges

The military challenges facing Taiwan are well-known and, since 2008, in spite of the new détente across the Strait, have continued to grow. The PLA threat has intensified unabated; Taiwan's defence effort has been stagnating in spite of the January 2010 and September 2011 US weapon package announcements as well as a few new initiatives, such as the phasing out of the drafting system. Taiwan's will to fight seems to depend increasingly upon US commitment to the island's security, and Taiwan's military is becoming more and more vulnerable to China's espionage. Nevertheless, Taiwan has the capability, with US support and assistance, to maintain a credible defence system served by an asymmetrical military strategy.

The PLA's growing threat

Most experts agree that the military balance in the Taiwan Strait tilted in favour of China in around 2005. The PLA's capability to project forces across the Taiwan Strait has since then continued to expand. While, according to US military sources, the number of conventional missiles pointed at Taiwan reached a ceiling in 2010 (over 1,000), their sophistication and accuracy have continued to improve (Office of the Secretary of Defense 2014: 6, 36). In any event, ballistic missiles as opposed to cruise missile and other more modern weapon systems are just one small feature of the military balance. The ability of the PLA Navy and Air Force to take control of the Taiwan Strait and impose a blockade on the island, even if not to successfully launch a landing operation, has become much more credible, forcing the US to review its own counter-strategy (Shlapak 2009). The PLA has also beefed up its coastal air defence, especially in Fujian, and can now directly threaten Taiwanese fighters entering airspace over the northern Taiwan Strait. Moreover, China's capability to eavesdrop on Taiwan's military and intercept the island's electronic signals has been upgraded, enhancing the PLA's edge in digital warfare.

It is clear that in the same period of time, PLA missions have diversified: for example, to mention just a few, maintaining a stronger presence in the South and the East China Seas, anti-piracy operations in the Gulf of Aden and military operations other than wars (such as disaster relief operations), which have served to divert the Chinese military from the Taiwan theatre, at least to some extent. However, the PLA has also continued to include Taiwan among its priority military targets as well as the probability of US military involvement in any war over the island. While building aircraft carriers, J-20 stealth fighters and anti-ship ballistic missiles DF-21D (1,500 km) – three of the most advanced and symbolic PLA modernization projects – is part of a wider and more ambitious empowerment plan, it also underscores China's willingness to impose a new and more advantageous military balance on both Taiwan and US forward deployment forces (Cordesman and Yarosh 2012).

Taiwan's defence policy adjustment and weaknesses

As a consequence, since the middle of the 2000s, Taiwan has been compelled to put together an *asymmetric* military strategy that is aimed at deterring any unprovoked PLA attack. To be credible, Taiwan's military must ensure that the cost of such an attack remains prohibitive for the PLA and China, or *at least* much higher than the expected benefits of this operation, and, as a result, forces Beijing to think twice before contemplating any 'non-peaceful' option for 'solving the Taiwan issue'.

Enshrined in the TRA, the US commitment to Taiwan security has remained very strong, although deliberately vague; the daily cooperation between the Pentagon and the Taiwanese armed forces is, today, much closer and better than before the 1996 missile crisis. Ma's 2008 electoral promises to build a 'hard ROC', to increase the defence budget to three per cent of GDP and to move towards an all-volunteer military were well received in Washington. This came after nearly a decade of cuts in military expenditures – by around 40 per cent between 1999 and 2008 – and political bickering in the Legislative Yuan (Taiwan's parliament) about the relevance and financing of the unprecedented arms package granted by George W. Bush in 2001 (including for the first time diesel submarines, which the US has, however, been unable to manufacture). However, during his first term, Ma did not keep his promises, and he has not done so in his second term so far.

This does not mean that he has not taken defence seriously. Although he initially adopted a purely defensive strategy inspired by the US expert, William Murray (Murray 2008), under the pressure of the military, he has maintained and modernized the Taiwanese armed forces' offensive capability. And since 2008, the US and especially the Obama Administration have committed more arms sales to Taiwan than the Bush government in the seven previous years (US$18.3 billion and US$12.25 billion respectively).

It is true that as formulated in March 2009, in the Taiwan Defence Ministry's first Quadrennial Defence Review (QDR), Ma's defence strategy restored the pre-2000 order of priorities: 'resolute defence and effective deterrence' (*fangwei gushou, youxiao hezu*), as opposed to the 'effective deterrence and resolute defence' and 'active defence' strategies put forward under Chen Shui-Bian.

Nonetheless, for many reasons, including resistance among the Taiwanese military, both the QDR and the National Defence Report (NDR) published in October 2009 made recommendations stating that Taiwan should maintain an offensive capability and continue to develop conventional weapons, such as Hsiung-feng-2E cruise missiles (650–800 km), that were capable of striking and neutralizing targets on the other side of the Strait.[1] In other words, Chen's 'active defence' has not been completely shelved; only the ambitious and unrealistic objectives of moving the 'decisive battle outside the territory' (*jingwai juezhan*) and developing offensive weapons such as long-range missiles (over 1,000 km) targeting non-military objectives have clearly been abandoned (Chen 2009: 8–12). In addition, the Ma government has continued to invest heavily in the Navy and the Air Force. Since 2009, it has developed high-tech fast-attack missile corvettes, dubbed 'carrier killers', which are also equipped with powerful supersonic anti-ship Hsiung-feng III cruise missiles and are more capable of posing a threat to the PLA surface ships in the Strait. And in 2011, the Obama administration accepted to retrofit Taiwan's current 145 F-16 A/N for a price-tag of US$5.8 billion.

Nevertheless, in spite of Ma's promises, Taiwan's defence budget has not just stagnated but has decreased in real terms. Amounting US$10.5 billion in 2008, the budget fell to US$9.6 billion in 2009 and US$9.3 billion in 2010 before slightly increasing again to US$10.2 billion in 2011 and to US$10.6 billion in 2012. In 2013 and 2014, the defence budget amounted to US$10.5 billion and US$10.4 billion respectively, confirming the lack of additional investment in defence. But more importantly, between 2008 and 2014, Taiwan's defence budget share decreased from 2.5 per cent to 2.0 per cent of GDP and from 20.2 per cent to 16.2 per cent of total government expenditures (Kan 2014: 33–34). Although the financial crisis was used to justify the 2009 drop, the subsequent reductions have been the result of higher social welfare expenditures (22 per cent of the state budget in 2014) as well as a mixture of savings and misallocations of funds for weapons systems that could not be delivered as anticipated.

Similarly, the transition to an all-volunteer force by 2015 has revealed itself to be much more expensive and slower than originally planned – it was postponed until 2017: the 2011 personnel budget has been able to support less than half (5,000) of the additional volunteer personnel that need to be recruited according to the already revised target (11,000 instead of 15,000). And owing to the projected budget increase, in 2014, only 20 per cent of the recruitment objective will be met (9,000) (Mei 2011: 7–10).

Another growing danger for Taiwan's security is the PRC intensification of espionage activities on the island, qualified by the Premier, Wu Den-Yih, as a 'war without gunfire' in November 2010. The deepening interconnections between the two societies – the increasing number of retired Taiwanese officers that travel to and settle down on the mainland and the unprecedented surge in Chinese tourists – have made counter-espionage work more arduous. Rather than retired officers who may hold information that rapidly becomes outdated, active military officers are certainly privileged to be the targets of Chinese espionage. And Taiwan's political divisions and faltering ideological loyalties in the context of a rising China have contributed towards making easy prey of a larger number of Taiwanese professional military personnel. Although some additional restrictive measures (targeting, in particular, retired military personnel) have recently been adopted by the Ma Administration, the game seems to be becoming increasingly asymmetrical, and also perhaps hopeless, compelling the US military to think twice before transferring its most sophisticated and advanced weaponry to Taiwan.

Finally, and not without relation to the previous problem, there have been increasing doubts about the Taiwanese people's will to fight and invest in the island's military defence. The so-called 'peace dividend' that Ma and the KMT are expecting from the overall decrease in military tension with China has helped to convince many Taiwanese that less investment is required for defence (Huang 2010: 5). Moreover, the KMT's strong tendency, since 2008, to regard the mainland Chinese as 'brothers' (*xiongdi*) rather than 'enemies' (*diren*) has fuelled these doubts, especially in the US. Obviously, the PRC is both an economic partner and a military threat – which I have qualified elsewhere as 'Taiwan's strategic paradox' – and the growing influence of the PRC over Taiwan has been making many ROC citizens increasingly schizophrenic (see below). For instance, while on a scale from 1 to 10, war with China remains for most Taiwanese quite unlikely (3.2), 54 per cent of them have a negative impression of the PRC government, which they describe as 'authoritarian' and 'corrupt'.[2] Moreover, in a poll conducted in March 2014, 50.8 per cent of the Taiwanese stated that they still think that Beijing is hostile (the MAC now uses 'unfriendly') to the 'ROC government' (against 53.1 per cent in August 2008 and 39.5 per cent in December 2009) and 42.8 per cent of them think that it is hostile ('unfriendly') to the 'people of Taiwan' (against 45.1 per cent and 41.1 per cent respectively).[3]

Arguably, a professional military force would be better trained to use the sophisticated armaments that are in its possession and more ready to fight in case of war. But the bond with the nation is vital. For this reason, while accelerating the transition towards an all-volunteer force that is intended be completed by 2015, Taiwan's defence ministry has decided to retain a four-month basic training requirement for all male citizens when they reach 18 years of age. However, can an economy that is more interdependent on mainland China and a society that is culturally closer to mainland China than, say, France is to Germany, generate the material and moral support that would be necessary for its soldiers to defend Taiwan's sovereignty and de facto independence? At this stage, it is impossible to fully answer these questions. Studies have shown that US support and involvement would be a decisive factor, which is not surprising. In any event, since 2008, there has been a troubling lack of communication with the US (which has remained deliberately ambiguous about its potential involvement in any armed conflict in the Strait), as well as unrealistic assessments of the Taiwanese military's capabilities.

An underdeveloped security dialogue

As the current armed détente demonstrates, security constitutes a particularly important set of issues that have not yet been genuinely addressed by Beijing and Taipei. Although as early as 2004, China had shown the intention of including confidence-building measures (CBMs) in cross-Strait talks, an intention that was reiterated by Hu Jintao at the Eighteenth Chinese Communist Party (CCP) Congress in November 2012, military CBM negotiations have not been able to get off the ground, partly because they are still perceived, on both sides of the Strait, as closely connected to more sensitive political discussions, and partly because of other difficulties and limitations mentioned below (Glaser 2010). And after Xi Jinping succeeded Hu in late 2012, there is little chance for these obstacles to be overcome. China's more assertive foreign policy and the prospect of a DPP return to power in 2016 have on the contrary added more hurdles to any prospect of such a negotiation.

Since (and even before) 2008, some informal and, more importantly, secret talks have taken place. Simultaneously, non-official contacts and discussions involving academics and experts on political and security issues have also rapidly increased since then. Channels of communication already exist, for instance, between the coast guard forces of both sides, to avoid and manage incidents in the Strait. In 2010, the Taiwanese Coast Guards and the PRC Maritime Safety Administration held their first joint search and rescue operation. On 30 August 2012, they organized a second, much bigger, coordinated exercise, involving 2 helicopters, 14 vessels, 300 personnel and even one deputy-minister from each side of the Strait, and decided to carry out such operations every two years. Moreover, when necessary, and in times of crisis in particular, both sides have been able to hold high-level secret talks (Tucker 2009). In other words, communication and incident management are less of a problem than many observers have suspected.

Nevertheless, the many obstacles to the opening of CBMs negotiations mentioned in earlier publications still hold (Cabestan 2010: 27–29). First, through CBMs, Taiwan would attempt to alleviate the current level of PLA threat while China does not wish to discuss this issue, arguing that its military buildup is targeting not Taiwan but the US and Japan (Glaser 2011). Second, for Ma

Ying-Jeou, the withdrawal of the missiles was, at least until October 2011, when he launched the idea of concluding a peace agreement with the mainland, a pre-condition to any 'political talks', including CBMs. Although in his October 2011 announcement, Ma was vaguer about the 'reassurances' that China should give to Taiwan – 'safeguard Taiwan's security and prosperity' – it remains to be seen whether he will be able to move forward on military CBMs, let alone peace talks, before the mainland makes any move or gesture. However, so far, for Beijing, adjustments to military deployment can only be one subject of the talks, must be reciprocal and based on improved trust, and must be balanced against meaningful concessions, such as the formal renunciation of de jure independence by Taiwan.

Third, Beijing and Taipei are following different objectives: by linking CBM talks to the adoption of a peace treaty or an end-of-hostility agreement, Taipei hopes that CBMs will consolidate the status quo; for its part, Beijing expects that it will serve unification, however indirectly, for instance 'in promoting bonds of common identity between the two militaries' (Glaser 2011: 21). But this linkage remains unacceptable not only to the pan-green camp but probably also to the majority of Taiwanese public opinion. As a consequence, Ma rapidly dropped his peace treaty idea and has avoided raising it again since he was re-elected in January 2012. In any event, opinion polls continue to show how much the Tai-wanese wish the decision to remain open-ended, regarding the future of their island: in the March 2014 poll, 61 per cent of them stated that they would support (against 57 per cent in August 2008) either the status quo in the Strait indefinitely (28.8 per cent against 22.4 per cent in August 2008) or the option 'status quo now and decision later' (32.2 per cent against 34.4 per cent), while another 17.6 per cent (against 17.5 per cent) favoured the status quo heading towards independence. The percentage of Taiwanese in favour of the 'status quo now, unification later' (10 per cent against 8.3 per cent) has remained stable, while the minority wishing for 'independence as soon as possible' has become even more marginal (4.7 per cent against 8.6 per cent).[4]

For all these reasons, those who are sceptical about the usefulness of military CBMs have remained influential (e. g. in the US, Steven Goldstein 2011: 42–43) and military CBM negotiations are unlikely to start any time soon. Only second-track discussions among military experts from the two sides are likely to continue and will perhaps become more meaningful in the next few years.

The limited impact of military CBMs

Even if military CBMs would be most welcome because of their contributions towards enhancing stability and predictability, they would not be able to fully address the issue of Taiwan's growing insecurity. At a time that would suit its interests, for instance, in order to facilitate the election of a KMT candidate in 2016, the PRC may contemplate the partial relocation or even the dismantling of the (oldest) missiles that are targeted against the island. This unilateral CBM would nevertheless constitute more of a political and symbolic gesture than a strategic decision, given that the conventional missiles aimed at Taiwan form only a small portion, and arguably a decreasing part, of the PLA forces that could be projected against the island today and in the coming years (Shichor 2008, Shlapak 2009). Thus, even if the partial demilitarization of the Taiwan Strait is possible, the military balance will continue to be less and less favourable to Taiwan, forcing the island to invest more in its defence, rely more on the US, and consequently take into greater consideration the perceived long-term interests of the US in the region.

Taiwan's strategic partnership with the USA

As has been seen, there is a strong security and military dimension to Taiwan's non-official relationship with the US. However, there is also an important political facet to it. Nevertheless, it seems that the military-to-military relations between the ROC armed forces and the Pentagon are closer and more trusting, in other words in better shape, than the political relations between the Taipei civilian authorities (Presidential Office, NSC, MOFA) and Washington (both the State Department and the NSC). To be sure, no junior partner in any security arrangement shows all its cards to its senior partner – and vice versa, of course. Taiwan never did – when ruled by the Chiang family or later under Lee Teng-Hui or Chen Shui-Bian – and probably never will, but since Taiwan's national security and survival are becoming increasingly dependent upon the US, it is in the island's interests to enhance communication and understanding with its only protector. At the end of his first term, President Ma seemed to have realized this and adjusted his communication methods with the Obama administration. In his second term, however, it is far from certain that he has been able to fully reassure the US.

The cross-Strait 'rapprochement' and the US debate on Taiwan's future

As far as the US is concerned, this so-called 'rapprochement' is obviously feeding doubts among some segments of the US political elite about Taiwan's long-term intentions. It is understandable that, as a small and ill-recognized nation-state situated on the doorstep of the PRC, Taiwan does not enjoy the same freedom as the US to confront China, when need be. In other words, China's influence over Taiwan is becoming more and more unavoidable. The question is whether the accommodations made by Taipei since May 2008 on several commercial (e. g. direct air links, opening Taiwan to PRC investments), political (e.g. restraint on criticism of China' human rights record and its policies in Tibet and Xinjiang), and security (downgrading of military manoeuvres and field training exercises, Quemoy's demilitarization) issues will place the island in a situation of dependency, jeopardizing its security and de facto sovereignty, and, as a result, shaking the foundations of the US–Taiwan security relationship and, particularly, the TRA. So far, the accommodations accepted by the Ma administration have not, per se, put the island in danger (see below). But they have contributed towards narrowing Taiwan's options and capacity to say 'no', modifying its outside perception and fueling the debate, in the US and elsewhere, about the risk to Taiwan of 'Hongkongization'.

The debate that has been initiated in some US circles since 2009 on the 'unsustainability' of the US–Taiwan security arrangement may be perceived as marginal (Gilley 2010, C. Glaser 2011, Swaine 2011a and 2011b, Tucker and Glaser 2011, Mearsheimer 2014). Nevertheless, it underscores the growing US doubts about Taiwan's lack of commitment to its security as well as the island's willingness to adopt a strategy of asymmetrical warfare on the one hand, and the military capability of the US to provide enough protection for Taiwan on the other. The question is not so much the US military's capacity to sustain a war and prevent Taiwan from being subjected to military constraints. It is more about the growing potential cost of deploying such a capacity in view of China's unabated assertiveness and her unification plan for Taiwan, the PLA's rapid modernization drive and the risks attached to any armed conflict involving two nuclear powers. As China is growing more powerful and assertive, the discrepancy between what Taiwan represents for Beijing and for Washington is widening: Taiwan is a vital and 'core' interest for the former, but not for the latter. For instance, although the Obama administration has not compromised, it tends to factor in more of China's 'sensitivities' than the previous administrations, especially regarding arms sales that Beijing, ironically, does not blame Ma for buying (Dreyer 2011). And there is little chance of any reversal of this trend.

The US's Asia-Pacific 'pivot' or 'rebalancing' and Taiwan

In launching the idea, in November 2011, that the Asia-Pacific region has become the 'pivot' of US strategy, the Obama Administration was in some sense addressing the concerns expressed by a number of American experts regarding the exaggerated prudence that was being exercised towards China. Highlighting the growing importance of this region for America's security interests, the pivot theory was replaced in June 2012 by a 'rebalancing' project, presented by the Defence Secretary, Leon Panetta, at the Shangri La strategic dialogue in Singapore, and according to which 60 per cent of US military forces, especially Navy ships, will be gradually deployed in Asia, against 40 per cent in Europe and elsewhere. The dispatch of 2,500 marines to Darwin, Australia, announced in late 2011, has also been described as an indication of the willingness of the US to highlight and confirm its 'return' to Asia. What are the consequences of this policy for Taiwan?

Since 2009, all the US allies (especially Japan, Korea and the Philippines) and most of China's neighbours in Asia have intensified their pressure on the US to strengthen its military and strategic presence in Asia, and it is striking that Taiwan, under the Ma Administration, has appeared as the only exception, the only government not to do so, busy as it was apparently to effect a reconciliation with the Beijing authorities. Simultaneously, Ma Ying-Jeou has very mildly criticized Xi Jinping's *fait accompli* policy in China's claimed maritime domain, its repeated coastguard incursions in the Senkaku-Diaoyu area since 2012, the establishment of a new Air Defence Identification Zone (ADIZ) that overlaps with Japan's own ADIZ in the East China Sea in November 2013 and its gradual control of more land features in the South China Sea. Although Taipei decided not to cooperate with Beijing with regard to the territorial disputes and clashes that have intensified in the South and East China Seas since 2010, Ma Ying-Jeou has remained particularly subdued, if not silent, about Obama's new policy. In particular, he has shown more interest in joining the Trans-Pacific Partnership (TPP) and solving the beef issue than in praising this new security development.[5]

In any event, the rhetoric around the US-Asian 'pivot' and 'rebalancing' does not modify the more dangerous equation that is taking shape for the US in the context of a Taiwan scenario, especially at a time when the US government is announcing unprecedented cuts in defence expenditures. Nor does Washington's new policy hide the increasing difficulties, in the long term, for its Navy to continue to dominate the seas around China. In these circumstances, how can the US expect to be able to balance the growing strength and capability of the PLA's navy to navigate the high seas, and especially to gradually dominate the seas surrounding it, including the Taiwan Strait?

In other words, the US' 'rebalancing' strategy is unlikely to give Taiwan any additional security guarantee from the US and it will not reverse the current power transition from the US to China, especially in the Western Pacific and therefore around Taiwan. Finally, since Japan is worried about the PLA's rapid modernization drive and China's increased pressure on the Senkaku-Diaoyu-archipelago, it will probably invest more in defence, particularly in the Navy, and take up a greater share of the US security burden in East Asia. However, even then, Japan's role in strengthening Taiwan's security is likely to remain marginal.

Non-military security challenges

Non-military security challenges are much harder to apprehend and keep in check. These challenges stem not only from the deepening and increasingly asymmetrical interdependence across the Taiwan Strait but also from the ambiguities and weaknesses of Taiwan's international status, identity and nation-building process. To put it differently, economic and people-to-people interdependence between two nation-states of uneven size, population, resources and power that still recognize each other and live in peace can create difficulties and bear consequences for security, including the need for the smaller country to obtain protection from a greater power. Nevertheless, this does not usually affect the smaller country's future and survival. In Taiwan's case, the unbridgeable divisions within society and among the political elite about 'what is Taiwan?' – its past, its present (ROC or Taiwan) and its future (permanent separation from China or some kind of unification) – directly weaken the island's security vis-à-vis the PRC and ease the latter's united front activities.

Taiwan's asymmetrical dependence upon China

Taiwan's unprecedented level of economic dependence on the mainland economy (around 40 per cent of the island's exports and 60 per cent of its FDIs) does not represent, in itself, a security challenge. This situation and the emerging trends make it easier for Beijing to coerce the island without using military means, for instance, through economic sanctions (Kastner 2011: 12). Ma's 'rapprochement' policy, the Economic and Cooperation Framework Agreement (ECFCA) signed in June 2010 as well as the 21 accords concluded between Taipei and Beijing since 2008 have deepened this dependence and directly contributed towards multiplying the Taiwanese constituencies that have a vested interest not only in maintaining a close and stable relationship with Beijing but also in pushing further the island's dependency upon its major source of revenues: the tourist and service industries as well as the fruit, vegetable and fish farmers, who are probably the best known beneficiaries of Ma's policy. But the latter are far from being the only ones: the main beneficiaries are the most advanced industries that have partly relocated their production lines to the mainland but have also continued to manufacture many key items and high added-value items on the island (electronics, computers, nanotechnologies) (Rosen and Wang 2011).

This does not mean that the PRC authorities have been as successful as some DPP officials argued during the 2012 election campaign in 'buying' the support of the voters representing those constituencies. For instance, a great deal of evidence has surfaced to show that the areas that have benefited from the ECFA's 'early harvest', such as the Southern Taiwan milkfish farmers, have not really modified their voting behaviour. And economic sanctions are tricky weapons to use, particularly for an economy that is as globalized as the Chinese economy (Tanner 2007). However, this growing dependence has increased the pressure on both the political elite and society to adjust their views about a whole range of issues, from mainland policy all the way to, arguably, the identity and the future of Taiwan.

The KMT's new Chinese nationalism

Since Ma came to power in 2008, the KMT has revived, to some extent, its traditional and somewhat old-fashioned Chinese nationalism, a nationalism that once again places the unity, if not the unification of the Chinese nation/race (*Zhonghua minzu*), at the heart of its ideological discourse. This new/reborn narrative is not only aimed at denouncing and reining in what the KMT and Beijing describe as Chen Shui-Bian's 'desinicization' (*quzhongguohua*) policy but also at negating Lee Teng-Hui's earlier attempted localization – or Taiwanization – of the KMT and the ROC. Although Ma has not endorsed the dark blue view, according to which Taipei, since 1949, has merely been the provisional capital of the ROC and unification should take place rapidly, he and the KMT have contributed towards creating tensions between their brand of Chinese nationalism and the need to cultivate the local Taiwanese identity and voters (Hughes 2014).

The KMT's new or revived Chinese nationalism is officially aimed at anchoring Taiwan in the Chinese nation, bridging the gap with the PRC and, last but not least, favouring the mainland's democratization. At the same time, the KMT has effected a reconciliation and developed a privileged relationship with the CCP. These new discourses and priorities raise many questions: are there factors of political unity or division on the island? Are they prone to consolidate or, on the contrary, weaken Taiwan's nation-building process as well as Taiwan's determination to maintain a credible defence? I would like to argue, here, that the KMT's new Chinese nationalism, its concurrent deconstruction of the ROCOT – the Republic of China on Taiwan, an inclusive and distinct acronym coined under Lee Teng-Hui – and its rapprochement policy have contributed towards the weakening of Taiwan's statehood and international status, notwithstanding the lack of progress on the latter front since 2008, as well as towards forfeiting a domestic political consensus and endangering national security. It has also contributed towards persuading Beijing to tighten the screws: at the 8th KMT-CCP Forum held in Harbin on 28 July 2012, a Politburo Standing Committee member, Jia Qinglin, declared that both Taiwan and the mainland belonged to 'one country' (*liang'an yiguo*) instead of 'one China' (*liang'an yiZhong*), which triggered endless discussions and criticism on the island (Brown 2012). In any event, reflecting the growing PRC impact on the KMT, these developments have placed the DPP and the electorate as a whole under additional constraints, narrowing their options vis-à-vis China and for the future (Beckershoff 2014). In this context, the success of the March 2014 Sunflower movement, led not by the DPP but by student activists, that opposed the speedy adoption by the Legislative Yuan of the Service Trade Agreement signed in June 2013, has underscored the growing anxiety of Taiwanese society vis-à-vis the KMT's rapprochement policy.

The DPP and the electorate's narrowing room for manoeuvre

The greatest impact of the growing dependence associated with Ma's 'rapprochement' policy has clearly been on the DPP and the electorate. Although before the beginning of the 2012 electoral campaign, Ma was still perceived by many Taiwanese voters as a weak and incompetent (*wuneng*) president, he was rather easily re-elected: part of the reason for this was that the DPP candidate, Ms. Tsai Ying-Wen, was unable to reassure not only her potential voters but also the Taiwanese business community and the US about her future mainland policy and her ill-defined 'Taiwan consensus' (*Taiwan gongshi*). One of the key outcomes of her defeat has been the dilemma that the DPP, if it wants to increase its chances of regaining power, cannot afford to either ignore China's requests or endorse, in one way or another, what Su Chi and later the KMT and the PRC have called the '1992 Consensus'. As a matter of fact, the DPP has remained deeply divided on this issue (Romberg 2012b): while Frank Hsieh Chang-Ting has continued to promote the concept of a 'constitutional one China' (*xianfa yizhong*)[6] and in October 2012, paid a 'private' but icebreaking visit to the mainland, followed by another visit to Hong Kong and Shenzhen in June–July 2013, the Party's Chairman, Su Chen-Chang (until March 2014), continued to adhere to the 1999 Resolution on Taiwan's Future, according to which the ROC equates to Taiwan (Romberg 2012a: 3).

Tsai's re-election as DPP chair in March 2014 may help the main opposition party to endorse a new China policy. However, the report adopted by the DPP's China Affairs Committee in January 2014 has not fundamentally modified the party's view of its relations with China (Democratic Progressive Party 2014). And in her subsequent statements, Tsai has refused to formally endorse the '92 Consensus'. Hu Jintao's reference, at the Eighteenth Party Congress, to the 'one China framework' (*yige Zhongguo de kuangjia*) as well as the 'one China principle' may help the CCP and the DPP to reach some kind of understanding.

In any event, the last few years have made the DPP and Taiwanese society at large 'prisoners', if not of the '1992 Consensus' at least of the 'one China' fiction or unreality. In other words, the changes in the Strait since 2008 have contributed towards narrowing Taiwan's options for the future and have made the island more dependent upon Beijing's good will; they have weakened Taiwan's de facto independence and, as a result, Taiwan's security.

The mainstream inclination of the Taiwanese business community

In the 2012 election, for the first time, a broad majority of business leaders openly endorsed the '1992 Consensus' and consequently placed the DPP in a more difficult position. These business people included entrepreneurs, such as Chang Yung-Fa, Evergreen's owner, who had previously sided with the green camp (except on direct air and sea links with China). More worrying has been the evolution of some media outlets such as the *China Times* (*Zhongguo shibao*), bought by Tsai Eng-Meng's Want Want group (*Wangwang tuanti*) in 2008, which have become less critical of the PRC authorities than even the dark-blue and KMT-supported *United Daily News* (*Lianhebao*). The acquisition in November 2012 of around one-third of Jimmy Lai's New Media Group and especially the *Apple Daily* newspaper by Tsai Shao-Chung, Tsai Eng-Meng's son and the president of Want Want group, have deepened these concerns. Although many Taiwanese have kept their distance from the Want Want media and have recently become more vocal in their protests against Ma's mainland policy, these developments highlight another facet of Taiwan's 'Hongkongization': the unprecedented emergence of a pro-Beijing discourse on the island.

A changing Taiwanese identity

It is often argued that in spite of these trends, the Taiwanese identity has continued to strengthen and, therefore, to consolidate the island society's attachment to the status quo and de facto independence. According to Chengchi National University's Election Study Centre, in 2013, 57 per cent of the respondents considered themselves to be Taiwanese (against 17.6 per cent in 1992), 36 per cent both Taiwanese and Chinese (46 per cent) and less than 4 per cent only Chinese (26 per cent).[7] But these perceptions are becoming increasingly disconnected from the political options available to Taiwan's political and economic elites and the two major parties, the KMT and the DPP. They are also becoming more and more disconnected from the professional and personal options that the Taiwanese, especially the youth of Taiwan, can contemplate. Or to be more accurate, Taiwan's identity is being increasingly constrained by this reality and, as a consequence, gradually disconnected from Taiwan's independence and quest for full statehood: in other words, the Taiwanese identity is becoming more and more 'Hongkongized'.

There are still major differences in terms of identity between Hong Kong and Taiwan, since the latter is a de facto state and the former is not. However, related to this changing content of the Taiwanese identity, several studies have shown that young Taiwanese have a more flexible approach to the PRC: their professional careers often include at least a temporary relocation to the mainland, since the local employment market remains sluggish and offers less well-paid jobs (see also the chapter by Yen-Fen Tseng in this volume). In case of war, most would prefer to flee rather than to face conscription and fight for the survival of the ROC, and they are becoming increasingly open-minded about the long-term solution of the cross-Strait conflict, especially the prospect of unification (Le Pesant 2011 and 2012).

Finally, the growing number of PRC spouses and other residents in Taiwan and the Taishang (Taiwanese business people) on the mainland include a security dimension. While around 350,000 mainland Chinese spouses have married Taiwanese citizens in the last 20 years or so (roughly 320,000 of them reside in Taiwan, the others mainly on the mainland), it is by definition impossible to assess the total number of PRC nationals living on the island (see also the chapter by Jian-Bang Deng in this volume).[8] The number of illegal PRC nationals is also increasing and difficult to track. Conversely, between 1 and 2 million Taiwanese people are living on the mainland and some of them have married local spouses. In any event, these two distinct but growing communities and their offspring have already started to influence Taiwan's view of the PRC (and China's view of Taiwan). The sheer magnitude of these interactions and cross-marriages cannot be discounted as marginal, especially in a society whose fertility rate has continuously decreased during the last 20 years (1.07 births per woman in 2013, down from 1.27 the previous year).[9] While this phenomenon may remain a long-term issue, it is prone to facilitate Beijing's united front work on the island. Although the Taishang and the Taiwanese business community are probably not 'agents of unification', they have certainly become what I would call 'agents of accommodation' (Lee 2011, Schubert 2010, Keng and Schubert 2010).

Beijing's more efficient 'united front' strategy

Little is known about the CCP's united front work (UFW) on Taiwan. It is indeed easier to identify UFW objectives and actors on the mainland: the united front cadres mainly target the Taishang and use all the Taiwan-related agencies

(Taiwan Affairs offices, Taiwanese business associations) that report in one way or another to the Central Committee United Front Department (*tongzhanbu*) to influence them. Today, the UFW's key objectives are to persuade the Taishang or any Taiwanese personality, group or individual that they meet outside Taiwan, if not to support unification, to at least vote for the KMT, endorse the '1992 consensus' and preferably the 'one China principle', and oppose the DPP and Taiwan independence. On the island, the PRC's united front's main objectives are probably identical. However, on whom can they rely? Which political parties, business organizations or social movements do CCP united front bureaucrats concentrate on? Do they have agents undercover in Taiwan? This is almost impossible to answer, although pro-unification groups, such as the Chinese Integration Association, which issued an invitation to Wang Zaixi in June 2012 (see above), are probably part of this growing network (Brown 2012).

At this stage, we do not have any evidence of Beijing's specific and direct UFW activities on the island, although the Hong Kong and Macau Special Administrative Regions can be used as a precedent and as a source of inspiration and comparison. There is a strong argument to substantiate the claim that the PRC authorities are concentrating on the KMT, a more friendly, accessible and easy target; however, if they want to win over the hearts and minds of the majority of the Taiwanese people, they also need to work on the DPP.

Since 2008, if we judge the UFW by its results, the Taiwanese business community has clearly been targeted as a prime objective. Beijing has therefore concentrated on weakening their anti-China sentiments by offering Taiwanese business people a well-known series of general benefits (such as the ECFA's early harvest) and a more discreet number of specific advantages when negotiating particular deals.

In any event, since 2008, Beijing's UFW has also targeted the DPP elite. A growing number of DPP leaders and former ministers have been invited to 'academic conferences' and other non-official gatherings on the mainland or in Hong Kong, to facilitate, through dialogue and other activities, the construction of a more trusting and amicable relationship. Since Ma's re-election in 2012, the DPP has been targeted more openly by the UFW because its chances of coming back to power in 2016 are likely to increase over time. The warm welcome reserved by the Chinese authorities for Hsieh Chang-Ting in October 2012 and again in July 2013 illustrated this new priority.

There has always been a risk when dealing with Taiwan that Beijing's UFW might backfire and actually contribute towards building a separate Taiwanese identity and polity, consolidating the quest for de facto independence, at least unless and until mainland China undergoes democratization. However, as we have seen, the current environment on the island and in the region is rapidly changing, strengthening Beijing's diplomatic and economic hand as well as its united front strategy towards Taiwan. And since the CCP's immediate objective is not unification but accommodation, it seems that its UFW has at least helped to achieve this latter and less ambitious goal. The most evident success of this strategy, so far, has been the KMT's unwillingness to build a consensus with the

DPP on a common mainland China and security policy. Another is the growing inclination of Taiwan's main opposition party to move closer to the '1992 consensus' or a similar commitment (the ROC constitution) in order to increase its chances of winning back the presidency – with the risk of splitting its own organization and ending up weaker in the parliament in the future.

All in all, Taiwan's non-military security challenges cannot be discounted. They are becoming increasingly palatable and, in the middle term, may well start to pose a greater threat to Taiwan's de facto independence and options for the future than its military challenges.

Conclusion

Taiwan's security is facing growing challenges and the looming debate in the US is fueling a sense of insecurity and uncertainty about the island's mid-term and long-term future. The good news is that the increasing flow of economic and quasi-governmental exchanges as well as people-to-people contacts across the Strait is strengthening interdependence and understanding between Taipei and Beijing; it is also consolidating stability and peace across the Taiwan Strait. The likely opening, in the coming years, of SEF and ARATS offices in both capitals is, in this respect, an encouraging development. The stabilization and 'creeping normalization' of the cross-Strait relationship is also contributing towards creating non-military CBMs across the Strait. In other words, for each of the three actors involved – Taiwan, China and the US – the cost of war is becoming more unbearable every day and the risk of war is therefore becoming more unlikely. The bad news is that the asymmetry between China and Taiwan is widening, and not only from a military point of view; time seems to be on the PRC's side with regard to gradually compelling Taiwan to become more accommodating and, eventually, to give in to the PRC's political demands without having to resort to any kind of armed conflict.

To contain or manage these dangerous trends, Taiwan still holds four trump cards: a meaningful defence system, US support, democracy, and what I have elsewhere called a 'sovereignist consensus' on the survival of the 'Republic of China on Taiwan' (Cabestan 2010). If Taiwan plays these cards well, national security will be guaranteed and the island will hold on until the PRC changes, hopefully, and becomes a democratic country. Among these four cards, maintaining a credible defence system is clearly Taiwan's top objective, because the other three cards can only be played if this 'ace' remains in Taiwan's hands. In spite of China's and the PLA's growing power, this goal is not out of reach if the Taiwanese military's asymmetric strategy and strong deterrence are consolidated, if Taiwan's political authorities decide to invest more in defence modernization and consolidation, and if they manage to persuade the United States to stay committed to the island's security and to the status quo in the Strait, at least in the mid-term future or for the next 20 years.

However, a strong defence system is not enough, especially in the increasingly asymmetrical game in which Taiwan is involved. The island is facing a growing number of non-traditional security challenges originating in China, particularly the CCP's united front strategy and its increasing capacity to influence the island's political and business elites, media, opinion leaders and public opinion at large. To counter this strategy, the Ma Administration has enhanced protective measures and has started to more actively promote Taiwan's 'soft power' and to use it as a lever. But will these initiatives be sufficient to keep Taiwan safe from the PRC's UFW?

The final and probably most important objective for the current government, however, is to achieve domestic consensus on Taiwan's mainland policy and security. This is not an easy task, since the main political divide still cuts through identity issues and the island's short-, mid- and long-term relationship with the PRC. Having forced the Ma Administration to accept a stronger Legislative Yuan supervisory role in April 2014, the Sunflower movement has underscored the depth of the divisions remaining in Taiwanese society and also the depth of the concerns over the KMT's rapprochement policy on the island.

All in all, Taiwan's military and non-military security challenges have intensified during the last decade and particularly since the KMT's return to power in 2008. Nevertheless, although its options are narrower than before, Taiwan is far from being in a desperate situation, since its future depends on many factors and variables which have by no means all manifested themselves on the island, in China, in the US and elsewhere.

Notes

1 The QDR released in March 2013 has strengthened this offensive capability (Ministry of National Defence of the Republic of China 2013: 38–41).
2 *China Post*, 12 September 2010, 1.
3 Mainland Affairs Council opinion polls, www.mac.gov.tw (accessed 18 June 2014).
4 www.mac.gov.tw (accessed 18 June 2014).
5 *China Post*, 15 November 2011, 1.
6 Hsieh recognizes that, according to the ROC constitution, there is only one China, the ROC. This view concurs with that of the KMT.
7 Taiwanese/Chinese Identification Trend Distribution in Taiwan (1992/6–2013/12), available at http://esc.nccu.edu.tw/course/news.php?Sn=166 (accessed 18 June 2014).
8 *China Post*, 11 April 2013; *Women of China*, 17 February 2014, available at www.womenofchina.cn/html/womenofchina/report/169809–1.htm (accessed 19 June 2014).
9 *Focus Taiwan*, 9 January 2014, available at http://focustaiwan.tw/news/asoc/2014010 9000 9.aspx (accessed 18 June 2014).

References

Beckershoff, André (2014) 'The KMT-CCP Forum: Securing Consent for Cross-Strait Rapprochement', *Journal of Current Chinese Studies*, 43, 1: 213–241.
Brown, David G. (2012) 'China–Taiwan Relations: A Year for Consolidation', *Comparative Connections*, 14, 3, available at http://csis.org/files/publication/1202qchina_taiwan.pdf (accessed 4 August 2014).
Cabestan, Jean-Pierre (2010) 'The New Détente in the Taiwan Strait and its Impact on Taiwan's Security and Future: More Questions than Answers', *China Perspectives*, 3: 22–33.

Chen, York W. (2009) 'The Evolution of Taiwan's Military Strategy: Convergence and Dissonance', *China Brief*, 9, 23: 8–12.

Cordesman, Anthony H., and Yarosh, Nicholas S. (2012) *Chinese Military Modernization and Force Development. A Western Perspective*, Washington DC: CSIS.

Democratic Progressive Party (2014) *China Policy Review: Summary Report*, available at www.scribd.com/doc/198143800/DPP-2014-China-Policy-Review-Summary-Report (accessed 3 August 2014).

Dreyer, June Teufel (2011) *Why Taiwan Matters* (testimony before the House Committee on Foreign Affairs), available at www.fpri.org/articles/2011/07/why-taiwan-matters (accessed 29 July 2014).

Gilley, Bruce (2010) 'Not So Dire Straits: How the Finlandization of Taiwan Benefits U.S. Security', *Foreign Affairs*, 89, 1: 44–56, 58–60.

Glaser, Bonnie S. (2010) *Building Trust Across the Taiwan Strait: A Role for Military Confidence-building Measures*, Washington DC: CSIS.

Glaser, Bonnie S. (2011) 'China's Approach to CBMs with Taiwan: Lessons from China's CBMs with Neighboring Countries', in Cliff, Roger, Saunders, Phillip C., and Harold, Scott (eds) *New Opportunities and Challenges for Taiwan's Security*, Washington DC: Rand National Defense Research Institute, 17–23.

Goldstein, Steven (2011) 'Cross-Strait CBMs: Like a Fish Needs a Bicycle?' in Cliff, Roger, Saunders, Phillip C., and Harold, Scott (eds) *New Opportunities and Challenges for Taiwan's Security*, Washington DC: Rand National Defense Research Institute, 33–43.

Hu, Jintao (2012) *Report at Eighteenth Party Congress*, available at http://news.xinhuanet.com/english/special/18cpcnc/2012-11/17/c_131981259.htm (accessed 3 August 2014).

Huang, Alexander Chieh Cheng (2010) 'The United States and Taiwan's Defense Transformation', *Taiwan-US Quarterly Analysis*, available at www.brookings.edu/research/opinions/2010/02/taiwan-defense-huang (accessed 29 July 2014).

Hughes, Christopher R. (2014) 'Revising Identity Politics Under Ma Ying-Jeou', in Cabestan, Jean-Pierre, and deLisle, Jacques (eds), *Political Changes in Taiwan under Ma Ying-Jeou: Partisan Conflict, Policy Choices, External Constraints and Security Challenges*, London and New York: Routledge, pp. 120–136.

Kan, Shirley (2014) *Taiwan's Major U.S. Arms Sales since 1990* (Congressional Research Service), available at http://fas.org/sgp/crs/weapons/RL 30957.pdf (accessed 29 July 2014).

Kastner, Scott L. (2011) 'The Security Implications of China–Taiwan Economic Integration', in Cliff, Roger, Saunders, Phillip C., and Harold, Scott (eds) *New Opportunities and Challenges for Taiwan Security*, Washington DC: Rand National Defense Research Institute, pp. 9–16.

Keng, Shu, and Schubert, Gunter (2010) 'Agents of Unification? The Political Role of Taiwanese Businessmen in the Process of Cross-Strait Integration', *Asian Survey*, 50, 2: 287–310.

Le Pesant, Tanguy (2011) 'Generational Change and Ethnicity among 1980s-born Taiwanese', *Journal of Current Chinese Affairs*, 40, 1: 133–157.

Le Pesant, Tanguy (2012) 'A New Generation of Taiwanese at the Ballot Box', *China Perspectives*, 2: 71–79.

Lee, Chun-Yi (2011) *Taiwanese Business or Chinese Security Asset: A Changing Pattern of Interaction between Taiwanese Businesses and Chinese Governments*, London and New York: Routledge.

Mearsheimer, John J. (2014) 'Say Goodbye to Taiwan. Time is Running Out for the Little Island Coveted by its Gigantic, Growing Neighbor', *National Interest*, available at http://nationalinterest.org/article/say-goodbye-taiwan-9931 (accessed 3 August 2014).

Mei, Fu S. (2011) 'Taiwan's Defense Transformation and Challenges Under Ma Ying-Jeou', *China Brief*, 11, 7: 7–10.

Ministry of National Defence of the Republic of China (2013) *Quadrennial Defence Review*, Taipei.

Murray, William S. (2008) 'Revisiting Taiwan's Defense Strategy', *Naval War College Review*, 61, 3: 13–38.

Office of the Secretary of Defense (2014) *Annual Report to Congress: Military and Security Developments Involving the People's Republic of China*, Report to the Congress Pursuant to the FY2000 National Defense Authorization Act for Fiscal Year 2000, Washington DC.

Romberg, Alan D. (2012a) 'Shaping the Future. Part I: Domestic Developments in Taiwan', *China Leadership Monitor*, 38: 1–19.

Romberg, Alan D. (2012b) 'Shaping the Future. Part II: Cross-Strait Relations', *China Leadership Monitor*, 39: 1–25.

Rosen, Daniel H., and Wang, Zhi (2011) *The Implications of China–Taiwan Economic Liberalization*, Washington DC: Peterson Institute for International Economics.

Schubert, Gunter (2010) 'The Political Thinking of the Mainland Taishang. Some Preliminary Observations from the Field', *Journal of Current Chinese Affairs*, 39, 1: 73–110.

Shichor, Yitzhak (2008) *Missiles Myths: China's Threat to Taiwan in a Comparative Perspective*, Taipei: CAPS Papers 45.

Shlapak, David A., Orletsky, David T., Reid, Toy I., Tanner, Murray Scot, and Wilson, Barry (2009) *A Question of Balance: Political Context and Military Aspects of the China–Taiwan Dispute*, Washington DC: Rand National Defense Research Institute.

Swaine, Michael D. (2011a) 'Enough Tough Talk on China', *National Interest*, available at http://nationalinterest.org/commentary/enough-tough-talk-china-5934 (accessed 4 August 2014).

Swaine, Michael D. (2011b) *America's Challenge: Engaging a Rising China in the Twenty-First Century*, Washington DC: Carnegie Endowment for International Peace.

Tanner, Murray Scot (2007) *Chinese Economic Coercion Against Taiwan: A Tricky Weapon to Use*, Santa Monica CA: Rand Corporation.

Tucker, Nancy Bernkopf (2009) *Strait Talk: United States–Taiwan Relations and the Crisis with China*, Cambridge MA: Harvard University Press.

Tucker, Nancy Bernkopf, and Glaser, Bonnie (2011) 'Should the US Abandon Taiwan?' *Washington Quarterly*, 34, 4: 23–37.

16 Conclusions

Assessing the China impact

Gunter Schubert

This volume has undertaken a thorough preliminary analysis of China's political and social impact on Taiwan. A number of research questions are formulated in the Introduction as a guide to the various chapters:

- What precisely is the China impact on Taiwan in the research area with which each author is concerned?
- To what extent is Taiwan's political and social space constrained and/or enlarged by the China impact?
- What kinds of challenges and/or opportunities arise from the China impact for Taiwan's future, and how should Taiwan respond to them?

These questions have been addressed in the individual chapters, and it is now the task of the editor, in these concluding remarks, to highlight the 'deep structure' or, to express this less ambitiously, the core issues of the China impact as these have been identified and analysed by the authors who have contributed to this volume. This will involve cutting across the three thematic blocs – domestic politics, society and security – in which the chapters have been categorized. Four core issues present themselves.

1 China's impact on policy preferences and cross-Strait policy-making in Taiwan

The authors who have contributed to this volume generally agree that the way in which most Taiwanese citizens cast their ballots in the 2008 and 2012 presidential elections was indicative of the warm welcome being extended to cross-Strait economic integration – and not only by constituencies with vested interests, such as the entrepreneurs and white-collar workers who are looking for investment opportunities and jobs on the mainland. China's rise and the promise that all Taiwanese would benefit from the intensification of cross-Strait trade, as well as the offer of a 'peace dividend' accompanying the political rapprochement across the Taiwan Strait, served to convince not only those who usually take an independent or middle-of-the-road stance in terms of party support but also those who would usually be rather cautious, if not reluctant, to side with the 'blue camp' and its pro-China approach. The Ma administration's China policies since 2008 have generally received majority support, although this deserves a caveat in the light of the repercussions of the Sunflower movement, which surprised Taiwan's political establishment in early 2014 (see below). In fact, as Dafydd Fell has argued in his chapter, public opinion in Taiwan has never been prepared to tolerate the complete liberalization of cross-Strait trade because awareness of the potential risks, both economic and political, has always stretched across the party camps.

Nevertheless, as has been highlighted repeatedly by Nai-Teh Wu and others in this volume, the impact is of particular significance for the DPP, which will have to formulate a convincing China policy if it is to have any hope of fulfilling its ambition to become the ruling party again. As Jih-Wen Lin has emphasized in his chapter, a negative correlation has developed between Taiwan's increasing economic dependence on the Chinese mainland on the one hand and the DPP's political support base on the other, and this will remain at least while the party continues to adhere to the ideology of independence. This contention might be debatable, but the fact that the DPP faces an arduous task in trying to politically navigate the dynamics of regional economic integration with China as the gravitational centre of this process certainly is not. At the time of writing, the DPP has not yet delivered on this front and although the party seems to be on a promising track after its strong showing in the nine-in-one local elections,[1] there is much uncertainty over whether it will be able to secure a presidential majority without a clear China policy stance.

2   China's impact on social class and (national) identity formation in Taiwan

The above-mentioned points are directly related to the Chinese impact on the formation of social class and identity in Taiwan. Apparently, as Thung-Hong Lin has argued in his chapter, a link can be observed between cross-Strait economic integration and income and asset concentration in the hands of the capitalists and the new middle classes, while the self-employed and unskilled workers seem to be losing out. This translates into class-based voting, since the former groups support the 'blue camp' identified with pro-China policies and the latter groups side with the 'green camp', which is supposed to reject such policies. Class-based party and policy preferences are confirmed by Chih-Jou Jay Chen, who finds that most of the opposition to cross-Strait agreements, such as the contested Trade in Services Pact, has formed among the students and white-collar workers, even if they do not apply class terminology to make their point. However, cross-Strait trade liberalization does tend to intensify class formation in Taiwan rather than act as a root cause. Taiwan lacks a tradition and ideology of state-induced redistribution, and in these times of increasing income disparity caused by structural changes in the Taiwanese economy due to economic globalization, Taiwan has long been confronted with (meagre) growth and (rising) inequity. China's economic impact has accelerated this process, and it will be interesting to see whether social class formation will eventually change the current party land-scape, which is primarily based on contending stances concerning cross-Strait policy and national identity.

With respect to identity, the picture is more complex. In line with the established wisdom, scholars have drawn on sound longitudinal survey data[2] to show that people in Taiwan overwhelmingly consider themselves to be 'Taiwanese' rather than 'both Chinese and Taiwanese' or even 'Chinese' and that this draws a clear line between Taiwan and China. However, Shelley Rigger in her chapter claims that the trend takes on a different aspect if the figures are broken down into generations of respondents. 'Fifth generationers', i.e. those young Taiwanese born after 1982, who came of age when Chen Shui-Bian was elected president in 2000 and have grown up with China's rise, certainly strongly identify themselves as Taiwanese – but they are nevertheless ready to engage with China and 'ride the tiger' instead of trying to escape or 'hedge' it. Their Taiwanese identity is firmly entrenched, and they are therefore self-confident enough to deal with the China impact, as opposed to simply turning it to their own benefit by investing in China or entering the mainland's job market. At the same time, as Chih-Jou Jay Chen's findings show, the younger generation's support for cross-Strait liberalization has declined since 2008, and particularly since 2014, as was highlighted by the recent Sunflower movement. Apparently, increasing cross-Strait exchange is not necessarily conducive to strengthening mutual understanding and overall support for even more exchange. It has has rather had the effect of sharpening the awareness of younger Taiwanese of the risks accompanying the China impact: for example, unaffordable real estate, decreasing salaries, the penetration of Taiwan's economy by Chinese capital, the manipulation of the media by mainland-based business interests, etc. A self-confident Taiwanese identity may reduce the fear of a rising China, but not necessarily the opposition to increasing cross-Strait integration – rather, on the contrary, when the net results of the China impact become clearer over time and then are subjected to controversial debates in Taiwan's lively democracy.

3 China's impact on migration patterns and policies in Taiwan

As has already been indicated, the China impact signifies not only risk-as-danger but also risk-as-opportunity, and this fact has been spelled out most clearly in those chapters that deal with cross-Strait migration patterns. China's economic rise and market-induced integration across the Taiwan Strait has not only generated new opportunities for Taiwan's entrepreneurs and managers who went to the mainland very early on in order to engage in business and earn the huge profits that were becoming increasingly difficult to make in the structurally changing Taiwanese economy. The road to China has also become a new and challenging route for Taiwanese skilled labour as well. This has profoundly impacted Taiwan's economy, which has lost much investment and human capital, although it has survived this drain surprisingly well and has managed to remain a successful export economy. Cross-Strait migration, however, has presented the Taiwan state with new challenges in the form of decisions that need to be made on how to respond to the phenomenon of increasing migration to China. Should obstacles be devised to discourage skilled labour from crossing the Taiwan Strait in order to maintain Taiwan as a distinctive political community – particularly since China is doing its best to attract young and highly educated Taiwanese in the hope of driving forward the process of unification? For the time being, the Taiwan state is manoeuvring cautiously, if not restrictively: double nationality for Taiwanese citizens residing on the Chinese mainland has been taken off the agenda, and if they wish to retain their membership in Taiwan's universal health coverage system, Taiwanese migrants have to return to Taiwan every two years in addition to paying their premiums. Hence the Taiwan state still stands firm against China's centrifugal pull on skilled labour migration and may be able to outlive the pressure, as China's economy matures and life in China gradually loses much of its former attraction as a result of jobs becoming less well paid and the labour market becoming more competitive than in the early days of China's market transformation.

However, China does not only interfere in Taiwan's labour market. The regulation of cross-Strait marriages poses another challenge that is equally difficult to tackle. On the one hand, this has forced Taiwan to reform its immigration policies to satisfy the strong social demand for the integration of mainland spouses into Taiwan's society, as explained in Jian-Bang Deng's chapter. On the other hand, the Taiwan state finds it hard to accommodate the fact that not all mainland spouses find the existing requirements attractive enough to settle in Taiwan. This may be a strategy for capping the inflow of mainland Chinese into Taiwan, but for Deng it produces contradictions that are detrimental to people's interests and life choices. In the shadow of China, Taiwan must acknowledge that not only is it an emigrant country but it has become an immigrant country, too. This presupposes, as Ping Lin argues in his chapter, the de-demonization of China as well as a more realistic understanding of the country, since 'any relationship with China can be beneficial or detrimental to Taiwan', and people have to acquire the necessary knowledge to make reasonable judgments when they face the China impact.

4 China's impact on Taiwan's security

Nowhere else is the China impact so clearly visible for international observers than in the realm of regional security. China's rise and cross-Strait rapprochement have placed Taiwan under considerable stress as a result of Beijing's demands for Taipei to adopt a common stance with them on sensitive issues related to sovereignty claims in the South and East China Seas. At the same time, the US is displaying an ambivalent attitude towards the détente across the Taiwan Strait because Taiwan is still considered a potential geostrategic asset in the seemingly inevitable confrontation with the 'Chinese dragon'. Japan, for its part, is also politically important for Taiwan. Cheng-Yi Lin has shown, in his chapter, how difficult it is for Taiwan to walk this tightrope, and no alternative has yet presented itself as a way for Taipei to balance competing power interests in the region and continuously calibrate the China–Taiwan relationship to safeguard Taiwan's security interests. Jean-Pierre Cabestan's chapter confirms Taiwan's delicate position in East and Southeast Asia's sensitive security structure and contends that Taiwan's quest for sovereignty has become barely tenable in the context of China's rise. This is due not only to Chinese military power but also to a 'united front alliance' that incorporates part of Taiwan's political and business elites and is able to steer, if not manipulate, Taiwanese public opinion to some considerable extent. This makes it all the more important for Taiwan to play its trump cards well: a meaningful defence system, US support, its democratic system and 'sovereignist consensus' on the existence and uncompromising survival of the 'Republic of China on Taiwan'. These trump cards, in the view of Cabestan, should be strong enough to help Taiwan successfully deal with the China impact in the future. Most importantly, however, Taiwan must achieve domestic consensus on its China policy and security concept to safeguard its sovereignty, freedom and prosperity, and this may be the greatest challenge facing Taiwan in its efforts come to terms with the China impact.

In conclusion

These few concluding remarks certainly do not do justice to the rich empirical findings presented in each of the chapters, and more could be cited to illustrate the four core issues of the China impact on Taiwan discussed here, an impact that is a 'moving target' given the dynamic evolution of cross-Strait relations. More research is required to show how China is shaping Taiwan's destiny, and the only certainty is that the China impact will continue. However, Taiwan should not be afraid; although unable to escape the 'Chinese dragon', the island's vibrant democracy, healthy-enough economy and international support should be more than adequate to ensure its survival in the dragon's looming shadow.

Notes

1 The DPP garnered 47.55 per cent (KMT: 40.70 per cent) of all the votes for the 22 top positions of municipality mayor, county commissioner and city mayor, winning 13 positions, six more than in the previous election held in 2010, against only six positions defended by the KMT, who lost seven. Three positions went to independent candidates, including the mayorship of the capital, Taipei city.
2 See, for instance, the data regularly gathered by National Chengchi University's Election Study Centre (http://esc.nccu.edu.tw/main.php).

Index

Page numbers in *italics* denote tables, those in **bold** denote figures.

1992 Consensus 9, 32, 65, 138, 145, 293–4, 296–7; accepting 59, 112, 267; Chinese government attitude 137; construction 136; DPP position 131–2; endorsement 15; support for 68n38, 139, *140*, 144, *147*; voter attitude 134, *138*, 141

Academia Sinica 99; Institute of Sociology 3, 10n5, 153, 172n2, 181, 199
Air Defence Identification Zone (ADIZ) 264, 272, 291
air-sea battle concept (ASBC) 266
Ansolabehere, S. 36
anti-access and area denial (A2AD) capability 266–7
ASEAN 271, 273–6; Regional Forum (ARF) 265, 273–4
Asia-Pacific Economic Trade Pivot 62; pivot of US strategy 290; region 262–3, 266; Regional Operations Hub 57–8; US security role 261
Asian Infrastructure Investment Bank (AIIB) 263
assimilation 218; segmented 240
Association for Relations Across the Taiwan Strait (ARATS) 26, 63, 104n3, 136–7; opening of office 297; SEF-ARATS talks 65
Association of Taiwan Investment Enterprises on the Mainland (ATIEM) 95–6, 105n14

Babb, S. 179, 191, 193n3
Bader, J. (former National Security Council director) 268
ballots 19–20, 96, 105n11, 105n12, 301
Barth, F. 246

Bartley, A. 241
BBC Chinese 165
blue 71, 75, *76*, 86, 106n24, 155–6, 158, *161–2*, *164*, *166–8*, 175, 183, 192; camp supporters 159, 302; dark 15, 292, 294; non-blue *166–8*; non-blue voters 159–60, 162, 167; parties 176; support 165; voters 160, 162, 167, **182**; *see also* pan-blue
Brazil, Russia, India, China and South Africa (BRICS) 261
Brooks, D.J. 36–8
Brown, D.G. 293, 296
Brzezinski, Z. (former National Security Advisor) 268
Bush, President G.W. 269, 284; Bush government 285
Bush, R.C. 3, 270
business environment 91; marginalized 201

Cabestan, J.-P. 9, 287, 297, 305
Campbell, K. (Assistant Secretary of State for East Asian and Pacific Affairs) 269, 274
capabilities 180; American intelligence 45; China's A2AD 266–7; Chinese electronic 284; military 266, 269, 287, 290; PLA combat 9; PLA power projection 282–3, 291; Taiwan defence 282–3; Taiwanese offensive 285, 298n1; women's 205
career 7–8, 211, 239–40; advancement 200–1; change 207; in China 226, 250; opportunities 202, 229, 231; plans 9, 61, 197, 216, 248; professional 254n14, 295; pursuit of 91, 199; women 204

Carmines, E.G. 37, 39–40, 54
Carnegie Endowment for International
  Peace 267
Central Leading Group for Taiwan Affairs
  (CLGTA) 19, 33n16
Central News Agency 33n18, 210
Chan, L. 42, 44, 137
Chang, Chin-Fen 176
Chang, G.A. 75
Chang Chun-Hsiung 62
Chang Hsien-Yao 45
Chang Jung-Fa 68
Chang Yung-Fa 57, 131, 294
Chen, C.J.J. 169–70
Chen, J. 211
Chen, K. 242–3
Chen Chun-Hung (KMT councillor) 46, 50
Chen Ming-Wen (Chiayi County
  magistrate) 46–8, 50
Chen Shui-Bian, President 1, 27, 41–2, 44,
  47, 62, 65, 81, 84, 86, 91, 93–4, 128n28,
  271, 282, 285, 289, 303
Chen Yun-Lin 44–5, 48–9
Chiang, L. 248
Chiang Ching-Kuo, President 21, 25, 283;
  family 289
China Benpost 207
China factor 37, 83, 130–2; in Taiwanese
  elections 133–6, 145
China Post 126n5, 232, 298n8
China rising 239, 252, 261, 286, 303
China Times Group 99; deal 107n28
Chinese Communist Party (CCP) 1, 19, 26,
  42, 57, 63, 80, 270, 294; Eighteenth
  Party Congress 287; invasion 55; KMT-
  CCP Forum 293; politics 170; united
  front work (UFW) on Taiwan 295–6,
  298
Chinese identity 4, 79, 130, 164; non-
  Chinese identity 251
Chinese military 130, 284, 305;
  intervention 268; power 305; rise 9,
  282; ship 273; PRC action 274; PRC
  Commission 26; Taiwan confrontation
  270
Chinese National Association of Industry
  and Commerce (CNAIC) 97, 106n17,
  106n18
Chinese National Federation of Industries
  (CNFI) 97, 106n17, 106n18, 106n19;
  White Book 101
Chinese visitors to Taiwan 53, 151, 162–3
Chow, P.C.Y. 1, 43
Chu, Y.H. 6, 32n4

CNFI (Chinese National Federation of
  Industries) 97, 106n17, 106n18, 106n19;
  White Book 101
Commonwealth Magazine 196, 200
communists 40, 42, 83; Chinese
  Communist authority 136; collapse 191;
  Chinese history 263; *see also* Chinese
  Communist Party
confidence-building measures (CBMs) 9,
  269, 282, 287; cross-Strait 274–6, 297;
  military 288
conflict 20, 114, 126n13, 239, 261; armed
  32, 264, 287, 290, 297; cross-Strait 110,
  295; industrial interest 192; labour 95;
  maritime and diplomatic 265; military 4,
  125n1; party 183; political 32n5;
  potential 208; risk 56; South China Sea
  271, 274–6
Congressional-Executive Commission on
  China (CECC) 228, 230
Conradson, D. 200–1
Constable, N. 221, 232, 234n5
Control Yuan Bulletin 106n23
convergence 53; economic 59; partisan 67
Cross-Strait Bilateral Investment
  Protection and Promotion Agreement
  100, 107n31
Cross-Strait Common Market 60–2
Cross-Strait Economic Cooperation
  Agreement 100
cross-Strait policies 1, 7, 54, 156, 303;
  Chen guideline 127n14; China impact
  301; conciliatory 23; DPP 65–6;
  government 163; government–business
  dialogue 101; Jiang Ping affair 121;
  KMT 62, 152; Ma's 64, 170, 174; party
  preferences 153; policy-making 67, 92,
  105n15; public opinions *154*, 155, *164*,
  166, 168; regime 117; reserved attitude
  165, 169; Taiwan's 151; trends 67n2
cross-Strait relations 1, 17, 25–6, 30, 32n3,
  32n4, 37–9, 84, 100, 103, 110–11, 130,
  152, 156, 164, 240, 275; changes 74,
  121; changing 5, 151; China impact
  153; confrontational period 114; debate
  55; deflated tensions 91; DPP claims 24;
  dynamic evolution 305; handling 58, 62;
  impact on practical politics 16;
  improved 266; improvements 272;
  improving 9, 64–5, 107n28; independent
  voters stance 143, *144*; indicators *24*;
  liberalization 170; normalization 297;
  payoffs 123; peaceful 19, 112, 116,
  271; political developments 242;

cross-Strait relations *continued*
  political stalemate 53; political
  unpredictability 268; practical issues 96;
  shaping the future 104; solutions 56;
  strengthening 165; Taipei conciliatory
  approach 113; Taiwanese
  entrepreneurial influence 216; US
  declining influence 267, 269; warmer
  261, 274
Cross-Strait Trade in Goods Agreement
  100–1
Cross-Strait Trades in Services Agreement
  (CSTSA) 29
Cross-Straits Economics Statistics Monthly
  104n1

defence budget 125n1; Taiwan 9, 284–5
democratic 2, 5, 130; Chinese activists
  113; countries 179, 191, 297; debate 67;
  elections 42, 55; movement 81; political
  entity 283; politics in Taiwan 70;
  process 74; reform 38; rights 68n7;
  Taiwan 72, 75, 83; transition 54, 60, 132
Democratic Progressive Party (DPP) 1,
  3–4, 7, 9, 16, 22–4, 30, 49, 53, 56, 60,
  71–2, 74, 83, 91, 94, 117, 131, *144*, 145,
  155, *157–8*, *160*, *164*, 268–70, 295, 297;
  administration 111, 128n28;
  advertisements 65; Budai Harbour issue
  46–8, 50; came to power 27; candidates
  18, 38, 55, 126n6, 175, 293; chairperson
  57, 174; chairwoman Tsai Ing-Wen 64,
  127n18, 174, 294; China Policy
  Conference 57–8; cross-Strait charter
  flights 68n33; cross-Strait economic
  issues 67; defeat 132, 140; government
  5, 42, 47, 59, 62–5, 92, 233, 271, 275;
  headquarters 43; identifiers 134, *138*,
  139, *140*; leaders 81, 296; leaning media
  95, 99, 105n10; national security 57;
  nuclear power station referendum
  68n36; officials 292; One China
  Common Market 61; opposed to China
  141, *142–3*, *147*; political support base
  302; presidency 86; presidential
  candidate 65, 68n16, 126n11; pro-
  independence 72, *76*, *87*, 137; protests
  against the ECFA 181; regime 114;
  Resolution on Taiwan's Future 58;
  return to power 66, 112, 266, 287; rule
  136; support 6, **16**, 29, *58*, 79–80, 84,
  85, 93, *133*; vote 19, 107n32, *135*,
  142–3, 170, 305n1; working-class
  identification 176, 183, 192

democratic system 305; theorists 147n3;
  values 261; Western states 261
Deng, J.-B. 230, 239–40
Deng Xiaoping 282
Dent, C.M. 2, 112
diaspora 207; state–diaspora relations 209;
  Taiwanese 210–11, 243, 251
Directorate General of Budget *24*, **175**
division of labour 27; international 215

East Asia economic and political
  integration 10; investment in South East
  Asia 53; security dilemma 19; Sino-
  American conflict 276; tourists from
  South East Asia 68n37; US security
  burden 291
East Asian 216; Assistant Secretary of
  State for East Asian and Pacific Affairs
  269; free trade regimes 2; regionalism
  112; Southeast Asian countries 57, 219,
  221
East China Sea 276, 291; Air Defence
  Identification Zone (ADIZ) 264, 272;
  China's A2AD capability 266–7; island
  disputes 9, 271; PLA missions 284;
  sovereignty claims 304
Economic Cooperation Framework
  Agreement (ECFA) 1, 4–7, 23, 25,
  28–9, 53, 63–5, 67, **73**, 91, 110–14,
  116–17, 119, 124–5, 126n6, 126n11,
  127n18, 128n29, 151–6, *157–8*, *160*,
  163, *164*, 165, *166*, 169, *171*, 174, 177,
  180–1, 189, 268–9; early harvest 292,
  296; post-ECFA 115, 118, 121
economic integration 1, 10, 32n5, 54–6,
  58–9, 66–7, 91, 174, 176, 252, 282, 302;
  access to 112; with China 60, 128n29,
  131, 145; closer 53, 57; cross-Strait 5–6,
  62, 130, 132, 182, 301; increasing 4, 7;
  regional 117
Economist, The 107n27
education 83, 155, *161–2*, *164*, 166, 170,
  183, 211, 250; better 200; Chinese-
  identity-reinforcing 79; Chinese
  qualifications 61; college *147*; continued
  253n10; denied access 230; different
  trajectories 241; higher 243, 247–8;
  level 156, *157–8*, 159, *160*, 163;
  problems 216; Taishang Schools 242,
  245–6; Taiwanese government policy
  231; tertiary 196
educational 84; divide 241; exchanges 151,
  154, 158–9, 163, 165–7; influence of the
  KMT 164; levels 103

elections 1, 36, 40, 42, 50n2, 58–9, 62, 64, 66, 72, 94–5, 99, 105n11, 137, 282–3, 294; advertising 54–6; campaigns 60, 144, 148, 248, 292; Central Commission (CEC) 32n2, **176**; coming 20, 29; domestic 92–3; facilitate 288; level 41; local 57, 175, 302; national 6; National Assembly 44, 49; National Chengchi University Election Study Centre (ESC) **16**, 305n2; oriented politicians 83; post-2000 65; to the presidency 84; previous 305n1; recent 177, 181; reelection 22, 270, 296; results 30, 67; run-up 96, 138; standing for 98; support group 43; Taiwan 37, 133, 182, 189, 269; TEDS 70, 79, 89n3; threat 101; turnouts 131, 143; voters 170, 183; winning 3, 61, 126n6, 132
electoral turnouts 131, 174–5
emigrant country 8, 210, 232–3, 304
employment market 295; access to China's 231
entrepreneurs 97, 102–3, 104n1, 107n34, 216, 239, 242, 294, 301, 303; influential 98, 101; initiative 198; leading 57; Taiwanese 6, 91–3, 95
Erikson, R. 179, 181
Exclusive Economic Zones (EEZs) 264; Chinese 265–6, 272–3; US military use 265
expatriates 197, 201; Chinese spouses 217, 221–3, 229–32; education for children 242; female Taiwanese 223; management trainee 228; organizations for wives 212n1; population 205; residing in China 215; Taiwanese 216, *224*, 226–7, 233n3

Fell, D. 3, 5, 302
Ferguson, N. 125, 263
Fielding, A. 201
Forbes Magazine 198
Freedom House 106n25
free trade 15, 18, 21, 28, 179; agreement 20, 23, 112–13, 118, 124, 174; conditions 177; East Asian regimes 2; opposing 180; policies 178, *181*; ports 59; pros and cons 189

Geer, J.G. 36–8
General Chamber of Commerce of the Republic of China (ROCCOC) 97, 106n17, 107n33
Gilley, B. 32n4, 268, 290
Glaser, B. 43, 48, 265, 267, 287–8, 290

Glaser, C. 268, 290
Glick Schiller, N. 222, 241
global hypergamy 221, 234n5; *see also* marriage
Goldstein, S. 32n4, 288
Goldthorpe, J.H. 179, 181, 191
'go slow, be patient' guidelines 53, 57–60, 67
graduates 9, 205–6, 228; Chinese graduate institutes 207; junior or senior high school 234n6; Taishang Schools 241–3, 247, 249–50, 253n9; Taiwanese 8, 207; university 249–50
green 75, 85–6, 155–6, *161–2*, *164*, 175–6, 183; camp 71, 95, 106n24, 192, 294, 302; camp supporters 159; dark 15; supporters 165; Taishang 107n32; tilt *76*, 80; voters 167, **182**; *see also* pan-green
gross domestic product (GDP) 284–5; Chinese 199, 261, *262*
Grossman, G.M. 111, 127n17
Group of Two (G-2) 263
Grugel, J. 54, 68n7

Herman, J. 206
Hiscox, M.J. 178–9; Rogowski-Hiscox theory 179–80, *181*, 183
Ho, S.Y. 2, 32n7
Hong Kong 53, 89n5, 99, 151, 234n8, 268, 295–6; Chinese visit 294; economic agreement with China 63; legislation 41; marriages *218*; migration to US 222; One Country, Two Systems unification model 68n29; Taiwan–China negotiations 136
household registration (rural/urban) 8, 202, *226*, 227–9; residents without 220, *221*; system 209, 230; *see also* hukou
Hout, M. 181, 191
Hsiao, M.H.H. 175, 233n1
Hsieh, J.F.-S. 71, 298n6
Hsieh Chang-Ting, F. 293, 296
Hsu, C.J. 99–100, 107n28
Hsu Hsin-Liang 57–8
Hu, A. 174, 182, 189
Hu Jintao 45, 61, 263, 265, 287, 294
hukou (rural or urban) 8, *226*, 227–32
Human Bank 199, 200; survey 206
Huntington, S.P. 175

immigrants 8, 232; bride 169; country 8, 232, 304; new 216–18; policies in Taiwan 233; Taiwanese 203, 232, 241

income 7, 21, *157–8*, 159, *160*, 165–6, 170, 181, 184; distribution 177–8, 180, 189, 191, 262; higher 159, 184, *186*, 187, 199; household 65, 155, *161–2*, **175**; individual 156, 159; inequality 174, 177, 180, 182, **187**, 189; middle 227
Indonesia 215
insecurity 82, 168, 200, 288, 297; job 197
integration 53, 60, 103, 282, 240; Chinese Association 296; cross-Strait 2, 59, 303; diaspora 210; EU-style 27; increasing 101; of mainland spouses 304; market 193n3; models 42; political 10, 180, 211, 239, 251; positive consequences 64; pressures to accelerate 67; pro-integration stance 5, 7, 94; regional 32; reintegration 248; social 91, 170; world market 6, 114
International Monetary Fund (IMF) *262*, 263
international relations 267; literature 177; Taiwan 53
investment 49, 53, 59, 92, 102, 104n5, 112–14, 253n1; Asian Infrastructure Investment Bank (AIIB) 263; ATIEM 95, 105n12; banking 198; Budai Harbour 47; in China 57, 60, 231; Chinese 2, 46–7, 58, 63, 239; cross-Strait *24*, 151; cross-Strait agreements 94, 100–1, 107n31; decisions 98, 115, 118, 121, 128n24; in defence 285–6; dependency ratio 174; foreign 124, 126n13, 199, 227; increase 114, 125n1, 126n12; investment lost 303; lacking 282; limiting 21, 127n14; mainland 6, 101; move to the mainland 23, 29; from non-Chinese sources 125n4; opportunities 301; optimization 106n24; PRC 289; private 110; Taishang 103, 105n10; in Taiwan 123; Taiwanese 4, 96; wave 196
IONPA (Immigration Office of the National Police Agency Ministry of the Interior) 219; White Paper *220*

Japan 9, 53, 64, 243, *262*, 263–6, 273, 287, 290, 291, 304; ADIZ 272, 291; Democratic Party (DPJ) 271–2; tourists 68n37; US–Japan security alliance 271–2, 276
Japanese 271; colonial era 5, 71; colonial rule 74, 79; colonization 132; government 270, 272; PM 61; Sino-Japanese rift 264, 271

jobs 199, 206; available 25; better 196, 200; change 227; in China 8, 199, 205, 207, 231, 301; demand and the supply 197; less well paid 304; loss 23, 25, 198; in low-end sectors 203; in Taiwan 231; take over 206, 211; threat to 28; well-paid 91, 201, 295

Kan, S. 274, 285
Kasinitz, P. 240–2
Kastner, S. 114, 127n14, 269, 282, 292
Keng, S. 32n5, 82, 95, 103, 216, 239–40, 295
Kim Jong-il (North Korean leader) 265
KMT (Kuomintang or Nationalist Group) 1, 4–6, **16**, 22–3, 30, 38, 42, 44, 46–8, 50, 53, 58, 67, 71–2, 74–5, *76*, 79–80, *87*, 91, 93, 104n4, 110–11, 131–2, *133*, 141, 152, 155, *157–8*, *160*, *164*, 170, 183, 268, 270, 274, 276, 283, 286, 295; advertisements 38, 58–9, 64–5; authoritarianism 132; candidate 56, 288; China policies 94, 99; China support 41, 49; critical reporting 106n25; cross-Strait policies 60–2, 66; government 1, 7, 57, 63–4, 232–3, 266, 271–2; identifiers *138*, 139, *140*; ideology 83, 107n32; KMT-CCP Forum 293; leaders 81, 105n15; legislators 43, 48; loyalists 25, 269; nationalism 9; National Unification Guidelines 68n16; new Chinese nationalism 292–3; partisan preference *78*, 79, 82, 84, *85*; position on China *143*, *147*; proposal for unification 55; rapprochement policy 293, 298; return to power 53, 91–2, 110, 137, 267, 283; sloppiness 29; supplementary member seat 106n16; support 105n8, 145, 176; supported newspaper 294; supporters 138; top priorities 172n1; voters 140, 142, *144*; votes 126n11, 134, *135*, 296, 305n1; win 28, 175
Koo Chen-Fu (chairman of SEF) 26, 136
Korea 290; *see also* North Korea, South Korea
Korean Peninsula 265, 267, 270
Kuo, J. 66

labour 2; deregulation 191; mismatched supply and demand 23; more competitive 211, 304; skilled 197; Taiwan 63, 304; vulnerable position 164
labour migration 2, 206, 215; Chinese 56; female 203; pattern 201; skilled 8, 304

Lan, P.C. 196, 207, 240
lawmakers 92, 98
Lee, Chun-Yi 2, 92, 95, 240, 295
Lee, D.R. 125n1
Lee, Y. 196, 212n4
Lee Ching-An 45
Lee Hung-Chun (PFP legislator) 44
Lee Teng-Hui, President 21, 25–7, 56, 58, 61, 81, 86, 137, 282, 289, 292–3; administration 59; KMT 60; policies 67
Lee Ying-Yuan (DPP deputy secretary general) 43
Lee Yung-Ping (PFP legislative whip) 44
Legislative Yuan 10n3, 26, 29, 42, 60, 104n4, 106n16, 112, 284, 298; caucus leader 131; Cross-Strait Service Trade Agreement passed 270, 293; Meeting Records 208; occupation 174, 192
legislature 152; bills delayed 172n1; KMT seats 28; Taiwan 104n3, 107n31, 151
Leng, T.L. 2, 104n5
Levitt, P. 240–1
liberalization 53, 58; cross-Strait 101, 103, 170; economic 2, 55, 57–9, 67, 161, 164; market 6, 102; trade and investment 1, 4, 63, 107n32, 180, 183, 302; younger generation support 303
liberalizing 2, 53, 60, 102
Lin, Cheng-Yi 9, 304
Lin, Jih-Wen 4, 233n1, 302
Lin, J.W. 17
Lin, P. 239–40, 242
Lin, P. 3, 89, 304
Lin, R.H. 71, 95
Lin, Thung-Hong 7, 23, 82, 174–6, **182**, 189, 206, 230, 233n1, 240, 302
Liu, I.C. 33n7
Lu, M. 216, 221–2

Ma Ying-Jeou 15, 22, 28, 63, 81, 94, 126n8, 128n8, 133, *147*, 174, 270–2, 282, 287, 290–1, 299; cross-Strait policies 64; defence strategy 285; election promises 284; election success 170, 283; first and second terms 29, 63, 66–7, 112; mainland China policy 111, 275, 294; One China Common Market 61–2; position on Taiwan 28; presidency 266; presidential inauguration 124, 271; rapprochement policy 292–3; re-election 296; 'three nos' 65, 69n40
Macau 68n29; Special Administrative Regions 296

Mainland Affairs Council 33n18, 96, 104n3, 173n4, 174, 233n3, *263*
Mainland Taishang Ma Wu Campaign Support Association 65
Malacca Strait dilemma 265
Malaysia 215, 2723
Mannheim, K. 73–5, 7
Manning, C. 215, 233n2
marginalized 27, 112, 117; business environment 201; socially 9; temporarily 267
marriage 7, 166, 168, 221–2, 226–9, 295; to a Chinese citizen 202; cross-Strait 3, 8, 223, *224–5*, 230–3, 304; market 169, 216; mobility 232, 234n5; registered 217, *218*; status 165, 183; to Taiwanese citizens 219–20
marriage migration 217, 221, 223, 226, 230; migrants 216, 219–20, 222, 232–3
martial law lifted 53, 74, 239
Massey, D.S. 215
Mearsheimer, J.J. 3, 267–8, 290
Memorandum of Understanding (MOU) 273
migrant 8, 198, 201–2, 209, 222; Chinese 56, 265; employee 212; to find jobs 207; homeless 61; liberal policy 179; marriage 216–17, 219–22, 232–3; overseas 208; returned 248; rural 228, 230; skilled 200, 215; teenage 240–1; women 197, 204, 212n1; young 242–3, 251–2; *see also* emigrant country; immigrants; National Immigration Agency
migrant communities 8, 241; of skilled labour 196
migrant Taiwanese 10, 196, 200, 202–3, 207–12, 230, 240, 304; female 204; return to Taiwan 209; young 197, 243, 252
migrant workers 179; Chinese 94, 265; Taiwanese 203
military 4, 79–80, 125n1, 265–6, 268, 275, 283–6, 289; capabilities 269, 287, 290; challenges 297; conflict 114; defence 10; deployments 288; incidents 282; joint actions 276; means 292; personnel 274; presence 273; strength 74; Taiwan 2; Taiwan–China confrontation 270; tensions 6, 85, 125; threat 9, 18, 31, 75, *76*, *86–7*, 267; *see also* Chinese military; US military
military confidence-building measures (CBMs) 269, 282; negotiations 287–8
Milner, H.V. 177, 179

Ministry of Commerce of People's
Republic of China 196
Ministry of Economic Affairs **175**
Ministry of National Defence of the
Republic of China 298n1
Mo, Y.-C. 272
Mou, S. 242–3
Murray, W.S. 285
Mutz, D.C. 38

National Bureau of Statistics of the
People's Republic of China 233n3
National Chengchi University 104n6;
Election Study Centre **16**, 305n2
national identity 70–2, 189, 192; China
impact 8, 130–1, 302–3; Chinese 184;
general public *146*, 151, 155–6, 159,
165; NP position 56–7, 59; party
positions 62, 134, *135*; president's
stance 21; Taiwanese 15, 75, 81, 174,
182, 183
National Immigration Agency (NIA) 217,
218–19, 223, 233, 234n9
National Unification Guidelines 55, 68n16
New Party (NP) 5, 56–9, 61–2, 66–7,
68n27, 68n29, *78*, 183
New York Times 45, 105n11
North Korea 265–6

Obama, President B. 61, 261, 265, 269,
276n10, 291
Obama administration 261, 266, 268–70,
272–3, 285, 289–90
Office of the Secretary of Defense 273,
283
One China 15, 131, 136–7, 139, *140*, 293,
298n6; Common Market 61; framework
294; Principle 26–7, 59, 61, 136–7, 268,
275, 294, 296
Ong, A. 222, 230
Ong, W. 112
O'Reilly, K. 241
Overseas Chinese News 215

pan-blue 47, **176**, 180; alliance 16; camp
17, 93, *181*, 183; China support 43,
105n8; leader 45; parties 4, 42, 189;
supporters 7, *184–5*, *190*; voters 18, 175
pan-green **176**; camp 4, 7, 16–17, *181*,
183, 191, 288; coalition 111; parties
180, 189; supporters 15; voters 18, 175
peasants and workers 174–6, 180
People First Party (PFP) 41–2, 44–5, 47,
133, 155, *164*, 183; Chinese assistance

49; legislative whips 43; legislators 42;
officials 48; partisan preference *78*, *85*
People's Liberation Army (PLA) 9, 19,
271, 284; growing power 297;
modernization drive 290; Navy 264–5,
291; power projection capability 282,
289; satellite interception 265; ships
285; threat 283, 287; US weapons
systems 269
People's Republic of China (PRC) 16–17,
29, 32n1, 43, 80, 83, 136, 196, 215, *225*,
233n3, 262, 269, 282, 293, 297; anti-
PRC 93; ARATS 26; authorities 292,
294, 296; balance of power 270;
citizenship 8, 217, 226–7, 229–32,
234n7; claim to represent China 74;
conflict with US 275; drive for
unification 211; ECFA 28; economic
power 263; government 15, *24*, 286;
hardliners 30; investments 289;
Maritime Safety Administration 287;
people 219, 253n11; policies 32n5;
relocation of missiles 288; sovereignty
claims 271, 273; UFW (united front
work) 295–6, 298; view of DPP 59, 63;
White Paper on National Defence 27
People's Republic of China (PRC) military
274, 282; Commission 26; threat 19, 75,
78, *86*, 267–8
People's Republic of China (PRC) and
Taiwan *24*, 81; economic dependence
19–21, 26, 28, 30; espionage activities
286; exports from Taiwan 23, 25, 28;
independence 31; military threat 75, *78*,
86; potential for trouble 72; relations
283, 289, 291; spouses in Taiwan 295;
Taiwanese working in PRC 82; talks 32
Philippines 215, 265, 273–4, 276n8, 290
Pomfret, J. 41, 47, 273
Portes, A. 240–1
poverty 221; rate in Taiwan 174, **175**
presidential elections 32n2, 37, 66, 112,
136, 144; 1996 93; 2000 93, 182; 2004
42, 94, 105n12, 137, 175, **176**, 182;
2008 60, 94, 105n12, 170, 301; 2012 6,
15, 64, 94, 126n6, 126n11, 131–2, 134,
135, 145, 175, **176**, 270, 301; 2016
10n3, 270; campaigns 38; decisive 58;
defeat 140; direct 25, 56–7; period 43;
Taiwanese 5, 15, 17, 26; turnout **176**;
votes 16, 30; winning 17–18, 30–1, 42,
131, 137
professional 200; achievement 199;
autonomy 207; bureaucrats 102;

disadvantages 197; experience 103, 203; group 170; life 198; licensing exams 231; productivity 82; skill 205; specialist 227; Taiwanese Professional Women's Society (TPWS) 204; trained 229; white-collar workers 8

professional careers 295; in China 240; future 254n14

professional military 286; Taiwanese personnel 286

professionals 179, 198, 215; mid-level 202; Taiwanese 91, 230; trained in Taiwan 61

pro-unification 84, 159; constituencies 110; groups 296; KMT candidates 93; stance 26; supporters 126n11

Putnam, R.D. 17, 29, 32n7, 177

rapprochement 119; costless 119–20; cross-Strait 91–2, 114, 122, 282, 289, 301, 304; policy 292–3, 298; Taipei–Beijing 1, 9, 104

relocation 2; Futenma marine base 272; of manufacturers 196; of missiles 288; of the nuclear family 197, 229; temporary 295

Renminbi transactions 102, 151

Republic of China (ROC) 9, 10n4, *24*, 27, 31, 32n1, 40, 79–80, 83, 86, 97, 136, 276, 286, 291–5, 298n1, 305; armed forces 289; capability to defend 282; Chinese spouses *225*; citizenship 222, 226; constitution 297, 298n6; constitutional framework 283; defence budget 284; expatriates *224*; government 74; ID cards 62; Mainland Affairs Council 104n3; Ministry of Foreign Affairs 277n24; registered marriages *218–19*, 221; ROCCOC (Chamber of Commerce) 97, 107n17, 107n33; sovereignty claims 274, 277n24

restrictions immigration policy in Taiwan 217; legal 106n21; marriage 222; on pro-independence speech 84

restrictions lifted 60; on bank transfers 127n14; for Chinese tourism 153, *154*; cross-Strait trade 100; inheritance 232; martial law 53, 74, 239; on travel 74, 239

reunification 155–6, *157–8*, *160*; advocate 28; of China 26; family *219–20*; pro-reunification platform 164

Rigger, S. 5, 70, 270, 303

ROCCOC *see* Republic of China

Rogowski, R. 178

Rogowski-Hiscox theory 179–80, *181*, 183

Romberg, A.D. 293–4

Rose, A.K. 112, 127n16

Rumbaut, R. 240–1

salaried workers 197–8

salaries 200, 207; Chinese 61, 202; higher 229; shrinking 211, 303; in Taiwan 206

school *147*, 155, *157–8*, *160–2*, 231, 234n6, 244, 253n2, 253n5; anthem 248; business 205; campus 143, 146, 251; Chinese 250; community centre 245; junior high 86; high 163, *164*, 227; life 252; records 253n9; schoolmates 249; Taiwanese overseas 241–2; teacher 242–3, 246

schooling *184–6*, *188*, *190*; access to 230

Schubert, G. 1, 3, 6, 93–4, 216, 233n1, 239–40, 295

security 2, 9, 266, 287, 289, 297, 301; Asian landscape 112; challenges 283, 292; commitments 267–8; competitive strategy 269; development 290; dilemma 19; dimension 295; East and Southeast Asia's structure 305; economic 111, 263; environment 275; externalities 125, 128n29; firms 107n33; issues 270; job 203; military 282; national 29, 54–5, 57–8, 101, 233, 293; non-military challenges 291, 298; planners 72; Public Bureau 202; ramifications 276; regional 262, 304; specialist 261, 267, 290; threatened 168; vessels from China 273; *see also* US security

Shambaugh, D. 267–8

Shanghai 8, 96, 105n9, 105n12, 151, 201, 206–7, 211, 249; booming economy 196; local dialect 246; local insurance system 234n8; migrant career women 204–5; schools for Taiwanese immigrants 241; Shanghai-Kunshan metropolitan area 94; Taishang School 243, 247, 251, 253n2; Taiwanese expatriates *224*; Taiwanese migrants 197–8, 200; work 227

Shangri La strategic dialogue 290

Shen, H.H. 169, 196, 202

Shenzhen 93, 228, 294; city government 229, 234n6; Dongguan-Shenzhen axis 94; Taiwanese expatriates *224*

Shih, H.C. 268, 272

Shlapak, D.A. 270, 284, 289

Sina News 234n8
Singapore 26, 136, 215, 290
Six-Party Talks 265
slander 40, 43–4, 47, 62
Sobieraj, S. 38
Soong, J. 42, 44
South China Sea 265–7, 270, 273; Air
    Defence Identification Zone (ADIZ)
    291; China-US standoffs 272; Chinese
    legal claims 271; Declaration on the
    Conduct of Parties 274; island disputes
    9; sovereignty claims 304; ROC
    government line 276; US involvement
    261, 275
South Korea 58, 264–6
sovereignty 2, 27, 131, 160, *171*, 289;
    Chinese claim 19, 130, 265, 274;
    competing claims 91, 271, 304; disputes
    17; issues 31; national *157*; political
    111, 159; Taiwan claim 9–10, 10n4, 46,
    94, 103, 156, 210, 287, 305
state-to-state special relationship relations
    24, 26–7
Straits Exchange Foundation (SEF) 26,
    101, 297; officials 105n15; SEF-ARATS
    talks 63, 65, 104n3, 136
Su, C. 136, 147n2
Su Chen-Chang 294
Sullivan, J. 37–9, 50n1
Sunflower student movement 1, 6, 10n3,
    29, 54, 67, 88, 91, 101, 104n4, 152, 164,
    170, 174, 192, 270, 293, 298, 302–3
Sutter, R. 261, 270
Suzhou City Government 226
Swaine, M.D. 261, 267, 290

Taipei Times 106n25, 125n2, 126n6, 174,
    181
Taishang 6, 56, 64, 66, 91, 97, 101–4,
    105n10, 105n12, 295–6; green 107n32;
    informal power 98–100; investment
    optimization 106n24; lack of collective
    identity 107n34; mainland 95–6,
    105n15, 106n16, 107n33; mainland
    investment 104n5; Mainland Ma Wu
    Campaign Support Association 65;
    Operations Headquarters 62; political
    agency 92, 105n6; presidential advisor
    107n30; School-based Taiwanese
    community 246; vote 93–4; Studies 216,
    234n3, 240
Taishang Schools 8, 240, 242–7, 249–51,
    253n3, 253n7, 253n13; Dongguan
    School 253n2, 253n5, 253n9; Huadong

School 253n2, 253n10; Shanghai School
    253n2
Taiwan 174; Central Election Commission
    32n2, **176**; Defence Ministry
    Quadrennial Defence Review (QDR)
    285, 298n1; Directorate General of
    Budget *24*, **175**; Mainland Affairs
    Council 10n2, 33n18, 96, 104n3, 173n4,
    174, 233n3, *263*, 298n3; Ministry of
    Economic Affairs **175**; Ministry of the
    Interior *218–19*, *221*, 232–3, 234n4;
    Relations Act (TRA) 269, 275, 282,
    284, 289; Social Change Survey (TSCS)
    174, 199, 202
Taiwan military 283–4; asymmetric
    strategy 297; security challenges 2, 282,
    298
Taiwan security 2, 9, 282, 288, 298;
    challenges 297; China impact 304–5;
    endangered 59, 286, 294; environment
    261; Japanese role 291; Japan–US
    arrangements 276; US guarantee 270,
    283
Taiwan Solidarity Union (TSU) 6, 60,
    62–3, 66, 127n18, 132, *133*, 155, *164*,
    183; partisan preference *78*, *85*
Taiwan Strait 3–4, 6–7, 91, 95, 111,
    125n1, 125n4, 198, 267, 269, 275, 284,
    291; ARATS 26, 63, 104n3, 136;
    bargaining power with both sides 104n5;
    consolidating stability and peace 297;
    cross-Strait visitors 253n5; destabilized
    72; détente 266, 270, 304; economic
    liberalization 161; economic and
    political ties 110; economic scale 126n9;
    elites on both sides 98; gateway to
    reconciliation 112; integration 101;
    interaction across 5, 10; job market 200,
    212; market-induced integration 303;
    marriage migration 223, 228, 232;
    military balance 268, 283; MOU 273;
    move across 180, 184, 187, 202, 206,
    231, 250–2; official contact 92; partial
    demilitarization 289; rapprochement
    282, 301; reduction in tension 113;
    relations across 2, 24; situation 276;
    Taiwanese business community 124;
    tensions 6, 122, 125, 271; two sides 16,
    27–8; US maintaining peace and
    stability 261
Taiwanese 105n7; business associations
    (TBAs) 92–5, 97–8, 100–1, 103,
    105n12, 105n14, 105n15; campaign
    rallies 105n8; compatriots 91, 248;

nationalism 80, 104n4, 107n34, 130;
officials 96, 105n9, 106n19
Taiwanese identity 5, 22, 30, 33n7, 73,
78–9, 85–6, 88, 130, 165, 231, 242–4,
303; changing 294; Hongkongized 295;
local 292; separate 296; student 245–6,
248, 250–1
Tanner, M.S. 2, 292
Thailand 215
Three Links (direct postal, trade and
transport links) 41, 47, 57, 60, 68n22, 91
tourism 53, 107n33; Chinese 153;
promoting 151
tourists 166, *167*; centre 206; Chinese 4, 7,
62–5, 67n1, 68n33, 151–3, *154*, 155–6,
161–2, 163, 167, *168*, *171*, 173n4, 267,
286; group *164*, 165–7; industry 292;
from Japan and South East Asia 68n37;
visas 202, *219–20*, 232
trade dependence 21, 53, **175**; exploiting
53; increasing 4
trade and investment 53, 121; attracting
126n4; bilateral agreements 94; Chinese
57; cross-Strait *24*, 151; dependency
ratios on China 174
trade relations 156, 158; with China 53;
cross-Strait 56, 59, 157; expanding 177
Trade in Services Agreement 1, 10n3,
107n31; controversial 104n4; Cross-
Strait 100, 170
trading partners 53, 111–12, 125
transmission belts 95, 98
Trans-Pacific Partnership (TPP) 291
Tsai, Ming-Chang 169, 215
Tsai Cheng-Yuan, KMT spokesperson 43
Tsai Eng-Meng 99–100, 102, 107n28, 294
Tsai Ing-Wen 64–6, 126n6, 127n18, *147*,
174, 270
Tsai Ying-Wen 1, *133*, *135*, *142–4*, 293
Tseng, Y.F. 7–8, 210, 216, 230–1, 233n1,
239–40, 242–3, 295
Tucker, N. 287, 290
Tung, C.Y. 104n2

UFW (CCP's united front work) 295–6,
298
unification 32, 63, 70–1, *76–7*, 80, 82–3,
85–6, *87*, 91, 103, 107n28, 135, 141,
146, *161–2*, *171*, 288, 291, 295–6, 304;
Chinese 53, 134, 292; Chinese proposal
68n29; debate 84; immediate 18;
imposed 92; issue 75, 79; National
Council (NUC) 26, 136; National
Guidelines 55, 68n16; new hopes 275;

peaceful 59; pledge against 69n40; PRC
drive for 211, 290; preference 71, 78,
81; support 137, 159; *see also* pro-
unification, reunification
United Nations: Chinese seat 74;
Commission on the Limits of the
Continental Shelf (CLCS) 273, 277n24;
Convention on the Law of the Sea
277n24; membership 62
US 44–5, 209, 243, 247, 263, 287, 293,
297–8; air-sea battle concept (ASBC)
266; American voters 137; Asia-Pacific
pivot 290–1; attitude on cross-Strait
détente 304; citizenship 222; conflict in
waters in East Asia 276; cross-Strait
relations influence 267; defence
community 274; gendered response 168;
intervention 268; involvement in the
East and South China Seas 271, 275;
segmented assimilation 240; support 10,
283, 305; trade *262*; USNS Impeccable
265, 272; wars in Iraq and Afghanistan
261, 266; *see also* Washington
US arms 261, 267–8; sales 110, 265–6,
269, 275; sales to Taiwan 285;
US government 269–70, 272, 275, 291;
Congress 269, 272, 276n10; Office of
the Secretary of Defense 273, 283;
Pentagon 264; President 269; Secretary
of State 262, 273
US military 283, 286; capacity to sustain a
war 290; CBMs 288; forces 290;
intervention 267–8; intervention in
Chinese EEZs 265; involvement in war
over Taiwan 284; sources 283; supplies
276n10
US politics 36–7; party identification 132;
policy 269; policy-makers 274; political
elite 289; politicians 128n28;
presidential candidate 61
US relations 3, 9; China 269; Japan
security alliance 271–2; with Southeast
Asian countries 274
US security 261, 270; guarantee 282, 284,
291; interests 290; Japan alliance 271–2,
276; Taiwan arrangement 289–90

Vietnam 265, 272–4
Vietnamese ships 265, 273

wage gap 177–8
Wang, Cher 131
Wang, Daohan 26, 136
Wang, H.Z. 216

Wang, T.Y. 32n7, 75
Wang Daohan (chairman of ARATS) 26, 136
Want Want China Times Group 99–100
Want Want Group (Wang Wang jituan) 99, 106n25, 107n26, 294; president Tsai Shao-Chung 294
Washington 3, 9, 26, 48, 266, 268; arms sales friction 267, 269; Consensus 263; guarantor of security for Taiwan 270; policy-makers 275; visit to 44–5; *Washington Post* 41, 43–4
wealth disparities 152, 156, *157–8*, *160*, *171*; distribution 29, 174; generate 198; growing inequality 170; national 210
Wealth Magazine 199; survey 200, 203
wealthy 189, 234n5; entrepreneurs 98
Wen Jiabao 126n9, 126n10
women 161, 168, 197; career 204; Chinese 169, 232; cross-border marriages 221, 234n5; DPP Department of Women's Development 43; elderly 79; migrants 204, 212n1; respect 205; support for liberalization 170; Taiwanese 7, 165, 169, 203, 233; warriors 203
women and girls girl 249, 254n14

Wong, Tze Wai Kevin 176, 182, 184
Wong Chung-Chun (KMT legislator) 46–8
Wood, A. 178–9
workers *181*, 191–2, 211; Chinese migrant 94, 265; co-workers 216; deprivation 176; female skilled 297; middle-management 200; migrant 179, 203; skilled 7, 177–8, 180, 189, 197–9, 215; unemployed 61, 206; unskilled 7, 177–9, 180, 182, 184, 187, 189; white-collar 8, 170, 204, 301–2; young 197, 205–6
working-class identity 176, 183
Wright, E.O. 178–81
Wu, Joseph Chao-Hsieh 42–3
Wu, N.T. 130, 132, 182–3
Wu, Y.S. 32n3, 32n4
Wu Sangui 46–7, 49

Xi Jinping 2, 287, 290
Xinxinwen [*The Journalist*] 106n16

Yang, W.Y. 168
Yangtze River delta 196, 223

Zhou, M. 240

CPSIA information can be obtained
at www.ICGtesting.com
Printed in the USA
JSHW011436221219
3113JS00001B/51

9 781138 945920